Pra[ise for PassPorter]

"A nifty [...] that wo[...] as a planner, organizer and journal..."
— Jacky Runice
Daily Herald–Chicago

[...]the most practical, sanity-saving guide you could take along to Disney World."
— Stephanie Gold, Amazon.com

"[PassPorter] has become the Bible for those of us who want to experience Walt Disney World to the max."
— Kim Cool, Venice Gondolier Sun

"Vacationers who want to enjoy all that Disney World has to offer should make sure they take along this PassPorter guide."
— ForeWord Reviews

You've spoiled me! Can't you do books for every place on Earth?
— Ann Weber in Ohio

PassPorter has everything you need in one book! Even as self-proclaimed experts, we learned new things!
— Craig Krause in Tennessee

The maps are the most comprehensive that I've had access to yet! Having all this information in one place is priceless.
— Melissa Hall in West Virginia

A place for everything and everything in its place. The entire trip can be planned using the PassPorter.
— Beth Casey in Nova Scotia

What's Unique in PassPorter

✳ **Comprehensive yet concise information** is packed into our pages—PassPorter is information rich and padding free!

✳ **Blending of personal experience** from your authors and the collective wisdom from tens of thousands of readers means a guidebook that's full of heart and soul.

✳ **Well-organized chapters and pages** make it easy to find what you need. We edit our information carefully so that sections always begin at the top of a page and end at the bottom.

✳ **Worksheets** to jot notes and make travel arrangements.

✳ **Coverage of the most recent changes** throughout Walt Disney World—thanks to our later production schedule, this is the most up-to-date 2005 guidebook available!

✳ **Floorplans of Disney resort hotel rooms** to give you a better sense of the layout.

✳ **Full color, fold-out maps** of the four major Disney theme parks, printed on heavy paper to stand up to rugged use.

✳ **Custom-designed attraction charts** provide all the information you need at a glance.

✳ **Allie's KidTips and TweenTips** offer advice for fellow kids.

✳ **Original photos**—many of which include your authors in the picture, too. No stock photos here!

✳ **Magical memories** from fellow vacationers to convey the spirit and wonder of Walt Disney World.

✳ **Disney changes highlighted** with a light gray background to mark significant additions and changes to Walt Disney World since our last edition.

✳ **Expert peer reviewers** to ensure accuracy and thoroughness.

Our original PassPorter editions (spiral and deluxe) also include ⌐e unique features:

✳ ⌐ famous organizer **PassPockets** to plan your trip, store ⌐aps and papers, and record your vacation memories.

✳ ⌐-stick tabs to mark your chapters in whatever way ⌐quick and easy reference.

✳ ⌐labels and fun stickers to custom-design your ⌐our own vacation.

PassPorter®
Walt Disney World® Resort

2005 Library Edition

The library-friendly travel guide and planner

Jennifer Marx,
Dave Marx,
and
Allison Cerel Marx

PassPorter Travel Press

An imprint of MediaMarx, Inc.
P.O. Box 3880, Ann Arbor, Michigan 48106
877-WAYFARER
http://www.passporter.com

PassPorter® Walt Disney World® Resort—2005 Library Edition
by Jennifer Marx, Dave Marx, and Allison Cerel Marx

P.O. Box 3880, Ann Arbor, Michigan 48106
877-WAYFARER or 877-929-3273 (toll-free)
Visit us on the World Wide Web at http://www.passporter.com

Publisher's Cataloging Data.
    Marx, Jennifer; Marx, David; Marx, Allison Cerel
    PassPorter Walt Disney World Resort: the library-friendly travel guide and planner. Ann Arbor, MI: PassPorter Travel Press, copyright 2005.
    Revised and updated edition of PassPorter Walt Disney World (1999)
    Includes 28 maps.
    PARTIAL CONTENTS: Magic Kingdom. -Epcot. -Disney-MGM Studios. -Disney's Animal Kingdom. -Downtown Disney & the water parks.
    Walt Disney World, Florida--Description and travel--Guidebooks. 2. Walt Disney World, description and travel--Tours. 3. Theme parks, Orlando region, Florida--Guidebooks. 4. Epcot --Description and travel--Guidebooks. 5. Disney-MGM Studios Theme Park, Florida--travel--Guidebooks. 6. Travel--Guidebooks (for parents and children). I. Title. II. Title: vacation. III. Title: Disney World vacation. IV. PassPorter Travel Press.

About the Authors

Jennifer Marx fell in love with Walt Disney World on her first visit as a teenager in 1983. She has since returned more times than she can count on her fingers and toes, visiting every park, attraction, resort, and restaurant at least once. As author of over a dozen popular books, she yearned to write one about Walt Disney World but felt no interest in churning out yet another travel guide when there were so many excellent books already available. When she hit upon the idea of the PassPorter, she knew she could offer her fellow vacationers something unique and valuable. With the help of the PassPorter, Jennifer has organized gatherings at Walt Disney World for individuals, groups, and families of all ages. Jennifer lives in Ann Arbor, Michigan where she makes her home with husband Dave, step-daughter Allie, newborn son Alexander, and their Alaskan Malamute dog, Kippi.

Name: Jennifer Marx
Date of birth: 10/09/68
Residence: Ann Arbor, MI
Signature: *Jennifer Marx*

Dave Marx may be considered a Renaissance Man, a jack-of-all-trades, or a dilettante, depending on how you look at things. He took a 20-year hiatus between his early journalism training and the commencement of his full-time writing career. Beyond co-authoring numerous books with Jennifer, he's been a radio writer/producer; recording engineer; motion picture music editor; broadcast engineering supervisor; tax preparer; cab driver; whitewater safety and rescue instructor; developer and instructor of online publishing courses; and newsletter editor and promotions chief for an online forum. He has also co-authored and contributed to numerous books about America Online and the Internet. He discovered the "World" (Walt Disney World, that is) in 1997 and spent more than six months there over the following five years. Dave is from New Jersey, and now makes his home in Ann Arbor, Michigan.

Name: Dave Marx
Date of birth: 04/07/55
Residence: Ann Arbor, MI
Signature: *Dave Marx*

Allison Cerel Marx ("Allie") is a veteran visitor to Walt Disney World (and Dave's 12-year-old daughter). She has a maniacal grin, especially when spinning one of Mad Hatter's teacups at top speed. She's camped at Fort Wilderness, hung out in the Treehouses at the Disney Institute, celebrated New Year's Eve 1999/2000 in the Magic Kingdom, and photographed animals at the Animal Kingdom Lodge Resort. She shares her "A-ok!" ratings and her popular tips for kids and "tweens" (pre-teens) on the attractions in the Touring the 'World' chapter. Allie also offers her thoughts on the childcare clubs on property. (Allie is pictured here with her baby brother, Alexander... a future co-author!)

Name: Allison C. Marx
Signature: *Allison*

PassPorter Team

Our Expert Peer Reviewers and Researchers—These experts painstakingly checked our text and maps and helped us ensure PassPorter's accuracy, readability, and thoroughness. Thank you for helping to make PassPorter the best it can be!

Maureen Austin is co-owner of Grand Getaways Travel and is a PassPorter message board guide. A Florida native and mom of four, she travels to Walt Disney World several times a year with her husband Kevan.

Joanne and Tim Ernest are message board guides at PassPorter, where they enjoy discussing the magic of Disney with readers. They have two boys, David and Andrew, and are veterans of more than 25 trips to Disney.

Debbie Hendrickson first visited Walt Disney World in 1988 and has since returned four times, savoring the wide variety of experiences she's acquired there. Debbie is married to Lee and is a PassPorter message board guide.

LauraBelle Hime enjoys traveling to Disney any time of the year with family, friends, or solo, but especially with her grandchildren Alexis, Olivia, and Caleb. She enjoys helping friends plan on the PassPorter message boards and at home.

Deb Koma, a Virginia-based writer, discovered the magic of Walt Disney World relatively recently. Since then she has made up for lost time, and is now a veteran of more than 30 Disney trips, with many more on the horizon.

Susan Kulick just returned from her eleventh trip to Walt Disney World. She and her family—husband Steve and stepson Mike—are Disney Vacation Club members and love all things Disney. She is a PassPorter message board guide and loves helping others!

Bruce Metcalf has loved and studied Disney parks since 1958. He works at a major Central Florida theme park and co-writes the delightful "Iago & Zazu's Attraction of the Week" at http://aotw.figzu.com.

Michelle Nash, an Instructional Technologist, has been to Walt Disney World more than twelve times; the last ten trips being taken with her son, Todd, in just the past six years. On their last trip, they enjoyed Walt Disney World for a month at Ft. Wilderness.

Cheryl Pendry and her husband Mark usually visit Walt Disney World every year, despite the fact they live in England. They became Disney Vacation Club members in 2002 and Cheryl is also a PassPorter message board guide.

Ann Smith is a PassPort message board guide and lives in Pittsburgh with her husband Jim and three children, Jamie, Brendan, and Shelby. The Smiths are Walt Disney World fanatics and visit at least once a year.

Donna Sonmor is planning her first trip to Walt Disney World, but caught the Disney magic years ago with a couple of trips to Disneyland. She is the mother of two wonderful teenagers and wife to Dan. She is also a PassPorter message board guide.

Jeff Spencer, a veteran of more than thirty Disney World trips, enjoys helping family, friends, and fellow Disney fans plan their vacations. For Disney trip reports, tips, links, and other Disney information, visit http://home.hiwaay.net/~jlspence.

Scott Thomas, the creator of the Priority Seating Calculator (http://pscalculator.net), has helped numerous Disney fans plan their meals. He has been visting Walt Disney World over the past twenty years and, obviously, enjoys eating at the many fine restaurants.

Deb Wills is widely recognized as a Walt Disney World expert by the national press and also by others in the Disney travel planning field. She is the founder of AllEarsNet.com, the most comprehensive unofficial Disney World site. She also publishes the AllEars* newsletter.

Sandy Zilka is a proofreader for a Big Four accounting firm who enjoys writing and scrapbooking. She has taken more than twenty Disney trips and is currently planning three more. Sandy is a PassPorter message board guide.

Acknowledgments

A "world" of thanks to our readers, who've contributed loads of tips and stories since PassPorter's debut. A special thanks to those who generously allowed us to include their contributions in this edition:

Ann Weber, Craig Krause, Melissa Hall, and Beth Casey (page i); Mark Zeis, Jeneice Seagraves, Dianne Cook, and Maureen Austin (page 12); Karen Miller, Melissa Jarvis, and Rhoda Smith (page 24); Fran Skall, Tom Anderson, Dene Gatewood, Jeff Haney, and LeighAnn Brown (page 112); Tara Sydow, Jamie Dailey, Wendy Bloedt, and Thomas Blom (page 198); Pamela Etheridge and Karin Dunn (page 240); and Elizabeth Shannon and Dana Slusher (page 260). May each of you receive a new magical memory for every reader your words touch.

PassPorter would not be where it is today without the help and support of the many members of the Internet Disney fan community. Our thanks to the friendly folks below and to all who we didn't have room to include!

- All Ears Net (http://www.allearsnet.com). Thanks, Deb and Deb!
- Adults at Walt Disney World (http://www.adultsatwdw.com). Thanks, Rose!
- Badger's Disney Countdown (http://nhed.com/countdown). We'll miss you, Ed!
- DIS—Unofficial Disney Information Station (http://www.wdwinfo.com). Thanks, Pete!
- Disney Vacation Planning (http://www.solarius.com/dvp). Thank you, Paul!
- Disney World: The Unofficial Online Guide (http://wdisneyw.co.uk). Thanks, Joanne!
- DisneyZone (http://www.disneyzone.actusa.net). Thanks, Kimmi!
- eGuides to Go (http://www.eguidestogo.com). Thanks, Andy!
- Hidden Mickeys of Disney (http://www.hiddenmickeys.org). Thanks, Tom!
- Intercot (http://www.intercot.com). Thank you, John!
- LaughingPlace.com (http://www.laughingplace.com). Thanks, Doobie and Rebekah!
- Magictrips.com (http://www.magictrips.com). Thank you, Ada!
- MouseEarVacations.com (http://www.mouseearvacations.com). Thanks, Beci and Jami!
- MousePlanet.com (http://www.mouseplanet.com). Thanks, Mike!
- MouseSavers.com (http://www.mousesavers.com). Thanks, Mary!
- Our Laughing Place (http://www.ourlaughingplace.com). Thanks, Ahnalira!
- Priority Seating Calculator (http://pscalculator.net). Thanks, Scott!
- RADP (news://rec.arts.disney.parks newsgroup)
- Spencer Family's Disney Page (http://home.hiwaay.net/~jlspence). Thanks, Jeff!

Big thanks to the Guides (moderators) of our own message boards: Maureen Austin, Kelley Baker, Michelle Clark, Joanne and Tim Ernest, Douglas Famy, Kristin Grey, LauraBelle Hime, Debbie Hendrickson, Christina Holland-Radvon, Robin Krening-Capra, Susan Kulick, Marcie LaCava, Tara McCusker, Michelle Nash, Allison Palmer-Gleicher, Cheryl Pendry, Tina Peterson, Susan Rannestad, Donna Sonmor, Ann Smith, Nate Stokes, Suzanne Torrey, Sara Varney, Margo Verikas, Dave Walsh, Suzi Waters, Brant Wigginton, Debbie Wright, Sandy Zilka, and the 9000+ readers in our amazing community at http://www.passporterboards.com.

A special thanks to these important folks "behind the scenes" at PassPorter:
Office Assistants: Nicole Larner and Carey Viviano
Printer: Magnum Printing, Ltd., Hong Kong (thank you, Anita Lam!)
Visibility Specialists: Kate and Doug Bandos, KSB Promotions
Assorted Pixies: Tom Anderson, Holly Benke, Mariska Elia, Dave Hunter, Kim and Chad Larner, Josh Pettit, Than Saffel, Bob Sehlinger, Susan Shumaker, and Dirk Uhlenbrock.

A heartfelt thank you to our family and friends for their patience while we were away on trips or cloistered at our computers, and for their support of our dream: Alexander Marx; Carolyn Tody; Tom Anderson; Fred and Adele Marx; Kim, Chad, Megan, and Natalie Larner; Dan, Jeannie, Kayleigh, Melanie, and Nina Marx; Gale Cerel-Marx; Jeanne and David Beroza; Gordon Watson and Marianne Couch; George Louie; Ben Foxworth; and Marta Metcalf.

Last but not least, we thank Walter Elias Disney for his dream.

Contents

List of Maps, Worksheets, and Charts

Touring the "World" 113

Contents
(continued)

Congratulations!

First, congratulations are in order—you're going to Walt Disney World! You are about to embark on an experience that will amaze and, hopefully, delight you. This isn't an ordinary, run-of-the-mill trip—after all, you're going to spend your vacation in the heart of Mickey Mouse land!

The Walt Disney World Resort is a world unto itself, full of heralded amusements and hidden gems. Yet the very fact that it is so vast can make a visit to Walt Disney World seem more like a race in a maze than a relaxed vacation. And worse yet, pleasant memories of a great vacation may disappear beneath the stress and worries that accompanied it.

Happily, after fifty-plus trips to Walt Disney World we've learned to dispel our stress with one simple and enjoyable task: **planning ahead**. In fact, it is no task at all—planning is as much fun as the vacation itself. Planning gave birth to the PassPorter concept. Originally, Jennifer made itineraries on her computer and placed them in a binder. During the trip she kept the binder handy, using it to store passes, brochures, and receipts. After the vacation, these organizers had turned into scrapbooks, full of pixie-dusted memories and goofy smiles. When Jennifer's writing career took off she didn't have the time to create binders for every trip. She wished for a simpler version that she could use each trip without a lot of fuss. It was on a Disney bus that the idea came to her. She could make an easy-to-use book and offer it as a resource to fellow vacationers!

Now, after much work, you hold PassPorter in your hands. The first edition of PassPorter debuted in 1999, creating a sensation in the Disney fan community, winning eight national awards, and helping tens of thousands plan great vacations. This edition, our seventh, is our best yet!

It is our greatest hope that PassPorter helps you "discover the magic" through your own eyes, as it did for us. To get you in the spirit, read "Disney Dreaming" on the next page and prepare for your adventure!

Smiles and laughter,

Jennifer, Dave, and Allison

We'd love to hear from you! Visit us on the Internet (http://www.passporter.com) or drop us a postcard from Walt Disney World!

P.S. This the Library Edition of PassPorter, which we designed for vacationers to borrow from their local library. This edition is missing some of the organizational features you may have heard about from others who have PassPorters. To learn about our other editions, see pages 284–285.

Disney Dreaming

A good part of the fun of going to the Walt Disney World Resort is the anticipation before your trip! To really get you into "Disney Dreaming," we present some of our favorite tips to feed your excitement and prepare you for the adventure that lies ahead. This is magical stuff—don't blame us if you get the urge to hop on the next plane to Orlando.

Watch a Movie

Disney movies—animations and live action alike—capture the Disney spirit wonderfully. Rent your favorite from the local video store and settle in for a cozy evening. You can also request a free vacation planning video of the Walt Disney World Resort— call Disney at 407-934-7639 to order your free video. (To get a free Disney Cruise Line video, call 888-325-2500.)

Go Shopping

You may enjoy a visit to The Disney Store—while many of these closed over the last few years and the chain was recently sold, plenty are still found in major shopping malls. The stores continue to offer delightful theming and foot-tapping music. You can buy park admission at a discount, and special offers may be had with the Disney Visa (see page 10).

Reminisce

If you've visited the "World" before, think back to your vacation and the things you enjoyed most about it. Dig out your souvenirs, photos, and home movies and view them with fresh eyes. If you used a PassPorter last time, go through your PassPockets carefully to refresh your memory and find the notes you made "for next time." If you haven't gone to Walt Disney World before, talk to all the friends and family members who have gone and get their impressions, tips, and stories.

Network With Others

Disney fans tend to gravitate towards online services and the Internet. If you've got an Internet connection, you'll find many Disney sites—even one for PassPorter planners! (See page 7 for more information.) No access to the Internet? Look to your communities for other vacationers who'd like to swap ideas and plans—try your workplace and school.

Plan, Plan, Plan

Few things are better than planning your own trip to the Walt Disney World Resort. Cuddle up with your PassPorter, read it through, and use it to the fullest—it makes planning fun and easy. PassPorter really is the ultimate in Disney Dreaming!

Planning Your Adventure

PREPARE the best possible vacation

MAKE the most of your PassPorter

LEARN where to find information on Disney

BUDGET your time, money, and resources $$$$$

Planning is the secret to a successful vacation. The vast Walt Disney World Resort is not designed for procrastinators or last-minute travelers. Good planning is rewarded by a far more magical Disney experience. Planning is also wonderful fun. It increases the anticipation and starts the excitement months before the vacation begins.

Planning begins with learning about the Walt Disney World Resort. Your PassPorter has all the information you need for a great vacation, and then some! Written to be complete yet compact, PassPorter can be your only guidebook or act as a companion to another. One unique aspect of this special Library Edition of PassPorter is how much information is available in such a seemingly small package—you won't find any other guidebook to Walt Disney World with so much detail in such a relatively slim volume. This makes PassPorter ideal for carrying about as you plan your trip!

This first chapter helps you with the initial planning stage: gathering information and budgeting. Your PassPorter then continues through the planning stages in order of priority. Sprinkled throughout are ways to personalize your trip, little-known tips, and magical Disney memories.

Above all else, have fun with your plans, both now and when you reach the Walt Disney World Resort. Leave room for flexibility, and include time to relax and refresh. Despite the temptation to see and do it all, an overly ambitious plan will be more exhausting (and frustrating) than fun. Don't get so bogged down with planning and recording that you miss the spontaneous magic of a Disney vacation. As Robert Burns so appropriately said, "The best laid plans of mice and of men go oft astray." Use your PassPorter to plan ahead so you can relax and enjoy your vacation, no matter what it brings.

Planning

Getting There

Staying in Style

Touring

Feasting

Making Magic

Index

Notes & More

Planning

Getting There

Staying in Style

Touring

Feasting

Making Magic

Index

Notes & More

Planning With Your PassPorter LE

While this version of PassPorter is known as the **Library Edition**, or LE, you may rest assured that it covers all the same topics and offers the same trusted advice found in the regular editions of PassPorter. The only features the Library Edition lacks are PassPorter's unique organizer pockets (known as PassPockets) and the sheet of tabs, labels, and stickers found in the other editions, features that are not appropriate in library books. For more information on the full-fledged editions, see the next page.

Each **important aspect of your vacation** is covered in this PassPorter. We recommend you read each chapter in order as we've organized the PassPorter in a logical fashion. Later, when you need to find a specific topic or refresh your memory, use the table of contents near the front of the book and the index in the back to find exactly what you need.

Our **special dedicated worksheets** cover everything related to planning the perfect vacation—budgeting, traveling, packing, lodging, touring, and eating. Naturally, since this is a library book, please don't write directly on the worksheets—you have our explicit permission to photocopy each worksheet for your personal vacation needs. These worksheets take the place of easy-to-lose scraps of paper because they are structured specifically for your vacation.

As this version of PassPorter does not have organizer pockets, you may find it helpful to keep your plans and papers in a **pocket folder** (the type you can get at any office supply store). You can also purchase organizer pockets directly from us at http://www.passporterstore.com/store/.

Additions and significant changes at Disney World since our 2004 edition are highlighted in gray, just like this paragraph! These higlights are not to be confused with general changes to PassPorter—almost every page has changed!

Your PassPorter is most useful when you keep it handy before and during your vacation. It fits compactly into backpacks and shoulder bags. Or, tuck your PassPorter into a **waist pack** (at least 6.5" x 9" or 17 x 23 cm).

Your PassPorter loves to go on rides with you, but try to **keep it dry** on Splash Mountain and Kali River Rapids. A simple resealable plastic bag (gallon size) is a big help.

If you're **borrowing this copy** of your PassPorter and decide you want your own just like it, you can purchase this Library Edition from us directly at http://www.passporterstore.com/store/libraryedition.aspx.

Organizing With PassPorter

If you're the type of vacationer who really loves to plan your trip, stay organized, and record memories, you may want to consider moving up to either the spiral edition or the deluxe edition of PassPorter. Both the spiral and deluxe edition offer fourteen unique "PassPockets" in the back of the book to help you plan before you go, keep items handy while you're there, and save memories for your return. You just pencil in your trip information and itinerary on the front, store brochures, maps, receipts, and such inside, and jot down impressions, memories, expenses, and notes on the back. You can even personalize your PassPockets with the included labels and stickers! Here's how they work:

Read the advice or tip.

Use the pockets as printed, or personalize with a label.

Write your itinerary here, including times, names, and confirmation numbers. Or just record what you did.

Jot down things you want to remember, do, or visit.

Make notes before you go or add notes during your trip.

Store items you want to have on hand during your trip, or things you collect along the way, in this roomy pocket. Guidemaps, brochures, and envelopes all fit inside.

Slip small items in this smaller slot, such as receipts, claim tags, and ticket stubs.

Write the day of the week and the date for quick reference!

Record memories of your vacation to share with others or to keep to yourself. You can jot these down as you go or reminisce at the end of the day.

Keep track of photos taken so you can find them later!

Watch your expenses to stay within a budget or to track your resort charge account balance.

Remember all those great (or not so great) meals and snacks by noting them here. You can even include the price of the meal or snack, too!

What did you forget? What do you want to do again? What would you like to try next time? What wouldn't you touch again with a ten-foot pole? Make a note of it here!

These organizer pockets are available with our spiral and deluxe editions, or may be purchased separately to put inside one of our deluxe, six-ring binders. To learn more about our other editions and planning products, please see pages 284–285.

(Side tabs: Planning, Getting There, Staying in Style, Touring, Feasting, Making Magic, Index, Notes & More)

Planning

Getting There

Staying in Style

Touring

Feasting

Making Magic

Index

Notes & More

Finding Disney Information

PassPorter can act as your **first source** of information for the Walt Disney World Resort. It can also be a companion to other Disney books you may already own or purchase later. Either way, we like to think it packs a lot of information into a small package. Everything you need to know to plan a wonderful Disney vacation can be found within its pages.

Do keep in mind that the Walt Disney World Resort is constantly changing. We've taken every step to ensure that your PassPorter is as up-to-date as possible, but we cannot foresee the future. So to help your PassPorter remain current, we **make free updates available** to you at our Web site (http://www.passporter.com/customs/bookupdates.htm). If you have ideas, questions, or corrections, please contact us—see page 260.

Oodles of **travel guidebooks** are available if you have a hankering for second opinions. We highly recommend these guidebooks: "The Unofficial Guide to Walt Disney World" (for irreverence, detail, and touring plans), "Birnbaum's Walt Disney World" (for the official line and color photos), "Walt Disney World for Couples" (for sweet romance), and "Hassle-Free Walt Disney World" (for touring plans). You'll find something different in each.

Call the **Walt Disney World Resort** at 407-WDW-MAGIC (407-939-6244) or e-mail them through their Web site (http://www.disneyworld.com) when you need answers to specific questions. In our experience, their representatives are very friendly, but they rarely volunteer information and won't offer opinions. Prepare questions in advance. If the person you reach doesn't have an answer, call back—several times if necessary. Don't hesitate to ask for a manager if you can't get the information you need.

Travel agents whom you know and trust can be an excellent source of information, such as the service-oriented MouseEarVacations.com (see coupon on page 282). Also check with **membership organizations** that arrange travel, such as AAA (see page 11).

Magazines and newsletters about Disney are also available. The "Disney Magazine" covers all things Disney, including the parks. Subscribe for $20 for eight issues (two years) at 800-333-8734. Annual Passholders in the U.S. (see page 10) receive a quarterly newsletter from Disney. ALL EARS® is a free unofficial e-mail newsletter that comes out weekly with news, reviews, and reports—subscribe at http://www.allearsnet.com. We also offer our own bi-weekly newsletter with updates, Disney and general travel features, and tips—subscribe at http://www.passporter.com/news.htm. "Mouse Tips" is a more traditional paper newsletter—subscribe for a special rate of $11/year at Box 383, Columbus, OH 43216.

Exploring a Whole New World Wide Web

The ultimate source of information, in our opinion, is the **Internet**. Of course, this requires a personal computer with a modem, a network connection, or "WebTV," but with this you can connect to millions of vacationers happy to share their Disney knowledge.

The Web offers hundreds of Disney-related sites. In fact, **PassPorter** has its own Web site with updates, tips, ideas, articles, forums, and links. Visit us at http://www.passporter.com. More details are on page 279.

As you might expect, Disney has a Web site for all things Walt Disney World at http://www.disneyworld.com. While **Disney's official Web site** doesn't offer opinions, it is an excellent source for basic information, including operating hours, rates, maps, and resort room layouts. Late changes to operating hours are best verified at 407-824-4321, however.

We also highly recommend several **unofficial Web sites**, which we frequent ourselves when planning a trip. We introduce these Web sites as appropriate throughout the book (check pages 272–273 in the index for a full list), but one special site deserves mention now: **AllEarsNet®** is a comprehensive and up-to-date collection of information about the Walt Disney World Resort, often contributed by other Disney vacationers and enthusiasts. All Ears Net is located at http://www.allearsnet.com. Tell Deb we said "Hi!"

Another source of information (and camaraderie) is **discussion groups**. PassPorter has its own set of message boards with an active, supportive community of vacationers at http://www.passporterboards.com—come chat with us and ask your questions! Fans also gather at Pete Werner's **Unofficial Disney Information Station** at http://www.wdwinfo.com, as well as at John Yaglenski's **Intercot** at http://www.intercot.com and Rich Koster's **DisneyEcho** at http://disneyecho.emuck.com. We also recommend the **rec.arts.disney.parks (RADP)** newsgroup at news://rec.arts.disney.parks. Last but not least, those of you on **America Online** should pay a visit to the Disney message boards at Keyword: TRAVEL BOARDS.

E-mail lists are yet another valuable Internet resource, allowing you to observe and participate in discussions from the safety of your e-mailbox. We host both a discussion list and a newsletter list with regular feature articles—subscribe for free at our Web site. Many other mailing lists are available, including **The Mouse For Less** (formerly DisneyDollarless) for Disney fans on a budget—visit at http://www.themouseforless.com.

Budgeting for Your Vacation

There's nothing magical about depleting your nest egg to finance a vacation. Too many Disney vacationers can tell you that money worries overshadowed all the fun. Yet you can avoid both the realities and worries of overspending by planning within a budget. Budgeting ahead of time not only keeps you from spending too much, it encourages you to seek out ways to save money. With just a little bit of research, you can often get **more for less**, resulting in a much richer, more relaxed vacation.

If you purchase a **vacation package**, you have the advantage of covering most of your major expenses right up front. And while package prices haven't offered a real savings in the past, they've recently gotten better and can be excellent deals. Beyond finding a package with a great deal, planning each aspect of your vacation yourself usually saves you more money, as we show you throughout this book. You can learn about vacation packages on page 30 and inquire into prices with the Walt Disney Travel Co. at 800-828-0228 or on the Web at http://www.disneytravel.com.

Your **vacation expenses** usually fall into six categories: planning, transportation, lodging, admission, food, and extras. How you budget for each depends upon the total amount you have available to spend and your priorities. Planning, transportation, lodging, and admission are the easiest to factor ahead of time as costs are more or less fixed. The final two—food and extras—are harder to control, but can usually be estimated based on your tastes and habits.

Begin your vacation budgeting with the **worksheet** on the following page. Enter the minimum you prefer to spend and the maximum you can afford in the topmost row. Establish as many of these ranges as possible before you delve into the other chapters of this book. Your excitement may grow as you read more about the Walt Disney World Resort, but it is doubtful your bank account will.

As you uncover costs and ways to save money later, return to this worksheet and **update it**. Think of your budget as a work in progress. Flexibility within your minimum and maximum figures is important. As plans begin to crystallize, write the amount you expect to pay (and can afford) in the Estimated Costs column.

If you purchase the optional PassPockets, you can **transfer the amounts** from the Estimated Costs column to the back of each PassPocket. Note that each PassPocket also provides space to record actual expenses, which helps you stay within your budget.

Planning

Getting There

Staying in Style

Touring

Feasting

Making Magic

Index

Notes & More

Budget Worksheet

Use this worksheet to identify your resources, record estimated costs, and create a budget for your vacation. If you've borrowed this copy of the book, you have our permission to make photocopies of this page for your personal vacation planning.

	Minimum		Maximum		Est. Costs	
Total Projected Expenses	$		$		$	
Planning:						
Phone Calls/Faxes:						
Guides/Magazines:						
Transportation:						
Rental Car:						
Fuel/Maintenance/Tolls:						
Airfare/Travel Tickets:						
Shuttle/Town Car/Taxi:						
Stroller/Wheelchair:						
ECV/Golf Cart:						
Parking:						
Lodging:						
En Route Motel/Other:						
Resort/Hotel:						
Admission:						
Theme Park Passes:						
Water Park Passes:						
DisneyQuest Passes:						
Pleasure Island Passes:						
Guided Tours/Other:						

Food:	Daily	Total	Daily	Total	Daily	Total
Breakfast:						
Lunch:						
Dinner:						
Snacks:						
Groceries/Other:						

Extras:						
Souvenirs/Clothing:						
Gratuities:						
Vacation Wardrobe:						
Photos:						
Other:						
Total Budgeted Expenses	$		$		$	

Money-Saving Programs

You can save real money on a Walt Disney World Resort vacation by taking advantage of these money-saving programs. Some require a membership fee, but they often pay for themselves quite quickly.

Disney Visa Card—This credit card from BankOne gives cardholders special discounts on Disney resorts and packages and onboard credits on the Disney cruise. The card itself has no annual fee and earns "Disney Dream Reward Dollars" equal to 1% or more of your purchases. You can redeem your dollars quickly for Disney travel, entertainment, and merchandise. Another perk is the "pay no interest for 6 months" offer on Disney packages and cruises. We have Disney Visa ourselves and while the "rewards" are just average, the available discounts can be great. Note that the Disney Visa is available to U.S. residents only. For more information, visit http://disney.go.com/visa or call 877-252-6576.

Annual Pass (AP)—An Annual Pass (regular or premium) saves big money on admission if you plan to visit for more than eight or thirteen days in a one-year period (depending on the pass), at which point it becomes less expensive than conventional admission. It may also deliver great discounts (up to 50%) at selected Disney resorts. The discounts alone may be worth it! See pages 116–117 for details and call Disney at 407-WDW-MAGIC for prices.

Florida Residents—Those of you with proof of Florida residency (such as a valid Florida driver's license) often enjoy great savings on Disney tickets, resorts, cruises, and more. The deals are so good we're almost tempted to move to Florida. Visit http://www.disneyworld.com for more details.

Disney Dining Experience (DDE)—Available only to Florida residents with a valid Florida driver's license or I.D. card, this program offers 20% discounts at most Disney table-service restaurants, plus free parking after 5:00 pm and half price Pleasure Island admission. Membership is $75/year (with an extra $5 off for annual passholders and cast members). Renewals are $60/year. Call 407-566-5858 to order (allow 2–3 weeks).

Disney Information Center at Ocala—If you're driving from the north, stop at Disney's Information Center off I-75 in Ocala for occasional deals on accommodations. Open 9:00 am to 6:00 pm. Call 352-854-0770.

Disney Vacation Club (DVC)—This timeshare program may save money for families who plan ahead. DVC members also get discounts on meals, admission, and backstage tours. See pages 102–103 for details.

Advance Purchase Park Admission Discounts—Buy your Disney park tickets in advance and save! At press time, you can save $8–12 off the price of certain passes (see pages 116–117 for pass details). Get your advance purchase discounts at Disney Stores outside of Florida, Disney Specialist travel agents (such as MouseEarVacations.com—see page 282), via the Web (http://www.disneyworld.com), or by phone (407-WDW-MAGIC). If the tickets need to be mailed, expect a mailing charge of $3 per order. If you do buy your tickets in advance, be sure to write down the pass reference number(s) in your PassPorter in the event you lose them.

Disney "Postcard" Specials and Advertisements—Disney frequently offers lodging discounts in direct mail and mass media advertisements. These offers may be sent to previous Disney guests and vacationers who've requested planning materials, or may appear in newspaper or TV ads. These offers usually have eligibility requirements, such as residence in a particular state, or can only be used by the person who received the mailing. If you receive an offer, be sure to save it for your records. You'll need the "coupon code" and perhaps an I.D. number to make your reservation. Be sure you are eligible for the offer—if you show up at Disney and can't prove eligibility, you'll lose your "deal." Visit http://www. mousesavers.com for an excellent listing of current offers.

Orlando Magicard—This free card offers discounts on many non-Disney shows and park tickets, as well as rental cars and hotels. Call 888-416-4026 or visit http://www.orlandoinfo.com/magicard and allow 3–4 weeks.

American Automobile Association (AAA)—Members enjoy discounts ranging from 10% to 20%, including tickets (when purchased in advance). Contact your local office, call 800-222-6424, or visit http://www.aaa.com.

Money-Saving Tips

- ✔ MouseSavers.com is a Web site dedicated to cataloging available Disney discounts and deals. Webmaster Mary Waring has built a huge following, both at http://www.mousesavers.com and through her free monthly newsletter.
- ✔ If you are flying, check the newspapers and the Internet for fare sales—they occur more frequently than you might think and offer savings. Expedia.com (http://www.expedia.com) also has great deals on fares and hotel rooms!
- ✔ If you are driving or arriving late in the evening, consider staying a night at a less expensive motel your first night.
- ✔ You can save money on meals by sharing entrees or by eating only two meals a day, as Disney portions tend to be quite large. Bring quick breakfast foods and snacks from home to quell the munchies and keep your energy up.
- ✔ Always ask about discounts when you make reservations, dine, or shop. You may discover little-known specials for AAA, Disney Visa Card, Florida residents, Annual Passholders, or simply vacationers in the right place at the right time.
- ✔ Join The Mouse For Less community for more money-saving tips—you can subscribe for free at http://www.themouseforless.com.

Plan It Up!

Use these tips to make planning your vacation fun and rewarding:

Use **traveler's checks** instead of credit, debit cards, or cash. Allocate an amount of money to spend each day and only take that amount with you, leaving the rest in a safe place. That way you never go over budget. Traveler's checks are better than cash because of the ability to get replacements if they are lost or stolen.
— *Contributed by Mark Zeis, a winner in our 2004 Reader Tip Contest*

If you have access to the **Internet**, make it a point to get online once a week for the latest dish on the "World." We have many trip reports from fellow vacationers posted on our message boards at http://www.passporterboards.com. MousePlanet also offers trip reports at http://www.mouseplanet.com/dtp/trip.rpt.

If you have children, create **lunchbox notes** with vacation countdown information and Disney stickers. I began doing this for my daughter Alyssa 101 days before our trip. All the lunch table kids always ask her, "Is there a Disney Note in your lunch?" They are so excited for her that they are giving their parents the Disney bug.
— *Contributed by Jeneice Seagraves, a winner in our 2004 Reader Tip Contest*

Magical Memories

"Our son, Andrew, had an emergency appendectomy for a ruptured appendix a couple of months before our Walt Disney World vacation. With a very high fever and infection, he was in the hospital for several days. When we came home, he had no appetite, no desire to do anything, and was unable to attend school for two weeks. Andrew just seemed so depressed. I was staying home from my job to take care of him and one day I had a brainstorm. I opened up our PassPorter, sat on the sofa next to Andrew, and asked him if he would like to plan our Disney trip. If you could only have seen his face light up! It was the first smile I had seen in days! Tears came to my eyes to see him take an interest in something and to be happy! For the next several days, Andrew and I planned what parks we would go to and when and where we would eat. He even sat next to me when I called for priority seatings and made other reservations. I will always remember the joy he expressed and the magical memories we made just spending time together doing something we both love. Thank you so much for bringing PassPorter into our lives."

...as told by Disney vacationer Dianne Cook

"While preparing for a vacation with my two sons, I came up with the idea of the Disney Question of the Night. Each night before bed, the kids asked two questions about Disney or told me two things they were hoping for, expecting, etc. This game gave me a much better idea of what attractions and restaurants to plan without really asking. As a result, the kids were more prepared ... and excited!"

...as told by Disney vacationer Maureen Austin

Getting There (and Back!)

So, you promised your family a trip to visit the Mouse, or for the tenth time today you've gleefully thought, "I'm going to Disney!" Eventually the moment of truth arrives: just *how* are you going to get there?

Traveling in this age of tightened security requires more planning and patience, but you'll discover it is quite easy to get to the Walt Disney World Resort. The path to Orlando, Florida is well traveled by cars, planes, trains, buses, and tours. On the other hand, "easy" isn't always convenient or inexpensive. Choosing the best and most affordable way to get to Disney can take some doing. And we can help!

In this chapter, we walk you through the process of making your travel arrangements. We brief you on weather, attendance levels, park hours, and seasonal rates so you can pick the best time to go or make the most of the date you've already chosen. You'll find descriptions of each major path to the Walt Disney World Resort and a worksheet to help you pick a route and make your reservations. Then it's time to get packing, with the help of our special packing lists. Finally, we help you smile and enjoy your journey with tips for having fun along the way.

What we won't do is take up space with the phone numbers of airline and car rental companies or travel directions from every city. You can find that information in your phone book or on the World Wide Web. Just jot down numbers and notes on a copy of the worksheet provided in this chapter.

It's important to note that traveling is generally less flexible than lodging, which is in turn more costly. Thus, we find it works much better to make traveling decisions before finalizing hotel arrangements. However, you may prefer to skip to the next chapter and shop for your lodging first. Just return here to tailor your travel plans to your lodging choice.

Your journey begins...

Planning

Getting There

Staying in Style

Touring

Feasting

Making Magic

Index

Notes & More

The Best of Times

Most Disney veterans can tell you, in no uncertain terms, that some times are much better than others to visit the "World." We wholeheartedly agree, but there's more to it. While there are certainly times of the year that are less crowded or more temperate, only you can decide the best time to visit. To help you decide, we charted the **fluctuating factors** for each month below. If you ask us, the best time to visit is November–February, but avoid the holidays, when parks fill to capacity. Three-day weekends are also to be avoided whenever possible. The latter half of August and September are uncrowded, though you'll battle the heat. For links to temperature and rainfall data, visit http://www.passporter.com/wdw/bestoftimes.htm.

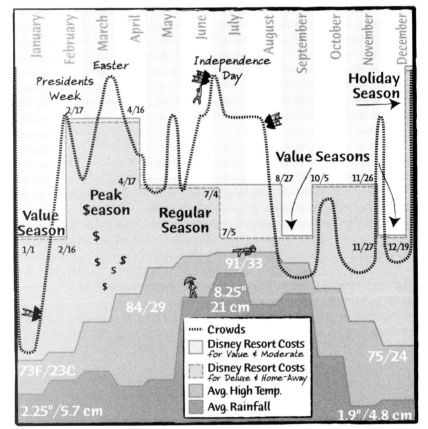

2005 Disney resort cost seasons are as follows:

Value Season is Jan. 1– Feb. 16 (all), Jul. 5–Oct. 4 (deluxe and home-away), Aug. 28–Oct. 4 (value and moderate), Nov. 27–Dec. 19 (all); **Regular Season** is Apr. 17–Jul. 4 (deluxe and home-away), Apr. 17–Aug. 27 (value and moderate), Oct. 5–Nov. 26 (all); **Peak Season** is Feb. 17–Apr. 16 (all); **Pre-Holiday Season** is Nov. 18–Dec. 19 (Ft. Wilderness campsites only); and **Holiday Season** is Dec. 20–31 (all).

Disney's Animal Kingdom Area   Epcot Area   Downtown Disney Area   Magic Kingdom Area

Chapter 2: Getting There (and Back!)   Topic: How To Get There   15

Getting There

One of the major hurdles to a Walt Disney World Resort vacation is figuring out how to get there in the first place. Many of us think along the traditional (and expensive) lines first, and become discouraged. It doesn't have to be like that. There are **more ways** to get to Disney than you probably realize. Below we describe each, beginning with the most popular. At the end of the list, on pages 20–21, a worksheet gives you space to make notes, jot down prices, and note reservation numbers. When your travel plans are finalized, record them on the first PassPocket.

By Car, Van, Truck, or Motorcycle

Most vacationers arrive at Disney in their own vehicle. It's hard to beat the **slowly rising sense of excitement** as you draw closer or the freedom of having your own wheels once you arrive. Driving may also eliminate the concerns you or family members may have with air travel. And driving can be less expensive than air travel, especially with large families. Be sure to compare the costs of driving versus flying before you decide. On the down side, you may spend long hours or even days on the road, which cuts deeply into your time with Mickey.

If you opt to drive, carefully **map your course** ahead of time. You can do this with a AAA TripTik—a strip map that guides you to and from your destination. You must be a AAA member (see page 11) to get a TripTik, but that is easily done for $40-$55/year (visit http://www.aaa.com for more information). If you're driving, we heartily recommend "Along Interstate-75" (Mile Oak Publishing, http://www.i75online.com) and/or "Drive I-95" (Travelsmart, http://www.drivei95.com). I-95 drivers should also visit http://www.usastar.com/i95/homepage.htm. Or try a trip routing service, such as AutoPilot at http://www.freetrip.com **Tip**: Have exact change ready for the many Florida toll roads along your trip. You can get toll prices at http://www.dot.state.fl.us/turnpikepio/TollCalculator/tollrates.htm.

If you live more than 500 miles away, **spread out your drive** over more than one day, allotting one day for every 500 miles. Arriving at Walt Disney World overly road-weary is no way to begin a vacation. If your journey spans more than one day, decide in advance where to stop each night and make reservations accordingly. Check that your air-conditioning is in good working order. Secure rest areas are available once you hit the Florida border, making it a bit easier to drive at night.

Planning · Getting There · Staying in Style · Touring · Feasting · Making Magic · Index · Notes & More

By Airplane

Air travel is the fastest way for most vacationers to get to Orlando—and it's a great way to strengthen the air travel industry and the U.S. economy. Plus, air travel may be less expensive than you think if you know the tricks to getting an **affordable flight**. First, be flexible on the day and time of departure and return—fares can differ greatly depending on when you fly and how long you stay. Second, take advantage of the many "fare sales"—to learn about sales, visit airlines' Web sites or travel sites such as Expedia (http://www.expedia.com), Orbitz (http://www.orbitz.com), or Travelocity (http://www.travelocity.com). Third, try alternate airports when researching fares. Fourth, be persistent. Ask for their lowest fare and work from there. When you find a good deal, put it on hold immediately (if possible), note your reservation number on page 21, and cancel later if necessary. Finally, don't stop shopping. If your airline offers a cheaper fare later, you may be able to rebook at the lower rate (watch out for penalties).

Try your **airline's Web site**—you can experiment with different flights and sign up for fare sale e-mails, and it can be cheaper—many airlines now charge extra for telephone reservations. Try Priceline (http://www.priceline.com), where you name your own price for a round-trip ticket (but once your price is met, Priceline chooses your flight times and you can't cancel).

Once you reserve a flight, **make a note** of the reservation numbers, flight numbers, seat assignments, and layovers on your worksheet. To arrange **ground transportation** from the airport, see page 19.

Our Top 10 Flying Tips, Reminders, and Warnings

1. Visit http://www.tsa.gov for travel security news and updates.
2. Check the status of your flight before departing for the airport.
3. Pack (or pick up) a meal for the flight, as most domestic flights have discontinued meal service for security reasons.
4. Pack sharp or potentially dangerous items in checked luggage (or just leave them at home). This includes pocket knives, knitting needles, pointed scissors, nail files, sport sticks (i.e., pool cues), lighters, or flammable items such as aerosol hairspray. If you must bring needles or syringes, also bring a note from your doctor. Nail clippers and tweezers are now fine to keep in your carry-on.
5. Keep your luggage unlocked for inspections, or it may be damaged.
6. Limit your carry-ons to one bag and one personal item (purse, briefcase, etc.) and assume they will be searched.
7. Plan to arrive at the airport two hours prior to departure.
8. Curbside check-in may be available, but you may need to obtain a boarding pass from your airline's customer service desk anyway.
9. E-Ticket holders should bring a confirmation and/or boarding pass. If you don't have one, print it from your airline's Web site.
10. Keep your ID handy. We carry ours in PassHolder Pouches (see page 283).

Getting Around the Orlando Airport

Orlando International Airport is a large, sprawling hub and one of the better (and cleaner) airports we've flown into. When you arrive, your plane docks at one of the **satellite terminals** (see map below). From there, follow the signs to the automated **shuttle** that takes you to the main terminal—there you'll find **baggage claim** and ground transportation. Once you reach the main terminal (Level 3), follow the signs down to baggage claim (Level 2). Shuttles, taxis, town cars, rental cars, and buses are found down on Level 1 (take the elevators opposite the baggage carousels). Each shuttle and bus company has its own ticket booth, so keep your eyes open. If you get lost, look about for signs or an information desk that can get you back on track.

As your authors used to live in entirely different parts of the country, we became quite good at **meeting up at the airport**. It's best to meet your party at their baggage claim area as you won't be allowed past security without a valid boarding pass. The trick here is knowing which airline and baggage claim area. Use the map and airline list below, or call the airport directly at 407-825-2001. Be careful when differentiating between Side A and B's baggage claim. Gates 1-29 and 100-129 use Side A, while gates 30-99 use Side B. Check the arrival/departure boards in the main terminal for flight status, too! Other meeting spots are the Disney Stores inside the terminal (see stars on map below) or an airport restaurant (especially good for long waits).

For **more details** on the Orlando International Airport, call 407-825-2001 or visit http://www.orlandoairports.net. Page travelers at 407-825-2000.

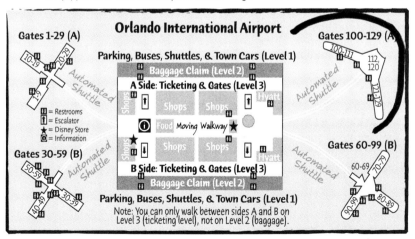

American Airlines, America West, ATA, Continental, SunWorld, Thomas Cook, and TWA use Gates 1-29; Air Canada, ANA, Northwest, Ted, United, and USAir use Gates 30-59; Delta, British Airways, Midwest, Song, Sun Country, and Virgin Atlantic use Gates 60-99; and AirTran, JetBlue, Southwest, and Spirit use Gates 100-129.

By Train, Bus, Tour, and Boat

By Train

The train is a uniquely relaxing way to travel to the Walt Disney World Resort. **Amtrak** serves the Orlando area daily with both **passenger trains** and an Auto Train, which carries your family and your car. The **Auto Train** runs between suburban Washington, DC and suburban Orlando (Sanford, FL). Other trains may go through to Kissimmee, which is a closer, less-crowded station for vacationers bound for Walt Disney World. Prices vary depending upon the season, the direction, and how far in advance you make your reservation. The Auto Train is also available one-way, and in many seasons, one direction is less expensive than the other direction. You may need to take a taxi or town car (see page 19) from the train station to the Disney property. Hertz rental cars are available from the Sanford and Orlando stations, but not the Kissimmee station. For Amtrak reservations, call 800-USA-RAIL or visit them at http://www.amtrak.com.

By Bus

Buses make good economic and environmental sense. **Greyhound** serves Orlando and Kissimmee. You can take the local LYNX buses from there, but it's not easy (for more information on LYNX, see the next page under "Riding a Bus"). Buses take longer to reach a destination than do cars driving the same route. Fares are lowest if you live within ten hours of Walt Disney World. For fares, schedules, and tickets, call Greyhound at 800-231-2222 or visit them at http://www.greyhound.com.

By Tour

A number of **special tours** go to the Walt Disney World Resort, which you may want to consider if you prefer to go with a large group or with like-minded folks. Check with the associations, organizations, and societies you belong to, or contact a travel agent.

By Boat

If you book passage on the **Disney Cruise Line**, your package may include a stay at the Walt Disney World Resort. The boat doesn't pull up to the Magic Kingdom, but Disney offers optional, prearranged transfers to and/or from the Walt Disney World Resort—this transportation may be included in your cruise package, or you may add it for an additional fee. See pages 100–101 for details on the Disney Cruise, and see page 285 to learn about our field guide to the Disney Cruise Line.

By Everything Else!

The list of ways to get to Disney is really endless. Consider traveling under your own power—bicycles! Combine business with pleasure, or make your pleasure your business, as we have.

Are We There Yet?

Once you reach Orlando, you need to continue about 20 miles before you actually reach the Disney property. Here are your options:

Taking a Shuttle or Town Car

A number of shuttle companies stay in business largely by transporting guests to and from Disney. Shuttle stands are located at the Orlando International Airport (Level 1), but all other pickup points require advance notice. The major shuttle operator is Mears (800-759-5219). We prefer and recommend a **town car**, however. The town car driver greets us at baggage claim, carries our luggage, drives us to our hotel, and charges less than it costs a family of four to use a shuttle, taxi, or rental car. We love Tiffany Towncar (888-838-2161) and recommend their services (we've included a great coupon for a roundtrip on page 280). If you'd like to stop at a grocery store or if you need a car/booster seat, request this at reservation. Visit http://www.tiffanytowncar.com. Two more services we've used with good results include YourRide (866-240-RIDE, http://www.yourride.net) and Happy Limo (888-394-4277, http://www.happylimo.com)

Driving a Car

If you're driving to Walt Disney World, you'll need specific directions. You can find detailed directions through a trip routing service (see page 15) or Disney (call 407-939-4636). Fliers planning to drive a car while in Orlando should rent at the airport. We don't feel a rental car is needed if you stay only on Disney property as their internal transportation system works well (see pages 118–119) and even an occasional taxi fare can be cheaper than a rental car. If you plan to go off-property often, you may find a rental car helpful. Alamo (Disney's official rental car agency), Avis, Budget, Dollar, and National are located right at the airport on Level 1 (in-airport rentals incur a 10% fee). Enterprise, Hertz, and many others are off-site and you'll need to take a shuttle on Level 1 to reach them (off-site rentals carry an 8.67% fee). The Dolphin Resort and several off-property hotels offer rental car desks, too. Inquire about all taxes and surcharges.

Riding a Bus

The regional bus system, LYNX, has limited service to the Walt Disney World property. Call 407-841-LYNX (5969) or visit http://www.golynx.com. And if you need to get from your hotel to any other theme park in the Orlando area, Mears offers shuttles ($12 roundtrip)—call a day in advance.

Using a Taxi

While taxis are available, we don't recommend them for travel due to cost. Large parties may be able to ride in a taxi mini-van economically, however.

Travel Worksheet

Use this worksheet to jot down preferences, scribble information during phone calls, and keep all your discoveries together. Don't worry about being neat—just be thorough! You have our permission to make a photocopy of this worksheet for your personal vacation planning. 💡 Circle the names and numbers once you decide to go with them to avoid confusion.

Arrival date: _____   Alternate: _____

Return date: _____   Alternate: _____

We plan to travel by: ❑ Car/Van   ❑ Airplane   ❑ Train   ❑ Bus   ❑ Tour
❑ Other: _____

For Drivers:

Miles to get to Orlando: _____ ÷ 500 = _____ days on the road

We need to stay at a motel on: _____

Tune-up scheduled for: _____

Rental car info: _____

_____

For Riders:

Train/Bus phone numbers: _____

Ride preferences: _____

Ride availabilities: _____

Reserved ride times and numbers: _____

Routes: _____

For Tour-Takers:

Tour company phone numbers: _____

Tour preferences: _____

Tour availabilities: _____

Reserved tour times and numbers: _____

Routes: _____

For Fliers:

Airline phone numbers: _____

Flight preferences: _____

Flight availabilities: _____

_____

_____

_____

Reserved flight times and numbers: _____

_____

For Ground Transportation:

Town car/shuttle/rental car phone numbers: _____

_____

Town car/shuttle/rental car reservations: _____

_____

Package ground transportation details: _____

_____

Additional Notes:

Reminder: Don't forget to confirm holds or cancel reservations (whenever possible) within the allotted time frame.

Packing List

You have our permission to make a photocopy of this worksheet for your personal vacation planning.

Packing for a vacation is fun when you feel confident you're packing the right things. Over the years, we've compiled a packing list for a great Disney vacation. Just note the quantity you plan to bring and check items off as you pack. Consider carrying items in **bold** on a daily basis around the parks.

The Essentials

❏ Casual clothing you can layer—the dress code nearly everywhere at Disney is casual, even at dinner. One "nice" outfit is usually enough.
   ___ Shorts/skirts   ___ Pants/jeans   ___ Shirts   ___ Sweaters
   ___ Underwear   ___ Socks   ___ Pajamas

❏ Jacket and/or sweatshirt (light ones for the warmer months)
   ___ **Jackets**   ___ Sweatshirts   ___ Sweaters   ___ Vests

❏ Comfortable, well-broken-in shoes ... plus a second pair, just in case!
   ___ Walking shoes   ___ Sandals   ___ Sneakers   ___ _____

❏ Swim gear (bring one-piece suits for water slides)
   ___ Suits/trunks   ___ Cover-ups/towels   ___ Water shoes   ___ Goggles

❏ Sun protection (the Florida sun can be brutal)
   ___ **Sunblock**   ___ **Lip balm**   ___ **Sunburn relief**   ___ **Sunglasses**
   ___ **Hats w/brims**   ___ **Caps**   ___ **Visors**   ___ _____

❏ Rain gear (compact and light so you don't mind carrying it)
   ___ Raincoat   ___ **Poncho**   ___ **Umbrella**   ___ **Dry socks**

❏ Comfortable bags with padded straps to carry items during the day
   ___ **Backpacks**   ___ **Waist packs**   ___ Shoulder bags   ___ **Camera bag**

❏ Toiletries (in a bag or bathroom kit to keep them organized)
   ___ **Brush/comb**   ___ Toothbrush   ___ Toothpaste   ___ Dental floss
   ___ Favorite soap, shampoo, and conditioner   ___ Deodorant   ___ **Baby wipes**
   ___ **Aspirin/acetaminophen/ibuprofen**   ___ **Band aids**   ___ **First aid kit**
   ___ **Prescriptions** (in original containers)   ___ Vitamins   ___ Fem. hygiene
   ___ Hair dryer/iron   ___ **Anti-blister tape**   ___ Makeup   ___ Hairspray
   ___ Razors   ___ Shaving cream   ___ Cotton buds   ___ Lotion
   ___ Nail clippers   ___ Spare eyeglasses   ___ Lens solution   ___ **Bug repellent**
   ___ Mending kit   ___ Small scissors   ___ Safety pins   ___ **Insect sting kit**

❏ Camera/camcorder and more film/tape than you think you need
   ___ **Camera**   ___ **Camcorder**   ___ **Film/tapes**   ___ **Storage cards**
   ___ **Batteries**   ___ Chargers   ___ **Camera case**   ___ _____

❏ Money in various forms and various places
   ___ **Charge cards**   ___ **Traveler's checks**   ___ **Bank cards**   ___ **Cash**

❏ Personal identification, passes, and membership cards
   ___ **Driver's licenses**   ___ **Other photo ID**   ___ **Passports**   ___ Birth certificate
   ___ **AAA card**   ___ **Discount cards**   ___ Air miles card   ___ _____
   ___ **Tickets/passes**   ___ **Insurance cards**   ___ **Calling cards**

Tip: Label everything with your name, phone, and hotel to help reunite you with your stuff if lost. Every bag should have this info on a luggage tag as well as on a slip of paper inside it. Use our Luggage Tag Maker at http://www.passporter.com/wdw/luggagelog.htm.

For Your Carry-On

❑ Your **PassPorter**, **tickets**, **maps**, **guides**, and a **pen** or **pencil**! ✏ Remember to pack any sharp or potentially dangerous items in your checked luggage, not your carry-on.
❑ **Camera** and/or **camcorder**, along with **film**, **tapes**, and **batteries**
❑ Any **prescriptions**, important toiletries, **sunblock**, **sunglasses**, **hats**, **bug repellent**
❑ Change of clothes appropriate to your destination's weather
❑ **Snacks**, 🥤 **water bottle**, **juice boxes**, gum, favorite books, **toys**, **games**, blankets

For Families

❑ Snacks and juice boxes
❑ Books, toys, 🎮 and games
❑ Stroller, carrier, and accessories 🚼
❑ **Autograph books** and **fat pens**
❑ EarPlanes (http://www.earplanes.com)

For Couples

❑ Corkscrew and wine glasses 🍷
❑ Candles and matches
❑ Evening wear for nights out
❑ (Jacket for Victoria & Albert's)
❑ Portable CD player and CDs

For Connected Travelers

❑ Laptop and power supply
❑ Extension cord/surge suppressor
❑ Phone/network cables, coupler, splitter
❑ Security cable with lock
❑ **Cell phones** and chargers
❑ **Two-way radios**
❑ Local access numbers 📱
❑ **Handheld/Palm organizer**

For Heat-Sensitive Travelers

❑ **Personal fans/water misters**
❑ **Water bottles** (frozen, if possible)
❑ **Washcloth** to cool off face and neck
❑ Loose, breezy clothing
❑ **Hats** with wide brims
❑ **Sunshades** (for baby strollers)
❑ **Elastics** to keep long hair off neck
❑ **Sweatbands**

Everyone Should Consider

❑ Big beach towels (for pools and water parks)
❑ **Penlight** or flashlight (for reading/writing in dark places and to alleviate kids' fears)
❑ **Water bottles** and personal **fan/water misters**
❑ **Snacks** for any time of the day (plus gum, if you chew it)
❑ Plastic cutlery for snacks or leftovers 🍴
❑ **Quarters** and **pennies** (and a way to hold them) for the coin presses and/or laundry
❑ Plastic storage bags that seal (large and small), plus trash bags
❑ Address book, stamps, and envelopes ✉
❑ Laundry detergent/tablets, bleach, dryer sheets, stain stick, and a laundry tote
❑ **Binoculars**
❑ Collapsible bag or suitcase inside another suitcase to hold souvenirs on your return

Your Personal Packing List

❑ _____ ❑ _____
❑ _____ ❑ _____
❑ _____ ❑ _____
❑ _____ ❑ _____
❑ _____ ❑ _____
❑ _____ ❑ _____
❑ _____ ❑ _____
❑ _____ ❑ _____
❑ _____ ❑ _____

Planning | Getting There | Staying in Style | Touring | Feasting | Making Magic | Index | Notes & More

Adventuring!

Your journey is more pleasant when you consider it an adventure rather than a tiring trek. Here are our tried-and-true adventuring tips:

Listen to **audio books**. Rent, purchase, or even "borrow" from Cracker Barrel restaurants (return them for a partial refund). You may also want to purchase/rent a VCR or DVD player and movies!

Map your course as you go. Create a travel journal to show your friends and to recall your adventure.

Bring your own **beverages and snacks** aboard the plane and live in the lap of luxury. Why not bring gum (to offset air pressure), lotion (to offset dry air), and a tape/CD player (to offset boredom)?

When driving to Disney from a distance, **pick a few hotels** along the way to stay. As you drive and gain a better idea of how much longer you will be able to go in one day, phone and cancel the extra hotels before the cancellation time (usually 4:00 or 6:00 pm). This helps when there is unexpected traffic and/or no traffic at all.
— *Contributed by an anonymous winner in our 2004 Traveling Tip Contest*

Pack an **extra glide-on deodorant** just for your feet. Yes, your feet! Roll it on each morning before hiking out to the parks and it keeps feet dry, cool, and, most important of all, blister-free!
— *Contributed by Karen Miller, a winner in our 2004 Traveling Tip Contest*

Magical Memories

"My entire family fell in love with all the wonderful aspects of vacationing at Walt Disney World, but my daughter (then 9) summed it up as only a little kid could. After a wonderful week, we sadly made the trip home and landed back at the Atlantic City airport in New Jersey. Making a bathroom stop in the airport, my daughter came out of the bathroom stall with a glum look. As we washed up, I asked her what was wrong. She looked up at me and said, 'You know you're not in Disney anymore when you have to flush your own toilet.' I laughed so hard that I made her burst into laughter, too. In the eyes of a child, the smallest luxuries are appreciated, even when it's toilets that 'magically' flush when you stand up!"
...as told by Disney vacationer Melissa Jarvis

"Before our trip, I made a label with my cell phone number and stuck it on the inside of a Disney Princess watch. We then taught my 4-year-old what to do if she became lost: approach someone with a white Disney name tag and show them her 'special watch' with the phone number inside. One day at Disney-MGM Studios while playing in the 'Honey I Shrunk the Kids' playground, she got separated from us! Instead of panicking, she went right up to the cast member nearby. He was just about to call our cell phone when my sister found her. We all felt great knowing we would have been quickly reunited!"
...as told by Disney vacationer Rhoda Smith

Staying in Style

Nowhere in the "World" is Disney magic more evident than at the resort hotels on Walt Disney World property. In fact, the resorts are so impressive that we do not often consider staying "off-property" (as hotels outside of Walt Disney World are known), and we frequently plan our visits around our favorite resorts rather than our favorite parks. Staying in a Disney resort is unlike any other hotel experience we've had, and we've visited both the exotic and the expensive. It isn't just that staying at a Disney resort provides total immersion in the Walt Disney World experience. The resorts are miniature theme parks in their own right, with hidden surprises and a remarkable attention to detail.

With more than 31,000 guest rooms and campsites throughout the Walt Disney World Resort, it would take more than 80 years to stay once in each room. (Sign us up!) There's something for every taste and budget. Whether you want a romantic setting, space for a family reunion, disabled access, bunk beds, or non-smoking rooms, you can find it somewhere in the "World." There are enough choices to preclude staying at a non-Disney hotel, but bargains off-property are also a factor. If you visit with friends or family, prefer to stay in another hotel, or even take a cruise, your PassPorter still serves you well—you can record your arrangements here with the same ease. We include basic information on the Disney Cruise Line, Disney Vacation Club, and off-site hotels at the end of the chapter, too.

If you've already decided to stay at a Disney resort, your PassPorter puts you a step ahead! Our Walt Disney World resort descriptions are the most comprehensive of any guidebook, and our resort maps, photos, floor plans, tips, notes, and recommendations can help the veteran vacationer as well as the novice get the most out of their resort.

To help you find your way through the staggering array of choices, we've prepared a detailed guide to choosing your resort. We heartily recommend you turn the page and take advantage of it.

Choosing a Resort

Ah, this is the fun part! Deciding which resort to stay at reminds us of choosing a dessert from a tray laden with every imaginable, mouth-watering goodie. Some are too rich for us, others aren't quite sweet enough, but there are enough choices left over to make us feel spoiled. Sometimes we stay at two or more resorts in one visit. Are you surprised?

Start with the exhaustive **Resort Checklist** on the next page. Compare it with your preferences to uncover the resorts that meet your needs. Then carefully read the resort descriptions, beginning on page 35. Each description follows the same format, allowing you to find exactly what you seek as you **compare resorts**. The first and second pages of each description list resort essentials, along with floor plans and transportation times. The third page lists the best tips, notes, and ratings for each resort—this is the "good stuff" to help you make the most out of your experience. In the Ratings section, we and our readers grade each resort for value, magic, and satisfaction. An explanation of the ratings is at the bottom of this page. The fourth page features a detailed resort map and our ideas for the best rooms in the resort. Rates, addresses, and phone/fax numbers are listed at the end of each description. **Tip:** When researching resorts, use the darkest "stamp" (tab) at the top of the page to locate parks and eateries in the vicinity, which will have the same "stamp" at the top of their pages.

When you're ready, use the Lodging Worksheet on pages 110–111 to record your dates, preferences, and reservation options.

Resort Ratings Explained
We offer a variety of resort ratings in PassPorter to help you make the best decisions. Even so, we recommend you use these ratings as a guide, not gospel.

Value Ratings range from 1 (poor) to 10 (excellent) and are based on **quality** (cleanliness, maintenance, and freshness); **accessibility** (how fast and easy it is to get to attractions); and **affordability** (rates for the standard rooms)—**overall value** represents an average of the above three values. **Magic Ratings** are based on **theme** (execution and sense of immersion); **amenities** (guest perks and luxuries); and **fun factor** (number and quality of resort activities)—**overall magic** represents an average of the above three values. We use a point accumulation method to determine value and magic ratings.

Readers' Ratings are calculated from surveys submitted by experienced vacationers at our Web site (http://www.passporter.com/wdw/rate.htm).

Guest satisfaction is based on our and our readers' experiences with how different types of guests enjoy the resort: ♥♥♥♥♥=love it ♥♥♥♥=enjoy it ♥♥♥=like it ♥♥=tolerate it ♥=don't like it

Resort Comparisons

*Kitchen facilities are present only in the villas of indicated resorts

	All-Star Resorts	Animal King. Lodge	Beach Club/Villas	BoardWalk Inn/Villas	Caribbean Beach	Contemporary	Coronado Springs	Dolphin	Fort Wilderness	Grand Floridian	Old Key West	Polynesian	Pop Century	Port Orleans	Saratoga Springs	Shades of Green	Swan	Wild. Lodge/Villas	Yacht Club
Deluxe		✓	✓	✓		✓		✓		✓		✓					✓	✓	✓
Home-Away			✓	✓					✓		✓				✓			✓	
Moderate					✓		✓							✓					
Value	✓												✓						
Rooms and Amenities																			
Total Rooms	5760	1293	785	910	2112	1041	1967	1509	1195	900	761	853	5760	3056	1040	586	758	864	634
Occupancy	4	4-5	4-8	4-12	4	5	4	5	4-10	5	4-12	5	4	4-5	4-12	5	5	4-8	5
Mini Bars								✓											
Coffeemakers •					✓		✓		✓	✓					✓	✓		✓	
Hair dryers •		✓	✓	✓	✓	✓	✓			✓					✓	✓	✓	✓	✓
In-Room Safes •	✓	✓	✓	✓	✓	✓	✓	✓		✓	✓	✓		✓	✓		✓	✓	✓
Kitchen Facilities*			✓	✓							✓				✓			✓	
Turndown (on req.)		✓	✓	✓				✓		✓							✓	✓	✓
Hi-Speed Internet			✓	✓		✓		✓							✓		✓	✓	✓
Eating and Drinking																			
Restaurants/Cafes	–	2	3	7	1	5	1	2	2	7	3	3	–	1	1	4	3	3	3
Character Meals •			✓			✓			✓	✓							✓		
Lounges	3	3	3	4	1	3	2	1	1	3	1	2	2	4	2	1	2	2	2
Food Court	3	1			1		1	1					2	2					
Room Service		✓	✓	✓	✓	✓	✓	✓		✓		✓			✓	✓	✓	✓	✓
Pizza Delivery	✓										✓			✓					✓
Recreational Activities																			
Beach (no swim)			✓		✓	✓	✓	✓	✓	✓		✓					✓	✓	✓
Pools	6	1	3	3	7	2	4	2	2	2	4	2	6	7	3	2	2	2	3
Kid Pool	3	1	1	1	1	1	1	1	1	1	1	1	2	2	1	1	1	1	1
Spa (Hot Tub)	–	2	5	3	1	2	1	1	–	1	2	–	–	2	4	1	1	3	5
Spa (Services)			✓	✓			✓	✓		✓		✓			✓		✓	✓	✓
Health Club •		✓	✓	✓		✓		✓		✓					✓	✓	✓	✓	✓
Marina •			✓	✓	✓	✓	✓		✓	✓	✓	✓		✓	✓			✓	✓
Tennis •			✓	✓	✓	✓		✓	✓	✓	✓				✓		✓	✓	✓
Jogging Path •	✓		✓	✓	✓	✓	✓		✓	✓	✓			✓	✓			✓	✓
Playground •	✓	✓	✓	✓	✓	✓	✓		✓	✓	✓			✓	✓			✓	
Kids' Program		✓				✓				✓		✓						✓	
Access and Facilities																			
Monorail						✓				✓		✓							
Disabled Rooms	288	66	10	51	22	6	99	43	13	5	67	17	126	34	16	22	8	46	10
Conf. Center		✓			✓		✓	✓		✓					✓		✓	✓	✓
Your Favorites																			

Planning · Getting There · Staying in Style · Touring · Feasting · Making Magic · Index · Notes & More

Reserving a Room

Once you have an idea of where you want to stay at the Walt Disney World Resort, it's time to **make reservations**. A travel agent is not needed, but if you have a great travel agent, by all means consult him or her—we recommend MouseEarVacations.com, as they can often get excellent deals you may not have known about. Here's the lowdown on reservations:

Before you make your reservations, **use the worksheet** on pages 110–111 to jot down the dates you prefer to visit along with any alternates. Even a one-day change in your travel dates can open the door to a great deal. Be familiar with all resorts in your price range.

Make reservations for all Walt Disney World resort hotels at **407-WDW-MAGIC** (407-939-6244) or 800-828-0228 (Walt Disney Travel Company). Disney representatives can offer assistance in English, Spanish, Japanese, French, Portuguese, and German. If you have Internet access, you can research room rates and make reservations online at http://www.disneyworld.com (click on "Resorts")—discounts are sometimes available on the Web site, but you must follow the specific links for the specials or you'll be charged regular rates. You may also want to try Expedia or Travelocity, both of which are popular Internet reservation systems—you can visit them at http://www.travelocity.com (or keyword: TRAVEL on America Online) and http://www.expedia.com. Be sure to look for promotional rates while you're there, too! If you prefer, you can also make reservations through the mail by writing to Walt Disney World at Box 10100, Lake Buena Vista, Florida 32830.

You may be able to **hold more than one reservation** for the same date, but eventually you have to put down a deposit or lose the reservation. Most reservations can be cancelled for full credit up to 45 days prior to arrival (policies vary for some discount programs). Disney will send a confirmation of your reservation.

Research **special deals or packages** by visiting MouseSavers.com (see page 11) or by calling Disney Reservations. If you have a Disney Visa card, Annual Pass, or are a Florida resident or military family, ask about those discounts, too. If your dates aren't available, ask about alternates. Sometimes you can get a discount for part of your stay. Lock in whatever discount you can get, and book at full price for the remainder. Keep calling back, as cancelled reservations are released every morning. If a lower rate comes out later, you may be able to call back and get it applied.

Make any **special requests** at the time of reservation and again when you check in. If you need a smoking, non-smoking, barrier-free room, a refrigerator, or a crib, request this now. If you have a particular location or room in mind (we make many suggestions later on), make sure to tell the reservations agent. It's best to make your request as general as possible. You'll have better luck requesting a "high floor with views of fireworks" than simply "room 5409." If Disney doesn't know why you want room 5409, they can't choose a suitable substitute. Disney will not guarantee a particular room or view, but if your request is "in the system" they will try their best to make your wish come true. Call or fax your resort about three days before your arrival to confirm any requests you made. We've created an easy, fill-in-the-blanks form for you to use when making phone calls (or when standing at the check-in desk) at http://www.passporter.com/wdw/resortrequest.htm.

Finalize resort reservations after you make your **flight reservations**. Hotel room reservations may be changed or cancelled without penalty, whereas flight changes often incur a fee. If you wish to cancel your resort reservations without penalty, cancel no later than 45 days prior to your arrival. Cancellations within 6 to 45 days of your arrival incur a $100 fee. Cancellations 5 or fewer days before your arrival are $200.

Once you've made your reservations, **record the details**, including the name of the resort, dates, type of room, price, reservation number, and any special information you want to note. This is also an ideal place to note any special requests you want to check on at check-in. Use a pencil if plans aren't final.

Typically, Disney resort reservations are held 10-14 days without confirmation. Confirmation requires a deposit of $200, due in 14 days. Be sure to **pay your deposit** before midnight on the 14th day. Your deposit can be made over the phone with The Disney Credit Card, American Express, MasterCard, Visa, Discover, JCB, Diner's Club, or through mail or fax with the same credit cards or a personal check. The Lodging Worksheet at the end of the chapter (pages 110–111) has spaces to check off confirmations and deposits made, too! **Tip:** You may be able to request an extension on your deposit if needed.

Disney's Two Reservation Systems

Why make a toll call to Disney Central Reservations Office (CRO) at 407-WDW-MAGIC to reserve a room when you can dial the Walt Disney Travel Company (WDTC) toll-free at 800-828-0228? Each has its strengths and weaknesses.

Central Reservations (CRO) is Disney's hotel reservation system. Its specialty is room-only reservations and selected vacation packages (they'll be happy to sell you park admission, too). CRO cannot book air travel, car rentals, travel insurance, or ground transportation. CRO has the more liberal deposit policy—the cost of one night's lodging is all that's required (due in 14 days), with a no-penalty cancellation possible up to six days prior. With less than six days notice, you forfeit the full one-night deposit. Packages require full payment 21 days prior to your stay; room-only bookings can be paid up at check-in. There's no penalty for modifying an existing reservation. The only problem with CRO (besides the cost of the phone call) is that Disney is downsizing this operation. Even though you dial 407-WDW-MAGIC, you may be connected to a Disney Travel Company agent. Make sure CRO booking policies have been applied to your reservation before you finalize it.

Walt Disney Travel Company is a full-fledged travel agency. Its specialty is package vacations with all the trimmings (see page 30). It offers a wider range of package vacations than CRO and also has access to the same "pool" of room-only reservations as CRO. Airfare, car rentals, ground transportation, and other arrangements can also be part of their service. WDTC normally requires full payment for your vacation 45 days in advance (even for room-only bookings—ask to have that changed), charges $100 for cancellations made between 6 and 45 days prior, and $200 for cancellations made less than 6 days prior. There's a $50 charge for modifying reservations within 21 days of your arrival. So, WDTC can do more for you, but it comes at a price. Disney tells us that the bulk of their reservations are through WDTC, which is why we noted their policies in the above text.

Choosing a Package

Disney's vacation packages offer the promise of peace of mind and luxury. Package rates may be lower than the list price for each component, but may include more components than you can possibly use. A significant number of veteran vacationers tell us they love these packages! Note that everyone in your room must be on the same package and plan. For more information and reservations, ask your travel agent, call Walt Disney Travel Company at 800-828-0228, or visit http://www.disneyworld.com.

■ Basic Magic Your Way Package

Get three or more nights of accommodations at a Disney resort hotel, a Magic Your Way Base Ticket (see page 116), and one luggage tag per person. You may choose to add Park Hopping, Magic Plus, and/or No Expiration features to your Base Ticket. From $330/person.

■ Magic Your Way Plus Dining Package

Everything in the basic package described above plus dining at over 100 participating Disney restaurants*. For each night of your package you get one table-service meal, one counter-service meal, and one snack**—you can exchange a table-service meal for a character meal, or two table-service meals for a signature meal or a dinner show. From $435/person.

■ Magic Your Way Premium Package

Everything in the basic package, plus breakfast, lunch, and dinner per person per night at over 100 participating Disney restaurants*, unlimited recreation, unlimited admission to Disney childcare clubs, Cirque du Soleil tickets, Grand Gathering experiences (if there are at least 8 in your party), and unlimited admission to selected theme park tours**. Also note that the Magic Your Way Base Ticket is upgraded to a Premium Ticket. From $835/person.

Note that with the dining plans, kids ages 3–9 must order off the children's menu when available at an eatery.

* Participating Disney restaurants include all restaurants described in chapter 5 (see pages 199–240) **except** the following eateries: Big River Grille (BoardWalk); Pepper Market, Siesta's, Francisco's, and Maya Grill (Coronado Springs); Victoria & Albert's (Grand Floridian); Alfredo di Roma Ristorante, Bistro de Paris, Boulangerie Patisserie, Cantina de San Angel, Chefs de France, Lotus Blossom Cafe, Restaurant Marrakesh, Matsu No Ma Lounge, Nine Dragons, San Angel Inn, Tangierine Cafe, Tempura Kiku, Teppanyaki Dining, and Yakitori House (Epcot); Rainforest Cafe (Animal Kingdom); plus all snack, counter-service, and table-service at both Downtown Disney and Wide World of Sports with the exception of Cap'n Jack's Restaurant and All-Star Cafe which are both included.

** Table-service meals include appetizer, entree, dessert, non-alcoholic beverage, and gratuity. Counter-server meals include entree and non-alcoholic beverage. Snacks include either ice cream, cookie, popcorn, or a non-alcoholic beverage.

*** Selected theme park tours include all tours described on pages 242–243 except the Around the World at Epcot tour, Backstage Magic, VIP Tours, Welcome to the Magic Kingdom, and Yuletide Fantasy.

Resort Key

Resort Locations—The Disney resorts described in your PassPorter are all located within minutes of the theme parks. We organize them into four areas: Magic Kingdom, Downtown Disney, Epcot, and Disney's Animal Kingdom (use the map on the inside back cover for reference). Each resort's area is identified in its description. You can also use the blue "stamps" at the top of each page to locate all resorts in a neighborhood.

Room Locations—Room locations such as a building or room number can be requested, but are not guaranteed. However, if you note your preferences when you make your reservation, via phone or fax about three days before arrival, and again when you check in, there is a chance you will get the room you want. Resort maps and suggestions are given for each resort in this chapter. If you don't like the particular room you've been assigned, do as you would with any hotel and politely ask for another.

Room Occupancy—All resorts have rooms that hold at least four guests, plus one child under 3 in a Pack-N-Play crib. Port Orleans Riverside (Alligator Bayou) rooms accommodate up to five guests with an optional trundle bed, as do many of the deluxe resorts and the Ft. Wilderness Cabins. The two-bedroom villas in the Home-Away Resorts can accommodate up to eight. There may be an extra charge for more than two adults in a single room.

Amenities—All rooms have the basics: television with remote control, phone, drawers, clothing rod with hangers, small table, chairs, as well as simple toiletries. Additional amenities differ at each resort and are detailed later. **Tip:** If your room doesn't have a coffeemaker, alarm clock, or iron/ironing board, request it from housekeeping.

Check-In Time—Check-in time is 3:00 pm or 4:00 pm (varies by resort), although rooms may be available earlier if you inquire upon your arrival. If your room is not available, you can register, leave your luggage, and go play at the parks while your room is being prepared.

Check-Out Time—Check-out time is 11:00 am. If you need to check out an hour or two later, ask the Front Desk the morning of check-out. If the resort isn't busy, they may grant your request at no extra cost. Extended check-out may also be available for an extra fee. You can also leave your bags with Bell Services and go play in the parks.

Childcare—Children's childcare "clubs" for ages 4–12 are available in many of the deluxe resorts (refer to the chart on page 27). In-room sitting is also available. See pages 252–253 for details and opinions on childcare.

Concierge—All of the deluxe resorts offer concierge services, which give you extra perks like a continental breakfast, afternoon snacks, and planning services. Concierge services are associated with certain rooms (often on the higher floors) and come at a higher rate.

Convention Centers—Several resort hotels at the Walt Disney World Resort are popular among convention-goers due to their excellent facilities, including the BoardWalk, Contemporary, Coronado Springs, Grand Floridian, Swan, Dolphin, and the Yacht Club. For more details on convention facilities, call 407-828-3200. Business Centers are available at each of the above resorts.

Data Services (Internet)—All phones have data ports. Look for a local access number before you arrive. Each local call you make is 75 cents. You must include the area code (407) in all local calls. The front desk will also receive your faxes for a fee. Some resorts (see page 27) now have high-speed Internet access for $9.95 for a contiguous 24-hour period. Eventually, all resorts will have high-speed Internet access.

Resort Key: Disabled Access to Information

Disabled Access—All resorts offer accommodations and access for differently-abled guests. For details and reservations, call Disney's Special Requests Department at 407-939-7807 (voice) or 407-939-7670 (TTY). Be sure to ask that "Special Needs" be noted on your reservation. See page 27 for the number of barrier-free rooms at each resort, page 48 for a barrier-free guest room, and page 284 for our upcoming Special Needs guidebook!

Extra Magic Hour—Guests at Disney resorts and the Swan, Dolphin, Shades of Green, and Hilton can enter the parks up to one hour earlier or stay three hours later than everyone else. Disney resort ID is required for entry, along with a valid admission. Only certain parks and attractions are open for Extra Magic Hour on any given day, however. The schedule changes from week to week (check http://www.disneyworld.com for the schedule during your visit), but here's a sample Early Magic Hour schedule:

	Sunday	Monday	Tuesday	Wednesday	Thursday	Friday	Saturday
am	none	Epcot	Disney-MGM Studios	none	none	Magic Kingdom	Animal Kingdom
pm	Disney-MGM Studios	none	Animal Kingdom	Magic Kingdom	Epcot	none	none

Extra Magic Hour Attractions—In the Magic Kingdom, this usually includes Space Mountain, Buzz Lightyear Space Ranger Spin, Big Thunder Mountain, Stitch's Great Escape, Haunted Mansion, Pirates of the Caribbean, Splash Mountain, Magic Carpets of Aladdin, and most of Fantasyland. Epcot opens Mission:SPACE, Spaceship Earth, Test Track, Journey Into Imagination, "Honey, I Shrunk the Audience," Universe of Energy, El Rio del Tiempo, and Maelstrom. Disney-MGM Studios opens Rock 'n' Roller Coaster, Tower of Terror, Star Tours, Muppet*Vision 3-D, The Great Movie Ride, Voyage of The Little Mermaid, and Playhouse Disney. Disney's Animal Kingdom opens It's Tough to be a Bug!, Festival of the Lion King, Tarzan Rocks, Dinosaur, TriceraTop Spin, Primeval Whirl, The Boneyard, and Pangani Forest Exploration Trail (am only). Underlined attractions are open only during evening Extra Magic Hours. Attractions are subject to change.

Food—Every resort has places to eat within it, such as food courts, cafes, fine dining, and room service. All resort eateries are noted in each resort's dining section later in this chapter. Details on the table-service restaurants start on page 224. If you are looking for snack food or groceries, each resort has a general store with a small selection of foodstuffs and drinks. No gum is sold on property.

Guest Services—Each resort has a Guest Services desk where you can purchase park passes, make dining arrangements, and find answers to just about any question. You can also connect to Guest Services (and other Disney services) through a button on your in-room phone.

Housekeeping Services—Every Disney resort has daily "mousekeeping" services and happily provides you with extra towels, pillows, and blankets upon request, as well as a hair dryer, iron, and ironing board. If you require extra toiletries, just ask for them. For tipping suggestions, see page 34. Note: Disney Vacation Club (DVC) resorts provide reduced services to DVC members using their points.

Information—Check the Walt Disney World information channels on your in-room TV. These channels are available at every resort and offer a nice introduction for newcomers, plus a peek at what's new for veterans.

Resort Key: Ice and Soda to Recreation

Ice and Soda—All resorts have ice machines within easy walking distance. Most, but not all, also have soda machines. The rule seems to be the more plush the resort, the harder it is to find a soda machine. If soda is important, pick some up before you arrive (it's cheaper anyway). Another option is to purchase a refillable souvenir mug (offered at most resorts) for free (or low-cost) refills of soda, coffee, tea, and cocoa at your resort—see page 34.

Laundry—Every resort has either coin-operated machines in a laundry room near the pool (expect to pay 8 quarters/load) or a washer and dryer in your room. **Tip**: Old Key West, The Villas at Wilderness Lodge, and Beach Club Villas offer complimentary self-service laundry facilities (no coins needed). Laundry bags and forms are available in your resort room for same-day service (it's very expensive). **Tip**: Store your dirty laundry in the laundry bags.

Mail and Packages—Purchase stamps at Guest Services and in many shops; mail can be dropped off at Guest Services or placed in mailboxes. Federal Express also picks up and drops off packages. ✒ A full-service Post Office is at the Shoppes at Lake Buena Vista at 12133 Apopka-Vineland Rd., about one mile north of the Crossroads Shopping Center.

Merchandise Delivery—Resort guests can have park and Downtown Disney purchases delivered free to their resort, usually by the next day or the day after. Inquire before your purchase is rung up. Your package is delivered to your resort's gift shop for pick-up, not your room. (Includes Swan/Dolphin guests.)

Money—Cash, Disney Dollars, traveler's checks, The Disney Credit Card, MasterCard, Visa, American Express, Discover, Diner's Club, and JCB are accepted, as well as personal checks with proper I.D. ATMs are located near the front desk. Make your room deposit over the phone or fax with the above credit cards or by mail with a credit card or check.

Parking—Secured, free, gated parking lots are available at all Disney resorts; the deluxe resorts also offer valet ($6/day, free to those with disabled tags). Show your resort I.D. or confirmation at the security gate—parking is reserved for resort guests and those using a resort's restaurants or recreation.

Pets—Pets 🐾 are not allowed in the parks or resorts (except for a few campsites at Fort Wilderness—see page 61) unless you travel with a companion (service) animal. Fees are $6 per day or $9 per night per animal for Disney resort hotel guests ($11 per night for non-Disney resort hotel guests). Although the kennels are designed primarily for dogs and cats, they can also accommodate birds, ferrets, small rodents, rabbits, and non-venomous snakes. Pets in kennels must be walked three times per day by their owners. The Epcot kennel offers a dog-walking service for $2.50/walk.

Pools—Every Disney resort has at least one swimming pool. Hours vary, but usually the "theme" pools close in the evenings while the "quiet" pools may stay open all night. Only guests staying at a resort can use its pool, though some resorts share pools and Disney Vacation Club members using their points have access to all but Stormalong Bay at the Yacht & Beach Club and the pool at Animal Kingdom Lodge (unless they are staying there).

© MediaMarx, Inc.

Recreation—Every resort has something to do, with many offering a wide variety of outdoor activities. ☀ You can visit another resort to use its recreational facilities (with the exception of swimming pools). Be sure to note the operating hours upon arrival or by phoning ahead.

The theme pool at Saratoga Springs Resort

Planning | Getting There | Staying in Style | Touring | Feasting | Making Magic | Index | Notes & More

Resort Key: Refillable Mugs to Voice Mail

Refillable Mugs—Most resorts sell thermal mugs that can be refilled free or for a small fee at your resort for the length of your stay. If you drink a lot of soda, tea, coffee, or hot chocolate, these are a blessing—and they make fun souvenirs. Mugs are about $12 and can generally be refilled at a resort's food court or snack shop. Some resorts place mugs in your room, but if you use them, you'll be charged. Mugs can't be refilled at other resorts or parks, and neither milk nor juice is a refill option.

Refrigerators—In-room refrigerators are available on request, subject to availability. There is no charge at Disney's deluxe and moderate resorts, and a $10 fee at the value resorts.

Room Service—The deluxe resorts and some of the moderate resorts offer room service. Some resorts offer a pizza delivery service in the afternoon and evenings.

Security—Security at Disney has always been good, and since 9/11 security has visibly heightened. A gatehouse ☀ guards entry into every resort. If you arrive by car, show your resort ID, or show photo ID and explain that you are checking in, dining, or using the resort's recreational facilities. All resort rooms have electronic locks which open with your resort I.D. for added security. In addition, you can store small valuables in your in-room safe (most, though not all, rooms have them) or with the front desk.

Spa—Disney-speak for a hot tub. There's at least one spa at every Disney resort, with the exception of the All-Stars, Fort Wilderness, Polynesian, and Pop Century. Traditional spa facilities (massages and manicures) are available in some resorts.

Tax—Sales tax is 6.5% and is charged on all resort purchases and lodging. An additional Lodging tax is assessed on guest rooms: 6.5% in Osceola County (Pop Century and some parts of All-Star Resorts), 5% in Orange County (all other Disney resorts).

Telephones—All rooms have a phone 📞 and information on how to use it. Local, toll-free, and credit card calls are 75 cents each, while long distance calls are the cost of the call plus a 50% surcharge. Ouch! Use calling cards instead. Incoming calls are free.

Tipping—It's customary to tip valet parking attendants $1–2 upon arrival and departure, bell services $1–2/bag upon delivery and pick-up, and housekeeping $1/person/day. **Tip:** Leave your housekeeping tip on the sink in an envelope each day so it's easily spotted.

Transportation—Every resort provides its guests with complimentary transit to and from the parks via bus, boat, monorail, and/or walking path. We list each resort's options and in-transit times in this chapter.

© MediaMarx, Inc.

Wheelchairs—Wheelchairs can be borrowed from every resort (inquire at Bell Services). A deposit may be required, and availability is limited. Motorized wheelchairs (ECVs) may be rented at the parks for in-park-only use. Care Medical (800-741-2282–http://www.caremedicalequipment.com) or Walker Mobility (888-726-6837–http://www.walkermobility.com) both offer 24-hour rentals of wheelchairs and ECVs ... and they'll deliver!

Jennifer rented an ECV when she was 7 months pregnant at Disney

Voice Mail—Every resort offers free voice mail that can be retrieved from your room or any other phone in or outside of the Walt Disney World Resort. You can even personalize the message callers hear when they are connected to your room. ☎ If you are on the phone when a call comes in, the voice mail system still takes your caller's message.

Disney's All-Star Resorts

Both economical and magical, the All-Star Resorts bring movies, music, and sports to life in three independent yet connected resort hotels. The All-Star Movies, All-Star Music, and All-Star Sports Resorts are located near Disney's Animal Kingdom theme park and the Blizzard Beach water park (use the blue tab at the top of the page for parks and eateries in the vicinity).

AMBIENCE

A star-studded production awaits you at the All-Star Resorts. From the painted stars everywhere you look to the autographed photos of famous celebrities lining the lobby walls, each resort greets you as a star in its **main hall**—Cinema Hall in All-Star Movies, Melody Hall in All-Star Music, and Grandstand Hall in All-Star Sports. The halls house the registration desks, food courts, general stores, and arcades, each named and themed as only Disney can. Outside, the stars give way to larger-than-life movie, music, and sports icons, such as a towering Buzz Lightyear from Disney's Toy Story, a four-story high conga drum, and a Coke cup that could hold 240 million ounces. The themes continue with imaginatively designed pools and landscaping. Music plays in the background, providing you with an ever-changing soundtrack as you stroll through the grounds.

RESORT LAYOUT & ROOMS

The 5,760 guest rooms (1,920 in each resort) are situated in 15 differently themed areas encompassing a total of 30 buildings. **All-Star Movies Resort** showcases 101 Dalmatians, Fantasia and Fantasia 2000, The Love Bug, Toy Story, and Mighty Ducks; **All-Star Music Resort** features Calypso, Jazz Inn, Rock Inn, Country Fair, and Broadway; and **All-Star Sports Resort** sports Surf's Up!, Hoops Hotel, Center Court, Touchdown!, and Home Run Hotel. Each of the 15 areas features a themed courtyard created by two of the T-shaped buildings. The energetic and colorful themes of the resorts are echoed in the guest rooms, with themed bedspreads, drapes, wallpaper, and a vanity area with one sink. Rooms have either two double beds or one king bed, a TV, a small table with two chairs, and drawers. Rooms with king-size beds are also the barrier-free rooms; thus, some of these rooms have only showers (no tubs). Rooms are small— 260 sq. feet—but we found them adequate with the simple furnishings. Rooms have no private balconies or patios, but each offers individual climate controls. Amenities include soap, housekeeping, in-room safe, and voice mail. You can rent a small refrigerator for $10/night—request one at reservation time.

Standard Room Layout

Using the Amenities at Disney's All-Star Resorts

EATING & DRINKING

Food courts: World Premiere (Movies), Intermission (Music), and End Zone (Sports), each with four food stations plus a snack shop. Breakfast (6:30 am to 11:00 am) menu items typically include a Breakfast Platter for $5.59, a cheese omelet for $5.89, and child meals for $3.59. Lunch and dinner (11:00 am to mid.) items include a 16" supreme pizza for $17.99, a meatball sub for $5.99, a taco salad for $6.59, a cheeseburger for $5.49, and child meals for $3.99. Souvenir mugs (about $12) offer unlimited soft drink refills. A **pizza delivery service** may be available. **Walk-up bars** at each food court and main pool.

© MediaMarx, Inc.

Guest room at All-Star Music

PLAYING & RELAXING

For Athletes: Well-marked paths are ideal for walks and jogs.
For Children: Quiet playgrounds are located within each resort (locations vary—see map on page 38 for playground locations).
For Gamers: Each resort's main hall has an arcade—some games reward players with tickets that can be redeemed for small prizes.
For Shoppers: Donald's Double Feature (Movies), Maestro Mickey's (Music), and Sport Goofy (Sports) offer gifts and sundries.
For Swimmers: Each resort offers a main pool and a smaller pool. Movies' main pool conjures up the fun of Fantasia, Music's main pool is in the shape of a guitar, and Sports' main pool is styled after a surfing lagoon. All main pools have children's wading pools nearby.

GETTING ABOUT

Buses (see chart below for in-transit times) are found outside the main halls in each resort. Stops are well-marked and offer benches. We find the bus service efficient, but some guests complain of waiting too long. Destinations other than those below can be reached by changing buses at Disney's Animal Kingdom (daytime) or Downtown Disney (evening). Guests may find a car useful at this resort, and ample parking is freely available around the resort.

Magic Kingdom	Epcot	Disney-MGM Studios	Disney's Animal Kingdom	Downtown Disney
direct bus ~20 min.	direct bus ~10 min.	direct bus ~10 min.	direct bus ~10 min.	direct bus ~15 min.

Approximate time you will spend in transit from resort to destination during normal operation.

Making the Most of Disney's All-Star Resorts

TIPS

Walk around the three resorts to catch all the neat props and details that make these resorts so fun. Don't forget your camera, as photo opportunities abound! Even the walkways have fun designs.

If you need an escape from the activity of the All-Stars, look for the **quiet spots** around the resorts. Relax in a hammock behind a stand of palm trees in Fantasia at All-Star Movies, or try the picnic tables in Country Fair's courtyard in All-Star Music for a leisurely lunch.

The **food courts** can get crowded at traditional meal times, so stop there earlier or later in the day.

NOTES

Plan to either carry your own luggage or wait a while (often 45–60 minutes) for their **luggage assistance service** to drop it off at your building. Unlike other Disney resorts, luggage is delivered at their convenience, not yours. Arrangements to pick up luggage on your departure day should be made the night before. You can borrow a luggage cart from the luggage assistance desk in the main hall, and you may need to leave your I.D. while you use the cart.

Toiletries are limited to a bar of facial soap at the sink and a wall-mounted dispenser of bodywash and shampoo in the shower/tub. You may want to bring your own from home.

Towels are not provided near the pools, so bring your own or use your room **towels**. Contact housekeeping for extra towels.

All-Star Sports **may close for maintenance** in the near future—call to check to avoid disappointment.

Check-in time is 4:00 pm. Check-out time is 11:00 am.

RATINGS

Ratings are explained on page 26.

Our Value Ratings:		Our Magic Ratings:		Readers' Ratings:
Quality:	6/10	Theme:	6/10	42% fell in love with it
Accessibility:	5/10	Amenities:	4/10	35% liked it well enough
Affordability:	9/10	Fun Factor:	2/10	12% had mixed feelings
Overall Value:	**7/10**	**Overall Magic:**	**4/10**	11% were disappointed

The All-Stars are enjoyed by...		(rated by both authors and readers)
Younger Kids: ♥♥♥♥♥	Young Adults: ♥♥♥♥	Families: ♥♥♥♥
Older Kids: ♥♥♥♥♥	Mid Adults: ♥♥♥	Couples: ♥♥
Teenagers: ♥♥♥	Mature Adults: ♥♥	Singles: ♥♥♥

Planning · Getting There · Staying in Style · Touring · Feasting · Making Magic · Index · Notes & More

Finding Your Place at Disney's All-Star Resorts

ALL-STAR RESORT MAP

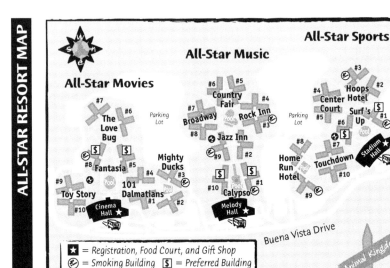

BEST LOCATIONS

Rooms at the All-Star Resorts vary only by location within the resorts and floor level. For convenience, we recommend **101 Dalmatians**, **Fantasia**, or **Toy Story** (at All-Star Movies), **Calypso** (at All-Star Music) and **Surf's Up!** (at All-Star Sports)—they are closest to the main pools, food, and transportation. Our personal preferences are **Fantasia** (at All-Star Movies), **Country Fair** (at All-Star Music), and **Hoops Hotel** (at All-Star Sports) as they are relatively quiet and have good views from most windows—the latter two are a good distance from the Main Hall, however. Quieter rooms are those that face away from the pools and are on the **second or third floors**.

RATES

2005 Sample Room Rates

Seasons are noted on page 14

Room Type	Value	Regular	Peak	Holiday
Standard Room	$77	$99	$109	$119
Preferred Room	$89	$111	$121	$131

Tax not included in above rates. Preferred rooms are in buildings closest to the main hall (Fantasia, Calypso, or Surf's Up). Rooms may face parking lots or courtyards.

INFO

Disney's All-Star Movies/Music/Sports Resorts

✉ 1901/1801/1701 W. Buena Vista Dr., Lake Buena Vista, FL 32830

☎ Phone: 407-939-7000/407-939-6000/407-939-5000

📠 Fax: 407-939-7111/407-939-7222/407-939-7333

📋 For reservations, call Central Reservations: 407-939-6244

Disney's Animal Kingdom Lodge Resort

Disney's Animal Kingdom Lodge shares the ambience of its neighboring park, Disney's Animal Kingdom (use the blue tab at the top of the page for parks and eateries in the vicinity). Guests at this deluxe resort can watch grazing mammals on 33 acres of African savanna from their balconies.

AMBIENCE

Your trek to the Lodge is rewarded as soon as you step into the atrium lobby, which offers a dramatic view to the animal reserve and "kopje" (rock outcrop) beyond. Sunlight pours in through high windows, painting the lobby's thatched ceiling and carved wooden decorations in a warm, intimate glow. African artwork, much of it museum quality, greets you at every turn. Designed by the architect behind Disney's Wilderness Lodge, the six-story hotel shares its sister resort's **rustic appeal**, but adds a welcome warmth and intimacy, even in the largest public spaces. Then, of course, there are the animals, which add a sense of delight unique to this resort.

LAYOUT & ROOMS

Standard Room Layout

This **horseshoe-shaped lodge**, inspired by African Kraal (corral) villages, gives all but 100 of the 1293 rooms a view of the private wildlife reserve. The rooms are vibrant with rich tapestries, hand-carved furniture, gauze hangings at the head of the beds, and Kente-inspired fabrics. Standard rooms (344 sq. ft.) have two queen beds; one king bed and a day bed; or one queen bed and bunk beds. Deluxe rooms (381 sq. ft.) add a daybed (most rooms), a make-up mirror, and a second phone. All rooms have a balcony, ceiling fan, table and chairs, armoire with 27" TV and drawers, double sinks, in-room safe, iron and ironing board, hair dryer, voice mail, and newspaper delivery.

DINING

A casual yet upscale restaurant, **Jiko**, is open for guests who want an elegantly inventive dinner. **Boma**, which means "place of refuge," offers an exciting, African-flavored dining adventure with all-you-care-to-eat buffets at breakfast and dinner. These two table-service restaurants are reviewed on page 224. **The Mara** is a quick-service cafe open all day—this is the perfect place for a fast meal. Typical breakfast menu items include breakfast pizza ($5.79), a croissant sandwich ($5.59), and a kid's breakfast ($3.99). Typical lunch/dinner items include Sugar Cane Chicken ($7.29), African House Salad ($6.59), and Fish and Chips ($9.49). Refillable mugs ($12) can be purchased (and refilled) at The Mara. Room service is also available.

Using the Amenities
at Disney's Animal Kingdom Lodge Resort

LOUNGING

Victoria Falls Lounge, which overlooks Boma, serves coffees, African wines, and international beer in the evenings. The **Cape Town Lounge and Wine Bar**, inside Jiko, serves remarkable wines from South Africa. **Uzima Springs** is a poolside bar offering beer and mixed drinks. Snacks, beer, and wine are at the **Zawadi Marketplace** and **The Mara**.

© MediaMarx, Inc.

The view from a fifth floor guest room at Disney's Animal Kingdom Lodge

PLAYING & RELAXING

For Animal Watchers: Bring plenty of film for your camera—you may also want a tripod. Binoculars are an excellent idea, too.
For Athletes: Keep in shape in the Zahanati Fitness Center near the pool. Massage treatments are also offered. There are no jogging paths—drive or bus to another resort (such as Coronado Springs).
For Children: Simba's Cubhouse is a supervised club for kids ages 4–12 (see page 252). There's also the Hakuna Matata playground near the pool, storytelling at the fire pit, and daily activities at Boma.
For Gamers: Pumbaa's Fun and Games has video games.
For Shoppers: The festive Zawadi Marketplace can outfit you with sundries, foodstuffs, books, clothing, and African crafts.
For Swimmers: Soak in the Uzima Pool, an 11,000 sq. ft. pool with an African theme, water slide (closes at 10:00 pm), kids' pool, and two spas (hot tubs). The pool features a zero-entry section where you can wade into the water. A pool wheelchair is available.
For Concierge Guests: Inquire in advance about the Sunrise and Sunset Safari experiences that include a special tour at Animal Kingdom park plus a breakfast at Tusker House or dinner at Jiko.

GETTING ABOUT

Buses to theme parks and Downtown Disney (see chart below for in-transit times) are a short walk out front (see the map on page 42). Travel to other resorts via Disney's Animal Kingdom theme park (daytime) or Downtown Disney (evening). Ample parking is available, as is valet parking. This is the only deluxe resort to lack boat or monorail access to a nearby park.

Magic Kingdom	Epcot	Disney-MGM Studios	Disney's Animal Kingdom	Downtown Disney
direct bus ~20 min.	direct bus ~15 min.	direct bus ~10 min.	direct bus ~5 min.	direct bus ~15 min.

Approximate time you will spend in transit from resort to destination during normal operation.

Planning | Getting There | Staying in Style | Touring | Feasting | Making Magic | Index | Notes & More

Making the Most of Disney's Animal Kingdom Lodge Resort

The Lodge's own **33-acre savanna**, which is distinct from the theme park, is home to 36 species of mammals and 26 species of birds—more than 330 animals in all. Guests can see zebras, antelopes, giraffes, gazelle, wildebeests, ostriches, cranes, vultures, and storks. Animals may come within 15 feet of the main observation area on the kopje, or as close as 30 feet from your balcony, day or night.

At night, the savanna is lit by **artificial moonlight**. Bring a bathrobe to visit your balcony without fear of binoculars or security cameras.

Refrigerators are available upon request at no additional charge.

African storytelling is held nightly around the firepit. In inclement weather, storytelling moves to one of the overlooks inside. "Safari guides" are also on hand to educate guests on the animals.

Tour the resort's **African art collection**, either on your own or on a free guided tour. Ask at the front desk.

There are **three separate savannas** (each about 11 acres) which can be viewed 24 hours a day. Each savanna has a few animal species that are unique to it. Each closes daily for cleaning and animal care, but at least two savannas are open at all times. Best viewing times are typically early to mid-morning, and dusk through sunset.

If your room doesn't have a view of the savanna, **watch the animals** from the kopje (the large observation area that extends into the savanna), the Sunset Overlook (a delightful room on the west side of the lobby), the overlook near the pool, and the alcoves along Zebra Trail and Kudu Trail (visit the second floor for outdoor viewing platforms that feature rocking chairs and high-powered binoculars).

Check-in time is 3:00 pm. Checkout is 11:00 am. No late checkouts.

Ratings are explained on page 26.

Our Value Ratings:		Our Magic Ratings:		Readers' Ratings:
Quality:	9/10	Theme:	10/10	70% fell in love with it
Accessibility:	5/10	Amenities:	5/10	23% liked it well enough
Affordability:	5/10	Fun Factor:	8/10	7% had mixed feelings
Overall Value:	**6/10**	**Overall Magic:**	**8/10**	0% were disappointed

Disney's Animal Kingdom Lodge is enjoyed by... (rated by both authors and readers)		
Younger Kids: ❤❤❤❤❤	Young Adults: ❤❤❤❤	Families: ❤❤❤❤❤
Older Kids: ❤❤❤❤❤	Mid Adults: ❤❤❤❤❤	Couples: ❤❤❤
Teenagers: ❤❤❤	Mature Adults: ❤❤	Singles: ❤❤❤❤

Sidebar tabs: Planning | Getting There | Staying in Style | Touring | Feasting | Making Magic | Index | Notes & More

Sidebar labels: TIPS | NOTES | RATINGS

Planning
Getting There
Staying in Style
Touring
Feasting
Making Magic
Index
Notes & More

Finding Your Place
at Disney's Animal Kingdom Lodge Resort

ANIMAL KINGDOM LODGE MAP

BEST LOCATIONS

Standard rooms are for up to four guests and are located on floors 1-4. Rooms come in three views: standard (Giraffe and Ostrich Trails), pool (Giraffe and Zebra Trails), and savanna (Zebra, Kudu and Ostrich Trails). **Deluxe rooms** are on floor 5 and accommodate up to five guests. If the animal watching is your main draw, reserve a savanna-view room. Rooms on the far ends of the Zebra and Kudu Trails require a long walk. **Concierge rooms** (floors 5 and 6) are also available in pool and savanna views, as are several one-bedroom, two-bedroom, and "royal" suites. Note that only the 6th floor is key-protected.

RATES

2005 Sample Room Rates

Seasons are noted on page 14

Room Type	Value	Regular	Peak	Holiday
Standard View	$199	$239	$289	$324
Standard Water/Pool View	$225	$265	$315	$355
Standard Savanna View	$280	$320	$370	$420
Deluxe Savanna View	$340	$385	$445	$510
Concierge	$435	$490	$555	$620

Tax not included in above prices. Suites start in the mid-$600's.

INFO

Disney's Animal Kingdom Lodge Resort
✉ 2901 Osceola Parkway, Lake Buena Vista, FL 32830
☎ Phone: 407-938-3000 📠 Fax: 407-938-7102
📋 For reservations, call Central Reservations: 407-939-6244

Looking for the Beach Club and Villas? See pages 93–97.

Disney's BoardWalk Inn & Villas Resort

BoardWalk Inn & Villas Resort enjoys a favored location in the middle of the action, fronting Crescent Lake between Epcot and Disney-MGM Studios (use the blue tab at the top of the page for parks and eateries in the area). The Villas are affiliated with the Disney Vacation Club (see pages 102–103).

This **"seaside" resort** takes you back to the heyday of the Atlantic City Boardwalk in the 1920s and 1930s, where carefree days floated by on the summer breeze. Reminiscent of an elegant bed-and-breakfast inn, the BoardWalk continues this impression inside with its old-fashioned furnishings and soft, muted colors. Outside, a stroll along the vibrant promenade offers great views, family fun, and more eateries, clubs, and shops than you can visit.

Standard Room Layout (Inn)

The two different sides of this resort offer varying accommodations, ranging from 359 to 2142 sq. ft. **BoardWalk Inn** has 378 rooms with one king or two queens plus a day bed or queen sofa bed, and suites. **BoardWalk Villas** feature 532 studios and one-, two-, and three-bedroom suites—studios have a kitchenette, suites have a full kitchen, big-screen TV, DVD player, and washer/dryer. All rooms in the resort have a balcony or patio, double sinks, a marble vanity, a table and chairs, a sofa, an armoire, TV, ceiling fan, toiletries, hair dryer, housekeeping, turndown service (on request), voice mail, valet parking, and, in most rooms, in-room safe and newspaper delivery.

Unique to this resort is a lively entertainment complex along the waterfront promenade. This innovative mini-park offers a variety of dining options. BoardWalk table-service restaurants, detailed on pages 224–225, include **Big River Grille & Brewing Works**, a modern brewpub; **ESPN Club**, an All-American sports cafe; **Flying Fish Cafe**, fine dining with an ever-changing menu; and **Spoodles**, delicious Mediterranean food. Spoodles also has an outside counter for take-out—pick up a slice of pepperoni pizza ($3.49) or a calzone ($5.99). The **Belle Vue Room** offers a quick bite in the mornings. Two quick-service cafes round out the menu. **BoardWalk Bakery** tempts you with baked goods and coffee—try the chocolate croissant ($2.79), breakfast burrito ($3.99), or a Lunch Bag (chicken salad sandwich, whole fruit, and chips for $6.59). **Seashore Sweets** offers ice cream, cookies, fudge, saltwater taffy, and coffees.

AMBIENCE

LAYOUT & ROOMS

DINING

Planning

Getting There

Staying in Style

Touring

Feasting

Making Magic

Index

Notes & More

Using the Amenities at Disney's BoardWalk Inn & Villas Resort

LOUNGING

The BoardWalk is rich with lounges and clubs. **Atlantic Dance Hall** and **Jellyrolls** (see page 193) serve up drinks and fun. In the resort itself is the **Belle Vue Room**, perfect for a quiet drink and a game of chess. **Leaping Horse Libations** is the pool bar near Luna Park. 24-hour room service is also available.

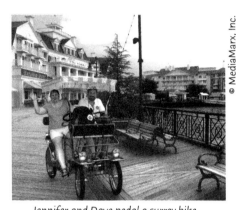

Jennifer and Dave pedal a surrey bike down the resort's wooden boardwalk

© MediaMarx, Inc.

PLAYING & RELAXING

For Athletes: Muscles and Bustles Fitness is a fitness center with exercise equipment, steam room, sauna, and massage therapies (for an extra fee). Rent bikes at Community Hall (the resort's recreation center) and surrey bikes on the BoardWalk (see photo above). There are also two lighted tennis courts and a walking/jogging circuit around Crescent Lake and along the path to Disney-MGM Studios.
For Children: A playground and wading pool is at Luna Park. Harbor Club kids' care club is closed, but may reopen (see page 252).
For Gamers: Side Show Games Arcade has video games. Rent video tapes at Community Hall (free to DVC members, $3.16 for guests).
For Shoppers: Dundy's Sundries and Screen Door General Store offer the basics, while Thimbles & Threads and Disney's Character Carnival stock apparel and gifts. Wyland Galleries has collectibles.
For Swimmers: Of the three pools, the largest is Luna Park with a 200-ft. wooden "coaster" slide. All pools have spas (hot tubs).

GETTING ABOUT

Buses are boarded in the front of the resort, while **boats** depart from the marina (see the chart below for in-transit times). Travel elsewhere via a park (daytime) or Downtown Disney (evening). You can **walk** to Disney-MGM Studios, Epcot, Yacht & Beach Club, and Swan & Dolphin. If you miss the Disney-MGM Studios boat, just walk to the Swan & Dolphin boat dock before your missed boat reaches it and hop on. Parking is available, as is valet ($6/day).

Magic Kingdom	Epcot	Disney-MGM Studios	Disney's Animal Kingdom	Downtown Disney
direct bus ~20 min.	walk/boat ~10/~5 min.	walk/boat ~15/~20 min.	direct bus ~10 min.	direct bus ~15 min.

Approximate time you will spend in transit from resort to destination during normal operation.

Making the Most
of Disney's BoardWalk Inn & Villas Resort

The **Belle Vue Room** is a marvel of nostalgia. It's tucked away in a corner down the hall from the lobby on the Inn side of the resort. You'll find backgammon, chess, and checkers tables (ask a cast member for game pieces), as well as a single-malt scotch menu.

Take a stroll through the grounds of the resort, away from the busy BoardWalk Promenade itself. The **landscaping** is meticulous and often original. If you prefer the bustle of the BoardWalk, rent a **surrey bike** and tour around the promenade and lake.

The BoardWalk Inn's **Garden Suites** have got to be the most romantic in the "World." Each of the fourteen suites looks like a two-story cottage. All suites have private entrances and most have a unique garden surrounded by a white picket fence with a trellised arbor gate. Suites have a separate living room, sleeper sofa, and a wet bar on the first floor, while the open second floor has a king-size bed, a separate shower, and a large whirlpool tub.

There are several quaint **sitting areas** scattered (and sometimes virtually hidden) throughout the resort's buildings.

Guests with rooms in the **small courtyard building** on the Inn side must use their room key to enter the building itself.

Noise and **light** levels are important considerations here due to the proximity of the BoardWalk Promenade. If these are concerns, request a room away from both the promenade and the pools.

Conference facilities are available at the BoardWalk.

Check-in time is 3:00 pm (BoardWalk Inn) or 4:00 pm (BoardWalk Villas). Check-out time is 11:00 am for both.

Ratings are explained on page 26.

Our Value Ratings:		Our Magic Ratings:		Readers' Ratings:
Quality:	9/10	Theme:	8/10	72% fell in love with it
Accessibility:	7/10	Amenities:	8/10	17% liked it well enough
Affordability:	3/10	Fun Factor:	6/10	8% had mixed feelings
Overall Value:	**6/10**	**Overall Magic:**	**7/10**	3% were disappointed

The BoardWalk is enjoyed by...		(rated by both authors and readers)
Younger Kids: ♥♥♥♥	Young Adults: ♥♥♥♥	Families: ♥♥♥♥♥
Older Kids: ♥♥♥♥	Mid Adults: ♥♥♥♥♥	Couples: ♥♥♥♥♥
Teenagers: ♥♥♥	Mature Adults: ♥♥♥♥♥	Singles: ♥♥♥

TIPS

NOTES

RATINGS

Planning · Getting There · Staying in Style · Touring · Feasting · Making Magic · Index · Notes & More

Finding Your Place
at Disney's BoardWalk Inn & Villas Resort

BOARDWALK RESORT MAP

Parking Lot

To Tennis Courts & Studios

Pool

Community Hall

★ = Registration
E = Elevators
🚌 = Bus Stop

Conference Center

Luna Park

Channel to Studios

Pool

E ★ E

Pool

Pool
Garden Suites
BoardWalk Inn

BoardWalk Promenade

BoardWalk Villas

Swan/Dolphin

Walk to Epcot

Boat to Epcot

Boat to Studios

Crescent Lake

BEST LOCATIONS

It's hard to get a bad room at either the BoardWalk Inn or Villas. Request a **water view** at the Inn if you want to watch the bustling BoardWalk Promenade, but keep in mind it can be noisy. Water views in the Villas may be over the Promenade itself, but are more likely to overlook the canal leading to the Studios. **Standard views** overlook attractive courtyards or the entrance driveway (which isn't so bad as trees shield the parking areas). **Preferred views** in the Villas can overlook anything but a parking area. Rooms around the quiet pools are more peaceful than those around Luna Park.

RATES

2005 Sample Room Rates

Seasons are noted on page 14

Room Type	Value	Regular	Peak	Holiday
Standard (Inn) or Studio (Villas)	$294	$334	$404	$459
Water View (Inn)	$370	$415	$480	$545
One-Bedroom (Villas)	$400	$450	$525	$590
Two-Bedroom (Villas)	$560	$725	$920	$1040

Tax not included in above prices. Concierge-level rooms at the BoardWalk Inn begin at the low-$400's and suites begin in the mid-$500's. The Grand Villas begin in the $1300's.

INFO

Disney's BoardWalk Inn & Villas Resort
✉ 2101 Epcot Resort Blvd., Lake Buena Vista, FL 32830
📞 Phone: 407-939-6200 📠 Fax: 407-939-5150
📋 For reservations, call Central Reservations: 407-939-6244

Disney's Caribbean Beach Resort

Planning

Getting There

The free spirit of the tropics greets you at the Caribbean Beach Resort, Disney's original moderately priced resort. Within easy distance of both Epcot and Disney-MGM Studios (use the blue tab at the top of the page for parks and eateries in the area), this large resort is popular with families.

The bright, sunny colors of the buildings and rooftops are your first sign of the **laid-back lifestyle** you'll find at the Caribbean. After you check in at the Customs House, you make your way to one of the six "islands" that encircle 45-acre Barefoot Bay. Lush tropical foliage, hidden courtyards, and white sand beaches are the setting for your lively Caribbean adventure.

AMBIENCE

The 2,112 rooms are well spread out among the six exotic **"islands"** of the Caribe—Aruba, Barbados, Martinique, Jamaica, Trinidad North, and Trinidad South. Each island has a cluster of stucco, pitched-roof buildings that make up the "village centers," all painted in their own distinctive colors. The rooms in the two-storied buildings are decorated in soft colors with oak furnishings. The beds (one king or two doubles) have posts carved into pineapples, the symbol of hospitality. Guest rooms have double sinks in the separate vanity area, a small table and chairs, an armoire with TV, a set of drawers, and a ceiling fan. There are no balconies or patios. The guest rooms here are the largest of all the moderately priced resorts at 340 sq. ft. Amenities include a coffeemaker, toiletries, housekeeping service, limited room service, and voice mail.

Standard
Room Layout

RESORT LAYOUT & ROOMS

The Caribbean Beach offers a new table-service restaurant, as well as a breezy food court and the ubiquitous pool bar. All are available in **Old Port Royale**, also called "Center Towne," housing the eateries, shops, main pool, and marina. The food court's hours are 7:00 am–11:30 pm. **Banana Cabana**, a pool bar located at Old Port Royale, offers a variety of specialty drinks ($6.50) and beer ($4.25–$5.25) during pool hours. **Bluerunner** is a limited room delivery service—typical menu items include domestic beer ($4.50), 16" pizza ($14.95), 8-piece chicken in a bucket ($13.50), tuna sub with chips ($5.49), a chef salad ($5.99), and cheesecake ($3.50). **Shutters**, the table-service restaurant, serves Caribbean-flavored fare for dinner only—see the restaurant's description on page 225.

DINING

Staying in Style

Touring

Feasting

Making Magic

Index

Notes & More

Using the Amenities at Disney's Caribbean Beach Resort

MORE DINING

A bustling village atmosphere sets the stage for **Market Street**, the resort's newly renovated food court. Fill your trays at the various food stations, then pay at a central check out area. Chicken, pasta, sandwiches, burgers, pizza, and baked goods are on the menu, as is French toast with bacon ($4.99), chicken Caesar salad ($5.99), double cheeseburger with fries ($6.19), veggie wrap ($5.49), kids' grilled cheese ($3.99), and carrot cake ($2.99). Get refills at the beverage island with a mug ($12).

© MediaMarx, Inc.

Relaxing in our king bed, barrier-free room (#2311)

PLAYING & RELAXING

For Athletes: The Barefoot Bay Boat Yard rents boats and "toobies" (motorized inner tubes). Rent a bicycle for a ride around the bay. Walkers and joggers enjoy the many beautiful paths, and will really enjoy the circuit around Barefoot Bay and the footbridges to Parrot Cay island.

For Children: There are playgrounds on the beaches in Barbados, Jamaica, and Trinidad South.

For Gamers: Goombay Games in Old Port Royale has video games.

For Shoppers: The Calypso Trading Post & Straw Market offers themed gifts, sundries, clothing, and Caribbean items.

For Swimmers: The theme pool near Old Port Royale features cannons and waterfalls, as well as a wading pool for kids, a spa (hot tub), and a water slide. Six quiet pools are in each of the resort's "islands."

For Sunbathers: Each "island" has a beautiful, white sand beach.

GETTING ABOUT

Transportation to the theme parks and water parks (see chart below for in-transit times) is via frequent **buses**. Other resorts are accessible by changing buses at a nearby theme park (daytime) or Downtown Disney (evening). You can also take an internal resort bus if you need to reach other areas within the resort. To go to the Customs House, get off at Barbados.

Magic Kingdom	Epcot	Disney-MGM Studios	Disney's Animal Kingdom	Downtown Disney
direct bus ~20 min.	direct bus ~15 min.	direct bus ~12 min.	direct bus ~20 min.	direct bus ~25 min.

Approximate time you will spend in transit from resort to destination during normal operation.

Making the Most of Disney's Caribbean Beach Resort

We stayed in this **beautiful resort** after its recent renovation and are delighted to report that it is looking wonderful! For those who visited prior to December 2002, note that the old restaurant, Captain's Tavern, has been replaced by Shutters (see page 225).

While you can't swim in the bay, the **white sand beaches** are great spots to relax. We found several hammocks set up along the beach—take some time to just kick back and watch the palm trees flutter.

You can catch a glimpse of the **Epcot globe** between Old Port Royale and Martinique—look in the evenings for a glimpse of IllumiNations.

There are "hidden" **courtyards** sporting tables with umbrellas in every "island" of the resort—finding these can be an adventure in itself, and they offer a very rewarding place to relax.

Be sure to take a trip across the bridge to **Parrot Cay** in the middle of Barefoot Bay. Beyond the lush gardens and dense bamboo stands, you'll find gazebos and picnic areas. Alas, the playground that used to reside here is gone, however.

In-room refrigerators are now no charge. Request when reserving.

One of the biggest drawbacks of this resort is how spread out it is, making it difficult to get to Old Port Royale to eat or shop. You may find it easier to **stock up** on snacks and quick breakfast foods. Board the bus marked "Internal" to move around the resort a little easier.

All rooms in Martinique and Trinidad North are **Preferred Rooms** and are priced the same as a water-view or king-bed room.

Check-in time is 3:00 pm. Check-out time is 11:00 am.

Ratings are explained on page 26.

Our Value Ratings:		Our Magic Ratings:		Readers' Ratings:
Quality:	6/10	Theme:	6/10	47% fell in love with it
Accessibility:	5/10	Amenities:	6/10	43% liked it well enough
Affordability:	8/10	Fun Factor:	6/10	8% had mixed feelings
Overall Value:	**6/10**	**Overall Magic:**	**6/10**	2% were disappointed

Caribbean Beach is enjoyed by...		(rated by both authors and readers)
Younger Kids: ❤❤❤❤❤	Young Adults: ❤❤❤❤	Families: ❤❤❤❤
Older Kids: ❤❤❤❤❤	Mid Adults: ❤❤❤❤	Couples: ❤❤❤❤❤
Teenagers: ❤❤❤❤	Mature Adults: ❤❤❤	Singles: ❤❤❤

TIPS

NOTES

RATINGS

Planning · Getting There · Staying in Style · Touring · Feasting · Making Magic · Index · Notes & More

Finding Your Place at Disney's Caribbean Beach Resort

CARIBBEAN BEACH RESORT MAP

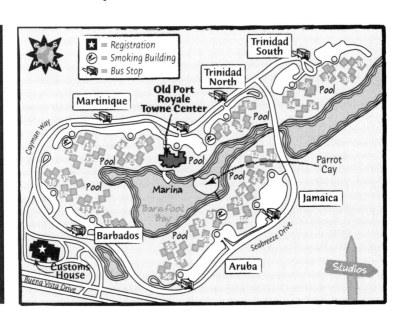

BEST LOCATIONS

Your "island" can make or break your experience. Though more expensive, we suggest you request **Martinique** or **Trinidad North**, both of which are close to Old Port Royale (dining and shopping). **Aruba** and **Jamaica**, across the Barefoot Bay bridge, are good choices if you wish to be a bit secluded. You don't need a **water view** to enjoy your room here, but if you prefer one, we found the following rooms to have outstanding water views: 2524, 2525, 2556, and 2557 in Martinique; and 3117, 3149, 3225–3228, and 3257–3261 in Trinidad North. Corner rooms (with king-size beds) seem larger as they often have an extra window.

RATES

2005 Sample Room Rates

Seasons are noted on page 14

Room Type	Value	Regular	Peak	Holiday
Standard View	$134	$149	$169	$184
Preferred, Water/Pool, or King	$149	$165	$194	$209

Tax not included in above rates. King-bed rooms come in both standard or water view, and both are the same rate as a water view room. Preferred rooms (any view, any bed size) are located in Martinique and Trinidad North.

INFO

Disney's Caribbean Beach Resort

✉ 900 Cayman Way, Lake Buena Vista, FL 32830

☎ Phone: 407-934-3400 ✏ Fax: 407-934-3288

🕐 For reservations, call Central Reservations: 407-939-6244

Disney's Contemporary Resort

The Contemporary Resort is one of the original and quintessential Walt Disney World hotels, built at the same time as nearby Magic Kingdom (use the blue tab at the top of the page for parks and eateries in the area). Bay Lake and the Seven Seas Lagoon surround the resort on three sides.

Every time we enter the Contemporary Resort, we get the sense we've entered the **center of the "World."** It isn't just the soaring architecture, the massive steel and glass tower, or the monorail running right through it, though those are all a part of it. Rather, it is akin to the feeling city dwellers boast about: everything you need, everyone you like, and every place that matters is right there. And that seems to be exactly the way Disney intended it, with the Grand Concourse housing most of the resort's services, restaurants, and shops. There's even a restaurant at the top of the tower, overlooking the "World" below. The Contemporary Resort is the future we dreamed of as children.

Standard Room Layout

The 1,041 guest rooms at the Contemporary are housed along the outside of the 15-story, A-frame **tower** or within the two flanking, three-story **garden wings**. Spacious rooms (about 436 sq. ft.) are decorated in eclectic, vibrant colors with two queen-size beds or one king-size bed, and a daybed. All rooms have spacious bathrooms with two sinks, a massage shower head, a small table and chairs, an armoire with drawers, and a TV. Some rooms have large patios or balconies. Amenities include housekeeping, toiletries, safe, newspaper delivery, hair dryer, turndown service (on request), voice mail, and valet parking.

If your stomach feels as cavernous as the Grand Concourse, the Contemporary has great dining. Table-service restaurants (see details on pages 225–226) include **Chef Mickey's**, a character dining experience; **Concourse Steakhouse**, traditional fare; and trendy **California Grill**, the Contemporary's centerpiece. The **Food and Fun Center Snack Bar** is open early and late. Typical menu items include biscuits and gravy ($4.99), fruit plate ($4.99), chicken strips ($6.59), California club wrap ($6.99), and kids' macaroni and cheese with fries, chips, or fruit ($4.29). Refillable mugs are available here for $12. The **Sand Bar** by the pool also offers drinks, sandwiches, and ice cream.

Planning · Getting There · Staying in Style · Touring · Feasting · Making Magic · Index · Notes & More

AMBIENCE

RESORT LAYOUT & ROOMS

DINING

Planning | Getting There | Staying in Style | Touring | Feasting | Making Magic | Index | Notes & More

Using the Amenities
at Disney's Contemporary Resort

LOUNGING

California Grill Lounge offers California wines and appetizers along with a magnificent view of the Magic Kingdom. The **Outer Rim Cocktail Lounge**, overlooking Bay Lake, offers a full bar and snacks. **Contemporary Grounds** is a coffee bar near the front desk. **Room service** is also available 24 hours a day.

© MediaMarx, Inc.

Our first-floor Garden Wing room was spacious and convenient

PLAYING & RELAXING

For Athletes: The Olympiad fitness center has exercise equipment, sauna, and massage therapies. Six lighted clay tennis courts are available. Boat rentals, waterskiing, and parasailing add to the fun. Volleyball and shuffleboard courts are available, plus jogging paths.
For Charmers: A full-service salon offers services by appointment.
For Children: A playground is by the North Garden Wing. The Mousketeer Clubhouse childcare club has closed (see page 253).
For Gamers: The biggest and best of the resort arcades is here in the Food and Fun Center, with pinball, video, and action games.
For Shoppers: The fourth-floor Concourse shops sell gifts and clothing. The marina pavilion offers swimming and sun protection.
For Swimmers: Two heated pools, two spas (hot tubs), and a water slide, as well as a sand beach for sunbathers.

GETTING ABOUT

The Contemporary Resort offers myriad transportation options (see the chart below for in-transit times). For the Magic Kingdom, board the **monorail** on the 4th floor or walk the **path** on the north side (see map on page 54). For Epcot, monorail to the Transportation and Ticket Center (TTC) and transfer to the Epcot monorail. For other parks, take the **direct bus** just outside the lobby. For the Polynesian or Grand Floridian, take the monorail. For Fort Wilderness or the Wilderness Lodge, take the **boat**. For other destinations, go to the Magic Kingdom (daytime) or Downtown Disney (evening) and transfer to the appropriate resort bus.

Magic Kingdom	Epcot	Disney-MGM Studios	Disney's Animal Kingdom	Downtown Disney
monorail/walk ~20/~10 min.	monorail x 2 ~15 min.	direct bus ~20 min.	direct bus ~20 min.	direct bus ~35 min.

Approximate time you will spend in transit from resort to destination during normal operation.

...king the Most ...Contemporary Resort

..., a whimsical parade of lighted barges
...he shore of Bay Lake at 10:00 pm.

...wo-bedroom suites and two concierge
...s. Among the many amenities in the
...ng, turndown service, etc.), the two-
...or those who use dataports often.

... by the tranquility of the grounds.
...dmire the view of Bay Lake.

...he obvious method of transportation to Magic Kingdom is via the
monorail, but consider **walking** instead on busy mornings or when the
park lets out—it's much faster! The monorail goes around the lagoon
clockwise, so it can take a while to reach the Magic Kingdom.

Guest rooms in the **Garden Wings** can be a hike from the Tower's
restaurants and services. If this is a concern, reserve a Tower room.
On the other hand, the North Garden Wing is very convenient to
the buses and to the walking path to the Magic Kingdom.

The **observation deck** on the 15th floor is closed to all but California
Grill guests. There's a fireworks viewing deck on the fourth floor.

For some, the Contemporary lacks the whimsy seen in most other
Disney resorts. It feels much more like a traditional hotel. Even so,
it is a very deluxe, modern, sparkling-clean hotel with a powerful
presence. You'll be delighted by **subtler details** and **little luxuries**.
Look for high-speed Internet access here in the near future!

Check-in time is 3:00 pm. Check-out time is 11:00 am.

Ratings are explained on page 26.

Our Value Ratings:		Our Magic Ratings:		Readers' Ratings:
Quality:	8/10	Theme:	4/10	50% fell in love with it
Accessibility:	9/10	Amenities:	9/10	24% liked it well enough
Affordability:	5/10	Fun Factor:	5/10	1% had mixed feelings
Overall Value:	7/10	Overall Magic:	6/10	16% were disappointed

Contemporary is enjoyed by...		(rated by both authors and readers)
Younger Kids: ♥♥♥	Young Adults: ♥♥♥♥♥	Families: ♥♥♥♥♥
Older Kids: ♥♥♥♥♥	Mid Adults: ♥♥♥♥	Couples: ♥♥♥♥
Teenagers: ♥♥♥♥♥	Mature Adults: ♥♥♥	Singles: ♥♥♥♥

TIPS
NOTES
RATINGS

Planning
Getting There
Staying in Style
Touring
Feasting
Making Magic
Index
Notes & More

12/08/05 3
2:30p
4:33PM
Another FASTPASS
ticket will be
available after
6:42PM
AND
5:42PM
Time Between
Enter Any

SOARIN'

Finding Your Place
at Disney's Contemporary Resort

CONTEMPORARY RESORT MAP

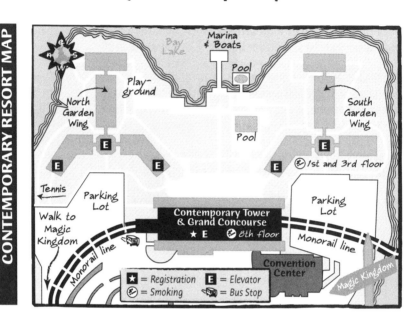

Bay Lake

Marina & Boats

Pool

Playground

North Garden Wing

South Garden Wing

Pool

E   E   E

E

E   ♿ 1st and 3rd floor

Tennis

Parking Lot

Walk to Magic Kingdom

Monorail line

Contemporary Tower & Grand Concourse
★ E   ♿ 8th floor

Parking Lot

Monorail line

Convention Center

Magic Kingdom

★ = Registration   E = Elevator
♿ = Smoking   🚌 = Bus Stop

BEST LOCATIONS

If you are drawn to the Contemporary by its proximity to the Magic Kingdom and you want to **see the castle** from your room, be sure to request this specifically when reserving—only certain **Tower** rooms get this breathtaking view. The **Garden Wing** may lack the tower's excitement, but we found the rooms delightful and relaxing, especially those facing the water. North Garden Wing rooms are closer to the Magic Kingdom. Rooms fronting Bay Lake feel far removed from the bustle of the Tower. Very few of the Garden Wing rooms have **balconies**, but first-floor rooms have **patios**.

RATES

2005 Sample Room Rates
Seasons are noted on page 14

Room Type	Value	Regular	Peak	Holiday
Standard View (Wing)	$244	$274	$319	$359
Garden/Water View (Wing)	$280	$315	$365	$405
Tower Room	$345	$380	$450	$490
Tower Club (concierge)	$405	$445	$520	$560

Tax not included in above rates. Concierge-level suites (floors 12 and 14) start at $1050. Suites come in garden and lake views, and start in the high-$800's.

INFO

Disney's Contemporary Resort
✉ 4600 North World Drive, Lake Buena Vista, FL 32830
☎ Phone: 407-824-1000   📠 Fax: 407-824-3539
📋 For reservations, call Central Reservations: 407-939-6244

Disney's Coronado Springs Resort

Coronado Springs is located near Disney's Animal Kingdom and Disney-MGM Studios (use the blue tab at the top of the page for parks and eateries in the area). The resort offers moderately priced rooms and convention facilities. The resort surrounds a 15-acre lake known as Lago Dorado.

The architecture and decor traces the travels of explorer Francisco de Coronado in colonial Mexico and the **American Southwest**. Adventure awaits around every corner, from the colorful, bustling market to the Mayan pyramid overlooking the main swimming pool. Your visit begins in a sunny plaza, which leads to the large, open lobby graced by beamed ceilings, elegant columns, and intricately inlaid floors. Around the corner, a festive market offers native foods, just the thing to eat on the lakeside terrace. The resort's buildings are clustered around sparkling Lago (Lake) Dorado, including the stately main building, El Centro.

The guest rooms in this 1,967-room resort are divided into three districts. Closest to El Centro are the **Casitas**, a bustling village of three- and four-story stucco buildings painted in soft pastels. Next around the lagoon are the rustic adobe-and-wood **Ranchos**. You could imagine Zorro dashing under the porch roofs and amid the cactus, while bubbling springs cascade into rock-strewn stream beds, ultimately to disappear into the parched desert earth. Finally, you reach the tropical **Cabanas**, vibrantly colored two-story buildings with the corrugated tin roofs of a rustic beach resort. Rooms are about 314 sq. ft. and offer two extra-long double beds or one king bed, a separate vanity area with just one sink, table and chairs, armoire, and a TV. Amenities include toiletries, housekeeping, limited room service, hair dryer, iron and ironing board, coffeemaker, in-room safe, and voice mail. Newspaper delivery is available for $1.50/day. A number of junior, one-bedroom, and executive suites are also available.

Standard Room Layout

The large 95,000 sq. ft. **Conference Center** is quite modern and generally lacks the regional character of the resort. It boasts the largest ballroom in the Southeast (60,214 sq. ft.). Several smaller-sized meeting rooms, another 20,000 sq. ft. ballroom, and patios round out the facilities. The center is currently undergoing a major expansion. A full-service business center is available.

Using the Amenities at Disney's Coronado Springs Resort

DINING

Coronado Springs' dining options are the real enchilada. **Maya Grill** (see page 226) is an upscale table-service restaurant open for breakfast and dinner. **Pepper Market** is a food court dressed up like a festive, outdoor market for breakfast, lunch, and dinner. Typical menu items include breakfast burrito ($6.99), cheese omelet ($6.99), catch of the day ($10.95), chicken fajitas ($11.95), ham and cheese sandwich ($6.99), and kids' chicken strips ($4.50). **Siesta's** is the

Home on the Ranchos

poolside bar serving sandwiches, nachos, fries, and various drinks. **Francisco's** is a large lounge where you can also get light snacks and appetizers. **Limited room service** is offered in the mornings and evenings. Refillable mugs ($12) are available at the Pepper Market.

PLAYING & RELAXING

For Athletes: La Vida Health Club has exercise equipment, whirlpool, and massage treatments. Boats, bikes, surreys, and fishing poles can be rented at La Marina, and there is a volleyball court. Enjoy a nature trail and the walk/jog around the lagoon.
For Charmers: Casa de Belleza offers beauty and hair treatments.
For Children: The Explorer's Playground is near the main pool.
For Gamers: Video games of all sorts are found at the two arcades: Jumping Beans (in El Centro) and Iguana (near the main pool).
For Shoppers: Panchito's has sundries, character items, and gifts.
For Swimmers: A quiet pool in each of the three districts, plus the Dig Site main pool, which is built around an ancient pyramid, and features a water slide, spa (hot tub), and kids' pool.

GETTING ABOUT

Transportation to the theme parks is by frequent, direct **buses** (see chart below for in-transit times). There are four bus stops (see map on page 58). For other destinations, transfer at a nearby theme park (daytime) or at Downtown Disney (evening). A sidewalk connects the resort to Blizzard Beach, and it's a quick drive to both Disney-MGM Studios and Disney's Animal Kingdom.

Magic Kingdom	Epcot	Disney-MGM Studios	Disney's Animal Kingdom	Downtown Disney
direct bus ~15 min.	direct bus ~15 min.	direct bus ~15 min.	direct bus ~10 min.	direct bus ~25 min.

Approximate time you will spend in transit from resort to destination during normal operation.

Making the Most of Disney's Coronado Springs Resort

The **Dig Site** is really a miniature water park with delightful scenery and fun water attractions. The pool itself is huge (10,800 sq. ft.) and there's a large sandbox that masquerades as the "dig site" of the Mayan pyramid. The 123-foot-long water slide has a jaguar atop it that spits water. Oh, and they have the largest outdoor spa (hot tub) of any Disney resort—it fits 22 people!

Small **refrigerators** are now available at no charge. Roll-away beds are available for $15/day (but rooms are still limited to four guests). Request these with your reservations and again at check-in.

The **Pepper Market** food court works differently than other food courts. Upon arrival, you are seated by a cast member and given a ticket. You then visit the various food stations, and when you find an item you want, your ticket is stamped. You pay after your meal. A 10% gratuity is added (unless you get your food to go).

This resort goes for the sun-drenched effect and, in the process, seems to **lack enough shade** to protect you from the scorching Florida sun. Use caution if you are fair-skinned (as Jennifer is) or are going during the summer months.

Coronado Springs strikes us as a bit more **buttoned-down** than the other moderate resorts, no doubt due to the conference center and business facilities. While we have no major complaints, it also didn't delight us in the same way that other moderate Disney resorts have. On the other hand, some of our fellow vacationers are very impressed with the resort, especially its quality service. We definitely feel this is a great resort for business travelers.

Check-in time is 3:00 pm. Check-out time is 11:00 am.

Ratings are explained on page 26.

Our Value Ratings:		Our Magic Ratings:		Readers' Ratings:
Quality:	7/10	Theme:	8/10	35% fell in love with it
Accessibility:	6/10	Amenities:	5/10	47% liked it well enough
Affordability:	8/10	Fun Factor:	4/10	15% had mixed feelings
Overall Value:	**7/10**	**Overall Magic:**	**6/10**	3% were disappointed

Coronado Springs is enjoyed by...		(rated by both authors and readers)
Younger Kids: ♥♥♥♥	Young Adults: ♥♥♥♥♥	Families: ♥♥♥♥
Older Kids: ♥♥♥♥	Mid Adults: ♥♥♥♥	Couples: ♥♥♥♥♥
Teenagers: ♥♥♥♥	Mature Adults: ♥♥♥	Singles: ♥♥♥♥

Planning · Getting There · Staying in Style · Touring · Feasting · Making Magic · Index · Notes & More

TIPS · NOTES · RATINGS

Finding Your Place at Disney's Coronado Springs Resort

CORONADO SPRINGS RESORT MAP

BEST LOCATIONS

The **Casitas** are the least interesting visually, but they are convenient to the Convention Center—in fact, they house the only rooms that you can reach from El Centro without leaving the protection of a roof or overhang. Building 1 is the closest to the Conference Center. The charming **Ranchos** are closest to the main pool, and farthest from El Centro. We recommend building 6B for its view and proximity to the quiet pool. The **Cabanas** are convenient to El Centro. We loved our room in building 8B (close to pools and the bus); building 8A has good views, and 9B is next door to El Centro.

RATES

2005 Sample Room Rates

Seasons are noted on page 14

Room Type	Value	Regular	Peak	Holiday
Standard View	$134	$149	$169	$184
Water View or King-Bed Room	$149	$165	$194	$209
Junior Suite (Double Beds)	$290	$335	$395	$435
One-Bedroom Suite	$580	$635	$705	$775

Tax not included in above rates.

INFO

Disney's Coronado Springs Resort

✉ 1000 W. Buena Vista Drive, Lake Buena Vista, FL 32830
☎ Phone: 407-939-1000 ✎ Fax: 407-939-1001
🗓 For reservations, call Central Reservations: 407-934-7639

Looking for Dixie Landings? Page 79. Dolphin Resort? Page 99.

Disney's Fort Wilderness Resort & Campground

Much more than tents and hookups, Fort Wilderness is a resort in every sense of the word. It is pleasantly situated in a shady forest on Bay Lake, connected by a scenic waterway to the nearby Magic Kingdom theme park (use the blue tab at the top of the page for parks and eateries in the vicinity).

Enveloped by pine, cypress, and oak, this 700-acre campground is a **relaxing haven** after the noise and excitement of a long day at the parks. Rough-hewn log common buildings are nestled among towering pine trees and flowering meadows. Wilderness this is not, however. There are enough daily conveniences and services that the tents may be the only reminder that you are camping.

All types of camping are available—tent, pop-up, trailer, and motor home (RV)—throughout the 788 **campsites**. Located on small loop roads connecting to larger thoroughfares, each site is relatively secluded by trees and shrubs and offers its own paved driveway, Coquina rock bed, charcoal grill, picnic table, and 110V/220V electrical service. Of the three types of campsites, partial hookups supply water, full hookups offer sewer and water, and preferred sites have cable TV, sewer, and water—preferred sites are also closest to the marina and eateries. Each site accommodates up to ten people and one car; pets are welcome at certain sites. All sites are close to very clean, air-conditioned "Comfort Stations" with restrooms, private showers, telephones, ice machines (extra fee), and laundry facilities. For guests without a tent or trailer, the 407 **Wilderness Cabins** are roomy, air-conditioned "log cabins" (504 sq. ft.) that accommodate up to six guests plus a child under 3 in a crib. Each cabin has a living room, bedroom, a full kitchen, and modern bathroom. Charmingly rustic yet comfortable, each cabin comes stocked with pots and utensils, plus a coffeemaker, stove, microwave, refrigerator, dishwasher, cable TV, VCR, phone, hair dryer, and safe. The living room has a pull-down double bed, while the bedroom has a separate vanity, a double bed, and a bunk bed. Outside is a charcoal grill, picnic table, and deck. Amenities include voice mail and housekeeping—they even do dishes! All guests staying in the Cabins must be accommodated within them; no tents are permitted outside the Cabin.

Cabin Layout

AMBIENCE

RESORT LAYOUT & ROOMS

Planning

Getting There

Staying in Style

Touring

Feasting

Making Magic

Index

Notes & More

Using the Amenities at Disney's Fort Wilderness Resort

DINING

Many guests cook at their sites or cabins. If cooking isn't your thing, try **The Chuck Wagon**—it's open during the nightly campfire and serves snacks. Typical menu items: a hot dog ($2.35), popcorn ($2.36), and s'mores ($4.93). **Hoop-Dee-Doo Musical Revue** is a dinner show (see page 234). **Trail's End Restaurant** is a buffeteria (page 226). **Crockett's Tavern** serves drinks and snacks.

Inside a Fort Wilderness Cabin

© MediaMarx, Inc.

PLAYING & RELAXING

For Athletes: You'll find two lighted tennis courts, plus volleyball, tetherball, basketball, and horseshoes. Rent a boat at the marina or a canoe or bike at the Bike Barn. Horseback rides ($32) at the livery (must be 9+ yrs., 48"+). Nature walks, too!

For Children: A free Petting Zoo with pony rides ($3) and a nearby playground delight kids. Free nightly campfires with Chip and Dale, and Disney movies, or go on a "hayride" ($8/adult and $4/kids).

For Fishers: Try a bass fishing excursion in Bay Lake for $169-197.

For Gamers: Two video arcades are within the resort.

For Romantics: Enjoy a relaxing, private carriage ride for $30.

For Shoppers: Gifts, sundries, and groceries at two trading posts.

For Show-Goers: Two dinner shows! See page 234 for details.

For Swimmers: Two heated pools, a wading pool, and a beach for sunbathers. Child-size life vests are at the pools (no charge).

GETTING ABOUT

Boats (see chart below) go to Magic Kingdom, Wilderness Lodge, and Contemporary. **Buses** to Disney-MGM Studios and the Transportation and Ticket Center (TTC)/Wilderness Lodge pick up/drop off at Settlement Depot. Buses for Epcot, Animal Kingdom/Blizzard Beach and Downtown Disney/Typhoon Lagoon pick up/drop off at Outpost Depot. Three bus routes—Yellow, Orange, and Purple—service locations within the resort and all stop at Settlement Depot and Outpost Depot. For resorts, transfer at Magic Kingdom or Downtown Disney. You can rent an **electric golf cart** to move about the resort easier.

Magic Kingdom	Epcot	Disney-MGM Studios	Disney's Animal Kingdom	Downtown Disney
boat ~15 min.	direct bus ~25 min.	direct bus ~30 min.	direct bus ~30 min.	direct bus ~35 min.

Approximate time you will spend in transit from resort to destination during normal operation.

Making the Most of Disney's Fort Wilderness Resort

Electric golf carts are very popular for moving about the resort but are hard to get. To reserve one up to a year in advance, call the Bike Barn at 407-824-2742. Rates are $44+tax per 24-hour period.

The **Electrical Water Pageant**, a light and music barge parade on Bay Lake, can be seen from the beach at around 9:45 pm.

Seasonal, weekly, and monthly **discount rates** may be available for campsites (but not cabins).

A **car** may come in handy at this resort. Disney transportation to and from Fort Wilderness requires a transfer from an internal to external transport, making it more time-consuming than most resorts. To reduce transit time, request a site in loops 100–800 as these are within walking distance of Settlement Depot and the marina.

Motor traffic is limited to vehicles entering or leaving the resort only, though there is 15-min. parking at the Meadows Trading Post.

Bring your **groceries**, or buy them at Gooding's at Crossroads near Downtown Disney. You can pick up some items from the Trading Posts.

Pets are allowed for $5/day, but only in loops 300, 700, 800, and 1600–1900 (request at booking). No pets in pop-ups or tents.

Creekside Meadow offers rustic **group camping** with a Comfort Station, grills, and fire pits. Tents and cots can be rented.

Campfires are not allowed at individual campsites.

Check-in time is 1:00 pm (campsites) or 3:00 pm (Cabins). Check-out time for all is 11:00 am.

Note: The two Affordability Ratings below correspond to lodging and camping.   *Ratings are explained on page 26.*

Our Value Ratings:		Our Magic Ratings:		Readers' Ratings:
Quality:	7/10	Theme:	6/10	80% fell in love with it
Accessibility:	4/10	Amenities:	5/10	7% liked it well enough
Affordability:	6 & 10/10	Fun Factor:	8/10	10% had mixed feelings
Overall Value:	**6 & 7/10**	**Overall Magic:**	**6/10**	3% were disappointed

Fort Wilderness is enjoyed by...		(rated by both authors and readers)	
Younger Kids: ❤❤❤❤❤	Young Adults: ❤❤❤❤	Families: ❤❤❤❤❤
Older Kids: ❤❤❤❤	Mid Adults: ❤❤❤❤	Couples: ❤❤❤
Teenagers: ❤❤❤❤	Mature Adults: ❤❤❤❤	Singles: ❤❤

Sidebar tabs: TIPS · NOTES · RATINGS

Planning · Getting There · Staying in Style · Touring · Feasting · Making Magic · Index · Notes & More

FORT WILDERNESS RESORT

Planning · Getting There · Staying in Style · Touring · Feasting · Making Magic · Index · Notes & More

Finding Your Place
at Disney's Fort Wilderness Resort

BEST SPOTS

Campsites and cabins are located on loops, which are circular drives with about 40 sites or cabins each. The most popular **Cabin** locations are on loops 2500–2700 near the west pool, though we loved our cabin on loop 2100 near a bus stop. The most popular **campsites** are on loop 400. Preferred sites are **closest to Pioneer Hall** in the 100–500, 700, and 1400 loops. **Full hookup campsites** are in loops 600, 800–1300, and 1600–1900—we highly recommend loop 800. **Partial hookups** are located in the 1500 and 2000 loops.

RATES

2005 Sample Campsite/Cabin Rates
Seasons are noted on page 14

Room Type	Value	Regular	Peak	Pre-Holiday	Holiday
Partial Hook-Up Campsite	$38	$54	$62	$42	$72
Full Hook-Up Campsite	$43	$64	$73	$47	$84
Preferred Campsite	$51	$69	$79	$55	$89
Wilderness Cabin	$234	$274	$309	$234	$339

Tax not included in above rates. There is an additional charge of $5/night for more than two adults in a cabin, or $2/night for more than two adults at a campsite.

INFO

Disney's Fort Wilderness Resort & Campground
✉ 4510 N. Fort Wilderness Trail, Lake Buena Vista, FL 32830
☎ Phone: 407-824-2900   Fax: 407-824-3508
For reservations, call Central Reservations: 407-939-6244
For details: http://home.hiwaay.net/~jlspence/faq_fw.htm

Disney's Grand Floridian Resort & Spa

The most luxurious of Disney's resorts, the Grand Floridian Resort & Spa is a breathtaking Victorian hotel with turrets and gabled roofs. It extends into the Seven Seas Lagoon between the Polynesian and the Magic Kingdom (use the blue tab at the top of the page for parks and eateries in the area).

From the moment you step into the **Grand Lobby**, you will feel as though you've been transported back to the 1890s and the days when the well-to-do wintered in style at grand seaside resorts. Like that unhurried time, the warm whites and soft pastels draw you in, just as the towering lobby and stained glass skylights draw your eyes upward. It is the picture of charm, romance, and luxury.

900 guest rooms are generously spread out among five **lodge** buildings and the Grand Lobby. The luxurious rooms are decorated in four different whimsical-yet-subtle themes: floral, cameo (fairies), swans (Wind in the Willows), and Alice in Wonderland. Rooms are about 400 sq. ft. and are resplendent with marble-topped double sinks and balconies or patios. Most guest rooms offer two queen-size beds and a daybed, accommodating five people. The lodge buildings also house the slightly smaller "dormer" rooms, plus suites. Amenities include signature toiletries, turndown service, mini bar, large in-room safe, hair dryer, newspaper delivery, valet parking, 24-hour room service—and best of all—big, fluffy robes to relax in after a long day at the parks.

Standard Room Layout

Culinary delights await you in any of the restaurants and lounges, largely located on the first two floors of the Grand Lobby. Table service restaurants, which are described on pages 227–228, include: **1900 Park Fare**, a festive character dining experience; **Cítricos**, sophisticated Floridian and Mediterranean cuisine; **Grand Floridian Cafe**, a sun-splashed cafe with traditional fare; **Garden View Lounge**, high tea in the afternoon; **Narcoossee's**, seafood with a view of Seven Seas Lagoon; and **Victoria & Albert's**, Disney's finest restaurant. Quick-service options include the **Grand Floridian Pool Bar** for snacks and **Gasparilla's Grill and Games** for light fare 24 hours a day. Typical menu items at Gasparilla's Grill include an egg croissant ($4.79), a cheeseburger and fries ($5.99), a whole pepperoni pizza ($15.88), and chili ($3.50).

AMBIENCE

RESORT LAYOUT & ROOMS

DINING

Planning

Getting There

Staying in Style

Touring

Feasting

Making Magic

Index

Notes & More

Using the Amenities at Disney's Grand Floridian Resort & Spa

LOUNGING

Lounges at the Grand Floridian include the **Garden View Lounge**, which offers drinks in the evening. **Mizner's** serves cocktails and light snacks within earshot of the musicians who often perform in the Grand Lobby. The **Grand Floridian Pool Bar** also serves drinks and snacks,

© MediaMarx, Inc.

Jennifer and Dave enjoy a Turret Suite

such as a cheeseburger with fries ($11.95) or a Cobb salad ($12.95). Visit **Gasparilla's Grill and Games** to purchase refillable mugs (about $12) and get refills.

PLAYING & RELAXING

For Athletes: Two clay tennis courts are available for a fee. Rent a variety of boats at the marina. You'll also find walking/jogging paths.
For Charmers: The Ivy Trellis Salon pampers you with hair and nail treatments. The Grand Floridian Spa & Health Club is a full-service spa facility. Call 407-824-2332 for information.
For Children: A playground is adjacent to the Mouseketeer Clubhouse, a supervised program for kids 4–12 (see page 253).
For Gamers: Gasparilla's Grill and Games has a video arcade.
For Shoppers: On the first floor, Sandy Cove stocks sundries and Summer Lace offers upscale women's clothing. On the second floor, M. Mouse Mercantile has gifts; Bally offers luxury leather goods; and Commander Porter's has men's and women's apparel.
For Swimmers: A moderately sized but relatively quiet pool and hot tub are available, as is a theme pool near the beach with a slide and play fountain. Sunbathers enjoy the beach (no swimming).

GETTING ABOUT

A **monorail** goes to Magic Kingdom as well as the Contemporary, Polynesian, and the Transportation and Ticket Center (TTC), where you can transfer to the Epcot monorail. **Boats** also take you to the Magic Kingdom and the Polynesian. For other parks (see chart below for in-transit times), use the **direct buses** in front of the resort. For other resorts, monorail to the Magic Kingdom (daytime) or bus to Downtown Disney (evening) and transfer to a resort bus.

Magic Kingdom	Epcot	Disney-MGM Studios	Disney's Animal Kingdom	Downtown Disney
monorail/boat	monorail x 2	direct bus	direct bus	direct bus
~3/~10 min.	~12+10 min.	~10 min.	~15 min.	~20 min.

Approximate time you will spend in transit from resort to destination during normal operation.

Making the Most of Disney's Grand Floridian Resort & Spa

The Grand Lobby is often filled with the sound of **live music**, ranging from solo pianists to full dance bands.

Many **children's activities** are offered, including scavenger hunts, arts & crafts, story time, fishing trips, as well as the Wonderland Tea Party, the Pirate Cruise, and a cooking class (see page 244). Ask at Guest Services about the Ladybug Release Program, too!

Private dining is available for a quiet or romantic evening. You can have a meal on your balcony, on the beach, or even on a boat in the lagoon. Make arrangements in advance with room service.

For a touch of magic, end your day with a romantic, nighttime **stroll along the beach**. You may even catch the Electrical Water Pageant on the Seven Seas Lagoon around 9:15 pm.

Four extra-special types of rooms are available. The **lodge tower** rooms have a separate sitting area, an extra TV and phone, and five windows. **Concierge** rooms offer personalized services, continental breakfast, evening refreshments, and a private elevator. Of the concierge rooms, special **turret rooms** (see our honeymoon photo on previous page) have wet bars and windows all around, while **honeymoon suites** pamper with whirlpool tubs!

The Grand Floridian Resort & Spa is also a **conference center**.

Even though this is a luxury resort, don't feel you need to dress up. **Casual wear** is the norm here. The only exception is Victoria & Albert's restaurant, which requires evening attire.

Check-in time is 3:00 pm. Check-out time is 11:00 am.

Ratings are explained on page 26.

Our Value Ratings:		Our Magic Ratings:		Readers' Ratings:
Quality:	10/10	Theme:	8/10	80% fell in love with it
Accessibility:	8/10	Amenities:	9/10	4% liked it well enough
Affordability:	2/10	Fun Factor:	6/10	11% had mixed feelings
Overall Value:	7/10	Overall Magic:	8/10	5% were disappointed

Grand Floridian is enjoyed by...	(rated by both authors and readers)	
Younger Kids: ♥♥♥♥	Young Adults: ♥♥♥♥	Families: ♥♥♥
Older Kids: ♥♥♥♥	Mid Adults: ♥♥♥♥♥	Couples: ♥♥♥♥♥
Teenagers: ♥♥♥	Mature Adults: ♥♥♥♥♥	Singles: ♥♥♥

Planning · Getting There · Staying in Style · Touring · Feasting · Making Magic · Index · Notes & More

TIPS · NOTES · RATINGS

Finding Your Place
at Disney's Grand Floridian Resort & Spa

GRAND FLORIDIAN RESORT MAP

Boat Dock

Seven Seas Lagoon

Conference Center

Monorail line

Sago Cay

Conch Key

Narcoossee's

Marina

Sugar Loaf Key

Boca Chica

Pool

Parking Lot

Grand Lobby ★

Big Pine Key
Floors 4&5

★ = Registration
☺ = Smoking Building
🚌 = Bus Stop

Path to Spa and Polynesian

Beach

Magic Kingdom

Theme Pool

Seven Seas Lagoon

BEST SPOTS

The **dormer rooms** on the top floors of the lodge buildings may be a bit smaller (they only fit 4 rather than 5), but they feature vaulted ceilings, a secluded balcony, and a charming window above the French doors. The **best views of Cinderella Castle** come in the lagoon view rooms in Sago Cay and Conch Key lodges. Sugar Loaf Key is the closest lodge house to the Grand Lobby, but also sees the most traffic and hears the most noise. Big Pine Key is near to the beach and its lagoon view rooms offer picturesque views.

RATES

2005 Sample Room Rates

Seasons are noted on page 14

Room Type	Value	Regular	Peak	Holiday
Garden View	$349	$394	$459	$534
Lagoon View	$410	$470	$555	$615
Lodge Tower	$430	$490	$580	$645
Lodge Concierge (Sugar Loaf Key)	$460	$535	$620	$685
Main Building Concierge	$605	$685	$765	$855

Tax is not included in above room rates. Honeymoon concierge rooms start in the low-$600's. Suites, which are available in one- and two-bedrooms, are upwards of $900.

INFO

Disney's Grand Floridian Resort & Spa

✉ 4401 Floridian Way, Lake Buena Vista, FL 32830
☎ Phone: 407-824-3000   📠 Fax: 407-824-3186
🗓 For reservations, call Central Reservations: 407-939-6244

Disney's Old Key West Resort

Formerly known as the Vacation Club, the large Old Key West Resort caters primarily (but not exclusively) to Disney Vacation Club members. Old Key West is located roughly between Downtown Disney and Epcot (use the blue tab at the top of the page for parks and eateries in the area).

AMBIENCE

If Disney's Grand Floridian and BoardWalk set the pace for elegant turn-of-the-century seaside resorts, this is the dressed-down, laid-back antidote. Lush vegetation and low, white **clapboard buildings** with sky blue eaves evoke authentic Key West style, and the public areas of the resort exude small-town intimacy. Quaint waterside shops and restaurants are connected by wooden walkways, and the Conch Flats Community Hall offers homey choices like table tennis and board games. The atmosphere is lively, friendly, and not at all hectic. Accommodations are spacious, comfy, and attractive.

RESORT LAYOUT & ROOMS

Intimate is not necessarily small. Old Key West is big enough to get lost in. (We speak from experience!) The resort's 761 guest "homes" range from **studios** (376 sq. ft.) with kitchenettes that sleep four adults, to spacious **one-bedrooms** (1086 sq. ft.) with full kitchens that sleep four adults, **two-bedrooms** (1392 sq. ft.) also with full kitchens that sleep eight adults, and the incredible three-bedroom/four bath **Grand Villas** (2265 sq. ft.) that sleep up to 12. All have a private patio or balcony perfect for breakfast, and all but the studios include a master suite with a large two-person whirlpool tub; a sprawling Great Room with full kitchen, dining area, and queen-sized sleep sofa (see photo on the following page); and washer and dryer. Villas sport views of the golf course, waterways, or woods. Amenities in all rooms include a TV, refrigerator, microwave, coffeemaker, and voice mail. One-bedroom and larger rooms boast a fully equipped kitchen, big-screen TV, DVD player, and in-room safe. These "homes" are an excellent choice for groups and families who wish to stay together.

One-Bedroom (unshaded)
Studio Layout (shaded)
Entire layout represents a Two-Bedroom Home

Using the Amenities at Disney's Old Key West Resort

DINING

Olivia's Cafe (see page 228) is a kind of casual, small-town place loved by locals. **Good's Food to Go** over by the main pool serves up breakfasts, burgers, and snacks—typical menu items include a tuna sandwich ($6.29) and a child's sandpail meal ($5.89). Refillable mugs are available for $12. Also by the main pool, the **Gurgling Suitcase** has drinks

Jennifer and Allie prepare a meal in a one-bedroom villa at Old Key West

© MediaMarx, Inc.

and appetizers like shrimp fritters ($5.99), buffalo wings ($6.99), and crab cake ($7.59). **Turtle Shack** by the Turtle Pond Road pool has snacks seasonally. **Pizza delivery** is also available.

PLAYING & RELAXING

For Athletes: Tennis, basketball, shuffleboard, and volleyball courts are available. Rent boats and bikes at Hank's Rent 'N Return. Golf at the nearby course, or try the walking/jogging path. A health club has Nautilus equipment, plus a sauna and massages.

For Children: The Conch Flats Community Hall offers games and organized events for kids. Playgrounds are near some of the pools.

For Gamers: The two arcades—Electric Eel Arcade and The Flying Fisherman—have plenty of video games to keep the kids happy.

For Shoppers: The Conch Flats General Store offers general and Disney merchandise, plus groceries and sundries.

For Swimmers: Three quiet pools and a large theme pool round out the "R.E.S.T. Beach Recreation Department." A children's wading pool is near the main pool. The theme pool closed in September 2004 for renovations and is expected to reopen in December 2004.

GETTING ABOUT

Direct **buses** to the four major parks and Downtown Disney (see chart below for in-transit times) stop at the resort's five bus stops. A **boat** from the marina also travels to Saratoga Springs and the Marketplace at Downtown Disney between 11:00 am and 11:00 pm—check the schedule. To get around the resort, hop on a bus as they always stop at the Hospitality House before heading out.

Magic Kingdom	Epcot	Disney-MGM Studios	Disney's Animal Kingdom	Downtown Disney
direct bus ~25 min.	direct bus ~10 min.	direct bus ~10 min.	direct bus ~15 min.	bus/boat ~5/~15 min.

Approximate time you will spend in transit from resort to destination during normal operation.

Making the Most of Disney's Old Key West Resort

Some one-bedroom homes have a slight variation that can make a big difference if your party is large: there is a **second door to the bathroom** through the laundry room (see layout on page 67), which avoids the master bedroom. If this is important, request buildings 30 or higher at reservation and again at check-in.

Buildings 62–64 are the newest—they opened in early 2000. These are also the only buildings that have elevators.

The **three-bedroom Grand Villas** are luxurious (and expensive). They are two-storied with private baths for each bedroom plus an extra one for guests sleeping on the sleeper sofa. They have all the amenities of the other vacation homes, plus a 32" television and a stereo. They are phenomenally popular with families, though, so reserve as early as possible.

Hank's Rent 'N Return offers more than just bikes and boats. You can rent videos, board games, balls, and more. There are often daily activities and games—inquire when checking in.

If you stay in a studio, you won't have a washer and dryer in your room but there are air-conditioned **laundry rooms** available near the pools at no extra charge. You can buy soap and bleach, too.

Studios guests also have **no in-room safes**, but there are safe deposit boxes at the front desk. Note that ice is available from ice machines at the bus stops.

The theme pool has been upgraded and gains a water slide.

Check-in time is 4:00 pm. Check-out time is 11:00 am.

Ratings are explained on page 26.

Our Value Ratings:		Our Magic Ratings:		Readers' Ratings:
Quality:	7/10	Theme:	7/10	85% fell in love with it
Accessibility:	5/10	Amenities:	6/10	15% liked it well enough
Affordability:	4/10	Fun Factor:	5/10	0% had mixed feelings
Overall Value:	5/10	Overall Magic:	6/10	0% were disappointed

Old Key West is enjoyed by...		(rated by both authors and readers)
Younger Kids: ❤❤❤	Young Adults: ❤❤❤❤	Families: ❤❤❤❤❤
Older Kids: ❤❤❤❤	Mid Adults: ❤❤❤❤❤	Couples: ❤❤❤❤❤
Teenagers: ❤❤❤❤	Mature Adults: ❤❤❤❤❤	Singles: ❤❤❤

TIPS · NOTES · RATINGS

Planning · Getting There · Staying in Style · Touring · Feasting · Making Magic · Index · Notes & More

Finding Your Place at Disney's Old Key West Resort

OLD KEY WEST RESORT MAP

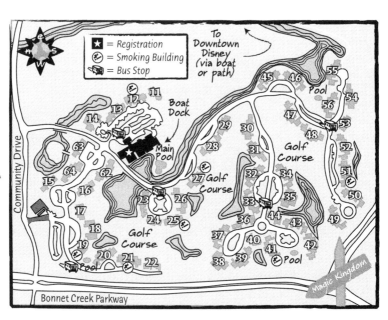

BEST LOCATIONS

Location is important in this sprawling resort. Though there are bus stops throughout the resort, we found staying near the **Hospitality House** to be a huge benefit. Buildings 11–14 and 62–64 are the closest (we loved our one-bedroom home in building 11), with buildings 15–16 and 23–26 also within reasonable walking distance. Most locations enjoy relative **peace and quiet**, but if you really want seclusion, 47–48 and 52–54 are nice as they are away from pools and roads, yet are near a bus stop. We suggest you avoid 30–44 as they feel remote, have traffic noise, and bus stops are often inconvenient.

RATES

2005 Sample Villa Rates
Seasons are noted on page 14

Room Type	Value	Regular	Peak	Holiday
Studio Villa	$259	$289	$339	$379
One-Bedroom Villa	$350	$395	$460	$525
Two-Bedroom Villa	$490	$575	$700	$805
Grand Villa	$1070	$1195	$1350	$1505

Tax is not included in the above rates. Three views are available—water, golf course, and woods—but with no difference in price.

INFO

Disney's Old Key West Resort
✉ 1510 North Cove Road, Lake Buena Vista, FL 32830
📠 Phone: 407-827-1198 Fax: 407-827-7710
📋 For reservations, call Central Reservations: 407-939-6244

Disney's Polynesian Resort

The Polynesian Resort is a lush, tropical paradise that brings the romance of the South Pacific to life. It rests tranquilly on the Seven Seas Lagoon between the Transportation and Ticket Center and the Grand Floridian Resort (use the blue tab at the top of the page for parks and eateries in the area).

The blooming gardens are your first hint of the beauty and color of the **tropics**, which are captured so splendidly here. You may not even notice that you've entered the main building, the Great Ceremonial House, with its atrium filled with falling waters and flowering tropical plants. "Aloha!" is more than a word here—it is a way of life—and you will be reminded of this again and again during your visit.

853 guest rooms are arranged throughout **longhouses** on eleven "islands" of Polynesia. The longhouses are two or three stories; the first-floor rooms have patios and many of the upper-floor rooms have balconies. The lush, laid-back feeling of the resort is carried into the rooms with wicker furnishings and canopied beds. Spacious rooms (409–448 sq. ft.) offer two queen-size beds and a daybed, accommodating five people in a room. We particularly like the roomy bathroom with its large mirror, tub, and toilet hidden around the corner. Suites and concierge-level rooms housed in the Tonga and Hawaii longhouses offer personal service and great views. Amenities for all resort rooms include toiletries, 24-hour room service, housekeeping service, turndown service (on request), voice mail, and valet parking.

Standard Room
Layout

Paradise offers bounty in food, too. Two table-service restaurants (see page 228) are **Kona Cafe**, offering a filling breakfast and inventive lunch and dinner, and **'Ohana**, serving up food and fun with skewered meats. **Captain Cook's Snack Company** is a good place for a quick breakfast and light meals. Typical items are French toast sticks ($3.99), Polynesian-style chicken sandwich ($6.69), and kids' chicken strips ($4.25). Refillable mugs are available for $12. A family-style **character breakfast** is served at 'Ohana, too. And let's not forget the Spirit of Aloha dinner show (page 235). **Tambu**, the lounge by 'Ohana, serves snacks and drinks, **Kona Island** is a coffee bar in the mornings, and the poolside **Barefoot Bar** has drinks.

Planning

Getting There

Staying in Style

Touring

Feasting

Making Magic

Index

Notes & More

AMBIENCE

RESORT LAYOUT & ROOMS

DINING & LOUNGING

Using the Amenities at Disney's Polynesian Resort

PLAYING & RELAXING

For Athletes: Boaters rent Sea Raycers and sailboats at the marina. Joggers enjoy the Walk Around the World that partially encircles the lagoon, and a 1.5-mile path winds through the resort (ask Guest Services for a map).

For Charmers: The Grand Floridian Spa & Health Club (see page 64) is north of the resort.

For Children: The Never Land Club is a childcare club (see page 253)—it's next to the arcade. A playground is near the main pool.

© MediaMarx, Inc.

Dave relaxes on a hammock near the Tokelau longhouse

For Gamers: Moana Mickey's Arcade offers some video games.

For Shoppers: On the first floor, News From Polynesia has newspapers and gifts; Polynesian Princess offers women's wear; Robin Crusoe's has men's apparel; Maui Mickey's has kid's apparel; and Wyland Galleries has collectibles. The second floor houses Trader Jack's (souvenirs and sundries) and Samoa Snacks.

For Show-Goers: Tucked in the back of the resort is Luau Cove, home to Polynesian-style dinner shows. More details on page 235.

For Swimmers: In addition to a quiet pool, the Nanea Volcano theme pool features a large pool "fed" by a spring, a water slide, warm water areas, underwater music, and a zero-entry section (pool wheelchair available). There's also a kids' play fountain. Alas, there is no spa (hot tub). There is a beach for sunbathing.

GETTING ABOUT

A **monorail** shuttles you to the Magic Kingdom (see chart below for in-transit times), Grand Floridian, and Contemporary, as well as the Transportation and Ticket Center (TTC). A **boat** also goes to the Magic Kingdom. To reach Epcot, take a short walk to TTC and board the monorail. To reach other parks (listed in chart below) and Downtown Disney, take **direct buses** (see map on page 74 for the bus stop). To reach most resorts, take a monorail to the Magic Kingdom and transfer to a resort bus (daytime), or take a bus to Downtown Disney and transfer to a resort bus (evening).

Magic Kingdom	Epcot	Disney-MGM Studios	Disney's Animal Kingdom	Downtown Disney
monorail/boat ~10/~5 min.	walk + monorail ~10+10 min.	direct bus ~15 min.	direct bus ~15 min.	direct bus ~25 min.

Approximate time you will spend in transit from resort to destination during normal operation.

Making the Most of Disney's Polynesian Resort

TIPS

On the beach in front of the Hawaii and Tahiti longhouses are several **bench swings** and **hammocks**. Not only are these heaven after a long day, they make ideal spots to watch the fireworks.

A **night stroll** through the resort is sublime. A very secluded spot over the rise on the beach's point is pure magic to us.

The **Electrical Water Pageant** passes right by the Polynesian around 9:00 pm. If you don't have a water-view room, take a stroll down to the beach or to the end of the dock near the marina.

The **lulling music** of the South Seas is all around you, with the notable exception of your room. If you'd like to keep these sounds, bring a portable CD player and purchase a CD in the gift shop.

Families love the Polynesian and it may get a bit **noisy** in the pool areas (near Samoa, Niue, Hawaii, Rarotonga, and Tokelau).

NOTES

The longhouses recently underwent **renovations** (completed in 2004) and are now all open.

Walk to the Transportation and Ticket Center for the **Epcot monorail**. The monorail around the lagoon adds 20 minutes otherwise.

The Polynesian Resort shares **bus routes** with the Contemporary and Grand Floridian resorts, picking up/dropping off guests at the Contemporary first and Grand Floridian last.

Daily activities are available for kids of all ages, such as coconut races and torch lightings. Ask for a schedule upon check-in.

Check-in time is 3:00 pm. Check-out time is 11:00 am.

Ratings are explained on page 26.

RATINGS

Our Value Ratings:		Our Magic Ratings:		Readers' Ratings:
Quality:	8/10	Theme:	9/10	62% fell in love with it
Accessibility:	9/10	Amenities:	7/10	29% liked it well enough
Affordability:	3/10	Fun Factor:	8/10	7% had mixed feelings
Overall Value:	7/10	Overall Magic:	8/10	2% were disappointed

The Polynesian is enjoyed by...	(rated by both authors and readers)	
Younger Kids: ♥♥♥♥	Young Adults: ♥♥♥♥♥	Families: ♥♥♥♥♥
Older Kids: ♥♥♥♥♥	Mid Adults: ♥♥♥♥♥	Couples: ♥♥♥♥♥
Teenagers: ♥♥♥♥	Mature Adults: ♥♥♥♥♥	Singles: ♥♥♥

Planning
Getting There
Staying in Style
Touring
Feasting
Making Magic
Index
Notes & More

Finding Your Place
at Disney's Polynesian Resort

POLYNESIAN RESORT MAP

- ★ = Registration
- 🚭 = Smoking Building
- 🚌 = Bus Stop

BEST LOCATIONS

All **first-floor rooms** have patios, and all **third-floor rooms** have balconies. Most **second-floor rooms** have no balconies, with the exception of Tahiti, Rapa Nui, Tokelau, and Tonga, which were built later. Particularly nice water views can be found in Tuvalu, Hawaii, Tahiti, and Fiji. The first-floor rooms in Tahiti facing away from the water have pleasant, secluded patios, as do those in Rapa Nui and Rarotonga. If you opt for a standard view, we recommend Aotearoa with beautiful landscaping and an up-close view of the monorail. For added **privacy**, request a room on the top floor.

RATES

2005 Sample Room Rates

Seasons are noted on page 14

Room Type	Value	Regular	Peak	Holiday
Garden-View	$304	$354	$419	$484
Lagoon-View	$400	$445	$520	$580
Garden-View Concierge	$410	$455	$530	$595
Lagoon-View/Suite Concierge	$510	$580	$645	$720
2-Bedroom Suite Concierge	$1232	$1340	$1510	$1690

Tax is not included in the above rates. One-bedroom suites start in the low-$500's.

INFO

Disney's Polynesian Resort
✉ 1600 Seven Seas Drive, Lake Buena Vista, FL 32830
📞 Phone: 407-824-2000 📠 Fax: 407-824-3174
📋 For reservations, call Central Reservations: 407-939-6244

There is no projected opening date for Pop Century Legendary Years.

Disney's Pop Century Resort

Auld acquaintance shall be remembered at Pop Century, the Walt Disney World Resort's newest value-priced resort. By the time the final phase of construction is done, each of the 20th Century's decades will be immortalized for its contribution to popular culture. Pop Century Resort is located in the Epcot area (use the blue tab at the top of the page for parks and eateries in the vicinity) on the northeast corner of Osceola Parkway and Victory Way. This resort opened in December 2003.

Whether you're eight or eighty, a **blast from your past** awaits at Pop Century. Actually twin-sister-resorts, Pop Century Classic Years and Pop Century Legendary Years surround a 33-acre lake and are connected by a scenic bridge (called the "Generation Gap"). Go from the quaint days of Main Street U.S.A. to infinity, and beyond, in eye-popping style. Each resort has its own, uniquely themed check-in lobby, food court/shop/lounge, and pool bar. Outside, giant cultural icons fill the senses, including a monumental Rubik's Cube®, a billboard-sized laptop computer, and the biggest Big Wheel ever parked in a front yard. The themes continue with six imaginative theme pools. Each guest lodge building is festooned with cultural icons and "groovy" catch phrases.

The 5,760 guestrooms (2,880 in each resort) are situated in 10 differently themed areas encompassing a total of 20 guest lodges. **Pop Century Classic Years** opened first, celebrating the decades of the 1950s, '60s, '70s, '80s and '90s. Opening later, **Pop Century Legendary Years** will take us back to the 1900s, '10s, '20s, '30s and '40s. Themed courtyards are formed between two or more of the ten T-shaped guest lodges. Each decade's theme is reflected in the guest room decor, but rich, wood-grain furniture adds elegance to the fun. Rooms have either two double beds or one king bed, a large TV with remote, a small table with two chairs, and a roomy chest of drawers. Rooms hold up to four guests plus one child under three in a crib (a folding crib is available on request). Rooms are small—about 260 sq. feet—but as with the All-Star resorts, furnishings allow adequate floor space. Rooms have no private balconies or patios, but each offers climate controls. Amenities include soap, housekeeping, large in-room safe, table-side modem jack, iron and ironing board, and voice mail. Inquire at check-in about renting a small refrigerator for around $10/night.

Standard Room Layout

AMBIENCE

RESORT LAYOUT & ROOMS

Planning

Getting There

Staying in Style

Touring

Feasting

Making Magic

Index

Notes & More

Using the Amenities
at Disney's Pop Century Resort

EATING & DRINKING

Each resort has a very large **food court**. Both food courts have a variety of food stations, plus a lounge. The eateries are open daily for breakfast, lunch, and dinner. Typical menu items include a breakfast platter ($5.59), a double cheeseburger ($6.69), and Shrimp Lo Mein ($6.99). Purchase a souvenir mug for about $12 and get unlimited

© MediaMarx, Inc.

Dave answers e-mail in his room at the Pop Century Resort

refills from the beverage bar. A pizza delivery service is available in the afternoons and evenings, along with seasonal snack carts.

PLAYING & RELAXING

For Athletes: The 12' wide lakeside path is ideal for walks and jogs. The lake does not offer a marina, but we hear that surrey bikes may be available for jaunts around the lake when the resort is done.
For Children: Quiet playgrounds and play fountains are located within each resort (see map on page 78 for locations).
For Gamers: An arcade is located in each resort's main building.
For Shoppers: Both resorts offer large shops with Disney logo merchandise, clothing, sundries, and some snack foods.
For Swimmers: Each resort offers a main pool with a wading pool, and two smaller themed pools. Classic Years' pools are shaped like a bowling pin, a flower, and a computer, Legendary Years' pools will resemble a crossword puzzle, soda bottle, and highway sign.

GETTING ABOUT

Buses (see chart below for estimated in-transit times) are outside the main buildings in each resort. Stops are well-marked and offer benches and shelter. Bus service is prompt and efficient. Destinations other than those below can be reached by changing buses at Disney-MGM Studios or Epcot (daytime) or Downtown Disney (evening). Ample parking is freely available, though you should study the map to find the closest lot to your room.

Magic Kingdom	Epcot	Disney-MGM Studios	Disney's Animal Kingdom	Downtown Disney
direct bus ~25 min.	direct bus ~20 min.	direct bus ~15 min.	direct bus ~15 min.	direct bus ~20 min.

Approximate time you will spend in transit from resort to destination during normal operation.

Making the Most of Disney's Pop Century Resort

TIPS

The **33-acre lake** between these resorts is an added perk for a value resort—the equivalent All-Star Resorts have no ponds, lakes or rivers. The lakeside promenade and Generation Gap bridge are a total delight. Frequent park benches line the path, and "roadside" signs note landmark cultural events of each era.

Epcot's **IllumiNations** fireworks are visible across the lake. Best views are from the '50s B & C buildings—try the fourth floor!

All pools at Pop Century are **full-sized "theme pools"** and all have lifeguards. The somewhat larger Hippy Dippy Pool (Classic Years) adds a wading pool and pool bar.

Food court patrons are treated to a **dance routine** performed by the resort's cast members at breakfast and dinner! They do The Twist at 8:00 am and the Hustle at 6:00 pm. Be there or be square!

While Mom or Dad checks in, the kids can enjoy a **big-screen video** theater. Be sure to take in the memorabilia exhibits, too.

A **children's pop jet fountain** is tucked away in a corner between the '60s and '70s—look for a statue of Goofy and a red corvette.

NOTES

Plan to either **carry your own luggage** or wait a while (perhaps 45–60 minutes) for the resorts' luggage service to drop it off at your building. Arrangements to pick up luggage on your departure day should be made the night before.

Coin-operated laundries are located near each pool. Bring lots of quarters—wash loads and dry cycles are $2.00 each.

Check-in time is 4:00 pm. Check-out time is 11:00 am.

Ratings are explained on page 26.

RATINGS

Our Value Ratings:		Our Magic Ratings:		Readers' Ratings:
Quality:	6/10	Theme:	6/10	63% fell in love with it
Accessibility:	5/10	Amenities:	4/10	18% liked it well enough
Affordability:	9/10	Fun Factor:	4/10	11% had mixed feelings
Overall Value:	7/10	Overall Magic:	5/10	8% were disappointed

Pop Century is enjoyed by...		(rated by both authors and readers)
Younger Kids: ♥♥♥♥♥	Young Adults: ♥♥♥♥	Families: ♥♥♥♥
Older Kids: ♥♥♥♥♥	Mid Adults: ♥♥♥	Couples: ♥♥
Teenagers: ♥♥♥	Mature Adults: ♥♥	Singles: ♥♥♥

Planning · Getting There · Staying in Style · Touring · Feasting · Making Magic · Index · Notes & More

Finding Your Place
at Disney's Pop Century Resort

POP CENTURY RESORT MAP

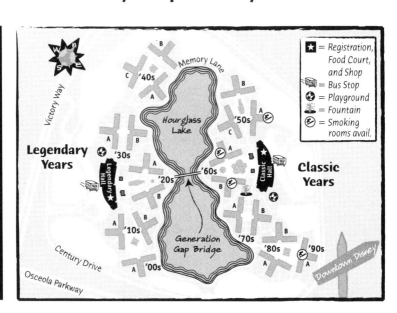

★ = Registration, Food Court, and Shop
🚌 = Bus Stop
🎠 = Playground
⛲ = Fountain
🚬 = Smoking rooms avail.

BEST LOCATIONS

Rooms at Pop Century **vary only by location** within the resorts and floor level. For convenience, we recommend the '50s, '60s, or '70s (Classic Years), and '10s, '20s, and '30s (at Legendary Years)—they are closest to pools, food, and transportation. Our personal picks are the '70s (at Classic Years) and the '30s (at Legendary Years) as they should be relatively quiet and have good views from most all windows. Note that several buildings offer excellent views of Hourglass Lake, notably '50s B & C, '60s, and '70s A. If you seek quiet, request a room on the third or fourth floors.

RATES

2005 Sample Room Rates
Seasons are noted on page 14

Room Type	Value	Regular	Peak	Holiday
Standard Room	$77	$99	$109	$119
Preferred Room	$89	$111	$121	$131

Tax is not included in above rates. Preferred rooms are in the guest lodges closest to the main buildings (the '60s at Classic Years and the '20s at Legendary Years). There is a $10 per person charge for the third and fourth adult in a room, but no extra charge for children under 18. Rooms may face parking lots or courtyards.

INFO

Disney's Pop Century Resort
✉ 1050 Century Drive, Lake Buena Vista, FL 32830
📞 Phone: 407-938-4000   📠 Fax: 407-938-4040
📋 For reservations, call Central Reservations: 407-939-6244

Disney's Port Orleans Resort
(and the former Dixie Landings)

In 2001, sister resorts Port Orleans and Dixie Landings merged into one resort known as Port Orleans. The large, moderately priced resort is located along the banks of the Sassagoula River, north of Downtown Disney (use the blue tab at the top of the page for other places in the same vicinity). Port Orleans is popular with young couples, families, and children, both for its value and for its fun atmosphere.

AMBIENCE

The romance of the Old South awaits you at Port Orleans. The resort is divided into two separate districts: the French Quarter (the smaller district and the original Port Orleans) and Riverside (the former Dixie Landings). The **French Quarter** recaptures the feeling and flavors of historic New Orleans as it prepares for Mardi Gras. The Mint is your first stop in the French Quarter, a large building with wrought ironwork details and a soaring glass atrium that safeguards the district's front desk, guest services, and shop. A step outside reveals narrow cobblestone lanes, complete with "gas" lamps, wrought-iron benches, and grand magnolia trees. A leisurely 10-minute walk along the Sassagoula takes you over to **Riverside**. Banjo music and southern hospitality greet you as you enter Riverside's Sassagoula Steamboat Company, a replica of an old riverboat depot. The depot is the crossroads of this quaint settlement, housing the district's front desk and services. Venture out along meandering paths and wooden bridges to antebellum mansions in one direction or the bayou in the other.

RESORT LAYOUT

The resort's 3,056 guest rooms are scattered among the two districts, with 1,008 in the French Quarter and 2,048 in Riverside. Rooms in the French Quarter are housed in six large buildings (see map on page 83), each designed to resemble **rows of townhouses** with differing architectural styles, varying rooflines, and facades bricked or painted in shades of blue, cream, or peach. Most buildings have their own yards and gardens in front, which are charmingly fenced with wrought iron. Down the Sassagoula in Riverside you'll find 1,024 rooms gracing "Gone With the Wind," plantation-style mansions in an area called **Magnolia Bend**. These three-storied, elegant buildings are situated majestically along the Sassagoula River. An equal number of rooms are housed within crackerbox-style dwellings in the **Alligator Bayou** section. These two-storied, rough-hewn dwellings peek through the trees, with quaint paths winding through the "bayous" interspersed among them. Alligator Bayou has a more intimate feel to it than its neighbor, Magnolia Bend.

Planning

Getting There

Staying in Style

Touring

Feasting

Making Magic

Index

Notes & More

Planning

Getting There

Staying in Style

Touring

Feasting

Making Magic

Index

Notes & More

Lodging and Dining at Disney's Port Orleans Resort

RESORT ROOMS

Rooms are 314 sq. ft. in size and **decorated in three styles**. In the French Quarter, you find faux French Provincial furniture, gilt-edged mirrors, and Venetian blinds. In Riverside's Magnolia Bend, antebellum rooms delight with cherry furniture and brocade settees. Riverside's Alligator Bayou rooms sport beds made of hewn "logs" and patchwork quilts. All rooms accommodate up to four and come with either two extra-long double beds or one king bed (king bed rooms are located on building corners);

© MediaMarx, Inc.

Allie watches TV at Port Orleans French Quarter

Standard Room Layout

963 Alligator Bayou rooms house up to five guests by offering a trundle bed for an extra $15/night (trundle beds slide out from under the double bed and fit a child or small adult). Rooms include a TV, armoire, table and chairs, ceiling fan, and a separate vanity area with double pedestal sinks. Every room has a window (corner rooms have two), but none have private balconies. Amenities include toiletries (soap and shampoo only), housekeeping, limited room service, in-room safe (most rooms), and voice mail.

DINING & LOUNGING

Port Orleans plays host to one of the more popular resort eateries: **Boatwright's Dining Hall**. This table-service restaurant in the Riverside district offers breakfast and dinner—see page 229. Two large food courts—**Sassagoula Floatworks and Food Factory** in the French Quarter and the **Riverside Mill** at Riverside—offer breakfast, lunch, and dinner. Typical menu items are croissants ($2.19), French toast with sausage ($4.99), beignets ($3.79 for six), roasted chicken ($8.99), chicken Caesar salad ($6.09), and kids' chicken strips ($3.99). Purchase a mug for $12 and get free refills at both food courts. The French Quarter's **Scat Cat's Club** is a full-service bar with live music on the weekends, while **Mardi Grogs** pool bar has drinks and snacks. In Riverside, the **River Roost** offers specialty drinks, appetizers, and music in the evenings, and **Muddy Rivers Pool Bar** has drinks and snacks. **Limited room service**.

Disney's Animal
Kingdom Area

Epcot
Area

Downtown
Disney Area

Magic Kingdom
Area

| Chapter 3: Staying in Style | Topic: Port Orleans Amenities | 81 |

Using the Amenities
of Disney's Port Orleans Resort

For Athletes: The Dixie Levee marina in Riverside rents pedal boats, rowboats, canopy boats, and bikes (including surrey bikes). Be sure to check the rental hours early on to avoid disappointment later. Both districts offer plenty of paths for walkers and joggers, too.

For Fishers: An old-fashioned fishin' hole on Ol' Man Island in Riverside lets you hang a cane pole over a pond stocked with catfish, perch, bass, and bluegill (catch and release only). For more adventure, you can book a fishing excursion down the Sassagoula.

For Children: Two playgrounds are near the two theme pools.

For Gamers: South Quarter Games (French Quarter) has plenty of video games, as does the Medicine Show Arcade (Riverside).

For Shoppers: Jackson Square Gifts & Desires (French Quarter) and Fulton's (Riverside) stock sundries, souvenirs, and snacks.

For Swimmers: The French Quarter's Doubloon Lagoon is a moderately sized theme pool with a huge dragon housing the water slide (you slide right down its tongue). A Mardi Gras band of crocodiles shoots water at unsuspecting swimmers. The French Quarter also has a wading pool for the young ones and a hot tub (spa) nearby. In Riverside, Ol' Man Island in the middle of the district offers a particularly nice "swimmin' hole" with a large free-form pool, complete with a water slide, a waterfall cascading from a broken sluice, and a fun geyser. A hot tub and kids' wading area are also available here. Riverside also has five quieter pools spread throughout Magnolia Bend and Alligator Bayou.

Direct **buses** to the major theme parks and Downtown Disney stop regularly (see chart below for in-transit times). Buses usually pick up guests at French Quarter's single bus stop first, then go on to the four stops in Riverside. To get to other resorts and destinations, take a bus to Epcot (when open) or to Downtown Disney (evening), and transfer to the appropriate bus. A **boat** also picks up guests from Riverside and the French Quarter and goes to and from Downtown Disney Marketplace until 11:00 pm (weather permitting). Boats run about once an hour until 4:00 pm and every 15 minutes thereafter. The trip is leisurely and relaxing. A **shuttle boat** also operates between the French Quarter and Riverside on a frequent basis, especially at meal times. Parking is available throughout the resorts.

Magic Kingdom	Epcot	Disney-MGM Studios	Disney's Animal Kingdom	Downtown Disney
direct bus ~10 min.	direct bus ~10 min.	direct bus ~15 min.	direct bus ~15 min.	direct bus/boat ~15/~20 min.

Approximate time you will spend in transit from resort to destination during normal operation.

PLAYING & RELAXING

GETTING ABOUT

Planning

Getting There

Staying in Style

Touring

Feasting

Making Magic

Index

Notes & More

Making the Most
of Disney's Port Orleans Resort

TIPS

The two **spas** (hot tubs) near the theme pools are heavenly after a long day at the parks. The spa in the French Quarter is a bit secluded (look near the laundry), but large enough for several people.

Explore the **resort's grounds** for the quaint parks and gardens scattered throughout. An evening stroll in the French Quarter when the "gas" lamps are lit is particularly magical.

Enjoy an **evening carriage ride** through the two sister resorts. Carriages depart from in front of Boatwright's in Riverside between 6:00 pm and 9:00 pm. Cost is $30 for a 30-minute ride for up to four adults or two adults and two to three children.

Mickey's Pin Trading Afternoon is held in the former Bonfamille's restaurant at French Quarter from 2:00 to 6:00 pm every Wednesday. This free event is open to all, including kids. Bring your pins!

Small **refrigerators** are now free of charge, and roll-away/trundle beds are $15/day. Request these when you reserve your room.

NOTES

The **beds** are pretty high off the floor. Watch young ones so they don't fall out. If you are concerned, note that some rooms in Alligator Bayou at Riverside come with a pullout trundle bed, which you can request upon reservation and check-in. In fact, this trundle bed allows for a fifth person, making Port Orleans the only moderately priced resort to accommodate five people. Do note that the trundle is small and is really intended for a child or very short person.

Due to the resort merger, Port Orleans has **two front desks**, one in each district. Be sure to check with Disney before arrival to find out which district's front desk you should arrive at.

Check-in time is 3:00 pm. Check-out time is 11:00 am.

Ratings are explained on page 26.

RATINGS

Our Value Ratings:		Our Magic Ratings:		Readers' Ratings:
Quality:	7/10	Theme:	8/10	65% fell in love with it
Accessibility:	7/10	Amenities:	6/10	22% liked it well enough
Affordability:	8/10	Fun Factor:	6/10	4% had mixed feelings
Overall Value:	**7/10**	**Overall Magic:**	**7/10**	9% were disappointed

Port Orleans is enjoyed by...		(rated by both authors and readers)
Younger Kids: ❤❤❤	Young Adults: ❤❤❤❤❤	Families: ❤❤❤❤
Older Kids: ❤❤❤❤❤	Mid Adults: ❤❤❤❤	Couples: ❤❤❤❤❤
Teenagers: ❤❤❤	Mature Adults: ❤❤❤	Singles: ❤❤❤

Finding Your Place
at Disney's Port Orleans Resort

The French Quarter has a more compact, orderly layout.

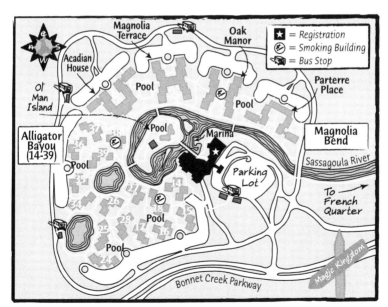

Riverside is large and meandering, with an island in the middle.

Choosing Your Room
at Disney's Port Orleans Resort

BEST LOCATIONS

Thanks to the merger between the two resorts, Port Orleans is exceptionally large and sprawling and **room location** can really make a difference in your resort experience. Each of Port Orleans' three distinctive sections is beloved by its fans. There's no right or wrong section. Request the style that suits you best—don't let Disney choose for you. When you make your reservation, you can specify whether you want a room in Riverside or the French Quarter.

Most rooms in the **French Quarter** are within easy distance of the guest services, the gift shop, and the food court. Buildings 2–5 are the nearest. If being close to the center of things is important, request such a room. The best views are of the Sassagoula River, as the opposite river bank is pristine—consider upgrading to a water view room (specifically request a river view).

The grand "mansions" and formal gardens of **Magnolia Bend** in Riverside add a luxurious air to your stay. The Magnolia Terrace building is a good pick for proximity to recreation and dining.

Our personal favorite is **Alligator Bayou** in Riverside. The buildings in Alligator Bayou are smaller (only two stories) and have lush landscaping that make this sprawling resort seem much more intimate. We often request building 14, which is near the main building, Ol' Man Island, a quiet pool, and a bus stop—it has no bad views as it is nestled between buildings and the river. Buildings 15 and 18 are also good choices—note that 18 is smoking-optional.

For a **quieter** room, request the second or third floor. Corner rooms are particularly nice as they provide two windows.

RATES

2005 Sample Room Rates

Seasons are noted on page 14

Room Type	Value	Regular	Peak	Holiday
Standard View	$134	$149	$169	$184
Water/Pool View or King-Bed	$149	$165	$194	$209

Tax not included in above rates. King-bed rooms come in both standard or water view and are available at the same rate as a water/pool view room.

INFO

Disney's Port Orleans Resort

✉ 2201 Orleans Dr. and 1251 Dixie Dr., Lake Buena Vista, FL 32830
☎ Phone: 407-934-5000 (French Quarter) or 934-6000 (Riverside)
📠 Fax: 407-934-5353 (French Quarter) or 934-5777 (Riverside)
📋 For reservations, call Central Reservations: 407-939-6244

Disney's Saratoga Springs Resort and Spa

The Disney Vacation Club's newest and largest resort is just across the lake from Downtown Disney. Opened in May 2004 and built on the grounds of the former Disney Institute, Disney's Saratoga Springs Resort and Spa offers vacation villas for vacation ownership and nightly rental.

Saratoga Springs stretches out over 65 acres of the former Disney Institute, adjacent to the Lake Buena Vista Golf Course and across Village Lake from Downtown Disney. This **Victorian-styled resort** is modeled on the historic vacation escape in Upstate New York. The fashionable elite of New York City journeyed up the Hudson on Commodore Vanderbilt's railroad to sip the health spa's waters, stroll its shady byways, and cheer their race horses to victory. Disney's architects soaked up the town's Arts and Crafts atmosphere to bring its essence (minus the horses) to Walt Disney World. When finished in 2007, 14 lodges will cluster around the resort's lakes in three districts—Congress Park (opening first), The Springs, and The Paddock, each representing the resort's theme of history, health, and horses. Other buildings survive from the former Disney Institute, including The Carriage House check-in and hospitality building, which also offers dining and shopping.

The four, first-phase buildings of **Congress Park** are directly across the water from the Marketplace. Studio villas (355 sq. ft.) accommodate up to four guests with one queen bed, a sofa bed, sink, microwave, and a small refrigerator. The one- bedroom (714 sq. ft.) and two-bedroom (1075 sq. ft.) villas hold up to 4 or 8 guests each and offer master suites with king beds and whirlpool tubs, DVD players, sofa beds, full kitchens, and washers/dryers. The Grand Villas (2113 sq. ft.) sleep up to 12 on two levels and feature three bedrooms—the living room, dining room, and master suite (with its whirlpool tub) are on the first level and, on the second level, two more bedrooms with queen beds and private baths. All villas have a laptop-sized safe.

One-Bedroom (unshaded)

Queen

King

Studio Layout (shaded)

Entire layout represents a Two-Bedroom Villa

Shower

Planning

Getting There

Staying in Style

Touring

Feasting

Making Magic

Index

Notes & More

AMBIENCE

LAYOUT & ROOMS

Using the Amenities at Disney's Saratoga Springs Resort

DINING & LOUNGING

Hungry? **The Artists' Palette** is a neighborhood eatery and market styled to resemble an artist's loft. Open all day, it has pizzas, salads, sandwiches, bakery items, meals, groceries, gifts, and sundries. You can dine-in or take-out, and it's more upscale than a typical food court. **The Rocks** pool bar is open daily. **The Turf Club** game room/lounge also has a bar.

© MediaMarx, Inc.

Allie and Jennifer relax in their one-bedroom villa at Saratoga Springs

PLAYING & RELAXING

For Athletes: Rent surrey bikes at Horsing Around Rentals. There are also two clay tennis courts, basketball, shuffleboard, jogging path, and golf at the Lake Buena Vista Golf Course.

For Charmers: Saratoga Springs Spa (formerly The Spa at the Disney Institute) has a fitness center and a full range of spa treatments.

For Children: Organized activities are offered at Community Hall. Children's playground. "Pop jet" play fountains are by the main pool. Board games are in The Turf Club near The Artists' Palette.

For Gamers: Win, Place, or Show Arcade games in Community Hall; board games in the lounge outside The Artists' Palette.

For Shoppers: Visit The Artists' Palette for groceries and sundries.

For Swimmers: The High Rock Spring theme pool features a zero-entry/children's wading area, a 125 ft. long water slide that passes through a 20 ft. high tumble of rocks and waterfalls, two free-form hot-tub spas, and an adjoining kids' play area. There are also two quiet pools with spas (hot tubs).

GETTING ABOUT

Direct buses to the four major parks, water parks, and Downtown Disney (see chart below for transit times) stop at the resort's three bus stops. These buses also provide internal transportation within the resort. A **boat** from the dock near the Carriage House goes to the Marketplace at Downtown Disney and Old Key West. **Walking paths** connect the resort with Downtown Disney Marketplace and West Side (West Side pathway crosses the footbridge near the boat dock). Generous parking is available next to each lodge building.

Magic Kingdom	Epcot	Disney-MGM Studios	Disney's Animal Kingdom	Downtown Disney
direct bus ~25 min.	direct bus ~10 min.	direct bus ~15 min.	direct bus ~20 min.	walk/bus/boat ~15/10/7 min.

Approximate time you will spend in transit from resort to destination during normal operation.

Making the Most
of Disney's Saratoga Springs Resort

The Downtown Disney Pleasure Island **fireworks** go off every night at midnight and can be viewed from many guest rooms and from the Fireworks Pavilion in Congress Park. If you're concerned about the (barely audible) noise of the fireworks, avoid lakeside villas.

The **Main Street Railroad Station** at Magic Kingdom was modeled on the former station in Saratoga Springs, New York. The Carriage House, theater, and other nearby buildings recycled from the Disney Institute were originally modeled on the architecture of another historic Upstate New York resort, Chautauqua.

Want to **relax**? A barbecue pavilion, fireworks pavilion, formal gardens, and gazebos/fountains for "taking the waters" all add to the relaxed resort atmosphere.

A **refillable mug** ($12) is available for purchase at The Artists' Palette—you can refill it here and also at The Rocks pool bar.

The classroom and meeting areas of the Disney Institute have been converted into the **main sales offices** and show-villas for Disney Vacation Club. The sales facility at Disney's BoardWalk closed when Saratoga Springs opened.

The **remaining villas** from the Disney Institute will not be offered to the public. The Fairway Villas and Grand Villas are being demolished to make way for the last phase of construction. The Treehouse Villas are being used for internal Disney needs.

Golf carts are *not* being offered for rental to resort guests.

Check-in time is 4:00 pm. Check-out time is 11:00 am.

Ratings are explained on page 26.

Our Value Ratings:		Our Magic Ratings:		Readers' Ratings:
Quality:	6/10	Theme:	6/10	67% fell in love with it
Accessibility:	6/10	Amenities:	6/10	18% liked it well enough
Affordability:	6/10	Fun Factor:	5/10	10% had mixed feelings
Overall Value:	**6/10**	**Overall Magic:**	**6/10**	5% were disappointed

Saratoga Springs is enjoyed by...		(estimated by the authors)
Younger Kids: ♥♥♥♥	Young Adults: ♥♥♥♥	Families: ♥♥♥♥♥
Older Kids: ♥♥♥♥	Mid Adults: ♥♥♥♥♥	Couples: ♥♥♥
Teenagers: ♥♥♥	Mature Adults: ♥♥♥♥♥	Singles: ♥♥

TIPS

NOTES

RATINGS

Planning

Getting There

Staying in Style

Touring

Feasting

Making Magic

Index

Notes & More

Finding Your Place
at Disney's Saratoga Springs Resort

SARATOGA SPRINGS RESORT MAP

★ = Registration
🚌 = Bus Stop

Buena Vista Drive

Resort Entrance

Disney Vacation Club Way

Fourth Phase: Opening 2007

Saratoga Lake

Quiet Pool

The Paddock
(opening later)

The Springs
(opening later)

Carriage House

Theme Pool

Spa

Dining

Boat Dock

Tennis Courts

Spring Pavilion

Congress Park
Quiet Pool
Fireworks Pavilion

Walkway to Downtown Disney Marketplace

Walkway to Downtown Disney West Side

Village Lake

Downtown Disney

BEST LOCATIONS

There are no "preferred" or premium-priced guest rooms. Requests for particular locations are honored when possible. Rooms in **Congress Park** (opened first) have views of Downtown Disney and/or gardens and offer a short walk to the Marketplace and Fireworks Pavilion, and a moderate walk to The Carriage House. Some garden views include parking lots. **The Springs** (second phase) offers closest proximity to The Carriage House and theme pool areas, with views of Saratoga Lake or gardens/parking. **The Paddock** (third phase) is most spread out and distant from other facilities. The **fourth phase** has yet to be named. Request to be close to the quiet pool and/or footbridge (to The Carriage House) if that's important.

RATES

2005 Sample Villa Rates

Seasons are noted on page 14

Room Type	Value	Regular	Peak	Holiday
Studio Villa	$259	$289	$339	$379
One-Bedroom Villa	$350	$395	$460	$525
Two-Bedroom Villa	$490	$575	$700	$805
Grand Villa	$1070	$1195	$1350	$1505

Tax is not included in the above rates.

INFO

Disney's Saratoga Springs Resort & Spa

✉ 1960 Broadway, Lake Buena Vista, FL 32830
📞 Phone: 407-827-1100 📠 Fax: 407-827-1151
📋 For reservations, call Central Reservations: 407-934-7639

Looking for Shades of Green? Page 98. Swan Resort? Page 99.

Disney's Wilderness Lodge and Villas Resort

The Wilderness Lodge and Villas are nestled in a dense forest of pines on Bay Lake, accessible by waterway from the Magic Kingdom (use the blue tab at the top of the page for parks and eateries in the area). The Lodge and Villas were inspired by the U.S. National Park lodges built in the 1900s.

Ah, wilderness! Rustic log buildings, swaying pines, babbling brooks, and the faintest whiff of wood smoke from the crackling fireplace. The Wilderness Lodge pays homage to the **grand log lodges** of the Pacific Northwest, with its towering lobby, 55-foot totem poles, and deluxe rooms. The Villas at the Wilderness Lodge offer home-away-from-home accommodations for Disney Vacation Club Members (see pages 102–103) and all other guests. Architecturally, the Villas predate the existing Wilderness Lodge and draw influences from the lodges created by America's railroad workers.

AMBIENCE

The Wilderness Lodge and the Villas offer varying accommodations, ranging from 340 to 1071 sq. feet. The **Lodge** houses 728 guest rooms and suites, with some encircling the cavernous lobby but most in the two wings. The cozy Lodge rooms are outfitted with pine furniture and quilted bedspreads. Most Lodge rooms have two queen beds, but some offer a bunk bed in place of the second bed. The **Villas** feature 136 studios, one- and two-bedroom suites, each with a kitchenette or full kitchen, VCR, and washer and dryer. All rooms have a balcony or patio, a small table and chairs, TV, double sinks, toiletries, in-room safe, housekeeping service, turndown service (on request), newspaper delivery, voice mail, and valet parking.

Standard Lodge Room Layout

LAYOUT & ROOMS

As you would expect from a Lodge, the food here is served in hearty, healthy portions. The two table-service restaurants (see page 230) are **Artist Point** for fine dining in the evening and **Whispering Canyon Cafe** for a fun, western-style adventure serving all-you-can eat meals throughout the day. **Roaring Fork Snack Shop** is a self-service café serving breakfast foods, burgers, sandwiches, and snacks—purchase a refillable mug here for $12 and get free self-serve refills. Typical menu items include breakfast pizza ($5.59), smoked turkey sandwich ($5.79), chili dog with fries ($5.39), and pecan sticky buns ($2.79). **Miss Jenny's In Room Dining** is available for limited room service at breakfast and dinner.

DINING

Using the Amenities
at Disney's Wilderness Lodge and Villas Resort

LOUNGING

Territory Lounge, a saloon adjacent to Artist Point, serves up beers, wines, and snacks. The **Trout Pass Pool Bar** offers cocktails and light snacks you can enjoy at tables overlooking the main pool and Bay Lake. Beer and wine are also available from the resort shop.

© MediaMarx, Inc.

A waterfall flows to Silver Creek in the Wilderness Lodge courtyard

PLAYING & RELAXING

For Athletes: Rent watercraft and bicycles at Teton Boat & Bike Rentals. A bike and jogging path extends about a mile to Fort Wilderness. A health club, Sturdy Branches, is available.

For Children: The Cub's Den is a supervised program for kids ages 4–12 (see page 253). A playground is located near the beach.
For Gamers: Buttons and Bells arcade, across from Cub's Den.
For Shoppers: The large Wilderness Lodge Mercantile in the Lodge carries clothing, sundries, foodstuffs, newspapers, and gifts.
For Swimmers: Cleverly designed to seem like part of Silver Creek, a free-form swimming pool is nestled among craggy rocks and waterfalls. A water slide and wading pool, as well as two hot tubs, are also available nearby. A quiet pool and another hot tub are located near the Villas. The white sand beach here on Bay Lake is ideal for relaxing upon, but swimming is not permitted.

GETTING ABOUT

You can take a direct **boat** to the Magic Kingdom (see chart below for in-transit times). Boats also ferry you to Fort Wilderness and the Contemporary. **Buses** take you directly to Epcot, Disney-MGM Studios, Disney's Animal Kingdom, Downtown Disney, and the water parks. To reach other resorts, go to the Magic Kingdom (daytime) or Downtown Disney (evening), and then transfer to a resort bus. Fort Wilderness and Wilderness Lodge share many of their bus routes, so travel to and from Fort Wilderness for the Hoop-Dee-Doo show (see page 234), horseback riding, etc. is quite convenient.

Magic Kingdom	Epcot	Disney-MGM Studios	Disney's Animal Kingdom	Downtown Disney
boat ~8 min.	direct bus ~10 min.	direct bus ~15 min.	direct bus ~15 min.	direct bus ~25 min.

Approximate time you will spend in transit from resort to destination during normal operation.

Making the Most of Disney's Wilderness Lodge and Villas Resort

Guests staying in the **Villas at the Wilderness Lodge** register at the main Lodge registration desk.

For good rainy day activities, ask for a **kids' activity/coloring book** at the bell station or a list of **Hidden Mickeys** at Guest Services. You can also get a list of the resort's music at the Mercantile shop.

Explore the resort. Indian artifacts, historic paintings, and survey maps are displayed. Follow Silver Creek from its indoor origin as a hot spring and onward outside as a bubbling brook and waterfall, eventually making its way to Bay Lake (see photo on page 90).

Ask about becoming a **Flag Family**. Each morning and a family is selected to go on the Lodge roof to help raise or lower the flag! This is popular, so inquire at check-in for a better chance.

Inquire about the **"Wonders of the Lodge" tour** at Guest Services. The walking tour explores the architecture, landscaping, totem poles, and paintings. Offered on Wednesdays–Saturdays at 9:00 am.

Watch **Fire Rock Geyser**, modeled after Old Faithful, erupt like clockwork every hour on the hour from 7:00 am to 10:00 pm. The **Electrical Water Pageant** is visible from the beach at 9:35 pm.

The lower courtyard can be **noisy** with the sounds of children and rushing water. Opt for a Lodge view if you prefer serenity.

About 37 Lodge rooms with **king beds** double as the barrier-free (handicap-accessible) rooms and have a large shower with no tub.

Check-in time is 3:00 pm. Check-out time is 11:00 am.

Ratings are explained on page 26.

Our Value Ratings:		Our Magic Ratings:		Readers' Ratings:
Quality:	9/10	Theme:	10/10	79% fell in love with it
Accessibility:	6/10	Amenities:	6/10	17% liked it well enough
Affordability:	6/10	Fun Factor:	8/10	3% had mixed feelings
Overall Value:	**7/10**	**Overall Magic:**	**8/10**	1% were disappointed

Wilderness Lodge is enjoyed by...	(rated by both authors and readers)	
Younger Kids: ♥♥♥♥	Young Adults: ♥♥♥♥♥	Families: ♥♥♥♥
Older Kids: ♥♥♥♥	Mid Adults: ♥♥♥♥♥	Couples: ♥♥♥♥♥
Teenagers: ♥♥♥♥	Mature Adults: ♥♥♥♥	Singles: ♥♥♥

Planning

Getting There

Staying in Style

Touring

Feasting

Making Magic

Index

Notes & More

Finding Your Place
at Disney's Wilderness Lodge and Villas Resort

LODGE AND VILLAS RESORT MAP

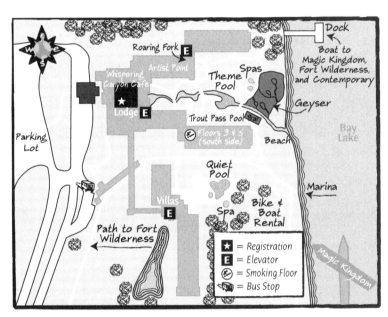

BEST LOCATIONS

Standard rooms overlook the parking areas yet are close to the Lobby. **Lodge views** overlook woods (north side) or the Villas (south side). **Top-floor rooms** facing the woods on the Magic Kingdom (north) side may catch a glimpse of fireworks. Rooms facing the **courtyard or lake** offer panoramic views and cheerful resort sounds. If you seek privacy, consider a **honeymoon suite** at the top of the Lobby, or a top-floor room with solid balcony railings. Concierge service is offered for suites and rooms on the seventh floor. **Villas** in the northeast corner offer views of the pool.

RATES

2005 Sample Room and Villa Rates   *Seasons are noted on page 14*

Room Type	Value	Regular	Peak	Holiday
Standard View	$199	$239	$289	$324
Lodge View (Woods)	$230	$265	$315	$350
Courtyard View	$255	$300	$355	$395
Studio Villa	$284	$324	$389	$449
One-Bedroom Villa	$390	$440	$535	$580

Tax is not included in the above rates. Suites and concierge start in the high-$300's.

INFO

Disney's Wilderness Lodge and Villas Resort
✉ 901 W. Timberline Drive, Lake Buena Vista, FL 32830
☎ Phone: 407-824-3200   📠 Fax: 407-824-3232
🗓 For reservations, call Central Reservations: 407-939-6244

Disney's Yacht and Beach Club and Villas Resorts

Offering luxury, convenience, and added amenities, the Yacht Club and Beach Club are sister resorts. Both resorts feature a relaxing atmosphere and are located on Crescent Lake within walking distance of Epcot (use the blue tab at the top of the page for parks and eateries in the area).

These resorts evoke the charm of **bygone seaside resorts**. The Yacht Club is housed in a dove-gray clapboard building, exuding elegance and grace. The Beach Club atmosphere is casual, bringing to mind sun-filled days you might have found along the eastern seaboard generations ago. Windows in the sky blue building may gaze out upon the "beachhouses" nestled alongside the beach. A recent addition are the Beach Club Villas, which are housed in a separate building evoking the charm of Cape May, New Jersey. The Villas' clapboard walls are painted in seafoam green with white railings and columns, and gingerbread trim. Colorful pennants flap in the breeze from atop the roofs and turrets, and strings of light bulbs dangle gracefully between old-fashioned street lamps.

Standard Room Layout

Each of the standard rooms at the Yacht and Beach Club is housed within five floors of one deceptively large yet creatively shaped building, while the villas are located within a free-standing addition. Covered walkways connect the Villas to the Beach Club lobby. Well-appointed and understated, the standard rooms are large (380 sq. ft.) and sunny. The 634 **Yacht Club** rooms are outfitted in ocean blues, floral patterns, and antiqued wood. The 580 **Beach Club** rooms are playfully decorated in seafoam greens and cabana-striped pinks. Guest rooms have one king-size or two queen-size beds, a day bed, double sinks, a make-up mirror, a small table and chairs, an armoire with a TV, and a small refrigerator. Some smaller rooms have a king-size Murphy bed and an extra sink and counter. Many rooms—but not all—have balconies or patios. Amenities include room service, hair dryers (most rooms), iron and ironing board, newspaper delivery, turndown service (on request), in-room safe, toiletries, voice mail, and valet parking. Beyond the standard rooms, both the Yacht Club and the Beach Club offer a luxurious concierge service with slightly larger rooms on the fifth floor. In addition, 40 special suites (20 in each resort) range in size from a junior suite to a two-bedroom suite to the ultimate Presidential Suite.

Side tabs: Planning · Getting There · Staying in Style · Touring · Feasting · Making Magic · Index · Notes & More

Vertical headings: AMBIENCE · RESORT LAYOUT & ROOMS

Lodging and Dining
at Disney's Yacht and Beach Club Resorts

VILLAS

Newly added in mid-2002 are the 205 Beach Club Villas with studio, one-, and two-bedroom **villas** for Disney Vacation Club members (see 102–103) and the public at large. Studios accommodate up to four guests with one queen-size bed, a double-size sofa bed, and a kitchenette (with a sink, microwave, and a small refrigerator). The

The full-size kitchen in our two-bedroom villa at the Beach Club Villas

© MediaMarx, Inc.

one- and two-bedroom villas accommodate up to four or eight guests each and offer full kitchens, DVD players, king-size beds

One-Bedroom (unshaded)

Studio Layout (shaded)

Entire layout represents a Two-Bedroom Villa

and whirlpool tubs in the master bedroom, double-size sleeper sofas in the living room, and washers/dryers. All villas are homey and feel like a cottage you might have on the ocean. Amenities for all villas include room service, iron and board, hair dryer, newspapers, turndown service (on request), in-room safe, toiletries, and voice mail.

DINING

With the Yacht and Beach Club sharing restaurants, there are more dining options here than at almost any other resort. Table-service options (see pages 230–231) include **Beaches and Cream**, a popular soda fountain; **Cape May Cafe**, a character breakfast and all-you-can-eat clambake; **Yachtsman Steakhouse** for dinner and the **Yacht Club Galley** for breakfast, lunch and dinner. The **Crew's Cup** offers a good snack menu. For a quick meal, try **Hurricane Hanna's**, a poolside grill. Typical menu items include a grilled chicken sandwich ($6.50), garden salad ($3.50), large cookie ($2.00), and a kids' cheeseburger ($4.50). Refillable mugs are available for $12.

Using the Amenities at Disney's Yacht and Beach Club Resorts

Several lounges will help you relax after a long day of playing. **Ale & Compass** and **Crew's Cup** in the Yacht Club serve drinks and munchies. At Beach Club, **Martha's Vineyard** features an award-winning wine list and appetizers, and **Rip Tide Lounge**, tucked away in a quiet corner, serves specialty drinks and continental breakfast. **Hurricane Hanna's** is a pool bar. Room service is always available.

For Athletes: The Ship Shape Health Club is a complete fitness club offering a spa, sauna, and massage therapies. The resorts also sport two lighted tennis courts and a sand volleyball court. The Bayside Marina rents watercraft for cruises, including "The Breathless," a boat named after Breathless Mahoney in "Dick Tracy" (see page 250), and surrey bikes to ride around the lake.
For Charmers: Periwig's Beauty and Barber Shop is a full-service salon for hair, skin, and nail care.
For Children: A playground is near Stormalong Bay. Sandcastle Club offers supervised activities for children ages 4–12 (see page 253).
For Gamers: Lafferty Place Arcade has video games.
For Shoppers: Atlantic Wear & Wardrobe Emporium (Beach) and Fittings and Fairings (Yacht) offer sundries and resort wear.
For Swimmers: The three-acre Stormalong Bay water park is resort swimming at its best. Three free-form, sandy-bottomed pools create deceptively complex waterways with whirlpools, bubbling jets, "rising sands," a water slide in a shipwreck, and two hot tubs. Stormalong Bay is for Yacht and Beach Club and Villas resort guests only (bring your resort ID). Quiet pools are located at the far ends of the resorts. The Villas has its own quiet pool, called "Dunes Cove," and a hot tub.

Boats (see chart below for in-transit times) depart from the marina for Epcot and Disney-MGM Studios. **Buses** outside the lobby go to the Magic Kingdom, Disney's Animal Kingdom, and Downtown Disney. Reach other destinations by transferring at a nearby theme park (day) or Downtown Disney (evening). Parking is available, as well as valet parking ($6/day). The BoardWalk, Dolphin, and Swan are all within **walking distance**, as is the International Gateway to Epcot. You could also walk to Disney-MGM Studios along the path beside the BoardWalk Villas (see map on page 46).

Magic Kingdom	Epcot	Disney-MGM Studios	Disney's Animal Kingdom	Downtown Disney
direct bus ~20 min.	walk/boat ~10/~10 min.	walk/boat ~20/~15 min.	direct bus ~20 min.	direct bus ~15 min.

Approximate time you will spend in transit from resort to destination during normal operation.

Making the Most
of Disney's Yacht and Beach Club Resort

TIPS

Enjoy a **waterfront stroll** around Crescent Lake using the boardwalks and bridges encircling it. This is a very lively place!

Request **turndown service** from housekeeping before you go out for the evening, and return to find your bedcovers turned down with a chocolate. You must specifically request this service.

A **bank of elevators** near each resort's lobby serves most rooms. If your room is at one of the far ends, look for a **single elevator or stairway** rather than trek down the hallways. If you're going to Epcot, the exit near Beach Club's quiet pool is convenient.

Yacht and Beach Club have **separate entrances** and **front desks**. Beach Club Villas guests check in at the Beach Club's front desk.

Explore the charming **public areas**, such as The Solarium (just off the Beach Club Lobby), The Drawing Room (near the Villas' entrance), and The Breezeway (near the Dunes Cove pool).

NOTES

Be sure to bring **resort identification** with you to Stormalong Bay. Note that it can be noisy with the sounds of happy children late into the night, so avoid it and places nearby if you seek peace.

All rooms on the first floor have pleasant patios. Most rooms on the top floor have full **balconies**, as do some on the intervening floors. Be aware that some balconies are standing room only, however. If a full-size balcony is important, request it.

A **conference center**, reminiscent of a town hall, is available.

Check-in time is 3:00 pm. Check-out time is 11:00 am.

Ratings are explained on page 26.

RATINGS

Our Value Ratings:		Our Magic Ratings:		Readers' Ratings:
Quality:	8/10	Theme:	8/10	55% fell in love with it
Accessibility:	8/10	Amenities:	9/10	34% liked it well enough
Affordability:	3/10	Fun Factor:	6/10	7% had mixed feelings
Overall Value:	6/10	Overall Magic:	8/10	5% were disappointed

Yacht and Beach Clubs are enjoyed by... (rated by both authors and readers)		
Younger Kids: ♥♥♥♥	Young Adults: ♥♥♥♥	Families: ♥♥♥♥
Older Kids: ♥♥♥♥♥	Mid Adults: ♥♥♥♥♥	Couples: ♥♥♥♥♥
Teenagers: ♥♥♥♥	Mature Adults: ♥♥♥♥♥	Singles: ♥♥♥

Finding Your Place
at Disney's Yacht and Beach Club Resort

RESORT MAP

Your room location can make or break your experience. We strongly recommend you indulge in a room with a **water view** at either the Yacht or Beach Club. Specifically, try to avoid the standard-view, even-numbered Beach Club rooms between 3662–3726, 4662–4726, and 5662–5726 which overlook an ugly rooftop. You may also want to request a room **closer to the lobby** for easier access. Rooms with a king-size Murphy bed are slightly smaller than other rooms. The slightly larger rooms on the Beach Club's fifth floor are concierge. Rooms at the **Beach Club Villas** have views of Epcot, gardens, or the pool, but rates are the same for all.

BEST LOCATIONS

2005 Sample Room and Villa Rates
Seasons are noted on page 14

Room Type	Value	Regular	Peak	Holiday
Standard View or Studio Villa	$294	$334	$404	$459
Water View	$355	$410	$470	$525
One-Bedroom Villa	$400	$450	$525	$590
Two-Bedroom Villa	$560	$725	$920	$1040

Tax is not included in the above rates. Concierge rooms start in the low-$400's.

RATES

Disney's Yacht and Beach Club and Villas Resorts
✉ 1700/1800 Epcot Resort Blvd., Lake Buena Vista, FL 32830
☎ Phone: 407-934-7000/8000   Fax: 407-934-3450/3850
🗓 For reservations, call Central Reservations: 407-939-6244

INFO

Planning · Getting There · Staying in Style · Touring · Feasting · Making Magic · Index · Notes & More

Shades of Green Resort

Shades of Green is a U.S. Armed Forces Recreational Center on Walt Disney World property, located near the Magic Kingdom theme park. Formerly The Disney Inn, this self-supporting resort is exclusively for active and retired military personnel in the Army, Navy, Air Force, Marine, and Coast Guard, as well as those in the Reserves and National Guard. Department of Defense civilians and U.S. Public Health Officers are also eligible. The resort closed for renovations in 2003 and reopened March 2004 with bigger and better accommodations.

ROOMS

Nestled in the woods **between two golf courses**, the new Shades of Green offers 586 rooms with deluxe accommodations. Guest rooms remain among the largest on property at 450 sq. feet, accommodating up to five guests. Features include two queen-size beds, an armoire, and a TV, plus a sitting area with a daybed or sleeper sofa and table and chairs. Rooms have a refrigerator, coffeemaker, iron and ironing board, hair dryer, and an in-room safe. Internet access is available via a dataport (no high-speed access), or through the TV for $9.95/day. All rooms have either a balcony or patio. The resort (and all rooms) are smoke-free (smoking may be allowed on the balcony/patio). Eleven 1–3 bedroom suites are available, sleeping 6–8 guests each.

AMENITIES

Dining choices include the Garden Gallery family restaurant, Evergreens sports bar, a new specialty Italian restaurant (Mangino's), the new Express Cafe for quick-service meals, and room service. There's also a lounge (Eagles). Resort amenities include two lighted tennis courts, two heated pools, wading pool, playground, exercise room, arcade, and laundry facilities. You can also purchase theme park tickets. Two **buses** are available, and you can walk to the Polynesian and Transportation and Ticket Center. You must show your Shades of Green resort I.D. or military I.D. to board their buses. A car is helpful at this resort, and a new, mult-level parking structure is available.

RATES

Rates are based on rank or pay grade and begin at **$72** for standard rooms and **$82** for pool views. You may reserve up to three rooms. Reserve up to 53 weeks in advance. **Tip:** If the resort is full for your preferred time, inquire about overflow rates and the wait list.

INFO

Shades of Green Resort
P.O. Box 22789, Lake Buena Vista, FL 32830
Phone: 407-824-3400   Fax: 407-824-3460
For more information, call 888-593-2242 or 407-824-3400
Web site: http://www.shadesofgreen.org

Swan and Dolphin Resorts

Crowned by five-story-high sculptures of swans and heraldic dolphins, the Swan and Dolphin resorts tower above nearby Epcot area resorts. Some find their design striking, others find it surreal. Westin and Sheraton, both of which are divisions of Starwood Hotels, jointly manage this pair of luxury hotels popular with business and international visitors.

Guest rooms feature either one king-size bed or two double-sized beds, separate vanity and bath areas, two 2-line phones, mini-bar, hair dryer, iron, and in-room safe. A mandatory "resort fee" adds a coffeemaker, free local phone calls, health club access, high speed Internet, and newspapers. In-room movies and Nintendo are extra. Some rooms have balconies, and 195 suites offer a bit more room. Guest rooms at both resorts were recently renovated and now sport a modern design (by Michael Graves) and "Heavenly Beds" with pillow-top mattresses and down comforters. The sister resorts offer concierge (Royal Club Level) and conference facilities, plus many of the same amenities and benefits found at Disney resort hotels.

Between the resorts, there are **15 eateries**, including Palio, Gulliver's Grill, Kimonos, and Shula's Steakhouse, plus two new restaurants: bluezoo, an upscale restaurant by chef Todd English, and Fresh, an innovative market-style buffet (see pages 229–230 for details). The BoardWalk entertainment district is just a stroll away, as is Fantasia Gardens miniature golf. Free **buses** serve Disney's parks and Downtown Disney, and boats run to Disney-MGM Studios and Epcot. Guests receive many of the benefits enjoyed at the Disney-owned resorts, including package delivery and the option to purchase Ultimate Park Hoppers. The only thing guests can't do is charge Disney purchases to their room.

Rooms begin in the **high-$200's**, but discounts and special rate programs are available—ask about discounts for AAA, Annual Passholders, teachers, nurses, and military. Great rates can be found on Hotwire.com, and won on Priceline.com (page 16). Starwood Preferred Guest members earn points (see http://www.spg.com).

Walt Disney World Swan and Dolphin Resorts

✉ 1200/1500 Epcot Resort Blvd., Lake Buena Vista, FL 32830
📞 Phone: 407-934-3000 (Swan) or 934-4000 (Dolphin)
📠 Fax: 407-934-4499 (Swan) or 407-934-4099 (Dolphin)
📋 For reservations, call 800-828-8850 or 407-939-6244
🖥 For more information, visit http://www.swandolphin.com

ROOMS

AMENITIES

RATES

INFO

Planning · Getting There · Staying in Style · Touring · Feasting · Making Magic · Index · Notes & More

Looking for more information? Get details on our full-length Disney Cruise guide on page 284.

Disney Cruise Line

The Disney Cruise Line set sail in 1998 with the same enthusiasm and energy you find at the Walt Disney World Resort. Each of the two ships (the Disney Magic and the Disney Wonder) have four uniquely themed restaurants, including one for adults only. Experience Broadway-quality productions, first-run and classic Disney movies, and nightclubs. Separate areas of the ship were designed exclusively for adults and children.

ITINERARY

Ships depart Disney's own terminal in Port Canaveral at 5:00 pm. Four-night **cruises** spend the next day in Nassau, followed by a full day at sea, and then a day at Castaway Cay, Disney's private island. Guests debark at Port Canaveral at 9:00 am the following morning. Three-night cruises follow the same plan, but skip the day at sea. Seven-night cruises offer different itineraries—one to the Eastern Caribbean (with stops at St. Maarten, St. Thomas/St. John, and Castaway Cay), one to the Western Caribbean (Key West, Grand Cayman, Cozumel, and Castaway Cay), and a "seasonal" itinerary on the West Coast that departs from Los Angeles (with stops at Puerto Vallarta, Mazatlán, and Cabo San Lucas).

STATEROOMS

Staterooms range from downright comfortable to out-and-out luxurious. Even the least expensive (there are no "cheap") rooms are decorated in glowing, warm woods, and include a television, phone, refrigerator, and in-room safe. The bright and cheery bathrooms include a hair dryer and tub. Deluxe staterooms include a split bathroom, which makes family travel especially comfortable, and 44% of all staterooms offer a verandah. Staterooms that sleep four usually have one queen bed, a single daybed, and a single berth—great for families but not so great for two couples. At the high end, the two-bedroom Walter E. and Roy O. Disney suites are a feast for the eyes, decorated with exotic wood paneling and cut crystal—they include a whirlpool tub!

RATES

Many vacationers book seven-day land/sea **packages** that include a three- or four-night cruise and three or four nights at Walt Disney World. 2005 value season packages start at $1030/person (for double occupancy) for a standard inside stateroom to more than $5,000/person for a Royal Suite. Third, fourth, and fifth occupants pay much less. Airfare and ground transfers are extra, but the land/sea packages include park admission. Packages with less expensive staterooms include a room at a moderate resort, while the more expensive rate a deluxe resort. Cruise-only vacations start at $412/person.

Making the Most of the Disney Cruise Line

Your cruise includes all food onboard (including room service) and lunch at Castaway Cay. Soft drinks are free at meals and at the Deck 9 beverage station. Alcoholic beverages are extra. Each night you'll be assigned to a different dining room. **Triton's** (Wonder) or **Lumiere's** (Magic) is the most formal dining room, which is also open daily to all for full-service breakfast and lunch. **Parrot Cay** is the informal, Caribbean-themed room, and also hosts a breakfast buffet. **Animator's Palate** is an extraordinary room, lined with black and white drawings of famous Disney characters that gradually blossom into full color. **Palo** is the ships' intimate, adults-only restaurant. The menu is elegantly continental, the service is marvelous, and the view at sunset is breathtaking. You must reserve a table at Palo ($10/person surcharge) on the afternoon that you board, and seats can go quickly. Breakfast and lunch buffets and snacks are served on Deck 9. Fountain drinks are now complimentary from the beverage station on Deck 9.

You'll receive your **cruise documentation** listing your stateroom assignment a few weeks before you sail. If you have preferences, state them upon reservation and again a month before you sail.

You must show passports or certified birth certificates plus photo I.D. before boarding. Get your **papers** in order long before you depart.

All shore-side food, transportation, and entertainment in every port of call except Castaway Cay is **at your own expense**. Unless you are especially adventuresome, we suggest you either book a shore excursion (listed in your cruise documentation) or stay onboard.

Dress is mostly casual, but have a nice dress or jacket for the Captain's reception, dinner at Triton's/Lumiere's, and Palo.

To trim your **costs** or custom-tailor your vacation, book a cruise-only passage. You can still book ground transfers through Disney.

Need to stay connected? The **Internet Cafe** has reasonable fees.

Your day at **Castaway Cay** is short. Be sure to wake up early!

Looking for more information? We have an **entire book** about the Disney Cruise! Visit http://www.passporter.com/dcl/guidebook.htm and see page 284. We also recommend the unofficial Magical Disney Cruise Guide at http://allearsnet.com/cruise/cruise.shtml.

For details, visit http://www.disneycruise.com or call 888-DCL-2500.

Disney Vacation Club

Can you ever get enough of Walt Disney World? Disney Vacation Club (DVC) members are betting that they can't. DVC is Disney's kinder, gentler version of a vacation timeshare, and offers several enticing twists on the timeshare experience. As with all timeshare offerings, the DVC offers the promise of frequent, reduced-cost Disney vacations in exchange for a significant up-front investment on your part.

RESORTS

Disney operates **seven Disney Vacation Club resorts**: Old Key West (see pages 67-70), Boardwalk Villas (see pages 43-46), Villas at the Wilderness Lodge (see pages 89-92), Beach Club Villas (see pages 93-97), Vero Beach (Florida coast), Hilton Head Island (South Carolina), and the new Saratoga Springs (see pages 85-88). Studios, one-, two-, and three-bedroom villas with kitchen and laundry facilities are offered (studios have kitchenettes and access to laundry rooms), as well as excellent recreational activities. Housekeeping is limited, with full services every eight days (consider these reduced housekeeping services when you compare the value of a regular hotel to a DVC ownership).

THE PROGRAM

With a typical vacation timeshare, you buy an annual one-week (or multiple-week) stay during a particular time period in a specific size of accommodation. DVC uses a novel **point system** that adds far greater flexibility and complexity to the process. You can use your points however you wish to create several short getaways or a single, grand vacation—at any time of the year and at any DVC or other Disney resort. Here's how it works: You buy a certain number of points at the going rate ($95 per point as of 9/2004). 150 points is the minimum and a typical purchase—so every year you'd have 150 points to apply towards accommodations. You might need 15 points/night for a one-bedroom at Old Key West weeknights during the off-season. 100 points/night may be needed for a two-bedroom at BoardWalk weekends in peak season. Just as with a regular resort room, rates are affected by size, view, location, season, and day. You also pay annual dues based on the number of points purchased. Rates vary, depending on your "home" resort—from about $3 to $5 per point—so dues on a 150-point purchase would be approximately $475-600. If you compare the combined cost of points and annual membership fees to renting comparable resort rooms at non-discounted rates, it could take about five years to recover the value of the points purchased. After that, vacations might cost half the prevailing rental rates. Membership contracts at Saratoga Springs Resort expire in 2054; all others expire in 2042.

Making the Most of the Disney Vacation Club

While you can reserve up to eleven months ahead of time at your **home resort**, you can only book seven months in advance at others.

You can **borrow points** from the next year, or save unused points until next year. You can buy more points from Disney at the going rate, or buy/sell points on the open market—we heartily recommend you try DVC By Resale (visit http://www.dvcbyresale.com or call toll-free 800-844-4099; see their details on page 281).

Don't let unused points expire! If you can't use all your points this year or prefer to use them later, you must file the appropriate form with DVC. Otherwise, those **points expire** at year's end.

You can use points to book **other Disney resorts**, Disney Cruise Line, Disneyland Paris, luxury hotels and adventure travel vacations, or barter points for conventional "swaps" at non-Disney resorts.

DVC members receive many **discounts**, including discounts at The Disney Store, resort rooms (based on availability), dining, etc.

Point values for various resorts and seasons may fluctuate from year to year, but the **average point value** of all DVC rooms cannot increase. For maximum value, stay Sunday through Thursday nights.

Vacancies at DVC resorts are made available to **non-members**—they are booked just like regular Disney resort reservations and daily housekeeping is included. Thus, it may be very difficult to use your DVC points at a resort if your intended arrival date is 60 days away or less. Plan as far in advance as possible. Keep in mind that you can stay at a DVC property without using points, too.

The **Eagles Pines Resort**, announced in 2001, is on "hold" and is being considered alongside other unannounced DVC projects.

For more information, visit the Disney Vacation Club forums at http://www.mouseplanet.com and http://www.wdwinfo.com.

Disney Vacation Club
✉ 200 Celebration Place, Celebration, FL 34747-9903
📠 Phone: 800-500-3990   ✆ Fax: 407-566-3393
☏ DVC information kiosks are at most Disney parks and resorts.
🖋 Sales offices and models are at Disney's Saratoga Springs.
🖥 http://www.disneyvacationclub.com

TIPS

NOTES

INFO

Planning

Getting There

Staying in Style

Touring

Feasting

Making Magic

Index

Notes & More

Planning

Getting There

Staying in Style

Touring

Feasting

Making Magic

Index

Notes & More

Hotel Plaza Resorts

Each of the following hotels are located on Disney property across from Downtown Disney, but are independently owned and operated. A variety of discounts may be available. Some of the Disney resort hotel benefits mentioned earlier in this chapter do not apply (such as Extra Magic Hour and package delivery). Do note that all the Hotel Plaza Resorts offer scheduled bus transportation to the parks (see sidebar on next page) and are within walking distance of Downtown Disney.

Hotel Name (in alphabetical order)	Starting Rates	Year Built	Year Renovated
DoubleTree Guest Suites Resort	**$99+**	**1988**	**1999**

This all-suite hotel offers 229 one- and two-bedroom suites. All rooms come with dining areas, kitchenettes (refrigerator, microwave, and coffeemaker), separate living rooms with sofa beds, double-size or king-size beds, three TVs, two phones, in-room safe, hair dryer, iron and ironing board, and toiletries (no balconies). Suites accommodate up to six people (up to four adults). Amenities include a heated pool, wading pool, fitness center, arcade, one restaurant, one lounge, one pool bar, and room service. Look for the freshly-baked chocolate chip cookies upon your arrival. Web: http://www.doubletreeguestsuites.com. Call 800-222-8733 or 407-934-1000.

Grosvenor Resort	**$139+**	**1972**	**1996**

A British-themed resort offering 629 rooms in a 19-story high-rise nestled beside Lake Buena Vista. All rooms come with a VCR and wet bar in addition to the standard two double-size beds or one king-size bed, satellite TV, coffeemaker (with coffee and tea), mini-bar, in-room safe, newspaper delivery, and toiletries (no balconies). Resort amenities include two heated pools, whirlpool spa, two tennis courts (as well as basketball, volleyball, and shuffleboard courts), a European spa, fitness center, arcade, one restaurant (with character breakfasts thrice weekly), one cafe, one pool bar, and room service. The MurderWatch Mystery Theatre is held here on Saturday nights (see page 236). Kids eat free with each paying adult. You can get great rates on Priceline.com. Web: http://www.grosvenorresort.com. Call 800-624-4109 or 407-828-4444.

The Hilton	**$109+**	**1984**	**1999**

This first-class business hotel is located right across the street from the Downtown Disney Marketplace. The 814 rooms are luxurious, each offering two double beds or one king bed, overstuffed chair, cable TV, two phones, hair dryer, iron and ironing board, coffeemaker, mini-bar, newspapers, and toiletries (no balconies or in-room safes). Amenities include two heated pools, kids water play area, two whirlpool spas, fitness center, arcade, shopping area, three eateries (one with character meals every Sunday), two cafes, and one lounge, one pool bar, and room service. The Hilton is the only Hotel Plaza Hotel to offer the Extra Magic Hour perk (see page 32). Web: http://www.hotel-inside-the-park.com. Call 800-445-8667 or 407-827-4000.

Holiday Inn	**$99+**	**1978**	**2004**

In 2004, this hotel changed from a Courtyard by Marriott to a Holiday Inn. With 323 standard rooms and one suite, this renovated 14-story hotel offers clean, basic accommodations. Standard rooms come with two double beds or one king bed, balconies, satellite TV, hair dryer, iron and ironing board, coffeemaker, a large in-room safe, newspaper delivery, toiletries, and high-speed Internet. Additional amenities include Nintendo games (for an extra fee), two heated pools, wading pool, whirlpool spa, fitness center, arcade, one restaurant, one cafe, and room service. Web: http://www.hiorlando.com. Call 800-223-9930 or 407-828-8888.

Hotel Name (in alphabetical order)	Starting Rates	Year Built	Year Renovated
Hotel Royal Plaza	**$99+**	**1975**	**2004**

This hotel offers 394 standard rooms which each accommodate up to five guests and have a sitting area, balcony or patio, coffeemaker, and phone in addition to the two double beds or one king bed, daybed, cable TV, in-room safe, hair dryer, iron and ironing board, newspaper delivery, and toiletries. Rooms in the tower are slightly larger and offer upgraded bathrooms. Hotel amenities include a heated pool, whirlpool spa, four tennis courts, arcade, a restaurant (kids 12 and under eat free with a paying adult), a lounge, a pool bar, and room service. Of all the Hotel Plaza hotels, this is the one that gets the most rave reviews from other vacationers. Note that hurricane damage in September 2004 has closed the hotel for renovations until early 2005. Web: http://www.royalplaza.com. Call 800-248-7890 or 407-828-2828.

Lake Buena Vista Best Western Resort	**$79+**	**1973**	**1997**

This 18-story, Caribbean-themed hotel is on the shores of Lake Buena Vista. The resort offers 321 standard rooms (345 sq. ft.) and four suites, all of which have balconies. Rooms come with two queen beds or one king bed, satellite TV, hair dryer, iron and ironing board, coffeemaker (with coffee and tea), in-room safe, newspaper delivery, and toiletries. Other amenities include Nintendo games and premium movies for an extra fee, one heated pool, a wading pool, privileges to the DoubleTree fitness center, two eateries, two lounges, and room service. Formerly a Travelodge. Web: http://www.orlandoresorthotel.com. Call 800-348-3765 or 407-828-2424.

Wyndham Palace Resort & Spa	**$229+**	**1983**	**1998**

A high-rise hotel with 1014 luxury guest rooms and suites. This is the largest of the hotels on Hotel Plaza Boulevard. It's also the closest hotel to Downtown Disney Marketplace. All rooms feature balconies or patios, two double beds or one king bed, cable TV, cordless phone, coffeemaker (with complimentary coffee and tea), in-room safe, hair dryer, iron and ironing board, newspaper delivery, and toiletries. High-speed Internet access, WebTV, Sony PlayStation games, and premium movies are available for an additional fee. Resort amenities include three heated pools, whirlpool spa, tennis and sand volleyball courts, full-service European-style spa with fitness center and beauty salon, arcade, three restaurants (one with character breakfasts every Sunday), a cafe, two lounges, a pool bar, and room service. Formerly known as Buena Vista Palace. Web: http://www.wyndham.com/hotels/MCOPV/main.wnt. Call 407-827-2727.

Hotel Plaza Resort Transportation to the Parks

Guests staying at these Hotel Plaza Resorts get free bus transportation to the four major Disney parks, Downtown Disney, and the water parks. Hotel Plaza buses—which differ from the standard Disney buses—run every 30 minutes and typically start one hour before park opening and continue up to 2 hours after park closing. Note that buses to the Magic Kingdom drop you off at the Transportation & Ticket Center (TTC) where you can take a monorail or boat to the park entrance or transfer to a another bus to another Disney destination. Disney's Animal Kingdom buses may operate only once an hour during the slower times of the day. Within walking distance is Downtown Disney, where you can also board Disney buses to other resorts. Those bound for the water parks should check with their hotel for bus schedules. Guests who want to venture off to Universal Studios/Islands of Adventure, SeaWorld, Wet 'n' Wild, or the Belz Outlet Mall can take a shuttle for $12/person round-trip—check with your hotel on pick-up times. Many guests who stay at these hotels recommend you get a rental car—all hotels but the Best Western and Hotel Royal Plaza have a rental car desk.

Planning · Getting There · Staying in Style · Touring · Feasting · Making Magic · Index · Notes & More

Hotels Near Walt Disney World

Below are several hotels and motels near Walt Disney World (but not on property) that either we've stayed in and recommend, or at which our readers report good experiences. More hotels are listed on following pages.

Hotel Name (in alphabetical order)	Starting Rates	Year Built	Year Renovated
Holiday Inn Family Suites	**$114+**	**1999**	**2005**

We had the pleasure of staying at this 800-suite resort in July 2002. Besides the resort's close proximity to Walt Disney World (just 3 miles/5 km.), the hotel offers unique and very convenient "Kidsuites" with a living room, kitchenette, master bedroom, and kids' room. The kids get a bunkbed, TV, Nintendo (fee applies), and a small table and chairs. Allie fell in love with it! If you don't have kids, you can get a room with a different configuration, such as the SweetHeart Suite (whirlpool tub and 50" TV), the CinemaSuite (60" TV with stereo surround), Residential Suite (full kitchen), or the Two-Bedroom Suite. Guests get a full, hot breakfast buffet from 6:30 am–11:00 am. Kids eat free when they dine with adults. The resort also has a large pool, water playground, two hot tubs, and a small miniature golf course. There is a free scheduled shuttle bus to Walt Disney World, but we found it more convenient to drive. The resort is being revamped with a Nickelodeon theme by spring 2005. Visit http://www.hifamilysuites.com or call 407-387-5437 or 877-387-5437. Hotel address: 14500 Continental Gateway, Orlando, FL 32821

Radisson Resort Parkway	**$79+**	**1987**	**2001**

We enjoyed our recent stay at this 718-room, 6-story deluxe hotel just 1.5 miles (2.5 km) from the gates of Walt Disney World. Guest rooms accommodate up to four guests with either one king-size bed or two double-size beds. Rooms come in either pool or courtyard views and feature modern Italian furniture and marble bathrooms. Amenities include a 25" TV, stocked mini-bar, in-room safe, coffeemaker, iron and ironing board, hair dryer, make-up mirror, voice mail, and data ports. For a fee, you can add WebTV and Nintendo. The resort has two pools, a water slide, a wading pool, and two hot tubs, as well as lighted tennis courts, fitness center, playground, and arcade. Food service includes a full-service restaurant (open for breakfast and dinner), a deli with Pizza Hut items, a sports bar, a pool bar, and room service. Note that kids under 10 eat free when accompanied by a paying adult. There is a free scheduled shuttle bus to attractions. For the best rates, visit http://www.radissonparkway.com/offers/index.asp?adsvc=02PASS or call 407-396-7000 and ask for the "Y-PASS" rate code. 2900 Parkway Boulevard, Kissimmee, FL 34747

Sheraton Safari Resort	**$85+**	**1994**	**1998**

While this isn't equivalent to Disney's Animal Kingdom Lodge, this safari-themed resort is a winner with kids and adults alike. The 489-room, 6-story hotel is located just 1/4 mile (1/2 km.) from the Disney property (you can't walk to it, but it is a short drive or ride on the scheduled shuttle). Guest rooms come in standard (one king-size or two double-sized beds), Safari Suites (with kitchenette and separate parlor), and deluxe suites (with full kitchens and large parlors). Standard rooms accommodate up to four guests, or five guests with the rental of a rollaway bed. All rooms have a balcony or patio, TV with PlayStation, two phones with voice mail, dataports, and high-speed Internet access, hair dryer, make-up mirror, coffeemaker, iron and ironing board, and in-room safe. The resort features a large pool with a 79-ft. water slide, wading pool, hot tub, fitness center, and arcade. One full-service restaurant (Casablanca's) offers breakfast and dinner (kids under 10 eat free with paying adults), along with the Outpost Deli (for lunch and dinner), the ZanZibar Watering Hole, and room service (6:30 am–10:00 pm). Visit http://www.sheratonsafari.com or call 407-239-0444 or 800-423-3297. Hotel address: 12205 Apopka-Vineland Road, Orlando, FL 32836

Hotels Near Universal Studios

Below are the three on-site hotels at Universal Studios Florida (about 7 miles/11 kilometers from Walt Disney World property). Note that guests staying in these hotels get special privileges at Universal Studios and Islands of Adventure, such as the "Universal Express" ride access system to bypass attraction lines, priority seating at some restaurants, complimentary package delivery, on-site transportation, and more. Each of these hotels accepts pets and offers pet-related services. All of these resorts are operated by Loews Hotels (http://www.loewshotels.com).

Hotel Name (in alphabetical order)	Starting Rates	Year Built
Hard Rock Hotel	**$229+**	**2001**

If you think Hard Rock Cafe is great, this 650-room hotel really rocks. Step inside a rock star's mansion filled to the rafters with a million-dollar rock memorabilia collection. Standard guest rooms (365 sq. ft.) feature two queen beds or one king bed, cable TV, stereo and CD player, 2-line cordless phones, mini-bar, coffeemaker, in-room safe, hair dryer, bathroom scale, iron and ironing board, and toiletries. There are fourteen Kids Suites with a separate sleeping area for the kids. Hotel amenities include a heated pool with a water slide and underwater audio system, wading pool, two whirlpool spas, sand beach, fitness center, two restaurants (including a Hard Rock Cafe with a concert venue), a cafe, a lounge, a pool bar, and room service. Web: http://www.hardrockhotelorlando.com/locations/hotels/orlando. Call 800-BE-A-STAR (800-232-7827) or 407-445-ROCK. Hotel address: 5800 Universal Blvd., Orlando, FL 32819

Portofino Bay Hotel	**$259+**	**1999**

Stay in this remarkably-themed resort and get a big taste of the Italian Riviera. The hotel is a deluxe recreation of the seaside village of Portofino, Italy, developed with the help of Steven Spielberg. There may be cobblestone streets outside, but luxury abounds inside. 750 rooms and suites are available, including several Kids Suites. Standard rooms come with either two queen beds or one king bed and double sofabed, cable TV, two phones, mini-bar, coffeemaker, in-room safe, hair dryer, iron and ironing board, and toiletries. Deluxe rooms offer a bit more space, an upgraded bathroom, a VCR, CD player, and fax machine. Resort amenities include three heated pools, a water slide, whirlpool spas, a full-service spa, fitness center, a Bocce ball court, four restaurants, three cafes, a lounge, and room service. Web: http://www.portofinobay.com. Call 407-503-1000 or 800-232-7827. Hotel address: 5601 Universal Blvd., Orlando, FL 32819

Royal Pacific Resort	**$209+**	**2002**

This relatively new hotel is Universal Studio's lowest-priced resort, boasting 1000 guest rooms with a South Seas theme and lush landscaping. Standard rooms (355 sq. ft.) accommodate up to five guests (four adults) and feature two queen beds or one king bed, cable TV, mini-bar, coffeemaker, in-room safe, hair dryer, iron and ironing board, and toiletries. The Club Rooms add robes, bathroom scales, turndown service, newspaper delivery, continental breakfast, and afternoon beer/wine/snacks. Resort amenities include a huge pool, kid's water play area, wading pool, two whirlpool spas, sand beach, volleyball court, putting green, fitness center, arcade, a supervised children's program, two restaurants, a cafe, a lounge, a pool bar, and room service. Web: http://www.loewshotels.com/hotels/orlando_royal_pacific or http://www.usf.com and click on "Lodging." Call 888-322-5541 or 407-503-3000. Hotel address: 6300 Hollywood Way, Orlando, FL 32819

More Hotels Outside Disney

We feel we can save more at a value or moderately-priced Disney resort as there is no need for a car and we can do more in less time. Even so, you may prefer to stay "off-property" to attend a conference, visit other parks, or pay a bargain rate. Below are 33 popular hotels, motels, and inns off property. We've included starting rates for standard rooms (off-season), driving distance to Downtown Disney, available transportation to Disney, the year it was built (plus the year it was renovated, if available), if it is a Disney "Good Neighbor Hotel" (able to sell multi-day passes), a short description, web site (if available), and a phone number.

Hotel/Motel Name (in alphabetical order)	Starting Rates	Distance to WDW	Trans. Avail.	Year Built	Good Neighbor
All Star Vacation Homes	$109+	4mi/6km	–	Varies	
Vacation home rentals, most with pools. http://www.allstarvacationhomes.com. 888-249-1779					
AmeriSuites LBV	$64+	3mi/5km	Bus	'00	
151-suite resort with free breakfast. http://www.amerisuites.com. 407-997-1300					
Caribe Royale Resort	$146+	4mi/6km	Bus($)	'97	✔
Ten-story suite hotel with living rooms and wet bars. AAA discount. 407-238-8000					
The Celebration Hotel	$140+	8mi/12km	Bus	'99	✔
Upscale business hotel within Disney's town of Celebration. 407-566-6000					
Clarion Hotel Maingate	$50+	8mi/12km	Bus	'86('99)	✔
Five-story, 198-room hotel. http://www.clarionhotelmaingate.com. 407-396-4000					
Comfort Inn Lake Buena Vista	$50+	3mi/5km	Bus	'87	✔
Five-story, 640-room hotel. Details at http://www.comfortinnorlando.com. 407-996-7300					
DoubleTree Castle Hotel	$149+	8mi/12km	Bus	'95	✔
216-room, themed hotel. All rooms have three phones and Sony PlayStation. 407-345-1511					
DoubleTree Club Hotel	$129+	1.5mi/2km	Bus	'86('99)	✔
246 rooms and kid suites. http://www.doubletreeclublbv.com. AAA discount. 407-239-4646					
Embassy Grand Beach	$269+	3mi/5km	–	'95	
Secluded suite hotel, each with three bedrooms, three baths, and kitchen. 407-238-2500					
Embassy Suites LBV	$111+	3mi/5km	Bus	'85	✔
All-suite hotel with a Caribbean theme in Lake Buena Vista. 407-239-1144					
Embassy Suites I-Drive	$199+	8mi/12km	Bus	'85('98)	✔
Two-room suites with free cooked-to-order breakfasts. International Drive. 407-352-1400					
Gaylord Palms	$269+	1mi/1.5km	Bus	'02	✔
1406-room luxury resort near Disney. http://www.gaylordpalms.com. 407-586-0000					
Hawthorne Suites LBV	$89+	1mi/1.5km	Bus	'00	✔
Rooms and suites, all with free breakfast. http://www.hawthornsuiteslbv.com. 407-597-5000					
Holiday Inn Express	$59+	8mi/12km	Bus	'90('99)	✔
217-room motel with free continental breakfast bar and local calls. 407-351-4430					
Holiday Inn Maingate East	$54+	6mi/10km	Bus($)	'73('99)	✔
Standard rooms and Kidsuites. Located in Kissimmee. 407-396-4488					

Hotel/Motel Name (in alphabetical order)	Starting Rates	Distance to WDW	Trans. Avail.	Year Built	Good Neighbor
Holiday Inn Nikki Bird	**$70+**	6mi/10km	Bus	'73('99)	✔

530-room hotel with microwaves and refrigerators, plus 75 Kidsuites. 407-396-7300

| **Holiday Inn SunSpree** | **$64+** | 6mi/10km | Bus | '90('97) | ✔ |

Standard rooms and Kidsuites. Details at http://www.kidsuites.com. 407-239-4500

| **Homewood Suites** | **$80+** | 6mi/10km | Bus | '91('00) | ✔ |

Two-room suites with kitchen, living area, and bedroom. AAA discounts. 407-396-2229

| **Howard Johnson Maingate** | **$39+** | 10mi/16km | Bus | '85('00) | ✔ |

435-room motel with three pools. http://www.orlandohojomaingate.com. 407-396-4500

| **Hyatt Regency Grand Cypress** | **$199+** | 3mi/5km | Bus | '84('97) | |

750-room hotel with balconies, private lake, nature trails, and golf. 407-239-1234

| **Marriott Orlando World Center** | **$254+** | 4mi/6km | Bus($) | '86('99) | ✔ |

28-floor, 2000-room resort with four restaurants and a convention center. 407-239-4200

| **Perri House** | **$165+** | 4mi/6km | – | '89 | |

Bed & breakfast with private baths. Details at http://www.perrihouse.com. 407-876-4830

| **Quality Inn Plaza** | **$69+** | 6mi/10km | Bus($) | '85('99) | ✔ |

1,020-room hotel with "semi suites." http://www.qualityinn-orlando.com. 407-996-8585

| **Quality Suites Maingate** | **$79+** | 6mi/10km | Bus | '90('99) | ✔ |

One- and two-bedroom suites with living rooms and kitchenettes. 407-396-8040

| **Radisson Inn LBV** | **$74+** | 2mi/3km | Bus | '90('00) | ✔ |

200-room hotel with balconies. Located in Lake Buena Vista. 407-239-8400

| **Ramada Inn Maingate** | **$49+** | 6mi/10km | Bus | '80('98) | ✔ |

391-room hotel with two pools, tennis, basketball, exercise room. 407-396-4466

| **Red Roof Inn** | **$40+** | 5mi/8km | – | '89('97) | |

Basic budget lodging with a good reputation. Located in Kissimmee. 407-396-0065

| **Residence Inn** | **$139+** | 8mi/12km | Bus | '86('98) | ✔ |

All-suite, business-oriented hotel with "family fun" suites and full kitchens. 407-345-0117

| **Rodeway Inn International** | **$49+** | 8mi/12km | Bus($) | '75 | ✔ |

315-room, budget hotel. Details at http://www.rodewayinnorlando.com. 407-996-4444

| **Sheraton's Vistana Resort** | **$149+** | 3mi/5km | Bus | '80('97) | |

One- and two-bedroom villas. Details at http://www.sheraton.com. 407-239-3100

| **Sierra Suites** | **$65+** | 2.5mi/4km | Bus | '98 | |

Studio-style suites with kitchens. Details at http://www.sierra-orlando.com. 407-239-4300

| **Summerfield Suites** | **$229+** | 2mi/3km | Bus | '93('98) | ✔ |

All-suite hotel with one- and two-bedroom suites and free breakfast. 407-238-0777

| **Travelodge Maingate East** | **$49+** | 3mi/5km | Bus | '84('97) | ✔ |

446-room hotel. Details at http://www.orlandotravelodgehotel.com. 407-396-4222

Tip: You really need a car when staying at off-property hotels. Even when shuttles to the parks are provided, the schedules and drop-off/pick-up points aren't accommodating. If you are flying to Orlando and staying off-site, be sure to factor in the cost of renting a car.

Planning

Getting There

Staying in Style

Touring

Feasting

Making Magic

Index

Notes & More

Lodging Worksheet

Use this worksheet to jot down preferences, scribble information during phone calls, and keep all your discoveries together. Don't worry about being neat—just be thorough! Circle your final choices once you decide to go with them (to avoid any confusion). You have our permission to make a photocopy of this worksheet for your personal vacation planning.

Arrival date: _____   Alternates: _____

Departure date: _____   Alternates: _____

Total number of nights: _____   Alternates: _____

We prefer to stay at: _____

Alternates: _____

_____

Using your preferences above, call Disney's Reservations phone line at 407-WDW-MAGIC (407-939-6244) and jot down resort availabilities in the table on the next page. It works best for us when we write the available days in the far left column, followed by the resort, view/type, special requests, rate and total cost in the columns to the right. Draw lines between different availabilities. Circle those you decide to use, and then record the reservation numbers, as you'll need them to confirm, cancel, or make changes later. The two columns at the far right let you note confirmations and room deposits so you don't forget and consequently lose your reservation.

Additional Notes:

Collect information on lodging in the table below. We've included some sample notes to show you how we do it, but you're welcome to use this space in any way you please.

Dates	Resort	View/Type/Requests	Rate	Total	Reservation #	Confirm by	Dep.
7/10 – 7/13	Port Orleans	Water View (Riverside)	$169	$507	2635 1419 8419	2/14/05 ✓	✓
7/11 – 7/14	All-Star Movies	Standard (Fantasia)	$99	$297		2/15/05	

The Last Resort

If you'll be **arriving at your resort before check-in time**, be prepared in the event your room is not ready. Have your sunscreen, sunglasses, and the right clothes and shoes easily accessible so you can go straight to the parks. The resort will hold your luggage for you until you return and your room is ready.
— *Contributed by Fran Skall, a winner in our 2004 Lodging Tip Contest*

Stay on track on vacation by continuing to worship or attend your meetings. Many houses of worship are nearby—get a full list at http://www.orlandowelcome.com/pray/pray.htm. Friends of Bill W. can find local meetings at http://aaorlandointergroup.org.

To put into **perspective** just how vast Walt Disney World really is, the cities of Buffalo, New York City, Grand Rapids, Miami, Newark, and San Francisco are all smaller. In fact, Walt Disney World is larger than the countries of Nauru and San Marino combined! Things are not just around the block here. — *Contributed by Tom Anderson*

Magical Memories

"We had just arrived at the Wilderness Lodge with our daughters (ages 3 and 5) and decided to take the boat over to the Magic Kingdom. The girls were so excited to see Cinderella castle they could hardly contain themselves. We got on the boat and as we made our way to the park, the girls started screaming "Cinderella Castle! Cinderella Castle!" everytime we passed a Disney resort hotel! Finally the real Castle appeared and the look in their eyes is a memory I'll treasure forever. It is my very favorite moment of our entire trip. To see Disney through your child's eyes is amazing."
...as told by Disney vacationer Dene Gatewood

"My wife and I try to visit Walt Disney World annually. For a recent trip, I purchased a copy of your guidebook hoping to find a little extra magic for our trip this year—I found it! While we were at our resort (All-Star Movies), we went for a lovely walk about 11:30 pm. I didn't tell her where we were going but I was on a hunt for a hidden hammock close to a Donald & Gang display (see tip on page 37). I found it and we had a wonderful time talking and enjoying one another's company under the stars. It was a magical moment to remember for years to come. Thanks for the advice of where to find those little bits of magic."
...as told by Disney vacationer Jeff Haney

"We stayed at the Caribbean Beach Resort, and our best memory from the hotel was simply swimming in the quiet pool by our room. My cousin and her family joined us at Walt Disney World, and our girls are the same ages and best friends. We all went to the pool together, and were so pleased and surprised to have it all to ourselves! It was truly magical to be able to take a break from the busy-ness of the parks, relax, and PLAY together. The quiet pool was exactly that—a quiet oasis of calm—that provided one of the most memorable experiences of our trip."
...as told by Disney vacationer LeighAnn Brown

Touring the "World"

The Walt Disney World Resort has been called many things—a world-class resort, an endless playground for young and old alike, and even a mecca to capitalism—but we have never heard it called boring.

The "World" (as it is known to insiders) began in 1971. Opening on October 1st of that year, it offered a small fraction of what we enjoy today: the Magic Kingdom park and the Contemporary, Polynesian, and Fort Wilderness resorts. It was the dream of an All-American leader, Walt Disney, who didn't live to see opening day. Yet his legacy flourished, becoming the 47-square-mile wonderland we know and love today.

One of the things that makes the Walt Disney World Resort so special is the attention to detail and service. It takes tens of thousands of people, known as "cast members," working together to stage the "show" we see as "guests." You'll notice that Disney often uses special words to describe their unique services and attractions. There's nothing mundane here.

To help you recognize these terms, we begin with Park Passwords, defining the "Disneyese" you'll hear and read, such as the much-touted "FASTPASS" ride reservation system. We then move on to practical matters, such as transportation and admission to the parks. Next come our detailed attraction descriptions for the four major theme parks. Descriptions and maps of the smaller parks follow, along with hints, tips, and a Touring Worksheet to help you decide what to do. Don't overlook our at-a-glance attraction lists and theme park touring plans. We've also tucked full-color, fold-out park maps (the largest found in any guidebook) in the very back of this book for quick reference.

May 5, 2005 marks the beginning of "The Happiest Celebration on Earth," a worldwide commemoration of Disneyland's 50th birthday. You can read more about Walt Disney World's contribution to the party throughout this chapter.

So let's go around the "World" in 86 pages!

Park Passwords

Admission Media—Park passes (tickets). See pages 116–117 for pass details and rates.

Attraction—An individual ride, show, or exhibit.

Baby Services—Special centers are found in each of the major parks. All restrooms (men's included) support diaper changing.

Cast Member—All Disney employees are "cast members"—they wear white name tags with their names and hometowns.

Disney Dollars—Disney's own currency, good throughout the Walt Disney World Resort.

ECV—Electric Convenience Vehicle. You can rent these four-wheel scooters at the parks and elsewhere. See "wheelchairs" on page 35.

Extra Magic Hour (Early Entry)—Resort guests can enter certain parks one hour early on certain days. See page 32 for details.

FASTPASS—Disney's popular ride "reservation" system (see below).

© MediaMarx, Inc.

A FASTPASS machine

Making the Most of FASTPASS

Tired of waiting in long lines? Disney's FASTPASS system reduces the amount of time you spend in line—and it's free to all park guests! Just slip your park pass into a machine near an attraction with FASTPASS. Out pops your pass and a printed ticket (see sample below) that promises you a ride during a particular period some time later in the day. Depending on how many tickets have been issued to other guests, you may be able to return in 25 minutes, or hours later. When you receive your FASTPASS, look for the time you can get your next FASTPASS (you can usually get another at 5-10 minutes after the return time of your current pass, or in two hours, whichever comes first). When your FASTPASS return time arrives, walk up to the attraction's "FASTPASS Return" entrance, show your FASTPASS to the cast member, and walk on in. There's usually still a short wait, and you'll experience most or all "pre-show" activities. Every FASTPASS attraction has a "Standby" line, which is the regular wait-in-line queue—the wait time for the Standby queue is typically half as long as the FASTPASS return time.

We recommend you get your first FASTPASS early in the day for one of the more popular rides, as FASTPASS tickets can run out on busy days. Our attraction descriptions later in this chapter indicate if an attraction has FASTPASS (look for the **FP** icon), and our touring plans give recommendations on which FASTPASSes to get throughout a day. Note that FASTPASS isn't always available, especially later in the day when all tickets have been issued. **Tip:** Enjoy the same ride twice! Get a FASTPASS, then get in the Standby queue. By the time your ride is over, your FASTPASS may be ready to use. Note that the FASTPASS system may be used for special events, such as during Super Soap Weekend.

Sample FASTPASS
Enter Any Time Between
9:45 pm
and
10:45 pm
Another FASTPASS ticket will be available after
9:50 am
10/09/04   9:25

Actual size: 2¼" x 2¾"

First Aid—First aid stations and Automatic Defibrillators are at every park.

Guest Relations—An information desk, located both inside and outside the front gates of all four major parks. Guest Services at resorts provide a similar range of services.

Guidemaps—Free maps available at the parks. See also "Times Guide."

Land—An area of a park organized around a common theme.

Lockers—Available for a fee ($5 + $2 deposit) in each park and at the Transportation and Ticket Center. Save your receipt for a new locker at another park on the same day.

Lost & Found—Lost items or children can be claimed at a central location in each park. Consult a guidemap or a cast member. Also see page 249.

Money—Pay with Disney Dollars, cash, traveler's checks, The Disney Credit Card, American Express, MasterCard, Visa, Discover, JCB, Diner's Club, and Disney Visa Reward Vouchers. Disney Dollars are sold at parks, resorts, and the Disney Store. ATMs are located in the parks, resorts, and Downtown Disney. Disney resort guests can charge to their room.

Packages—Purchases can be delivered or held for pickup near the park exit at all major parks, and Disney resort guests can have packages 🚢 delivered to their resort free of charge. Inquire about package delivery <u>before</u> purchasing.

Park—Disney's recreational complexes requiring admission, which include the four major parks (Magic Kingdom, Epcot, Disney-MGM Studios, and Disney's Animal Kingdom) and five minor parks (Blizzard Beach, Typhoon Lagoon, Pleasure Island, Wide World of Sports, and DisneyQuest). Descriptions begin on page 121.

Parking—Fee is $8 per day; free to Disney resort guests and Annual Passholders. Tip: Save your receipt to park free at another Disney park on the same day.

Queue—A waiting area or line for an attraction or character greeting.

Re-Entry—Guests may exit and re-enter the same park on the same day. Be sure to get your hand stamped as you exit, and hold on to your pass.

Security—All bags are searched before entering parks.

Shopping—Shops sell Disney items, themed products, and sundries. We list the best shops in this chapter.

Smoking—Prohibited in buildings, queues, and most areas of parks, except in designated smoking areas (see photo and park maps).

Strollers & Wheelchairs—Strollers ($7/single stroller, $14/double stroller, per day + $1 deposit), wheelchairs ($7/day + $1 deposit), and ECVs ($30/day + $10 deposit) can be rented at the parks. Limited availability—arrive early, bring your own, or rent elsewhere (see page 35). Save your receipt for a free rental at another park on the same day.

Tax—Florida sales tax is 6.5%.

Times Guide—Free weekly listing of hours and showtimes. Available when you enter the parks.

© MediaMarx, Inc.

A Magic Kingdom smoking area

Park Passes

On January 2, 2005, Disney revamped their admission options, bringing more flexibility and more confusion. It's safest to budget **$64**/day for ages 10+ (**$51**/kids ages 3-9), the single-day/single-park base price for the major parks in 2005. The new "Magic Your Way" multiday passes emphasize flexibility and savings, so you can do more at a lower price. Here's the deal on passes (prices include tax):

■ Magic Your Way Tickets	*Actual 2005 Rates*

*Magic Your Way tickets are available for 1, 2, 3, 4, 5, 6, 7 or 10 days (no 8 or 9-day options offered). Guests can stick to basic admission, or add one or more options at the time of purchase (see explanations below). Magic Your Way replaces single-day passes and all varieties of Park Hopper passes. A Magic Your Way **Base Ticket** ($64-$223) is good for entry to a single major park (Magic Kingdom, Epcot, Disney-MGM Studios, or Disney's Animal Kingdom) for each day of the ticket. Multi-day Base Tickets bring substantial discounts (see chart on page 117), so it pays to buy your admission all at once. Multi-day Base Tickets expire 14 days after the first use, but they do not have to be used on consecutive days. Buy only as much admission as you'll actually need for your visit to Orlando. Note that multi-day Base Tickets are imprinted with the guest's name, so they are not transferable. The **Park Hopping** option (add $37) lets you visit more than one major park on the same day, for the length of your ticket. Available with any Base Ticket, this option is costly unless you spend four or more days at the parks, but it's indispensible if you plan to visit all four parks in fewer than four days and it can maximize the enjoyment of any longer stay. The Magic Your Way **Magic Plus** option (add $48) adds a limited number of single-day, single-park admissions for the minor parks (Blizzard Beach, Typhoon Lagoon, Pleasure Island, DisneyQuest, and Wide World of Sports) to any Base Ticket. Each Magic Plus option is worth $10-36, depending on where you use it. Purchase this feature with 1-3 day Base Tickets and you receive 2 Plus Options, 4-5 day Base Tickets receive 3 options, 6 day Base tickets receive 4 options, 7 and 10 day Base Tickets receive 5 options. Regardless of how many Plus options you receive, the cost to add this feature is always the same. So long as you make a minimum of two visits to the more costly minor parks, you'll get your money's worth. The **Premium** option (add $85) is a combination of a Base Ticket, Park Hopping, and Magic Plus options (but at no additional savings). This is similar to the old Park Hopper Plus and Ultimate Park Hopper passes. The **No Expiration** option (add $10-$107) is best-suited for those who plan to save the unused portion of a multi-day ticket for a future vacation. The 14-day lifespan of a Base Ticket is generally enough for any one vacation. Prices for the various tickets are listed in the comparison chart on the next page.*

■ Annual Pass	*Actual 2005 Rates*

Unlimited admission to the four major parks for a full year, plus special privileges. An Annual Pass ($421/$358) costs less than two 3-day Magic Your Way Base Tickets with Park Hopping. Annual Passes also kick in great discounts on resorts (based on availability) and other privileges, such as a newsletter and events. See page 10 for details. There are also annual passes for the water parks ($106/$86), Pleasure Island ($59), DisneyQuest ($84/$67), and water parks plus DisneyQuest ($137/$105). You cannot share an Annual Pass (or any other multiday pass).

■ Premium Annual Pass	*Actual 2005 Rates*

A Premium Annual Pass ($548/$466) offers the same privileges as the regular Annual Pass plus unlimited admission to the minor parks (including DisneyQuest) for $128 more. Five minor park visits cover the added cost. A Premium Annual Pass costs less than two, 3-day Premium Magic Your Way Tickets with a No Expiration option, and it is good for a full year.

Old Ticket Media: Prior to "Magic Your Way," Disney issued "Park Hopper" passes. If you have an old Park Hopper with unused days on it, you may use or upgrade it.

Upgrades and Exchanges: Upgrade or apply the unused value of an unexpired park pass to a better pass. Visit Guest Relations (parks) or Guest Services (resorts) for details.

Magic Kingdom E-Ride Nights: With the Extra Magic Hour program for Disney resort guests being extended to evening hours (see page 32), E-Ride Nights appear to be discontinued. E-Ride Nights were a ticketed, after-hours event at the Magic Kingdom.

Advance Purchase Discounts: Discounts of between $8 and $12 are possible on tickets of five days or longer duration, if you purchase them in advance at Disney's web site, or include them in the cost of a vacation package. This is significantly less than the value of advance purchase discounts available in the past. Frankly, you could save more money by depositing the funds for your admission in an interest-bearing account prior to your vacation.

AAA: Members (see page 11) can expect some sort of discount (historically 5%) on some passes. You must purchase tickets directly from AAA to get the discount.

Florida Resident Discounts: It pays to live nearby. Florida Resident Seasonal Passes work like Annual Passes, but with blackout dates in busy seasons. There are some other special deals for Florida residents only.

Military Discounts: Discounts of roughly 7%–8% may be available on admission—check with your Exchange shop or MWR (Morale, Welfare, and Recreation) office. Some offices may need to pre-order your tickets, so we advise you check with them well in advance. Keep an ear out for special programs for active military personnel—in recent years, Disney offered all active military personnel a free five-day park hopper, with discounted admission for up to five family members or friends. To check on current specials and buy tickets, phone 407-939-4636, or just visit Shades of Green (see page 98) upon arrival.

Online Ticket Brokers—These folks sell legitimate, unused tickets at great rates. Try http://www.ticketmania.com (877-822-7299), http://www.floridaorlandotickets.net (888-723-2728), or http://www.mapleleaftickets.com (800-841-2837). Be wary of others hawking tickets, including eBay and timeshares.

Kids Ride Free (Well, Some Do): Kids under 3 are admitted into the parks for free (and get a free ride if the ride allows someone that small). Anyone 10 and over is considered an adult in the eyes of the ticket booth. Passes for kids ages 3-9 cost up to 20% less than adult passes. Also, the option-filled pass you buy for yourself is usually more than your child needs, especially if you use childcare programs (detailed on pages 252–253).

Pass Comparison Chart: Options and prices for your number of days in the parks. *(Prices are the actual 2005 costs of adult, non-discounted passes, including tax.)*

Pass Type	Days: 1	2	3	4	5	6	7	8	9	10	11	12	13	14
Base (single day/park)	$64	$127	$182	$197	$206	$209	$212	$223	$223	$223				
Base + No Expiration		$137	$193	$213	$243	$257	$271	$329	$329	$329				
Base + Park Hopping	$101	$164	$219	$234	$243	$246	$249	$260	$260	$260				
Base + Park Hop. + No Exp.		$175	$230	$250	$280	$294	$308	$366	$366	$366				
Base + Magic Plus	$112	$175	$230	$245	$253	$257	$260	$271	$271	$271				
Base + Magic Plus + No. Exp.		$185	$241	$261	$291	$305	$318	$377	$377	$377				
Premium *(see page 116)*	$149	$212	$267	$282	$291	$294	$297	$308	$308	$308				
Premium + No Exp.		$223	$278	$298	$328	$342	$356	$414	$414	$414				
Annual Pass										$421	→			
Premium Annual Pass											$549	→		

For more details and updates, visit http://www.passporter.com/wdw/passes.htm.

Planning

Getting There

Staying in Style

Touring

Feasting

Making Magic

Index

Notes & More

Getting Around the Resort and Parks

The internal **transportation system** at the Walt Disney World Resort is quite extensive, with buses, boats, and the famed monorail all doing their part to shuttle guests around the property. Transportation hubs exist at each major theme park and Downtown Disney, where you can reach nearly any other place in the "World" by bus, monorail, or boat. The Transportation and Ticket Center (TTC) near the Magic Kingdom forms another hub, where you can get the monorail, ferryboat, and various buses. For current route information, see our property transportation chart on the right, check with a transportation cast member, or call 407-WDW-RIDE (407-939-7433).

Bus service is the cornerstone of the Walt Disney World transportation system. It is efficient, if occasionally confusing. With a few exceptions, bus routes run every 15 to 20 minutes, from about one hour prior to park opening until about one hour after closing. Bus stops are clearly marked. Travel times vary by route. Be sure to build in extra time for travel. Tip: Special early morning "character breakfast" buses visit all Disney resorts to pick up guests—ask about it at your resort. Most buses are lift-equipped to accommodate wheelchairs and ECVs.

Monorail trains run along two circular routes for the Magic Kingdom. The express route visits the park and the Transportation and Ticket Center (TTC), while the resort route also stops at the Contemporary, Polynesian, and Grand Floridian resorts. A separate line connects the TTC to Epcot. Monorails run from 7:00 am until one and a half hours after park closing.

© MediaMarx, Inc.

Dave boards one of the new buses, which can lower its front step for guests who have difficulty negotiating it

If you **drive**, you'll find ample parking at the parks. Use the map on the back flap of your PassPorter to get around the "World." **Tip:** Jot the row number and name of your parking lot in your PassPorter so you don't forget where you parked your car. Also, if you intend to take advantage of Extra Magic Hour (see page 114), we recommend you avoid driving to the Magic Kingdom—it may be difficult to get into the park early enough. If you do drive, the gates at the TTC generally open between 7:15-7:30 am on Extra Magic Hour mornings.

From several locales, **boats** (also known as launches, ferries, cruisers, and Friendships) usher guests to the Magic Kingdom, Epcot, Disney-MGM Studios, Downtown Disney, and between some resorts. Boats generally depart every 15-30 minutes. At the Magic Kingdom, large ferries transport guests from the TTC to the gates, and a **railroad** encircles the park. Small boats run between the Magic Kingdom and the nearby resorts. At Epcot, a "**Friendship**" shuttles between points in the World Showcase.

By far the most reliable and common method of transportation within the "World" is **walking**. You can't walk between most parks and resorts—it's too far and there are few sidewalks, making it unsafe. You will, however, walk a lot around the parks, the resorts, and even between some parks and resorts. Bring comfortable, broken-in, walking shoes!

Disney Property Transportation Chart

Note: TTC = Transportation and Ticket Center (see previous page)

To get to the Magic Kingdom from...	Take the...
Polynesian or Grand Floridian	Monorail or boat
Contemporary	Monorail or walk
Wilderness Lodge or Fort Wilderness	Boat
All other resorts	Bus
Disney-MGM Studios or Animal Kingdom	Bus to TTC, then monorail or boat
Epcot	Monorail to TTC, then monorail or boat

To get to Epcot from...	Take the...
Polynesian	Monorail (or walk) to TTC, then monorail
Contemporary or Grand Floridian	Monorail to TTC, then monorail
BoardWalk, Yacht/Beach Club, Swan/Dolphin, Studios	Boat or walk (to World Showcase)
All other resorts	Bus (to Future World)
Disney-MGM Studios or Animal Kingdom	Bus (to Future World)
Magic Kingdom	Monorail or boat to TTC, then monorail

To get to the Disney-MGM Studios from...	Take the...
BoardWalk, Yacht/Beach Club, Swan/Dolphin, Epcot	Boat or walk
All other resorts	Bus
Epcot or Disney's Animal Kingdom	Bus (or bus from Epcot)
Magic Kingdom	Monorail or boat to TTC, then bus

To get to Disney's Animal Kingdom from...	Take the...
All resorts	Bus
Disney-MGM Studios or Epcot	Bus
Magic Kingdom	Monorail or boat to TTC, then bus

To get to Downtown Disney/Typhoon Lagoon from...	Take the...
Port Orleans or Old Key West	Boat *(DD Marketplace only)* or bus
Saratoga Springs	Boat *(DD Marketplace only)*, bus, or walk
All other resorts	Bus
All parks	Bus, boat, monorail, or walk (to a resort), then bus

To get to Blizzard Beach/Winter Summerland from...	Take the...
Disney's Animal Kingdom	Any resort bus going to Blizzard Beach
All resorts (or other theme parks)	Bus (or take resort bus and transfer)

To get to Fantasia Gardens from...	Take the...
All resorts *(guests at Swan, Dolphin, BoardWalk, and Yacht & Beach Club can walk)*	Travel to any park but Epcot, take a bus (or boat) to Swan, then walk

To get to Wide World of Sports from...	Take the...
All resorts	Go to Disney-MGM Studios, then bus

To get to Hoop-Dee-Doo Revue from...	Take the...
Magic Kingdom, Wilderness Lodge, or Contemporary	Boat to Fort Wilderness
Any other park	Bus to Fort Wilderness
Any other resort	Go to Magic Kingdom, then boat

To get to Disney Resort Hotel from...	Take the...
Any resort *(Swan, Dolphin, BoardWalk, Yacht & Beach Club are in walking distance of each other)*	Go to nearby theme park or Downtown Disney, then bus, boat, or monorail

Planning

Getting There

Staying in Style

Touring

Feasting

Making Magic

Index

Notes & More

Park Tips and Ratings

Check **park hours** by calling 407-WDW-INFO (407-939-4636) or by visiting http://www.disneyworld.com. Resort guests may also consult the "News, Hours, Extras" update sheet, park maps, and Times Guides on arrival. Park hours are typically published two months in advance. Once you know the park hours for your vacation, write them on the appropriate PassPocket.

Study the descriptions and maps to **familiarize yourself** with the names and themes of the lands before you arrive. We provide handy, fold-out, full-color maps for each major park in the back of the book. We designed these maps so they are large enough to view easily and positioned in the book for quick reference. And don't forget our favorite touring plans and a list of attractions in this chapter.

Check the **Tip Board** on the main thoroughfare in each major park and near the big slides at the water parks. Tip Boards are also located in Tomorrowland at the Magic Kingdom and in the Streets of America Set at Disney-MGM Studios. These Tip Boards are continuously updated with wait times and closings—even openings or sneak peeks of new attractions.

Plan your visit around the things that are **most important** to you or require advance planning (like restaurant seatings or show times). If you're just not sure, you can use our favorite touring plans included in each major park description as a starting point. In general, though, we feel it is more enjoyable to "go with the flow" from attraction to attraction within each land. Relax and have fun!

Park Ratings

We rate each park to help you make the best decisions. Even so, our ratings may differ from your opinions—use the ratings as a guide only.

Value Ratings range from 1 (poor) to 10 (excellent) and are based on **quality** (cleanliness, maintenance, and freshness); **variety** (different types of thing to do); and **scope** (quantity and size of things to do)—**overall value** represents an average of the above three values. **Magic Ratings** are based on **theme** (execution and sense of immersion); **excitement** (thrills, laughs, and sense of wonder); and **fun factor** (number and quality of entertaining activities)—**overall magic** represents an average of the above three values. We use a point accumulation method to determine value and magic ratings.

Readers' Ratings are calculated from surveys submitted by vacationers at our Web site (http://www.passporter.com/wdw/rate.htm).

Guest satisfaction is based on our and our readers' experiences with how different types of guests enjoy the park: ❤❤❤❤❤=love it
❤❤❤❤=enjoy it ❤❤❤=like it ❤❤=tolerate it ❤=don't like it

Magic Kingdom

The Magic Kingdom is a true fantasyland, playfully painted in bold strokes upon the canvas of the imagination. This is quintessential Disney and often the first park guests visit. It is located the furthest north of all parks, on the shore of the Seven Seas Lagoon.

The Magic Kingdom conjures up fantasy, nostalgia, youth, and most of all, **magic**. One thing it does especially well is blend the ordinary with the unusual, enhancing both to make it all seem better than reality. This giant, 107-acre playground attracts people of all ages to its bygone boulevards, tropical gardens, western saloons, living cartoons, and yesterday's vision of tomorrow. All roads lead to Cinderella Castle, the crown of the Kingdom.

Five "lands" radiate like spokes from the hub of Cinderella Castle, located in the center of the park, with two more lands added on for good measure (see the fold-out map on page 287). Below are the lands in clockwise order, along with descriptions and headline attractions. See page 123 for an at-a-glance list of attractions, page 124 for itineraries, and pages 128–136 for attraction details.

Main Street, U.S.A. *Headline Attraction:*	An early 1900s Main Street bustles with shops, eateries, a barbershop quartet, and City Hall. *Walt Disney World Railroad*
Adventureland *Headline Attractions:*	Walk to the beat of jungle drums in a paradise filled with pirates, parrots, crocs, and camels. *Pirates of the Caribbean, Tiki Room, Jungle Cruise, Aladdin*
Frontierland *Headline Attractions:*	Journey back to the American Frontier, complete with a fort and "mountain range." *Splash Mountain, Big Thunder Mountain Railroad*
Liberty Square *Headline Attractions:*	Step back in time to Colonial America with her presidents, riverboats, and a haunted house. *The Haunted Mansion, The Hall of Presidents*
Fantasyland *Headline Attractions:*	An enchanted, brightly colored "small world" where elephants fly and teacups spin. *Winnie the Pooh, Dumbo, Mickey's PhilharMagic*
Mickey's Toontown Fair *Headline Attractions:*	Walk through a cartoon world to Goofy's farm, Mickey and Minnie's homes, and Donald's Boat. *Mickey's Country House, The Barnstormer at Goofy's Farm*
Tomorrowland *Headline Attractions:*	The future as imagined in the 1930s, complete with space flights, aliens, and time travel. *Space Mountain, Buzz Lightyear, Stitch's Great Escape!*

Planning · Getting There · Staying in Style · Touring · Feasting · Making Magic · Index · Notes & More

Entertainment and Shopping at the Magic Kingdom

Don't miss the fold-out map in the back of the book!

ENTERTAINMENT

Fun and excitement surround you in the Magic Kingdom. Live entertainment fills the streets with parades, performers, bands, and fireworks. Every afternoon, the 20-minute-long **Share a Dream Come True Parade** highlights favorite moments captured inside giant snow globes (see the parade route on page 287). We like to watch the parade from Frontierland or Liberty Square. The dazzling **Wishes fireworks show** is generally held nightly whenever the park is open after dark. Stand in front of Cinderella Castle to see Tinker Bell fly towards

© MediaMarx, Inc.

"Hey, Baby Alexander, that's Dumbo. After you're born and grow up a bit, you can go on it with Daddy!"

Tomorrowland during the 12-minute fireworks show. Mickey's Toontown Fair, Tomorrowland (near Indy Speedway), and Liberty Square are good viewing locations, too. Fantasyland is also possible, but it is very loud. Cinderella Castle is the backdrop for live musical stage shows. In May 2005, **Cinderellabration** (see page 191), a big hit at Tokyo Disneyland, debuts as part of The Happiest Celebration on Earth. The **SpectroMagic** evening parade (if showing) adds lights and music to the fun and follows the same route as the day parade. Disney characters make appearances throughout the park, especially at park opening and after some shows. See the Times Guide for showtimes or visit Steve Soares' unofficial site at http://pages.prodigy.net/stevesoares.

SHOPPING

Sure stops for general Disney merchandise include much of Main Street, U.S.A.—shops here are open for 30–60 minutes after park closing. Here are some of our favorite **themed shops**:

Shop	Land	What makes it special
The Chapeau	Main Street, U.S.A.	Hats with embroidered names
Disney Clothiers	Main Street, U.S.A.	Upscale yet casual Disney clothes
Agrabah Bazaar	Adventureland	Themed, open-air marketplace
Plaza del Sol Caribebazaar	Adventureland	Pirate clothing and decor
Briar Patch	Frontierland	Great theme, Pooh & friends
Tinker Bell's Treasures	Fantasyland	Disney costumes and dolls
Mickey's Star Traders	Tomorrowland	Sci-fi toys and gadgets

Magic Kingdom
Attractions At-A-Glance
(alphabetical order)

Attraction	Type	Allow	Page
☐ Ariel's Grotto [D-2]	Playground	30-60	132-Fa
☐ Astro Orbiter [F-4]	Ride	20+	135-T
☐ Barnstormer at Goofy's Farm [F-2]	Coaster	30+	134-TT
☐ Big Thunder Mountain Railroad [A-2]	Coaster	50+	130-Fr
☐ Buzz Lightyear [F-4]	Track Ride	30+	135-T
☐ Carousel of Progress [F-4] (seasonal)	Show	30+	135-T
☐ Cinderella's Golden Carrousel [D-2]	Ride	15+	132-Fa
☐ Country Bear Jamboree [B-4]	Show	30+	130-Fr
☐ Donald's Boat [G-1]	Playground	20+	134-TT
☐ Dumbo The Flying Elephant [D-2]	Ride	30+	132-Fa
☐ Fairytale Garden [E-3]	Live Show	30+	132-Fa
☐ Frontierland Shootin' Arcade [B-4]	Arcade	15+	130-Fr
☐ Galaxy Palace Theater [F-5]	Live Show	30-60+	135-T
☐ Goofy's Country Dancin' Jamboree [B-3]	Live Show	30+	131-LS
☐ Hall of Presidents, The [C-3]	Show	30+	131-LS
☐ Haunted Mansion, The [B-2]	Track Ride	30+	131-LS
☐ "it's a small world" [C-2]	Boat Ride	25+	132-Fa
☐ Jungle Cruise [B-4]	Boat Ride	40+	129-A
☐ Liberty Belle Riverboat [B-3]	Boat Ride	30+	131-LS
☐ Mad Tea Party [E-2]	Ride	20+	133-Fa
☐ Magic Carpets of Aladdin [B-4]	Ride	30+	129-A
☐ Main Street Vehicles [D-5]	Vehicles	30+	128-MS
☐ Mickey's Country House [F-1]	Walkthru	60+	134-TT
☐ Mickey's PhilharMagic [D-2]	3-D Show	40+	133-Fa
☐ Mike Fink Keelboats [A-3] (seasonal)	Boat Ride	30+	130-Fr
☐ Minnie's Country House [F-1]	Walkthru	20+	134-TT
☐ Peter Pan's Flight [C-2]	Track Ride	40+	133-Fa
☐ Pirates of the Caribbean [A-4]	Boat Ride	30+	129-A
☐ Shrunken Ned's Jr. Jungle Boats [B-4]	Arcade	10+	129-A
☐ Snow White's Scary Adventures [D-2]	Track Ride	20+	133-Fa
☐ Space Mountain [G-3]	Coaster	40+	136-T
☐ Splash Mountain [A-3]	Coaster	60-90+	130-Fr
☐ Stitch's Great Escape! [E-4]	Show	50+	135-T
☐ Swiss Family Treehouse [B-4]	Walkthru	30+	129-A
☐ Tiki Room, The Enchanted [B-4]	Show	20+	129-A
☐ Timekeeper, The [E-4] (seasonal)	Show	25+	136-T
☐ Tom Sawyer Island [A-3]	Playground	60+	130-Fr
☐ Tomorrowland Arcade [G-3]	Arcade	20-40+	136-T
☐ Tomorrowland Indy Speedway [F-3]	Ride	50+	136-T
☐ Tomorrowland Transit Authority [F-4]	Track Ride	10+	136-T
☐ Toon Park [F-1]	Playground	15+	134-TT
☐ Toontown Hall of Fame [F-1]	Pavilion	40+	134-TT
☐ Town Square Exposition Hall [D-6]	Exhibit	20+	128-MS
☐ Walt Disney World Railroad [D-6, A-2, G-1]	Train Ride	30+	128-MS
☐ Winnie the Pooh, Many Adv. [E-2]	Track Ride	30+	133-Fa

The Allow column gives the amount of time (in minutes) you should allow for an attraction, assuming you don't have a FASTPASS and there are no breakdowns. The letters after the page numbers represent the first one or two letters (or acronym) of the land in which the attraction is located.

Our Favorite Touring Plans for the Magic Kingdom

NOTES

While we don't believe in the "commando" approach to fun, relaxing vacations we realize that you may want guidance. Use these touring plans, which focus on the highest-rated attractions, as a starting point. You can do these plans in one day if you start by 9:00 am. If you can start earlier or stay later, add in additional attractions. The plans work best if you go in the same order, but feel free to re-order based on showtimes and wait times. Vacationers with infants and toddlers, or thrill-shy adults, may prefer to skip all attractions with asterisks.

ITINERARIES

Touring With Adults
Enter Tomorrowland
Get FASTPASS for Buzz Lightyear or
    Space Mountain*
Visit Buzz Lightyear
Visit Stitch's Great Escape!
Visit Space Mountain*
Enter Adventureland
Get FASTPASS for Jungle Cruise
Visit Enchanted Tiki Room
Visit Pirates of the Caribbean*
Visit Jungle Cruise
Enter Frontierland (and have a snack)
Get FASTPASS for Splash Mountain*
Visit Big Thunder Mountain*
Visit Splash Mountain*
Eat lunch at Liberty Tree Tavern or
    Columbia Harbour House (about
    4 hours after entering park)
Enter Liberty Square
Visit Haunted Mansion*
Visit Hall of Presidents
Watch parade from Sleepy Hollow
Enter Fantasyland (and have a snack)
Get FASTPASS for Peter Pan's Flight
Visit Mickey's PhilharMagic
Visit Peter Pan's Flight
Enter Mickey's Toontown Fair
Visit Barnstormer at Goofy's Farm*
Take Walt Disney World Railroad from
    Toontown Fair to Main Street, U.S.A.
If the park is still open, do the following:
Eat dinner at Crystal Palace, Tony's Town
    Square, or Plaza Restaurant (about 8 ½
    hours into your day)
Watch nighttime parade from Main Street,
    Cinderella Castle, or Liberty Square
Watch fireworks from same spot

(Tour duration: About 10 ½ hours)

Touring With Kids
Enter Fantasyland
Visit Dumbo the Flying Elephant
Visit Peter Pan's Flight
Get FASTPASS for Mickey's PhilharMagic
Visit Winnie the Pooh
Visit Mickey's PhilharMagic
Eat lunch at Pinocchio Village Haus
Enter Mickey's Toontown Fair
Visit Barnstormer at Goofy's Farm*
Visit Minnie's Country House
Take the WDW Railroad to Frontierland
Enter Frontierland
Get FASTPASS for Splash Mountain* or
    Big Thunder Mountain Railroad*
Enter Adventureland
Visit Pirates of the Caribbean
Enter Frontierland
Visit Splash Mountain or Big Thunder Mtn.*
Enter Adventureland (and have a snack)
Get FASTPASS for Jungle Cruise
Visit Magic Carpets of Aladdin
Visit Jungle Cruise
Enter Liberty Square
Watch parade from Sleepy Hollow
Visit Haunted Mansion*
Visit Diamond Horseshoe Saloon
Enter Tomorrowland
Get FASTPASS for Buzz Lightyear
Visit Stitch's Great Escape!
Visit Tomorrowland Transit Authority
Visit Space Mountain*
Visit Buzz Lightyear
Eat dinner at Tony's Town Square, Crystal
    Palace, or Cosmic Ray's
    (about 8 hours after entering park)
Watch nighttime parade from Main Street
Watch fireworks from hub or Liberty Square

(Tour duration: About 10 ½ hours)

Making the Most of the Magic Kingdom

Take a **spin around the park** when you first arrive by boarding the train at the Walt Disney World Railroad station in Main Street, U.S.A. The 20-minute journey is a great introduction to the park.

Consider a **guided tour**. Three Magic Kingdom tours are currently offered. For tour details and information on making advance reservations, see Backstage Passes on pages 242–243.

Ask about **Magic Kingdom E-Ride Nights** (see page 117) which may be offered to resort guests during your stay.

Need a trim? You can get a **haircut** at the barber shop on Main Street. Try some colored hair gel and watch out for the pixie dust confetti! You may even be serenaded by a barbershop quartet.

Make time for the **Flag Retreat** in the Main Street town square, usually at 5:00 pm or 5:30 pm daily. A color guard takes down the American flag, and most days a band plays as well. Veterans may inquire at City Hall about assisting in the flag lowering, too.

Seniors traveling with grandchildren should visit the Magic Kingdom together. The look in the children's eyes will be worth the trip alone.

Dining options abound, although table-service isn't as prevalent as at Epcot. There are five table-service restaurants and many counter-service cafes and carts. See pages 205–207 for details.

If you have **young kids**, consider visiting other theme parks first—nothing else quite lives up to the wonder of the Magic Kingdom.

Main Street, U.S.A. closes a half hour later than the rest of the park. So while other folks fight the crowds in the parking lot, feel free to linger. We don't recommend you shop at the end of the day, however—the stores are extremely busy.

No alcohol is served within the Magic Kingdom. If you want an adult beverage, ride the monorail to the Contemporary, Polynesian, or Grand Floridian resorts, where there are several lounges.

Need a **good place to meet**? The covered patio near Ariel's Grotto and the waterside seating across from Plaza Restaurant are good choices. We recommend you avoid setting Cinderella Castle as your meeting point as it is sometimes inaccessible due to shows.

TIPS

NOTES

Planning · Getting There · Staying in Style · Touring · Feasting · Making Magic · Index · Notes & More

Planning | Getting There | Staying in Style | Touring | Feasting | Making Magic | Index | Notes & More

Getting to the Magic Kingdom

BEST TIMES TO GO

The park tends to be the **busiest on Sunday and Thursday**, which are the Extra Magic Hour days (see page 32). **Saturday** also tends to be very busy as the park attracts locals. We recommend you visit on **Monday**, with Tuesday and Wednesday also being good days. Popular attractions such as Space Mountain and Splash Mountain are best done first thing in the morning to avoid long lines. Visit lands on the west (left) side of the park **earlier in the day**. Parents of young children are best off doing Fantasyland (particularly Dumbo) or Mickey's Toontown Fair first as they get busier later in the day. If you go to Splash Mountain and/or Big Thunder Mountain **during parade times**, be aware that the area can be very congested—use the river boardwalk or railroad instead. **Shop in the afternoon** to avoid crowds (ask about sending packages back to your resort).

GETTING THERE

By Monorail—From the Contemporary, Polynesian, or Grand Floridian resorts, take the monorail directly to the park. From Epcot, take the monorail to the Transportation and Ticket Center (TTC) and transfer to a Magic Kingdom express monorail or boat.

By Boat—From the TTC, boats ferry guests to and from the Magic Kingdom. Guests at the Polynesian, Grand Floridian, Wilderness Lodge and Villas, and Fort Wilderness also have boat service.

By Bus—From all other resorts, buses take you directly to Magic Kingdom. From Disney-MGM Studios or Disney's Animal Kingdom, bus to the TTC and transfer to monorail or boat. From Downtown Disney, bus to the Polynesian and then take the monorail.

By Car—Take I-4 to exit 67 (westbound) or exit 62 (eastbound) and continue about four miles to the toll plaza. All-day parking is $8 (free to resort guests and annual passholders) and the pass is valid at other parks' lots on the same day. Park, take a tram to the Transportation and Ticket Center, and monorail or boat to the park.

By Foot—You can walk from the Contemporary Resort.

Ratings are explained on page 120.

RATINGS

Our Value Ratings:		Our Magic Ratings:		Readers' Ratings:
Quality:	7/10	Theme:	7/10	82% fell in love with it
Variety:	9/10	Excitement:	10/10	15% liked it well enough
Scope:	7/10	Fun Factor:	7/10	2% had mixed feelings
Overall Value:	**8/10**	**Overall Magic:**	**8/10**	1% were disappointed

Magic Kingdom is enjoyed by...		(rated by both authors and readers)
Younger Kids: ♥♥♥♥♥	Young Adults: ♥♥♥♥	Families: ♥♥♥♥♥
Older Kids: ♥♥♥♥♥	Mid Adults: ♥♥♥	Couples: ♥♥♥♥
Teenagers: ♥♥♥♥	Mature Adults: ♥♥♥	Singles: ♥♥♥

Understanding and Using the Attraction Descriptions and Ratings

PassPorter's custom-designed attraction charts include background, trivia, tips, restrictions, queues, accessibility details, enhanced ratings, and much more! We've organized this wide array of information into a consistent format so you can find what you need at a glance. Below is a key to our charts, along with notes and details. Enjoy!

Description Key

Icons[3]   Ratings[4]

[1] Attraction Name [D-3[2]] FP ⛹I A-ok!	☒ # #
Description offering an overview of the attraction, what to expect (without giving too much away), historical background, trivia and "secrets," our recommendations for the best seating/viewing/riding, tips on getting the most out of the attraction, waiting/queue conditions (i.e., covered, outdoor, etc.), wheelchair and stroller access, height/age restrictions, and Allie's KidTips (ages 7-10) and TweenTips (ages 11-12)—hints and tips from one kid to another!	Type[5]
	Scope[5]
	Ages[6]
	Thrill Factor[7]
	Avg. Wait[7]
	Duration[7]

[1] Each chart has an empty **checkbox** in the upper left corner—use it to check off the attractions you want to visit (before you go) or those you visited during your trip.

[2] **Map coordinates** are presented as a letter and a number (i.e., A-5). Match up the coordinates on the park's map for the attraction's location within the park.

[3] Icons indicate when an attraction has FASTPASS (FP) or a height/age restriction (⛹I).

[4] Our **ratings** are shown on the far right end. An **A-ok!** indicates that an attraction is Allie-approved as kid-friendly (as rated by Allie, Dave's daughter, when she was seven). The three boxes on the right side show ratings on a scale of 1 (poor) to 10 (don't miss!). The first is **Jennifer's** rating, the second is **Dave's**, and the third is our **Readers'** ratings. We offer our personal ratings to show how opinions vary, even between two like-minded people. You can also use our ratings as a point of reference—Jennifer appreciates good theming and dislikes sudden spins or drops, while Dave enjoys live performances and thrills. We both appreciate detail-rich attractions where we can learn something new.

[5] The boxes on the right below the numeric ratings give basic information. The first box is **attraction type**. The second box is always **attraction scope**, which we rate as follows:

E-Ticket   Headliner attraction; the ultimate; expect long lines
D-Ticket   Excellent fun, not-to-be-missed
C-Ticket   Solid attraction that pleases most guests
B-Ticket   Good fun, but easily skipped in a pinch
A-Ticket   A simple diversion; often overlooked

[6] **Age-appropriate ratings**. For example, we may say "All Ages" when we feel everyone, from infant on up, will get something out of the experience. More common is "Ages 4 & up" or "Ages 8 & up" for attractions we think will be best appreciated by vacationers who are at least 4 or 8. This is only our guideline and not a Disney rule.

[7] **Thrill/scare factor**, **average wait**, and **duration** follow the age ratings, though we eliminate these if they don't apply or expand them if deserving. We did our best to format this information so you can understand it without having to check this key, too!

Planning · Getting There · Staying in Style · Touring · Feasting · Making Magic · Index · Notes & More

Planning

Getting There

Staying in Style

Touring

Feasting

Making Magic

Index

Notes & More

Charting the Attractions at Main Street, U.S.A.

	Jennifer's Rating	Dave's Rating	Readers' Rating

☐ Main Street Vehicles [D-5]　　A-OK!　　| 3 | 2 | 5 |

Catch a one-way ride to the hub of the Magic Kingdom in vehicles fashioned after those popular at the turn of the century. We've seen horseless carriages, trolleys pulled by Belgian horses, and even a fire engine. These vehicles are fun to ride in if you're willing to wait in the slow, long lines. No time? Just walk instead. The vehicles tend to stop operating later in the day and during parade times. Must transfer from wheelchair. Allie's KidTip: "It's a little bit boring."

Vehicles
A-Ticket
All ages
Gentle ride
Long waits

☐ Town Square Exposition Hall [D-6]　　A-OK!　　| 3 | 5 | 5 |

Many guests overlook this museum showcasing the history of cameras, including a cinema showing historic cartoons, interactive kiosks, photo cutouts, and character greetings! This is also the Camera Center. Allie's KidTip: "Get your picture under Dopey, with aliens, and next to Dalmatians."

Exhibit
A-Ticket
Ages 3 & up
Simple fun

☐ Walt Disney World Railroad [D-6]　　A-OK!　　| 5 | 5 | 7 |

Circle the Magic Kingdom on a popular steam train, with stops at Main Street, U.S.A., Frontierland, and Mickey's Toontown Fair. You'll catch glimpses of all but Liberty Square and Fantasyland along the 1.5-mile journey. Ride the full route for fun, or disembark at any stop to travel through the park. Personal strollers must be folded before boarding. Replacement rental strollers may be available at other stops (hold on to your name tag!), but are not guaranteed. Attraction is closed during the fireworks. May need to transfer from large ECVs to wheelchair. Allie's KidTip: "Don't worry, the train doesn't go too fast. Kids will like this!"

Train Ride
B-Ticket
All ages
A bit loud
Gentle ride
Short waits
20 min. ride (roundtrip)

Attraction descriptions and ratings are explained on page 127.

🅙 What Is and Isn't an Attraction?

We defined an "attraction" on page 114 as an individual ride, show, or exhibit. These are the destinations at the park and almost invariably come with a queue. We cover virtually all the attractions that Disney lists in their own guidemaps, plus a few that aren't listed but we still think are deserving of the "attraction" title (such as Ariel's Grotto). Like Disney, we don't consider things like talking trash cans (yes, they exist!) to be attractions as they rarely carry names or need a queue. We also don't consider outdoor stage shows, parades, or fireworks to be attractions, either—we cover these in the Entertainment sections in the park introduction pages of your PassPorter. Character greeting areas are less straightforward—if Disney considers one to be an attraction (such as the Toontown Hall of Fame) or we feel it offers more than simple character greetings, we include a description of it. For a list of character greeting locations, refer to the guidemap upon your arrival, which contains the most up-to-date information. We also list popular spots to find favorite characters at Disney-MGM Studios on page 153b. For more specific information or hard-to-find characters, ask at Guest Relations in any of Disney's parks, and check the Times Guide.

Charting the Attractions at Adventureland

Jennifer's Rating *Dave's Rating* *Readers' Rating*

☐ "The Enchanted Tiki Room–Under New Management" [B-4]   A-ok!   7 7 6

A perfectly cool place to sit and rest while Audio-Animatronics creatures sing and cavort above you. The Enchanted Tiki Room has been a Disney fixture for many childhoods. Now those famous fowl—Iago (Aladdin) and Zazu (The Lion King)—have stepped in to jazz it up. This is a fun musical revue, which grew from Walt Disney's notion for an unusually entertaining Chinese restaurant. Don't miss the brief pre-show in the outdoor, covered queue area. Best views are on the left side. Wheelchair friendly. Assistive listening devices. **Allie's KidTip:** "Cool. Look for the Tiki gods." **TweenTip:** "It may seem lame, but it's not!"

Show / D-Ticket / Ages 4 & up / Dark, loud, angry gods / Short waits / 2 min. intro / 9 min. show

☐ Jungle Cruise [B-4]   FP   A-ok!   6 6 7

See the sights along the "rivers of the world" in the company of a silly skipper. You and your fellow explorers will go chug-chugging up river in an open-air, awning-covered river boat inspired by the "African Queen." Every skipper tells a slightly different tale. Audio-Animatronics animals and "natives" liven things up. You may get damp. After-dark cruises are particularly fun. Outdoor, covered queue—lines can be deceptively long. Transfer from ECV to wheelchair. **Allie's KidTip:** "There's lions, and tigers, and King Cobra!" (Oh my.) **TweenTip:** "One of my favorites!"

Boat Ride / D-Ticket / Ages 3 & up / Corny jokes / FASTPASS or long waits / 10 min. ride

☐ The Magic Carpets of Aladdin [B-4]   A-ok!   5 6 5

Take a spin through a whole new world. Colorful, rider-controlled carpets go around, up, and down—sit in the front to control the height, or sit in the back to make the carpet tilt forward and back. Similar to Dumbo (see page 132). Water-spitting camels add to the fun. Transfer from ECV to wheelchair. **Allie's KidTip:** "Sit in the front so you can zoom up and maybe get sprayed by camels."

Ride / D-Ticket / Ages 3 & up / Med. waits / 1½ min. ride

☐ Pirates of the Caribbean [A-4]   A-ok!   8 7 9

"Yo ho, yo ho!" The ride that inspired a movie! Take a slow, dark cruise through a subterranean world of Audio-Animatronics pirates and the townsfolk they plunder. Enjoy scene after riotous scene and fun special effects. Not 100% politically correct, but a longtime favorite. Lines can be long, especially on hot days since most of the wait is in a cool cellar. You aren't likely to get wet, but the seats can be damp. Transfer from ECV to wheelchair and transfer from wheelchair. **Allie's KidTip:** "One of my top 10!" **TweenTip:** "Very, very cool!"

Boat Ride / E-Ticket / Ages 6 & up / Gentle drop, dark, scary to young kids / 9 min. ride

☐ Shrunken Ned's Junior Jungle Boats [B-4]   3 4 3

Steer small, remote-controlled craft resembling the Jungle Cruise boats around a lagoon sporting fountains and river gods. $1 for 2 minutes. **Allie's KidTip:** "Steering was very stubborn. When I did something right it still didn't work."

Arcade / A-Ticket / Ages 6 & up

☐ Swiss Family Treehouse [B-4]   5 5 4

Walk through the home of the shipwrecked family from the Disney classic "Swiss Family Robinson." The branches of the huge (and very fake) banyan tree, known affectionately as "Disneyodendron eximus," cradle the family's heirlooms and contraptions. The treehouse has multiple levels that you need to climb. Thus, this attraction is not wheelchair or stroller accessible, and it can be tiring for some. The line of guests winds through slowly. **Allie's KidTip:** "This is boring."

Walk-thru / B-Ticket / Ages 4 & up / Lots of stairs / Allow 15-30 min. to tour

Planning · Getting There · Staying in Style · Touring · Feasting · Making Magic · Index · Notes & More

Charting the Attractions at Frontierland

Jennifer's Rating
Dave's Rating
Readers' Rating

☐ Big Thunder Mountain Railroad [A-2]   FP   🧍   A-ok!   7 8 9

Be prepared to grin as you ride this not-so-scary roller coaster through a wild western landscape. There is plenty of speed and lots of curves, but no fearsome drops on this 4-min. mine train ride. You'll shake and rattle, though! Look around and enjoy Disney's lovingly built scenes. Night rides are extra fun! Lines can be long, with only fans and shade to cool you off. 40"/102 cm height restriction, adult supervision required. Transfer from wheelchair. Health warning. **Allie's KidTip:** "Listen for the howls of the wolves. I loved this ride! Can we go again?"	**Coaster** E-Ticket Ages 6 & up Fast turns, dark caves FASTPASS or long waits

☐ Country Bear Jamboree [B-4]   A-ok!   5 4 5

A troupe of Audio-Animatronics bears sings, dances, and jokes in this loving country music sendup. Grownup city slickers might find the jokes and songs a bit corny, but the young 'uns just might take a hankerin' to 'em. This is another cool, dim place to duck out of the hot Florida sun. Wheelchair accessible. Reflective captioning. Assistive listening devices. **Allie's KidTip:** "Listen carefully for the words to the songs. They're funny!"	**Show** C-Ticket Ages 2 & up Loud Med. waits 15 min. show

☐ Frontierland Shootin' Arcade [B-4]   4 6 3

Have fun shootin' targets with electronic rifles. Aim at cactus, tombstones, and bits of the landscape. 50 cents for 25 shots. **Allie's KidTip:** "Shoot the red dots. The guns are heavy." **TweenTip:** "Awesome! Rest your elbow on the pad."	**Arcade** A-Ticket Ages 9 & up

☐ Mike Fink Keelboats (seasonal) [A-3]   2 1 3

You'll need pioneer spirit to cruise these small, double-decker boats, called the "Gullywhumper" and "Bertha Mae." Despite the fun names, the sights described by your captain are hardly scintillating. On hot days you'll broil on the top deck (the best view) or roast in the cabin. The Liberty Belle offers more interest. Open seasonally (closed at time of writing, and we have the feeling it won't reopen again).	**Boat Ride** B-Ticket All ages Gentle rides 15 min. ride

☐ Splash Mountain [A-3]   FP   🧍   4 6 9

Even bystanders can get soaked when riders slide down this five-story log flume into the Briar Patch. The first ten minutes of this attraction are a gentle ride through an Audio-Animatronics wonderland with all the "brer" creatures from "The Song of the South." Then, kersplash! 40"/102 cm height restriction, adult supervision required. Little ones can play in the charming Laughin' Place playground near the attraction's exit while big kids ride. Health warning. Must transfer from wheelchair to ride. **Allie's KidTip:** "Wow! I love Splash Mountain. On the last big drop you might want to lean back."	**Thrill Ride** E-Ticket Ages 9 & up Very steep drop at end! FASTPASS or long waits 11 min. ride

☐ Tom Sawyer Island [A-3]   A-ok!   6 7 5

Young 'uns can explore caves, tunnels, and Fort Langhorn as they scamper over Tom and Huck's legendary hangout. Kids love the bridges and air guns; oldtimers wander the winding paths and play checkers. Caves are fun, but can be very dark. Board a raft near Big Thunder Mountain to reach the island. This is a great place for a break–try Aunt Polly's Dockside Inn for a snack. Must be ambulatory. Closes at dusk. Tip: Look for the hidden whitewash brushes–if you find one, tell a cast member for a surprise! **Allie's KidTip:** "Follow the wolf howls to the fort."	**Playground** C-Ticket All ages Dark, scary caves Short waits Allow 1-2 hrs.

Tip: You can board the railroad (see page 128 for details) at the Frontierland Station [A-2].

Charting the Attractions at Liberty Square

	Jennifer's Rating	Dave's Rating	Readers' Rating

Diamond Horseshoe Saloon [B-3]   – – –

As we go to press, the "Goofy's Country Dancin' Jamboree" show in the Diamond Horseshoe Saloon has been replaced by "Woody & Friends" from Toy Story 2. The updated attraction appears to be a character meet-and-greet with Woody, Jessie, and Bullseye. The saloon still has its good looks from years past, but the old stage show with dancing girls and snack food service is gone for good. This attraction has had difficulty finding its place in recent years, and we wouldn't be surprised if it changes yet again in the near future. Let's hope they bring back a live show with audience participation. Wheelchair accessible.

Pavilion
A-Ticket
Ages 3 & up
Characters
Med. waits
Bring your autograph book!

The Hall of Presidents [C-3]   5 4 6

Ladies and gentlemen, the Presidents of the United States! The show begins with a 180° film presenting a patriotic, stirring view of our past. Every U.S. President is represented in full Audio-Animatronics glory—including President George W. Bush, who has a speaking part. A red brick colonial hall houses the 700-seat theater, a cool, quiet hideaway. Wheelchair accessible. Reflective captioning. Assistive listening devices. Shows are every half hour. **Allie's KidTip:** "You might like the movie because it talks about freedom."

Show
C-Ticket
Ages 10 & up
Dark theater
Short waits
23 min. show

The Haunted Mansion [B-2]   FP   A-ok!   9 8 9

Another movie-inspiring attraction! Go for a gore-free ride through a world of 999 grinning ghosts. The spooky visual effects are astounding, but the scares are served up with a wink and lots of chuckles. There are no terrifying, chainsaw wielding maniacs in this house. There's so much delicious detail here that you'll ride again and again. Just be sure to leave room in your two-to-three-person "doom buggy" for hitchhiking ghosts! May be too intense for young kids (even though Allie liked it, she was a bit scared). Transfer from wheelchair to ride. Visit http://www.doombuggies.com for more details. **Allie's KidTip:** "Can you find the dog skeleton? Hint: It's on a cliff in the graveyard."

Track Ride
E-Ticket
Ages 6 & up
Mild scares, very dark
FASTPASS or med. waits
3 min. intro
7 min. ride

Liberty Belle Riverboat [B-3]   5 6 5

Take a cruise on a steam-driven sternwheeler. Mark Twain narrates your spin around Tom Sawyer Island, but the real joy is the attention to detail. The boat and its steam power plant are more interesting than the scenery—be sure to tour the decks. The middle deck salon is a nice spot to dodge the sun. The "Liberty Belle" replaced the "Richard F. Irvine" in 1996. Wheelchair accessible. Adult supervision. Cruises depart on the hour and half-hour. **Allie's KidTip:** "Boring."

Boat Ride
C-Ticket
All ages
Gentle rides
Med. waits
20 min. ride

Attraction descriptions and ratings are explained on page 127.

Strollers: To Bring or Rent
See page 115 for more on rentals.
If you bring your own stroller (a boon for the airport and travel to and from the buses/parking lot), we recommend a compact, umbrella stroller, as it's easy to tote about. If you prefer to bring a larger, folding stroller (the kind with cup holders and serious cargo capacity), try to travel the buses at off-hours, when the stroller won't prevent you from getting onboard due to crowded conditions. Rentals are good for kids who only need an occasional ride and weigh less than the 70 lb. weight limit. All rental strollers are now either "jogging style" or molded plastic.

Planning | Getting There | Staying in Style | Touring | Feasting | Making Magic | Index | Notes & More

Charting the Attractions at Fantasyland

	Jennifer's Rating	Dave's Rating	Readers' Rating

⬛ Ariel's Grotto [D-1] A-ok! 3 3 3

Little mermaids love to meet Ariel at this character meet-and-greet and fountain play area. Fountains may be turned off in droughts, but even so kids enjoy having a place to frolic while the long line of parents waits patiently. Wheelchair accessible. Allie's KidTip: "You can play here even without water."

Playground
A-Ticket
All ages
Long waits

⬛ Cinderella's Golden Carrousel [D-2] A-ok! 5 5 6

This colorful, lovingly maintained carrousel painted with scenes from Cinderella sits at the center of Fantasyland. Many of the 84 horses were rescued from a historic New Jersey carousel, but you'd have a hard time telling which ones. The horses closer to the perimeter tend to rise higher. A recently added chariot (an original) holds six. Disney tunes make it a joy for the ears! Enchanting in the evening. Must transfer from wheelchair to board. Adult supervision of children required. Allie's KidTip: "Make sure you're fully secure on the horse."

Ride
B-Ticket
Ages 2 & up
High horses can be scary
Short waits
2 min. ride

⬛ Dumbo The Flying Elephant [D-2] A-ok! 5 5 5

Every child wants to ride around, up, and down on Dumbo. Two-seater flying elephants take you all for a short, fast spin. Show your child how to lift the control lever to go higher. Grown-ups will enjoy the pachyderm's-eye view. The lines are long and hot—the queue area offers some shade and diversions. Adults must ride with small children, and you know the kids will want to ride again—do this ride first thing in the morning. Must transfer from wheelchair. Allie's KidTip: "If you ride with a grown-up, pick someone who isn't too big—the seats are small!"

Ride
D-Ticket
All ages
Spins high in the air
Long waits
2 min. flight

⬛ Fairytale Garden [E-3] A-ok! 6 6 5

Meet characters such as Belle (from "Beauty and the Beast") in this quaint garden created in 1999. Sit on stools and benches among the rose bushes and listen to Belle read a story at various times throughout the day. Belle takes volunteers from the audience to help tell her tale. Arrive about 10 minutes early to get a seat. No shade. Character meet and greet, too. Wheelchair friendly. Allie's KidTip: "You might want to be in the show because it could be fun!!!"

Live Show
B-Ticket
All ages
Happy ending
15 min. story

⬛ "it's a small world" (reopens Spring 2005) [C-2] A-ok! 4 3 6

"It's a world of laughter, a world of tears..." Yes, these are Disney's famous singing and dancing dolls, who first debuted their act at the 1964-65 New York World's Fair. Their catchy song adapts to the local surroundings as your boat floats sedately past scenes depicting the world's continents and cultures. Disney is pouring big bucks into a complete overhaul of this classic, so plan to see it! Must transfer from ECV to wheelchair to ride. Allie's KidTip: "Ask your grownups for a seat at the end of a row so you can see more. Try to sing along."

Boat Ride
C-Ticket
All ages
That song!
Short to med. waits
11 min. cruise

🔟 What's Happening at the 20,000 Leagues Lagoon?

The Fantasyland Character Festival and the old 20,000 Leagues Lagoon behind it are gone for good. Demolition crews went to work in mid-2004 to make way for an as-yet unannounced new attraction. The 20,000 Leagues submarine ride has been closed for more than 10 years, so folks have been speculating about a replacement for a long time. Maybe we'll know soon.

Charting the Attractions at Fantasyland
(continued)

	Jennifer's Rating	Dave's Rating	Readers' Rating

☐ Mad Tea Party [E-2]   A-OK!   7 3 6

Spin and spin and spin some more inside a giant teacup. Young kids love to get dizzy, so this ride draws them like a magnet. Turn the metal wheel at the center of your teacup to make it spin even faster. You'll be as dizzy as the Mad Hatter. This is one ride that lasts a bit longer than you'd like. Sit this one out if you're prone to dizziness. Adult supervision of children under 7. Must transfer from wheelchair to ride. Allie's Kid Tip: "Look for the dormouse!"

Ride
C-Ticket
Ages 4 & up
Scares adults
Short waits
2 min. spin

☐ The Many Adventures of Winnie the Pooh [E-2]   FP   A-OK!   6 5 7

Take a gentle ride through the world of that fabulously popular bear. Blow through the Blustery Day, bounce along with Tigger, dream of Heffalumps and Woozles, and float away in a mighty spring flood, all in a four-seated "honey pot" that moves along an indoor track. Pooh fans will exit feeling warm and fuzzy—the better you know Pooh's tales the more you'll get from your tour through the cartoon cut-out scenery. The covered queue winds through pages blown away from a huge storybook. Lines can be long—we suggest you get a FASTPASS soon after the park opens. Transfer from ECV to wheelchair. Allie's Kid Tip: "Sit in the front." Tween Tip: "Good for toddlers. Not a top 10."

Track Ride
D-Ticket
All ages
Kid-friendly; dark could be slightly scary
FASTPASS or long waits
3 min. ride

☐ Mickey's PhilharMagic [D-2]   FP   A-OK!   8 9 9

Trouble's brewing in Fantasyland for Disney's latest 3-D movie experience, when Donald "borrows" (and loses) Mickey's sorcerer hat. The audience, assembled in front of a giant, 150-foot wide screen in PhilharMagic Concert Hall, awaits a concert conducted by Mickey. Donald, naturally, gets into deep trouble. Soon he's scurrying through scenes from Disney classic films, trying to regain the lost hat. Along the way he meets Simba, Peter Pan, Lumiere, Aladdin, Ariel, and other favorite Disney characters. Look for Donald at the "end." The 3-D movie effects and sensations are kid-friendly. Best seats in middle or back of theater. Covered queue. Wheelchair accessible. Assistive listening devices. Reflective captioning. Tween Tip: "Wow! Good for all ages."

Show
E-Ticket
Ages 5 & up
Intense effects may be scary
FASTPASS or med. waits
10 min. show

☐ Peter Pan's Flight [C-2]   FP   A-OK!   6 6 8

Climb aboard a flying, three-seat pirate ship that twists and turns sedately through the clouds. Follow Peter Pan and the Darling children from London to Neverland. Scenes featuring the Lost Boys, mermaids, Captain Hook's ship, and the crocodile unfold below, then you're safely home. Very dark, 4-minute ride. Covered queue area. Transfer from wheelchair to ride. Allie's Kid Tip: "Can you find the mermaids? One of them looks like Ariel!"

Track Ride
D-Ticket
Ages 3 & up
Dark, heights
FASTPASS or long waits

☐ Snow White's Scary Adventures [D-2]   A-OK!   4 6 5

What's the most underappreciated ride in all of Fantasyland? Snow White! Your wooden mining car carries you though scene after scene from Disney's classic animation. The Wicked Witch provides the scares, but just when things get too gloomy you'll be transported into the welcome arms of the Seven Dwarfs and Prince Charming. Kids' legs fit best in the front seat, which is lower. May be too intense for young children. Must transfer from wheelchair to ride. Allie's Kid Tip: "Look for the name on the front of your car!"

Track Ride
C-Ticket
Ages 5 & up
Dark, scary for kids
Short waits
3 min. ride

Attraction descriptions and ratings are explained on page 127.

Planning   Getting There   Staying in Style   Touring   Feasting   Making Magic   Index   Notes & More

Charting the Attractions at Mickey's Toontown Fair

	Jennifer's Rating	Dave's Rating	Readers' Rating

☐ The Barnstormer at Goofy's Wiseacre Farm [F-2] 🕴 A-Ok!　7 7 6

It's tough to find a finer "kiddie" roller coaster than The Barnstormer. Even grown-up coaster fans love this fast, swooping flight through (and we do mean "through") one of the goofiest barnyards you'll ever see. The queue is a delight, too, as you get to inspect Goofy's crops and livestock. Long lines move quickly through the uncovered queue. Cars may be small for big/tall adults. Closes often during inclement weather. Transfer from wheelchair. Minimum age is 3. **Allie's Kid Tip**: "Lift your hands in the air! You'll want to go on it again and again!"	**Coaster**
	D-Ticket
	Ages 4 & up (35" and up)
	Fast turns
	Med. waits
	1 min. flight

☐ Donald's Boat [G-1]　A-Ok!　4 3 4

Your little ducklings will have a hoot splashing about in Unca Donald's fountains and exploring his boat. Bring suits and towels (change at the Service Station restrooms beside Minnie's House). Fountains may be off in droughts. Wheelchair accessible. **Allie's Kid Tip**: "Pull the horn and bell in the boathouse!"	**Playground**
	A-Ticket
	All ages
	No wait

☐ Mickey's Country House and Judge's Tent [F-1]　A-Ok!　5 5 6

Mickey's house is chock-full of chuckles and "tchochkes" (knick-knacks). Look closely at his decorating—there are enough sight gags and delights to turn anyone into a gleeful kid. Long, slow lines snake in the front door, out the back, and through his garden, because Mickey himself is waiting to greet you in the Judge's Tent next door. If the house and garden are enough, exit through Mickey's garage. Wheelchair accessible. **Allie's Kid Tip**: "Meet Mickey afterwards!"	**Walk-thru**
	B-Ticket
	All ages
	Long waits
	Allow 20 min. to 1 hour

☐ Minnie's Country House [F-1]　A-Ok!　6 5 6

Walk through Minnie's in-home studio and office for a fascinating glimpse into the talents of this fabled celebrity. Her painting, sculpting, and quilting talents are remarkable, and her kitchen is a wonder (be sure to look in the fridge). Alas, she's not at home to greet you, but that also means the lines move faster than they do at Mickey's. Wheelchair accessible. **Allie's Kid Tip**: "Look for things you can play with in the house, like the cake and the popcorn."	**Walk-thru**
	B-Ticket
	All ages
	No scares
	Med. waits
	Allow 20 min.

☐ Toon Park [F-1]　🕴　5 5 6

Toddler playground with lots of pint-sized slides, tunnels, and playhouses. Soft padded ground guards against boo-boos. Restricted to kids 40" and under.	**Playground**
	A-Ticket

☐ Toontown Hall of Fame [F-1]　A-Ok!　3 2 6

Meet Minnie and many other Disney characters in three separate greeting areas located on the right-hand side of this big, candy-striped "tent" which doubles as a store. Lines, not surprisingly, are long. Wheelchair accessible. **Allie's Kid Tip**: "Bring your autograph book!"	**Pavilion**
	A-Ticket
	All ages
	Long waits

☐ Walt Disney World Railroad [G-1]　A-Ok!　5 5 7

Toontown Fair Station! All out for Mickey's Toontown Fair, Fantasyland, and Tomorrowland. Next stop, Main Street, U.S.A. See page 128. This is a fun shortcut when you're heading for the exit. Large ECVs may need to transfer to wheelchair.	**Rail Ride**
	B-Ticket
	All ages

Tip: To get from Mickey's Toontown Fair to Tomorrowland faster, take the path that starts at the railroad station in Mickey's Toontown Fair and ends beside the Tomorrowland Arcade.

Planning　Getting There　Staying in Style　Touring　Feasting　Making Magic　Index　Notes & More

Charting the Attractions at Tomorrowland

	Jennifer's Rating	Dave's Rating	Readers' Rating

Astro Orbiter [F-4] — A-ok!

Ratings: 1 / 3 / 3

Go for a short, fast spin in a two-seat rocket high above Tomorrowland. Often mistaken for a futuristic sculpture, the fanciful planets of Astro Orbiter go into motion with each launch. Think "Dumbo" with small, silvery space ships. Pull back on the stick to "soar" high. Get a dizzying view as your ship whirls. Must ride an elevator to board. Motion sickness warning. Outdoor, covered queue. Adults must accompany kids under 7. Transfer from wheelchair to ride. **Allie's Kid Tip:** "You can get a great view of the park." **TweenTip:** "Faster than Dumbo and Aladdin."

Ride
C-Ticket
Ages 5 & up
Heights
Long waits
1½ min. flight

Buzz Lightyear's Space Ranger Spin [F-4] — FP — A-ok!

Ratings: 8 / 8 / 8

All right, Space Rangers, it's time to help Toy Story's Buzz Lightyear defeat the evil Emperor Zurg! Buzz himself briefs new cadets before you're sent into battle in a Day-Glo, comic book world of planets and space creatures. Your two-seat space vehicle (an "XP-37 Space Cruiser") is equipped with a pair of "ion cannons" (laser pointers) mounted on the dashboard. Aim and shoot the electronic targets to accumulate points (aim for the higher targets for more points). Move the joystick to make your vehicle spin and hone in on your targets. Compare your score at the end. Covered queue area is mostly indoors. Wheelchair accessible. **Allie's Kid Tip:** "Look at your score when you're done. I made Space Cadet!"

Ride
D-Ticket
Ages 4 & up
Mild "space flight" effects
FASTPASS or med. waits
4 min. flight

Walt Disney's Carousel of Progress (seasonal) [F-4] — A-ok!

Ratings: 9 / 6 / 6

See the march of modern technology through the eyes of an American family. Each of the four scenes in this Audio-Animatronics show highlights another twenty years (or so) of progress in the 20th century. When the scene changes, the entire theater moves around to the next stage. One of Walt Disney's favorite attractions. (Jennifer loves it, too!) Limited hours. Outdoor, covered queue. Wheelchair accessible. Assistive listening devices. Closed captioning (pre-show only). This attraction is seasonal and may have limited operating hours.

Show
C-Ticket
Ages 6 & up
No scares
Short waits
22 min. show

Galaxy Palace Theater (seasonal) [F-5] — A-ok!

Ratings: 4 / 5 / 4

This outdoor, partially covered theater plays host to a variety of live shows and entertainment throughout the year, such as the "Galaxy Search" talent show or "Mickey's 'Twas the Night Before Christmas" show. Most Tomorrowland visitors don't even know it exists, and much of the time the theater is "dark." Check your Magic Kingdom Times Guide for current show listings. Wheelchair accessible. Assistive listening devices. **Allie's Kid Tip:** "Sounds like fun!"

Live Show
B-Ticket
All ages
Showtimes vary (seasonal)

Stitch's Great Escape! [E-4] (Opened October 2004) — FP

Ratings: – / – / –

As we go to press, that wonderfully scary Alien Encounter will soon be tamed by redesigning and renaming it around Stitch of "Lilo and Stitch" fame. Guests will be recruited to guard "Experiment 626" (Stitch), and all sorts of mischief can be expected when that wily captive escapes. Disney promises sights, sounds, smells, and some of the most amazing Audio-Animatronics to date. Other friends present from the movie include the Grand Councilwoman, Captain Gantu, and Pleakley. Even Skippy from Alien Encounter is said to have a part. While Alien Encounter was creepy-scary, Disney promises to put a kid-friendly spin on its replacement. Outdoor, covered queue. Potential height restriction. Accessibility features unknown

Show
E-Ticket
Ages 7 & up
Could be scary for young kids
FASTPASS or long waits
12 min. show

Attraction descriptions and ratings are explained on page 127.

Planning | Getting There | Staying in Style | Touring | Feasting | Making Magic | Index | Notes & More

Charting the Attractions
at Tomorrowland
(continued)

	Jennifer's Rating	Dave's Rating	Readers' Rating

Space Mountain [G-3]   FP ⫯ A-OK!   6 8 9

Blast off into the blackness of space on the Magic Kingdom's most exciting roller coaster. This fast, indoor ride has sudden turns and short drops, but no big, stomach-in-your-throat drops. The darkness makes it scarier than it really is. The indoor queue and ride loading areas are rich with visual detail—pay attention while you're waiting. There are two slightly different coasters—go left for one, right for the other when you reach the loading area. Single rider queue (when available) can cut wait time. Transfer from ECV to wheelchair, then transfer from wheelchair to ride. 44"/112 cm height restriction. Adult supervision. Health warning. Allie's KidTip: "I loved it! But it is bumpy. Try to sit in the middle. Ride it again if you can!"

Coaster / E-Ticket / Ages 8 & up / Dark, rough, jerky, fast / FASTPASS or long waits / 2½ min. flight

The Timekeeper (seasonal) [E-4]   A-OK!   7 7 6

Travel through time with the Timekeeper and his sidekick 9-Eye. These Audio-Animatronics robots—brought to life by the talents of Robin Williams and Rhea Perlman—take you, along with Jules Verne and H.G. Wells, on a journey through time and space. 9-Eye shows the sights in a Circle-Vision 360 movie. You must stand to view—best views in the front and middle. Indoor queue with a pre-show on monitors. Shows every 20 minutes. Wheelchair accessible. Assistive listening devices. Closed captioning. Reflective captioning. This attraction is seasonal and could close permanently. Allie's KidTip: "Watch for the year 3000."

Show / D-Ticket / Ages 4 & up / Dark, some scary scenes / Med. waits / 4 min. intro 16 min. show

Tomorrowland Arcade [G-3]   A-OK!   3 2 3

Play the latest in video games, as well as some old classics, in this large, very loud arcade at the exit of Space Mountain. Spending money is required. Wheelchair accessible. Allie's KidTip: "Try to play a Disney dancing game here and win!"

Arcade / A-Ticket / Ages 6 & up

Tomorrowland Indy Speedway [F-3]   ⫯ A-OK!   4 3 4

Every kid wants a chance to drive, and when they're tall enough they can at this popular attraction. Experienced drivers won't be as thrilled. Guide rails, shock-absorbing bumpers, and a low top speed (7 mph maximum) make these gas powered "race cars" safe. Family members can cheer from an enclosed grandstand (the entrance is to the right). Shortest waits are early in the morning. Covered outdoor queue. Transfer from wheelchair to ride. 52"/132 cm height restriction to drive solo. Health warning. Adult supervision required. Allie's KidTip: "Even if you're tall enough, make sure your feet can touch the pedals before you drive."

Ride / C-Ticket / Ages 4 & up / Cars may bump yours from behind / Long waits / 4 min. drive

Tomorrowland Transit Authority [F-4]   A-OK!   6 6 6

Take a grand tour of Tomorrowland on an elevated, automated people mover. The four-seat vehicles move sedately along a route that takes you through Space Mountain and past nearly every other attraction in Tomorrowland. Along the way you can look down upon Tomorrowland's crowds and view a scale model of Progress City (formerly of Disneyland's Carousel of Progress). It makes a great introduction to Tomorrowland. Outdoor, mostly covered queue. Must be ambulatory to ride. Allie's KidTip: "This is ok, but not one of my top ten. Look for the stars when you go through Space Mountain."

Ride / B-Ticket / All ages / Dark / Short waits / 12 min. grand tour

Tip: Ever hear a talking trash can? Look for one called "PUSH" wandering about Cosmic Ray's Starlight Cafe and all over Tomorrowland.

Epcot

Triple the size of the Magic Kingdom, Epcot opened its doors (and many minds) in 1982. Epcot is the ultimate world's fair, showcasing a future where technology improves our lives, the countries of the world live in peace, and dreams really can come true.

Striving to educate and inspire as well as entertain, Epcot introduces millions to new **technological and international frontiers**. Epcot began as Walt Disney's dream of an "Experimental Prototype Community of Tomorrow;" it's a far cry from the ordinary communities that most of us live in. The first of two "worlds," Future World greets you with its awe-inspiring, 180-foot-tall, geodesic sphere (Spaceship Earth). Streamlined structures and broad vistas transport you into the future of today's hopes and dreams. Beyond Future World is World Showcase, offering an inspiring glimpse into faraway lands, different customs, and exotic peoples.

The two worlds of Epcot offer a variety of attractions, all housed in "pavilions"—ten in Future World and eleven in the World Showcase (see the fold-out map on page 289). Below are the headline attractions in the west and east sides of Future World and World Showcase. See page 139 for an at-a-glance list of attractions, page 140 for our favorite itinerary, and pages 143–149 for attraction details.

Future World East *Headline Attractions:*	Science and technology take center stage with an up-close look at space travel, vehicle testing, communications, biology, and energy. *Mission:SPACE, Test Track, Spaceship Earth, Universe of Energy*
Future World West *Headline Attractions:*	Explore the nature of the world on land and in the sea, and the nature of imagination and perception in the recesses of our minds. *Honey, I Shrunk the Audience, Living With the Land, Soarin'*
World Showcase East *Headline Attractions:*	Cruise the river of time in Mexico, experience a maelstrom in Norway, see the wonders of China, celebrate in Germany and Italy, and explore the heritage of the American adventure. *Maelstrom, The American Adventure, Reflections of China*
World Showcase West *Headline Attractions:*	Hear drummers in Japan, view treasures in Morocco, see the sights in France, tour gardens in the United Kingdom, and explore the wonders of Canada. *Impressions de France, O Canada!*

Entertainment and Shopping at Epcot

Don't miss the fold-out map in the back of the book!

ENTERTAINMENT

Epcot presents a rich medley of sounds and sights for the strolling visitor. Guests may encounter acrobats, dancers, actors, and musicians—more than **two dozen groups** in all. Most shows last about 10-20 minutes. Favorites include the Voices of Liberty, American Vybe, and fife and drum corps at The American Adventure, Celtic rock and bagpipes in Canada, Beatles look-alikes in the United Kingdom, white-faced mimes in France, "living statues" in Italy, brass bands in Germany, and a fun mariachi band in Mexico.

© MediaMarx, Inc.

Tip: This is a fun photo to take! You just need a steady hand.

Dave "leans" against Spaceship Earth

You'll flip for China's acrobats, and Japanese and African drummers set your pulse pounding. The spectacular **Fountain of Nations** dances in time to the music (see page 146). Beyond casual entertainment, check your Times Guide for the schedule at the open-air **America Gardens Theatre** which offers half-hour performances, plus the Flower Power concerts in the spring, Eat to the Beat concerts in autumn, and Candlelight Processional in December (see page 257). Crowds throng the World Showcase every evening at park closing for the popular **IllumiNations** fireworks and light show (see page 150 for details).

SHOPPING

The World Showcase makes Epcot the center for unusual shopping, too. A wide array of **international gifts and crafts** grace every pavilion, from British woolens and Japanese silks to German cut crystal and Moroccan leather. Here are our favorite shops:

Shop	Location	What makes it special
Art of Disney	Near Innoventions	Collectibles and animation cels
Disney Traders	World Showcase	Disney-themed merchandise
MouseGear	Future World	Huge store with clothes and gifts
ImageWorks	Imagination!	Unique photos and photo gifts
Plaza de Los Amigos	Mexico	It just _feels good_ to shop here!
Yong Feng Shangdian	China	Huge store with a wide variety
Mitsukoshi Dept. Store	Japan	Authentic Japanese gifts, snacks
Tangier Traders	Morocco	Open-air, exotic shopping
La Maison du Vin	France	Two words: wine tastings!
The Crown and Crest	United Kingdom	Family name histories
La Boutique	Canada	Anne of Green Gables items

Epcot
Attractions At-A-Glance
(alphabetical order)

Attraction	Type	Allow	Page
☐ America Gardens Theatre [D-1]	Show	30–40+	148-WS
☐ The American Adventure [D-1]	Pavilion	(80+)	148-WS
☐ The American Adventure Show [D-1]	Show	(50+)	148-WS
☐ Body Wars [B-7]	Thrill Ride	20–30+	144-FW
☐ Canada [E-4]	Pavilion	30–40+	149-WS
☐ Cranium Command [A-7]	Show	20–25+	144-FW
☐ China [B-3]	Pavilion	(35+)	147-WS
☐ The Circle of Life [F-6]	Film	15–20+	145-FW
☐ El Rio del Tiempo [B-4]	Boat Ride	20+	147-WS
☐ Fitness Fairgrounds [B-7]	Playground	15+	143-FW
☐ France [F-2]	Pavilion	30–40+	149-WS
☐ Germany [B-1]	Pavilion	(15–30+)	148-WS
☐ Global Neighborhood [D-7] (closed)	Playground	20–30+	143-FW
☐ Ice Station Cool [D-6]	Walkthru	15–20+	145-FW
☐ Impressions de France [F-2]	Film	20–25+	149-WS
☐ ImageWorks [E-5]	Playground	20–30+	146-FW
☐ Innoventions East [C-6]	Playground	40–60+	143-FW
☐ Innoventions West [D-6]	Playground	40–60+	145-FW
☐ Italy [C-1]	Pavilion	(15–30+)	148-WS
☐ Honey, I Shrunk the Audience [E-5]	3-D Film	25–45+	146-FW
☐ Japan [E-1]	Pavilion	15–30+	148-WS
☐ Journey Into Imagination [E-5]	Track Ride	15–20+	146-FW
☐ The Land [E-6]	Pavilion	(90+)	145-FW
☐ The Living Seas [E-7]	Pavilion/Film	40–60+	145-FW
☐ Living With the Land [F-6]	Boat Ride	30–40+	146-FW
☐ The Making of Me [B-7]	Film	20–25+	144-FW
☐ Maelstrom [B-3]	Boat Ride	25–40+	147-WS
☐ Mexico [B-4]	Pavilion	(25+)	147-WS
☐ Mission:SPACE [B-6]	Thrill Ride	40–90+	144-FW
☐ Morocco [E-1]	Pavilion	20–30+	148-WS
☐ Norway [B-3]	Pavilion	(45+)	147-WS
☐ O Canada! [E-4]	Film	(20–25+)	149-WS
☐ Reflections of China [A-3]	Film	25–30+	147-WS
☐ Soarin' [F-6]	Ride/Film	30–35+	145-FW
☐ Spaceship Earth [D-7]	Track Ride	30–40+	143-FW
☐ Test Track [B-5]	Thrill Ride	40–90+	144-FW
☐ United Kingdom [E-3]	Pavilion	15–30+	149-WS
☐ Universe of Energy [B-7]	Film/Ride	40–60+	143-FW
☐ Wonders of Life [B-7]	Pavilion	(100+)	143-FW

The Allow column gives the amount of time (in minutes) you should allow for an attraction, assuming you do not have a FASTPASS and there are no ride breakdowns. Times in parentheses are approximate totals for all attractions in that pavilion—component times for that pavilion's attractions are also in the attraction list.

The letters after the page numbers stand for the first two letters of the land in which that attraction is located: FW for Future World and WS for World Showcase.

Our Favorite Touring Plan for Epcot

NOTES

Epcot is so large it's really difficult to do in one day, and we don't recommend it if at all possible. We recognize that many families may only have one day for Epcot, however, so we're sharing our best, one-day touring plan (which assumes entry by 9:00 am). If you can enter earlier, spend that extra time in Future World. Those lucky enough to have more time to spend at Epcot probably don't need a touring plan at all. But if you'd like to use ours anyway, you can easily split Future World and World Showcase into two days—just add in all the optional attractions and plan to sleep in on the day you do World Showcase (as it opens later than Future World). As with our other touring plans, you can skip items with asterisks if you're with young kids or sedate adults.

ITINERARY

Touring With Adults and/or Kids

Enter Future World East
Get FASTPASS for Mission:SPACE*
Visit Test Track*
Visit Mission:SPACE*
Enter Wonders of Life (seasonal)
Visit Body Wars*
(Optional: Visit Cranium Command and/or The Making of Me)
Visit Spaceship Earth
(Optional: Visit Ice Station Cool)
Enter The Land (Future World West)
Get FASTPASS for Soarin'
Enter The Living Seas
Visit The Living Seas
Enter The Land
Visit Soarin'
Visit Living With the Land
(Optional: Visit The Circle of Life)
Eat lunch at The Garden Grill or Sunshine Season Food Fair (*estimate lunch time at about 2 hours after you enter the park*)
Visit Living With the Land
Enter Imagination!
Visit Honey, I Shrunk the Audience
Visit Journey Into Imagination with Figment
Enter Canada
Browse Canadian pavilion
Enter United Kingdom
Browse United Kingdom pavilion
Enter France
Browse French pavilion
Visit Impressions de France
Enter Morocco
Browse Moroccan pavilion

Have a snack in World Showcase East (try a baklava in Morocco or Kaki Gori in Japan)
Enter Japan
Browse Japanese pavilion
Enter American Adventure
Visit The American Adventure
Eat dinner in World Showcase East. Try San Angel Inn or Cantina de San Angel in Mexico, or Restaurant Akershus in Norway (*estimate time at 7 1/2 hours after you enter the park*)
Enjoy any extra "free time" at the World Showcase
(Optional: Visit Maelstrom*—if you decide to do this, you may want to get a FASTPASS for it earlier.)
Find an IllumiNations viewing spot (the terrace of Cantina de San Angel can be good—see pages 150 & 250 for tips)
Watch IllumiNations
(*Tour duration: About 11 hours*)

Touring With Kids
Start at Wonders of Life rather than Mission:SPACE and visit Cranium Command and/or Making of Me. Proceed with the plan, omitting those items in blue that won't appeal to your kids. The extra time you gain can be used at the KidCot stations around the World Showcase.

Making the Most of Epcot

If you arrive at Epcot via the **monorail**, you get a wonderful aerial view of Future World and a glimpse of World Showcase as the monorail glides on a track several stories above the park.

Your little ones will adore the **Kidcot Fun Stops** at each World Showcase pavilion. Cast members offer kids masks to color and decorate with beads and cut-outs—there's something different to add to the mask at each country. Allie loved it! Kids also love the play fountains on the promenade between Future World and the World Showcase, and behind Innoventions East. Come prepared with bathing suits under clothing and/or dry clothes and shoes.

Looking for **characters** at Epcot? Watch for a double-decker bus loaded with many Disney characters making the rounds, as well as various character meet and greets. Check your Times Guide, too!

Seniors should try to make more time for Epcot—you'll love it here!

Consider an Epcot **guided tour**, such as Gardens of the World or Undiscovered Future World. See pages 242–243.

On your way out of the park in the evening, glance down at the path as you pass Innoventions—you'll discover **fiber optic lights** embedded in the pavement that make beautiful patterns.

Epcot is the dining capital of the "World." Nearly all the good stuff encircles the World Showcase Lagoon in an **international dining extravaganza**, offering everything from the upscale Bistro de Paris to tacos and beer at Cantina de San Angel. Future World offers less table-service dining, but it has a wide range of counter-service opportunities. See detailed descriptions on pages 208–214.

"**Friendships**" (boats) convey you to different points within World Showcase. You can usually get there faster if you walk, however.

Good viewing locations for **IllumiNations** go quickly. See page 150 for hints on getting the best possible view of the action.

After IllumiNations ends, step aside and wait for the crowds to thin. Take a **leisurely stroll** around the lagoon. Enjoy the music and the lights—you'll have a nice, quiet walk with very few people around. As a bonus, you'll miss the traffic in the parking lot and bus queues.

TIPS

NOTES

Planning · Getting There · Staying in Style · Touring · Feasting · Making Magic · Index · Notes & More

Getting to Epcot

BEST TIMES TO GO

The **best time to visit World Showcase** is when it first opens at 11:00 am, as most guests are still in Future World. It follows then that the **best time to tour Future World** is in the late afternoon and during dinner time (note that many attractions in Future World close at about 7:00 pm). World Showcase becomes congested in the evenings due to the many restaurants and IllumiNations show. Because of the focus on dining at Epcot, traditional lunch and dinner times are better spent at the attractions while others are eating. Along the same vein, you will find restaurants less busy and noisy if you dine before or after the normal lunch and dinner hour. **IllumiNations** is held nightly at park closing (usually 9:00 pm)—for a good view, start looking about one hour prior (see page 150). If you've already seen IllumiNations, consider **dining during it** for a quieter experience.

By Monorail—From the Magic Kingdom, Contemporary, Polynesian, or Grand Floridian, take the monorail to the Transportation and Ticket Center (TTC) and transfer to the Epcot monorail.
By Boat—From Disney-MGM Studios, Swan & Dolphin, BoardWalk, Yacht & Beach Club, boats go to Epcot's International Gateway.
By Bus—From other resorts, Disney-MGM Studios, or Disney's Animal Kingdom, buses take you directly to Epcot. From Downtown Disney, take a bus to a nearby resort and transfer to an Epcot bus, boat, or walk. (Tip: Bus to BoardWalk and walk/boat to Epcot.)
By Car—Take I-4 to exit 67 (westbound) or exit 62 (eastbound) and continue on to the Epcot toll plaza. All-day parking is available for $8 (free to resort guests and annual passholders).
By Foot—From the BoardWalk Inn & Villas, Yacht & Beach Club and Villas, Swan & Dolphin, and Disney-MGM Studios, Epcot is within walking distance. Follow the paths toward International Gateway—it emerges between United Kingdom and France. Walk through United Kingdom and Canada to reach Future World.

Ratings are explained on page 120.

Our Value Ratings:		Our Magic Ratings:		Readers' Ratings:
Quality:	8/10	Theme:	8/10	58% fell in love with it
Variety:	8/10	Excitement:	8/10	34% liked it well enough
Scope:	10/10	Fun Factor:	6/10	7% had mixed feelings
Overall Value:	**9/10**	**Overall Magic:**	**7/10**	1% were disappointed

Epcot is enjoyed by...		(rated by both authors and readers)
Younger Kids: ♥♥♥	Young Adults: ♥♥♥♥	Families: ♥♥♥♥
Older Kids: ♥♥♥	Mid Adults: ♥♥♥♥♥	Couples: ♥♥♥♥♥
Teenagers: ♥♥♥	Mature Adults: ♥♥♥♥♥	Singles: ♥♥♥♥♥

Charting the Attractions at Future World (East)

| | Jennifer's Rating | Dave's Rating | Readers' Rating |

☐ Spaceship Earth [D-7]   A-ok!   9 7 8

Go inside the huge geodesic sphere that towers above Epcot for a look at the development of communication technologies from cave paintings through the space age. Four-seat "time machine" vehicles take you up into the huge sphere past 65 Audio-Animatronics reenacting milestones in communication. The Global Neighborhood post-show exhibit has closed (see below). Adults should accompany and sit beside children. Visit at park opening or evening for shorter waits. Outdoor queue is mostly covered. Must transfer from wheelchair. Allie's Kid Tip: "You'll love all the lights. And it's good for learning."

Track Ride
E-Ticket
Ages 5 & up
Dark, steep incline, but gentle
Short waits
15 min. ride

☐ Global Neighborhood (closed until further notice) [D-7]   – – –

AT&T no longer sponsors Spaceship Earth, so the AT&T-themed Global Neighborhood post-show exhibit area is gone as well. There has been some speculation about a redesign (with a new name), but with no new sponsor in sight and no official announcements from Disney, we'll just have to wait and see.

Playground
B-Ticket
Ages 3 & up
Short waits

☐ Innoventions East [C-6]   A-ok!   6 5 6

If gee-whiz technology pushes your buttons, pay a visit to Innoventions—Epcot's two-part, high-tech, hands-on trade exhibit. Innoventions East hosts exhibits on Internet activities (send electronic and video mail back home), forestry (play the "Total Treevia" game show), UL product testing (test the limits of products like a real UL engineer), the House of Innoventions (see inventive products of the future), and the new Fantastic Plastics Works exhibit (design your own plastic robot). Short queues in some exhibits. Wheelchair accessible. Allie's Kid Tip: "There are games to play and shows to see."

Playground
B-Ticket
All ages
Noisy
Short waits
Allow about one hour to explore

☐ Universe of Energy (Ellen's Energy Adventure) [B-7]   A-ok!   5 6 7

Join Ellen DeGeneres for a humorous crash course in energy, the stuff that powers our world. Widescreen films, thunderous sound effects, and gigantic Audio-Animatronic dinosaurs help tell the tale, sponsored by Exxon/Mobil. Ellen's cast includes Bill Nye the Science Guy, Jamie Lee Curtis, and Alex Trebek. Shows start every 17 minutes. Indoor queue with uncovered, outdoor, overflow queue. Small children should be accompanied by an adult. Effects may be too intense for small children and some adults. ECV must transfer to wheelchair. Wheelchair accessible. Assistive listening. No flash photo or video lights. Allie's Kid Tip: "Dinosaurs!!! Oh, and it has a movie about energy, too. May be loud."

Film/Ride
E-Ticket
Ages 4 & up
Dark, loud, dinosaurs
Med. waits
8 min. intro 37 min. ride

☐ Wonders of Life (seasonal) [B-7]   A-ok!   7 5 7

Health and fitness take center stage at this pavilion with a thrill ride, shows, and hands-on exhibits. This pavilion and its attractions are seasonal (unfortunately, it's rarely open these days and its future is unclear).

Pavilion
D-Ticket

☐ Fitness Fairgrounds (seasonal) [B-7]   A-ok!   5 3 5

Hands-on health and fitness-oriented exhibits, including sports games, fitness tests, quizzes, and demonstrations. Good refuge from the crowds. May not always be open. Inside Wonders of Life pavilion. Wheelchair accessible.

Playground
B-Ticket
All ages

Attraction descriptions and ratings are explained on page 127.

Planning   Getting There   Staying in Style   Touring   Feasting   Making Magic   Index   Notes & More

Charting the Attractions
at Future World (East)
(continued)

Jennifer's Rating
Dave's Rating
Readers' Rating

Body Wars (seasonal) [B-7]   🚶 A-ok! | 7 | 6 | 6 |

Get "shrunk" for an incredible medical rescue mission through the human body, utilizing the same technology as airline flight simulators. You'll be strapped into your seat and experience a rough ride—without really going anywhere. Indoor queue inside The Wonders of Life. Monitors show 1-min. introduction. 40"/102 cm height restriction. Young children require supervision. Health warning. Transfer from ECV to wheelchair. Closed captioning. Motion sickness warning. Non-moving rides available for ECV-bound and motion-sensitive—ask a cast member. Allie's Kid Tip: "It's fun, but don't go on it after a big meal."	**Thrill Ride**
	D-Ticket
	Ages 6 & up
	Turbulent, bumpy, jerky
	Med. waits
	10 min. ride

Cranium Command (seasonal) [A-7]   A-ok! | 6 | 5 | 8 |

Follow the progress of an inexperienced "Cranium Commando," Captain Buzzy, as he gets inside the mind of Bobby, an adolescent boy. This is a funny, fanciful film with star appearances and Audio-Animatronic characters. This show is especially appreciated by teens and their parents. Pre-show is standing only, while theater has seats. The indoor queue is located inside The Wonders of Life. Wheelchair accessible. Assistive listening devices. Reflective captioning. Allie's Kid Tip: "It's funny. I liked the cartoon part best. It's loud in some parts."	**Show**
	D-Ticket
	Ages 3 & up
	Loud noises
	Short waits
	5 min. intro
	12 min. show

The Making Of Me (seasonal) [B-7] | 6 | 7 | 5 |

Join comedian Martin Short for a humorously touching and sensitively told film about childbirth and family life. Sex takes a backseat to romance, marriage, and family love. The "difficult" issues are deftly glossed-over. Indoor queue inside The Wonders of Life pavilion. Parental discretion advised. Wheelchair accessible. Reflective captioning. Assistive listening. Allie's Kid Tip: "Don't go. They talk too much." (As you can see, the finer points may be lost on the young.)	**Film**
	C-Ticket
	Ages 8 & up
	Touchy topic
	15 min. film

Mission:SPACE [B-6]   FP 🚶 | 4 | 9 | 8 |

Prepare for space flight at the International Space Training Center. As a civilian "astronaut," you board a four-person training centrifuge to experience the sensations of liftoff and zero gravity. Sensations are intense—you may get queasy like Jennifer. Heed the warnings and don't close your eyes or look to the side during the ride. If you'd rather not ride, you can experience the pre-show, skip the simulator and go straight to the post-show exhibits. Young kids enjoy the Space Base playground. Single-rider queue available. Indoor, themed queue. 44"/112 cm height restriction. Young kids must be with an adult. Health and motion sickness warnings. TweenTip: "It feels like you're actually taking off into space!"	**Thrill Ride**
	E-Ticket
	Ages 8 & up
	Disorienting
	FASTPASS or long waits
	7½ min. pre-show
	5 min. ride

Test Track [B-5]   FP 🚶 A-ok! | 8 | 8 | 9 |

Do you feel the need for speed? How does 65 miles per hour in a rapidly accelerating six-seat, open-air test vehicle on a tightly banked track sound? Learn how GM tests (and tortures) new vehicles and experience some of those tests. Wait in an incredibly noisy, slow queue and watch test gear whack auto parts. Get a FASTPASS early in the day, or use the "single-rider queue" on the left for the shortest wait. Front seat offers more leg room. Indoor/outdoor queue. 40"/102 cm height restriction. Young children must be accompanied by adult. Health warning. Must transfer from wheelchair to ride. Assistive listening. Closed captioning. Allie's Kid Tip: "Sit in the middle so you don't get sprayed!"	**Thrill Ride**
	E-Ticket
	Ages 7 & up
	Fast, jerky
	FASTPASS or very long waits or singles line
	3 min. intro
	5 min. ride

Charting the Attractions at Future World (West)

Jennifer's Rating — Dave's Rating — Readers' Rating

☐ Innoventions West [D-6]   5 5 6

This is the other half of Innoventions, Epcot's two-part, high-tech, hands-on trade exhibit. Tiny robot Tom Morrow 2.0 greets you at the entrance to introduce the exhibits on computing and high-speed Internet technologies, e-mail postcards, Disney's interactive games, home theater demos, and a new fire safety exhibit with an interactive game house. Some short queues. Wheelchair accessible. **Allie's KidTip:** "Boring. The games are for little kids."

Playground	
B-Ticket	
Ages 6 & up	
Noisy	
Short waits	
Unlimited	

☐ Ice Station Cool [D-6]   A-OK!   6 5 7

Hot and thirsty? Walk through a delightfully chilly ice cave and emerge into an area where you can sample free soft drinks from around the world. The entrance is a hot weather delight, and some of these Coca Cola-owned beverages are eye-openers in their own right. Self-serve machines let you sample away. You'll love some, hate others. "Beverly" will surprise you. (No telling!) Wheelchair accessible. **Allie's KidTip:** "Try the watermelon soda. It's the best!"

Walk-thru	
A-Ticket	
Ages 2 & up	
Noisy, cold, sticky floor	
Unlimited	

☐ The Living Seas [E-7]   A-OK!   6 7 6

This immersion in sea life starts with a 7 min. film. Afterward, explore hands-on exhibits and spend time marveling at the world's largest saltwater aquarium tank and artificial coral reef. View dolphins, sharks, manatees, and thousands of sea creatures. Check with a cast member for a demonstration schedule. For programs that explore the aquarium in more depth, see page 245. Nemo and friends (of "Finding Nemo" fame) are now featured. Indoor queue. Wheelchair accessible. Assistive listening. Reflective captioning. Closed captioning.

Pavilion	
D-Ticket	
All ages	
Sharks!	
Short waits	
Allow about one hour	

☐ The Land [E-6]   A-OK!   7 6 7

Agriculture and the environment take center stage, hosted by Nestlé. Rides, film, food court, and restaurant. "Behind the Seeds" guided greenhouse tour.

Pavilion	
D-Ticket	

☐ The Circle of Life [F-6]   A-OK!   6 5 6

Timon and Pumbaa from The Lion King set out to build the Hakuna Matata Village Resort—without regard to their ecosystem. Simba reminds them (and us) how important it is to protect the environment. Great photography. Indoor queue with benches. Inside The Land pavilion. Wheelchair accessible. Assistive listening. Reflective captioning. **Allie's KidTip:** "Simba tells us about the earth and how to take care of it." **TweenTip:** "It's great for everyone!"

Film	
C-Ticket	
Ages 3 & up	
Short waits	
12 min. film	

☐ Soarin' [F-6] (Opens May 2005)   FP 🧍   9 9 –

You'll be soaring over California's awesome scenery in Epcot's newest attraction, a copy of the headline ride at Disney's California Adventure theme park. Guests are strapped into oversized porch swings and rise from the floor for a simulated hang glider tour of the Golden State. An eye-filling, IMAX-quality movie screen, gentle motion, stirring music, and scented breezes combine for an exhilarating journey that we expect will end (as the original does) with fireworks over Disneyland (in honor of that park's 50th birthday). Inside The Land pavilion. 40"/102 cm height restriction. Must transfer from wheelchair to ride. Closed captioning.

Simulator	
E-Ticket	
Ages 7 & up	
Simulated heights	
FASTPASS or long waits	
5 min. ride	

Attraction descriptions and ratings are explained on page 127.

Side tabs: Planning | Getting There | Staying in Style | Touring | Feasting | Making Magic | Index | Notes & More

Charting the Attractions at Future World (West)
(continued)

Attraction		Jennifer's Rating	Dave's Rating	Readers' Rating
Living With the Land [F-6] FP A-ok!		7	6	7
Learn how modern agriculture serves the needs of a hungry world and protects the environment. Your boat cruises through a multimedia exhibit and Disney's amazing experimental hydroponic greenhouses. See veggies that may be served for dinner upstairs (more than 30 tons are produced annually). Flash photos are only allowed in the greenhouses. Indoor queues. Inside The Land pavilion. Must transfer from ECV to wheelchair to ride. Wheelchair accessible. **Allie's Kid Tip:** "They have American Alligators!" **TweenTip:** "Boring but educational."		**Boat Ride** / D-Ticket / Ages 4 & up / Dark / FASTPASS or med. waits / 13 min. ride		
Honey, I Shrunk the Audience [E-5] FP		8	8	8
Get shrunk by Dr. Wayne Szalinski (Rick Moranis) when a demonstration of his world-famous shrinking/enlarging machine goes awry. A funny story and spectacular visual and special effects make this a must-see show for those who aren't terrified by snakes, mice, and dogs. There's no need to sit up front. An indoor/outdoor queue leads to a touching and funny pre-show film sponsored by Kodak. This may be too intense for children and some adults. Wheelchair accessible. Assistive listening. Reflective captioning. **Allie's Kid Tip:** "It's scary. Take off your glasses when you get scared and just watch the TV."		**3-D Film** / E-Ticket / Ages 8 & up / Loud, intense / FASTPASS or long waits / 5 min. intro / 13 min. film		
Journey Into Imagination with Figment [E-5]		5	5	3
Figment, the cute purple dragon, comes roaring back to Epcot in a reenergized version of Journey Into Your Imagination. Figment and Dr. Nigel Channing (Eric Idle) team up to stimulate our imaginations with sight, sound, smell, a bit of whimsy, and music from Disney Legends Richard and Robert Sherman. Highlights include Figment's House and the final rendition of the theme song, One Little Spark. The ride still doesn't rate an "A," but you'll be charmed and tickled. Riders exit into the ImageWorks interactive playground. Indoor queue with outdoor overflow queue. Effects too intense for some children. Wheelchair accessible. **TweenTip:** "It's pretty lame!"		**Track Ride** / C-Ticket / Ages 5 & up / Portions are very dark, loud, with bright flashes / Med. waits / 6 min. ride		
ImageWorks: Kodak "What If" Labs [E-5] A-ok!		6	6	7
Hands-on sound and image exhibits and a gift shop, at the exit to Journey Into Your Imagination. Digital portraits (which can be sent via e-mail), inventive photo gifts, and a unique Kodak photo lab. "Backdoor" entrance through shop. **Allie's Kid Tip:** "It's cool! Check out the floor piano!"		**Playground** / B-Ticket / All ages / Allow 30 min.		

⊕ Fountain of Nations

You can't help but notice Epcot's spectacular Fountain of Nations at the heart of Future World. You may even have been cooled (or chilled) by its drifting mists. But have you really taken the time to savor this carefully choreographed water ballet? Every 15 minutes, the fountain dances to another musical number, with special seasonal music during the Christmas holidays. Thousands of water jets and lights are computer-synchronized to the rhythms and melodies. 30,000 gallons of water course through the fountain, and 2,000 gallons can be airborne at one time, shooting up to 150 feet high. While the mists are more chilling at night, the fountain's lights make the display that much more magical. Enjoy a pastry at Fountainview Café or a meal at Electric Umbrella, and catch the show!

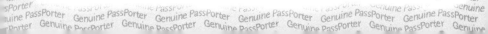

Planning | Getting There | Staying in Style | Touring | Feasting | Making Magic | Index | Notes & More

Charting the Attractions at World Showcase
(clockwise order)

Jennifer's Rating • Dave's Rating • Readers' Rating

Mexico [B-4] — A-OK! — 7 6 8

Enter Mexico's Mayan pyramid to find yourself in a magical, twilit village plaza with a volcano smoking ominously in the distance. Enjoy a fine exhibit of art and artifacts, eateries, a ride (see below), shops, and musicians. Allie's Kid Tip: "Don't worry, that's not a real volcano. Looks like it, though!"

- Pavilion
- D-Ticket
- All ages
- Low light

El Rio del Tiempo [B-4] — A-OK! — 4 4 5

Tour Mexico's past and present as your boat drifts down the "River of Time." A combination of Audio-Animatronics, music, and short film clips tell the tale of this thousands-of-years-old culture. Highlights include a skeleton-costumed band and a fiber optics fireworks display. Your boat floats past diners at the San Angel Inn restaurant. You could call this ride the Mexican version of "it's a small world," complete with dancing dolls. Not worth a long wait. Indoor queue inside the Mexico pavilion. Transfer from ECV to wheelchair to ride. Wheelchair accessible. Allie's Kid Tip: "Be sure to look up and see the fireworks!"

- Boat Ride
- C-Ticket
- All ages
- Dark, but very tame
- Short waits
- 7 minute cruise

Norway [B-3] — A-OK! — 6 6 7

This taste of Norway features a Viking ship play area, shops, the Maelstrom ride (see below), eateries, and an ancient wooden church. Tours available. Peek inside the church—it's open to the public. Allie's Kid Tip: "The ship is fun to play in. You'll feel like a Viking. If you see a troll, rub its nose for luck."

- Pavilion
- C-Ticket
- All ages
- Allow 30 min.

Maelstrom [B-3] — FP — A-OK! — 6 5 7

Board a boat for a refreshing ride through the Norway of fact and fancy. Trolls, Vikings, and a North Sea storm are all part of a fanciful ride that is much tamer than the name implies. The few "drops" are little more than a bounce. The Viking boats deposit you in an attractive indoor fishing village, prior to viewing a filmed travelogue. A new film is in production, set to debut sometime in 2005—walk right through the theater if you decide to skip the film. Indoor queue. Must transfer from wheelchair to ride. Assistive listening. Reflective captioning. Allie's Kid Tip: "Don't be scared of the life-size polar bears."

- Boat Ride
- D-Ticket
- Ages 5 & up
- Small drops and dark
- FASTPASS or med. waits
- 15 min. ride

China [B-3] — A-OK! — 4 5 6

Explore China through a film (see below), art and photography exhibits, gardens, eateries, and the Yong Feng Shangdian department store. Visit a half-scale model of Beijing's Temple of Heaven. Acrobats and gymnasts perform. Allie's Kid Tip: "When you walk into the temple to see the movie, look up."

- Pavilion
- C-Ticket
- All ages
- Allow 20 min.

Reflections of China [A-3] — 7 6 7

Experience marvels of China in a sweeping, 360° motion picture. Grand scenes of the Great Wall, the Yangtze Gorge, and Beijing's Forbidden City alternate with views of bustling cities. The film—previously called "Wonders of China"—was improved in 2003 with vibrant new footage of modern China including Macao and Hong Kong. You must stand to view. Indoor waiting area with wooden benches. Wheelchair accessible. Assistive listening devices. Reflective captioning. Allie's Kid Tip: "Don't sit down or you'll miss part of the movie."

- Film
- C-Ticket
- Ages 6 & up
- Could cause dizziness
- Short waits
- 13 min. show

Attraction descriptions and ratings are explained on page 127.

Charting the Attractions at World Showcase
(continued in clockwise order)

	Jennifer's Rating	Dave's Rating	Readers' Rating

☐ Germany [B-1]
3 4 7

Steep-roofed stone buildings, oompah bands, eateries, and shops evoke a quaint German square. Look for the model railroad, and listen for the glockenspiel that chimes on the hour. **Allie's Kid Tip:** *"Find the train set in the toy shop."*

Pavilion
C-Ticket
All ages

☐ Italy [C-1]
5 4 6

Disney captures the spirit and architecture of Venice in this Italian piazza. Eateries, shops, jugglers, music, and entertainers in a Mediterranean garden set the scene. **Allie's Kid Tip:** *"Make a good wish at King Neptune's fountain."*

Pavilion
C-Ticket
All ages

☐ The American Adventure [D-1]
6 5 7

This all-American pavilion is halfway around the lagoon from Future World. Home to the American Adventure show, theater, art gallery, a hamburger joint, wonderful singers, and shops. **Allie's Kid Tip:** *"See the fife and drum corps."*

Pavilion
D-Ticket
All ages

☐ The American Adventure Show [D-1]
7 7 7

Ben Franklin and Mark Twain take you on a patriotic tour of U.S. history. A large cast of Audio-Animatronic characters including Thomas Jefferson and Susan B. Anthony, while Martin Luther King Jr. takes center stage in filmed segments. Famous events are recreated and famous Americans share their ideas. Don't expect a critical view of history, however. The wide stage is easier to see if you don't sit in the front. See Times Guide for shows. Indoor queue. "Voices of Liberty" or "American Vybe" may sing. Wheelchair accessible. Assistive listening. Reflective captioning. **Allie's Kid Tip:** *"Look on the walls for the statues."*

Show
D-Ticket
Ages 5 & up
Dark at times
Med. Waits
15 min. intro with singers
30 min. show

☐ America Gardens Theatre (seasonal) [D-1]
6 7 6

Live, musical entertainment is the hallmark of this outdoor theater on the edge of the lagoon. Check the Times Guide for show times—usually three half-hour shows daily. Seating is free, but the front rows may be reserved for "package" guests (see page 236). Shows are visible from the promenade. Seating is on benches with sycamore trees providing some shade. Wheelchair accessible. **Allie's Kid Tip:** *"Sit in the front because it's covered and the back is just trees."*

Show
C-Ticket
Ages 2 & up
Short waits
Most shows 30 min.

☐ Japan [D-1]
A-Ok! **8 7 7**

The sound of Taiko drummers may draw you to this pavilion, featuring traditional Japanese architecture and gardens, entertaining exhibits, eateries, a lounge, and a Japanese department store. A beautiful and peaceful retreat. **Allie's Kid Tip:** *"Go through the Japanese garden. The goldfish are neat."*

Pavilion
C-Ticket
All ages
Allow 20 min.

☐ Morocco [E-1]
A-Ok! **7 6 7**

Morocco's Moorish architecture, art exhibits, exotic cuisine, live entertainers, and crafts beckon to the adventuresome traveler. Much is hidden from the casual visitor—take the "Treasures of Morocco" tour for a better look. You'll find a character meet-and-greet area virtually hidden across from Restaurant Marrakesh, plus artisans and cultural representatives scattered throughout. Excellent shopping opportunities. **Allie's Kid Tip:** *"You'll feel like you want to go to Africa. I like the entertainers here, too."*

Pavilion
C-Ticket
All ages
No scares
Allow about 20-30 min. to explore

Charting the Attractions at World Showcase
(continued in clockwise order)

	Jennifer's Rating	Dave's Rating	Readers' Rating

France [F-2]	A-OK!	7	7	7

The Eiffel Tower, cobblestone streets, eateries, shops, street performers, and a widescreen film (see below) combine to evoke the essence of France. **Allie's Kid Tip:** "The moving statue is cool, but it moved to Italy!"	**Pavilion** D-Ticket All ages

Impressions de France [F-2]	A-OK!	9	9	7

The beauty and romance of France's villages, cities, and countryside come to life in a breathtaking film. Fabulous scenery, wonderful 200° widescreen photography, and the best musical soundtrack at Walt Disney World (great French classical tunes), make this one of our favorites. Cool, dark theater offers seating and welcome relief. Shows on the hour and half-hour. Wrought-iron benches and small exhibits make even the indoor, air-conditioned queue enjoyable. Wheelchair accessible. Assistive listening. Reflective captioning. **Allie's Kid Tip:** "You get to see Notre Dame, like in 'Hunchback of Notre Dame.'"	**Film** D-Ticket Ages 5 & up Dark theater, loud music Short waits 18 min. film

United Kingdom [E-3]	A-OK!	7	6	7

This is Florida's British Colony, full of quaint shops, gardens, a restful park with live entertainment (check the Times Guide for The British Invasion band—they're excellent!), a busy pub, and deliciously British eateries. Well-themed. **Allie's Kid Tip:** "You gotta play in the hedge maze! And there's really cool music."	**Pavilion** C-Ticket All ages will enjoy

Canada [E-4]		5	5	7

The architecture and natural beauty of Canada are captured in a 360° movie (see below), nifty waterfall, gardens, shops, eateries, and live music.	**Pavilion** C-Ticket

O Canada! [E-4]	A-OK!	7	5	6

Experience the natural and manmade wonders of Canada by way of a Circle-Vision 360 film. Swooping aerials and dramatic scenery highlight this tour encompassing the Rockies and old-world Montreal. Shows start every 20 minutes. Stand to view. Indoor queue. Wheelchair accessible. Assistive listening. Reflective captioning. **Allie's Kid Tip:** "The animals are cute! But you can get tired of standing up for 18 minutes."	**Film** C-Ticket Ages 5 & up Dark, a little dizzying 18 min. film

Attraction descriptions and ratings are explained on page 127.

Epcot's Newest Art Gallery

As if Epcot wasn't already overflowing with cultural riches, the American Adventure pavilion is now home to the new American Heritage Art Gallery. The gallery's first exhibit, Echos of Africa, displays about 10–15 works from the Walt Disney-Tischman African Art Collection, reputed to be one of the finest collections of its kind in private hands. Other items from this collection are on display at Paris' Louvre, Washington D.C.'s Smithsonian, and the Museum for African Art in New York. These historic African works are contrasted with works by about a dozen contemporary artists. Other stops on the World Showcase's "Museum Circle" are the galleries in Mexico, China, Norway, Japan, and Morocco.

Planning
Getting There
Staying in Style
Touring
Feasting
Making Magic
Index
Notes & More

Making the Most of IllumiNations

IllumiNations: Reflections of Earth brings every night to a spectacular close. Brilliant fireworks and a rousing, original musical score fill Epcot's World Showcase Lagoon every evening at park closing, heralding the creation of Earth. A shower of sparkling comets paves the way, a huge globe glides across the lagoon to take center stage, and a pageant of breathtaking scenery, wildlife, and the peoples of the earth plays across a giant video display covering the continents of the globe. Lasers, blazing torches, and more fireworks tumble forth as the music builds to a rousing climax. Although the show is visible anywhere around the lagoon, there are definitely **better viewing sites**. You can judge a viewing site well in advance of the show as you stroll around the lagoon, or check our map on page 140. A clear view of the water (watch those tree limbs) at the center of the lagoon is critical, as is a clear view of the sky. It also helps if the wind is to your back or side (to avoid fireworks smoke). The bridge between France and the United Kingdom is a prime (and popular) location. Italy and Norway are other good viewing spots. Or try for a 7:30 pm priority seating at the Rose & Crown. Check-in at the podium early and request a patio table. You may get lucky with a great view. If not, enjoy your meal anyway—diners are invited outside to stand and enjoy the show. Another place to stay seated is at Cantina de San Angel in Mexico. Arrive at least 90 min. early for a lagoon-side table. We also highly recommend the excellent views from the lagoon-side patios in the United Kingdom and France, if they aren't already occupied by private parties.

© MediaMarx, Inc.

The World Showcase Lagoon at dusk

Ever-Changing Epcot

As with Walt Disney's original concept for EPCOT, the Epcot theme park continues to evolve, and we'll see more changes before the park's 25th anniversary in 2007. When Soarin' opens, Future World will have three big-ticket, long-queue attractions, where recently there was just one. Riders have to arrive early and work their FASTPASSes carefully to avoid very long waits. The Land pavilion may get an interior makeover before Soarin' opens, the time-worn film at China has been replaced, Norway's film is being remade (no release date yet), and Canada's film is also due for a remake. Alas, with these gains we have some losses. The Wonders of Life pavilion is only open during busy seasons and Spaceship Earth's Global Neighborhood is a ghost town, awaiting a new sponsor and name for the pavilion. Let's hope these, too, will be refreshed before too long.

Disney-MGM Studios

Disney-MGM Studios is the Hollywood that never was. Yet it always will be, on 154 acres that spotlight the golden era of the glamorous silver screen. Disney-MGM Studios is located southwest of Epcot and is connected to Epcot by Friendship boats and walkways.

Tinseltown never looked so good. All the glamour, glitz, and pageantry of Hollywood come out to greet you at the Disney-MGM Studios. Disney's rendition of Hollywood Boulevard is done up in 1930s art deco architecture, and an old-fashioned water tower (complete with Mickey ears) sets the stage. And you can't miss the 122-foot-tall version of **Mickey's Sorcerer's Hat**, representing the magic of show business and Disney animation. Disney-MGM Studios gives you a behind-the-scenes glimpse at movie-making as well as an opportunity to get involved in shows and tours. Celebrities may put in live appearances at Disney-MGM Studios as well, complete with a procession down Hollywood Boulevard and a handprint ceremony. There may also be chances to see upcoming movies being filmed on the actual soundstages that make their home here. The whole effect is of being a special guest at a major movie studio in the heart of Hollywood.

Unlike other parks, Disney-MGM Studios' layout is free-form, much like Hollywood's artistic personalities (see park map on page 154). See page 153 for an attractions-at-a-glance list, page 154 for daily touring itineraries, and pages 156–160 for attraction details.

Hollywood Boulevard Area *Headline Attraction:*	Stroll among the stars—this is the "main street" of Tinseltown in its heyday. *The Great Movie Ride*
Sunset Boulevard Area *Headline Attractions:*	Step back in time to the Hollywood that never was on this famous, palm-lined boulevard. *Rock 'n' Roller Coaster, Tower of Terror, Beauty and the Beast*
Echo Lake Area *Headline Attractions:*	Learn the magic behind spectacular stunts and effects, and go for a journey into outer space. *Star Tours and Indiana Jones Epic Stunt Spectacular*
Streets of America Area *Headline Attractions:*	Visit a movie set evoking famous urban skylines. It even has "towering" skyscrapers! *Muppet*Vision 3-D; Lights, Motors, Action! Extreme Stunt Show*
Mickey Avenue Area *Headline Attractions:*	Peek behind the scenes in soundstages, the "backlot," and animators' studios. *Millionaire, Voyage of the Little Mermaid, One Man's Dream*

Side tabs: Planning · Getting There · Staying in Style · Touring · Feasting · Making Magic · Index · Notes & More

AMBIENCE

PARK LAYOUT AND HIGHLIGHTS

Don't miss the fold-out map in the back of the book!

Entertainment and Shopping at Disney-MGM Studios

ENTERTAINMENT

Entertainment is simply a matter of course at the Disney-MGM Studios. The funny, unique **"streetmosphere"** performers make their home along famous boulevards of Hollywood and Sunset, as well as Echo Lake. Dressed in 1940s-style garb, they're responsible for all sorts of on-the-street shenanigans. Keep your eyes open—you don't know when they may appear. The **"Disney Stars and Motor Cars"** parade is held each afternoon, showcasing more than 60 Disney characters. The parade route is marked on

Dave and Allie play air guitar at Rock 'n' Roller Coaster

© MediaMarx, Inc.

the map on page 291. Be sure to stake out your viewing spot along the parade route about 30 min. in advance. Come evening, it's Mickey versus villains in **Fantasmic!** at the Hollywood Hills Amphitheater. Fantasmic! is a spectacular mix of live action, music, and fireworks. The huge outdoor amphitheater seats 6,900 at this nightly show. Fantasmic! may be held more often during busy seasons (later shows may have shorter waits and better seating). Fantasmic! is popular with many guests, though we can take it or leave it. A Fantasmic! Meal Package may be available with special seating—see page 217.

SHOPPING

General merchandise shopping is centered near the park entrance on Hollywood and Sunset Boulevards. Nearly every major ride and attraction has its own **themed shop**, too. All of the ride-related shops can be entered without going on the ride. Here are our favorite shops:

Shop	Location	What makes it special
Crossroads of the World	Hollywood Blvd.	Guidemaps, Times Guides, ponchos
Sid Cahuenga's	Hollywood Blvd.	One-of-a-kind movie memorabilia
Celebrity 5 & 10	Hollywood Blvd.	Custom embroidery and engraving
Keystone Clothiers	Hollywood Blvd.	Quality Disney clothes
Villains in Vogue	Sunset Blvd.	Disney Villain clothing and gifts
Animation Gallery	Mickey Avenue	Collectibles and animation cels
Stage One Company Store	Streets of America	Quirky shop with Muppets!
Writer's Stop	Streets of America	Books! (We can't resist 'em!)
Tatooine Traders	Echo Lake	Star Wars items, fun theme

Disney-MGM Studios Attractions At-A-Glance

Attraction	Type	Allow	Page
☐ Beauty and the Beast [G-4]	Live Show	40–55+	160-HS
☐ The Great Movie Ride [D-3]	Film/Ride	25–45+	160-HS
☐ Indiana Jones Epic Stunt [D-5]	Live Show	40–50+	157-EL
☐ Honey, I Shrunk the Kids [B-3] Movie Set Adventure	Playground	20–30+	158-SA
☐ Lights, Motors, Action! Extreme Stunt Show [A-3]	Live Show	45–60+	158-SA
☐ Magic of Disney Animation [F-3]	Walkthru	40-60+	159-MA
☐ The Making Of... [D-2]	Walkthru	35-55+	159-MA
☐ Muppet*Vision 3-D [B-4]	3-D Film	30–40+	158-SA
☐ One Man's Dream [D-2]	Walkthru	30–40+	159-MA
☐ Playhouse Disney [E-3]	Live Show	20–30+	159-MA
☐ Rock 'n' Roller Coaster [G-3]	Coaster	20–45+	160-HS
☐ Sounds Dangerous [C-4]	Film	15–25+	157-EL
☐ Star Tours [B-5]	Thrill Ride	20–40+	157-EL
☐ Streets of America Set [B-4]	Walkthru	20–30+	158-SA
☐ Studios Backlot Tour [B-2]	Tram Ride	30–40+	159-MA
☐ Toy Story Pizza Planet [B-5]	Arcade	15–20+	158-SA
☐ Twilight Zone Tower of Terror [H-4]	Thrill Ride	25–60+	160-HS
☐ Voyage of the Little Mermaid [E-2]	Live Show	25–40+	159-MA
☐ Who Wants To Be A Millionaire [D-2]	Live Show	45–60+	159-MA

The Allow column gives the amount of time (in minutes) you should allow for an attraction, assuming you do not have a FASTPASS and there are no ride breakdowns. The letters after the page numbers stand for the first one or two letters of the land in which that attraction is located: EL = Echo Lake, SA = Streets of America, MA = Mickey Avenue, and HS = Hollywood/Sunset Blvds.

Finding the Stars at Disney-MGM Studios

Disney-MGM Studios is the perfect star-gazing spot. The chart below shows typical locations of popular Disney characters.

Star(s)	Location(s)
☐ Mickey & Minnie Mouse	Mickey Avenue or Animation Courtyard
☐ Goofy	Goofy's Prop Stop (Streets of America)
☐ Pooh, Tigger, and friends	Mickey Avenue
☐ Cruella, Mulan, Aladdin	Hollywood Blvd.
☐ Toy Story characters	Al's Toy Barn
☐ Lilo & Stitch characters	Animation Courtyard or Hollywood Blvd.
☐ JoJo and Goliath	Mickey Avenue
☐ Various characters	Outside park entrance near opening time

Note: Greeting locations and characters vary (check your guidemap), but Mickey Avenue, Hollywood Boulevard near the Chinese Theater, Animation Courtyard, and Al's Toy Barn are the likely locations.

DISNEY-MGM STUDIOS ATTRACTION CHART

Planning · Getting There · Staying in Style · Touring · Feasting · Making Magic · Index · Notes & More

Our Favorite Touring Plans for Disney-MGM Studios

NOTES

While Disney-MGM Studios has fewer attractions than Magic Kingdom and Epcot, it's harder to see everything you want to visit due to show times and lengths. It is important to check your Times Guide or the Tip Board (on the corner of Hollywood and Sunset Boulevards) and note showtimes. We recommend you jot down these showtimes on this page once you know them—you'll find a fill-in-the-blank line for those attractions/events with specific showtimes. The plans work best if you go in the same order, but you should feel free to skip an attraction or two (and return to it later) if it makes sense for you. You should be able to accomplish either of these plans in one day if you start by 9:00 am. Those with infants and toddlers, or thrill-shy adults, may prefer to skip all attractions with asterisks.

ITINERARIES

Touring With Adults
Enter Sunset Boulevard
Visit Rock 'n' Roller Coaster*
Visit Tower of Terror*
Enter Echo Lake Area
Get FASTPASS for Star Tours
Enter Streets of America Area
Visit Lights, Motors, Action! @ _____
Visit Muppet*Vision 3-D
Enter Echo Lake Area
Visit Star Tours*
Visit Indiana Jones @ _____
Eat lunch at Studio Catering, Sci-Fi Dine-In, Backlot Express, 50's Prime Time, or Hollywood & Vine (about 3 hours after you enter the park)
Enter Streets of America Area
Visit Streets of America Set
Enter Mickey Avenue Area
Get FASTPASS for Voyage of the Little Mermaid @ _____
Visit One Man's Dream or Magic of Disney Animation
Visit Voyage of the Little Mermaid or watch Disney's Star and Motor Cars Parade @ _____
Visit Who Wants to be a Millionaire—Play It! @ _____
Eat dinner at Hollywood Brown Derby, Hollywood & Vine, 50's Prime Time, or Catalina Eddie's (about 7 1/2 hours after you enter the park)
Watch Fantasmic! @ _____
(Tour duration: About 10 hours)

Touring With Kids
Enter Echo Lake Area
Visit Star Tours*
Get FASTPASS for Indiana Jones
Enter Streets of America Area
Visit Lights, Motors, Action! @ _____
Visit Muppet*Vision 3-D
Enter Echo Lake Area
Visit Indiana Jones Epic Stunt Spectacular @ _____
Enter Mickey Avenue Area
Visit Playhouse Disney @ _____
Eat lunch at Hollywood & Vine, 50's Prime Time, ABC Commissary, or Backlot Exp.
Visit Studios Backlot Tour (about 3 1/2 hours after you enter the park)
Enter Streets of America Area
Visit Honey, I Shrunk the Kids Movie Set Adventure
Visit Al's Toy Barn Character Greeting
Enter Echo Lake Area
Watch Disney's Stars and Motor Cars Parade @ _____ and have a snack
Enter Mickey Avenue
Get FASTPASS for Voyage of the Little Mermaid
Enter Hollywood Boulevard Area
Visit Great Movie Ride
Enter Mickey Avenue
Visit Voyage of the Little Mermaid @ _____
Eat dinner at Hollywood & Vine, 50's Prime Time, or Catalina Eddie's (about 7 1/2 hours after you enter the park)
Watch Fantasmic! @ _____
(Tour duration: About 10 hours)

Making the Most of Disney-MGM Studios

If you're interested in the **live shows**, check the Times Guide for showtimes and plan accordingly to avoid long waits or mad dashes.

Autograph seekers, be prepared! Characters come out for meet-and-greets throughout the park. See page 153b for a "star" chart, and see page 246 for autograph tips.

Look for the **well** near Indiana Jones Epic Stunt Spectacular (when you're facing the attraction entrance, it's located to the left). Just don't pull the rope. (You've been warned!)

Many of the shows involve **audience participation**. If you like this sort of thing, volunteer enthusiastically for the fun!

If you love **Walt Disney and his legacy of animation**, plan to immediately follow your visit to Walt Disney: One Man's Dream (pages 157 and 159) with The Magic of Disney Animation (page 159). The two attractions complement one another very well.

Seniors won't want to rush through Disney-MGM Studios—make enough time to slow down and enjoy the ambience of the park.

Disney-MGM Studios has several **unique restaurants** and cafes, and many participate in a Fantasmic! Meal Package. See pages 215–217 for dining and package details.

Disney-MGM Studios is a **working production studio**—portions of the park may be closed occasionally. Check with Guest Relations, or call 407-939-4636 for details on any closings, studio audience opportunities, or special event packages. Television programs like Live with Regis and Kelly sometimes tape or broadcast live from the park. Passes for the shows are sometimes offered at one of the tickets booths outside the gates.

The focus at this park is on **independent shows and rides** rather than on a never-ending stream of entertainment. Be prepared for walking and waiting. Your reward is longer, lovingly produced shows, more intense rides, and fascinating backstage glimpses.

The pavement in front of Grauman's Chinese Theater (The Great Movie Ride) is full of **celebrity footprints** and handprints.

Planning

Getting There

Staying in Style

Touring

Feasting

Making Magic

Index

Notes & More

Getting to
Disney-MGM Studios

BEST TIMES TO GO

Disney-MGM Studios can be enjoyed in one day, although it is best to **visit the most popular attractions earlier** to avoid long lines. Arrive before the scheduled opening time for the best advantage. The most popular attractions—Rock 'n' Roller Coaster and The Twilight Zone Tower of Terror—generate very long lines. Make a beeline for these rides first thing, unless you've just eaten breakfast. Several of the shows have **limited seating capacity** (such as Voyage of the Little Mermaid) and can require a lengthy wait if busy. Whenever possible, get a FASTPASS! Check the entertainment schedule in the park Times Guide for show times. Take the length of show times into account when planning your route and keep in mind that several shows take a considerable amount of time. Many attractions and restaurants empty immediately before and during the parade, affording shorter lines or the chance to get a table without priority seating arrangements.

GETTING THERE

By Boat—From Epcot's International Gateway, BoardWalk Inn & Villas, Yacht & Beach Club & Villas, and Swan & Dolphin, take the boat.
By Bus—Take a direct bus from all resorts (other than those mentioned above), Epcot's main entrance, and Disney's Animal Kingdom. From the Magic Kingdom, catch a bus at the Transportation and Ticket Center (TTC). From Downtown Disney, Typhoon Lagoon, or Blizzard Beach, take a bus or boat to a resort and transfer to a Disney-MGM Studios bus.
By Car—Take I-4 to exit 67 (westbound) or exit 62 (eastbound) and continue on to Disney-MGM Studios parking. All-day parking is available for $8 (free to resort guests and annual passholders).
By Foot—You can walk from the BoardWalk, Swan & Dolphin, and Yacht & Beach Club, and even Epcot's International Gateway. Follow the marked pathways along the canal beside the BoardWalk Villas (see resort map on page 46 for path location).

Ratings are explained on page 120.

RATINGS

Our Value Ratings:		Our Magic Ratings:		Readers' Ratings:
Quality:	8/10	Theme:	8/10	64% fell in love with it
Variety:	7/10	Excitement:	9/10	33% liked it well enough
Scope:	6/10	Fun Factor:	7/10	2% had mixed feelings
Overall Value:	**7/10**	**Overall Magic:**	**8/10**	1% were disappointed

Disney-MGM Studios is enjoyed by... (rated by both authors and readers)		
Younger Kids: ♥♥♥♥	Young Adults: ♥♥♥♥♥	Families: ♥♥♥♥♥
Older Kids: ♥♥♥♥	Mid Adults: ♥♥♥♥♥	Couples: ♥♥♥♥♥
Teenagers: ♥♥♥♥♥	Mature Adults: ♥♥♥♥	Singles: ♥♥♥♥

Looking for The Great Movie Ride on Hollywood Boulevard? See page 160.

Charting the Attractions
in the Echo Lake Area

Jennifer's Rating   *Dave's Rating*   *Readers' Rating*

■ **Indiana Jones Epic Stunt Spectacular** [D-5] FP A-ok!	7 6 8	
The Indiana Jones films set the stage for an action show of epic proportions. Disney has built a huge indoor/outdoor set to demonstrate the stuntperson's craft, including the famous rolling boulder, an Egyptian marketplace, and a flaming German airplane. Adults may be picked to join the show—arrive early and show enthusiasm if this interests you. Theater opens 25 minutes before the show and guests sit in a covered, outdoor theater. Loud explosions and hot flames may scare young children. Wheelchair accessible. Assistive listening. **Allie's KidTip** and **TweenTip:** "This is a good show, but it is loud. Cover your ears."	**Live Show** E-Ticket Ages 4 & up Loud, fire, violence FASTPASS or med. waits 30 min. show	

■ **Sounds Dangerous** [C-4]	4 6 6	
Yes, it sounds dangerous, but you'll emerge totally unscathed from this entertaining sound effects demonstration hosted by comedian Drew Carey. Drew cooks up a detective mystery to demonstrate the art of sound effects. There's no audience participation—just sit back, put on the headphones, and enjoy the show. When you exit, be sure to try the SoundWorks hands-on exhibits—the Sound Station booths are a fine place to relax and cool off. You can enter via the SoundWorks back door if you'd rather skip the show. Outdoor queue is covered. Wheelchair accessible. Assistive listening. **Allie's KidTip:** "If you don't like it, take off the headphones. I didn't like it at all. It was too loud."	**Film** C-Ticket Ages 7 & up Total darkness and very loud noises Short waits 12 min. film	

■ **Star Tours** [B-5] FP ☆I A-ok!	8 8 8	
Take a flight to a galaxy far, far away in this "must ride" for all Star Wars fans. Although the flight simulator at the heart of this ride never really goes anywhere, you'll find it hard to believe as your StarSpeeder dives, banks, and speeds towards the Moon of Endor with a rookie pilot at the helm. But that doesn't mean the ride isn't rough. The roughest seats are in the back row, as we learned from riding it 27 times in a row. Indoor queue offers many visual delights, including R2D2 and C-3PO. Overflow queue outdoors is uncovered. 40"/102 cm height restriction. Young children should be accompanied by an adult. Health warning. Must transfer from ECV to wheelchair. Must transfer from wheelchair to ride. Closed captioning. Non-moving rides available for ECV-bound and motion-sensitive—ask a cast member. **Allie's KidTip:** "This is good, but hold on tight!" **TweenTip:** "The back seats really are the best."	**Thrill Ride** E-Ticket Far out fun Rough, rocky, may cause motion sickness FASTPASS or long waits 3 min. intro 5 min. flight	

Attraction descriptions and ratings are explained on page 127.

❾ Walt Disney: One Man's Dream

Explore the Man behind the 100 Years of Magic Celebration. The celebration ended in 2003, but the attraction continues indefinitely. Located on Mickey Avenue, this exhibit illustrates Walt's impact on his company and the world. Follow Walt's imaginings as they grow from notions to full-fledged reality, and learn how his boyhood experiences affected his life-long accomplishments. Hundreds of priceless and never-before-seen artifacts are on display, including Walt's entire California office and the "Project-X" (Walt Disney World) planning room. After the exhibits, settle in for a showing of "One Man's Dream," an inspirational film. Plan several visits. Photographs are now allowed.

Charting the Attractions in the Streets of America Area

Jennifer's Rating • *Dave's Rating* • *Readers' Rating*

Honey, I Shrunk the Kids Movie Set Adventure [B-3] — A-OK! | 6 | 5 | 6

Kids climb, cavort, and caper amidst huge plants, insects, and spider webs in this playground based on the popular movies and TV program. Keep cool with various water sprays (it does get very hot here) and crawl through a big Play-Doh can. Kids must be at least 4 years old to play, and adults must be accompanied by a child to enter. Wheelchair accessible. Note: Closed in September 2004 until further notice. Allie's Kid Tip: "Try to get wet by the giant Super Soaker!"

Playground
B-Ticket
All ages
Giant bugs, water
Short waits

Jim Henson's Muppet*Vision 3-D [B-4] — A-OK! | 7 | 7 | 9

Your 3-D glasses get a real workout as Kermit and his pals show you around the Muppet Labs. The Muppets are at their zany, pun-filled best in a frenetic good time that was Jim Henson's last production. The multi-screen videos and hilarious props shown in the pre-show area deserve your full attention. The theater is very large and air-conditioned, complete with comfy seats. There's no need to sit in front to get a good view. Some effects may be too scary for young children. Outdoor queue is mostly covered. Wheelchair accessible. Assistive listening. Closed captioning. Reflective captioning. Allie's Kid Tip: "It's better to keep your 3-D glasses on for this one. Don't be afraid."

3-D Film
E-Ticket
Ages 4 & up
Intense, loud, some violence
Med. waits
15 min. intro 17 min. film

Lights, Motors, Action! Extreme Stunt Show [A-2] (Opens May 2005) | — | — | —

Fresh from Disneyland Paris, prepare to be wowed by an epic display of the stuntperson's art. Cars, motorcycles, and jet skis roar across the set while a giant video screen shows how the special effects action is turned into movie magic. A 5,000-seat amphitheater is ready to pack in the audiences.

Show
E-Ticket
Ages 3 & up
Loud!

Streets of America Movie Set [B-4] | 6 | 6 | 6

Whether or not you've been to the big city, you'll enjoy the movie set-style renditions of New York, San Francisco, and Chicago, among other cities. The buildings are all facades, of course, but the detail is rich. You'll find familiar bits of Chinatown and a London street, too. Disney characters may appear on the Plaza Hotel-like steps for photos and autographs. The street set was updated with new facades in 2003 and 2004. Wheelchair accessible.

Walk-thru
A-Ticket
All ages
No scares
Few waits
Unlimited

Toy Story Pizza Planet Arcade [B-5] — A-OK! | 2 | 3 | 6

This is a spacious, pleasantly themed arcade adjacent to the Pizza Planet cafe with a typical selection of video games and try-to-hoist-a-toy games. There's a depressing lack of Toy Story-themed arcade games, however. Tokens are needed to play. Most games require 2 to 4 tokens, and the tokens are 25 cents each. Not very magical. Wheelchair accessible. Allie's Kid Tip: "Fun games."

Arcade
A-Ticket
Ages 5 & up
No scares
Few waits

Osborne Family Spectacle of Lights

Jennings Osborne's Christmas lights were too much for his Arkansas neighbors, so Disney invited him to the studio backlot, where his lights became a Thanksgiving through New Year's tradition. The lights went dark in 2003 to make room for the Stunt Show Spectacular, but the Osborne spirit cannot be dimmed! The five million lights returned in 2004 and moved to the city, gracing the Streets of America Set, hopefully for many holiday seasons to come.

Charting the Attractions in the Mickey Avenue Area

Jennifer's Rating
Dave's Rating
Readers' Rating

The Making Of... (seasonal) [D-2]	**5** **6** **6**
Tour the set of a recent Disney movie, view a making-of film, and/or see costumes. Attraction changes/closes often. Outdoor queue. Wheelchair accessible.	**Walk-thru** / B-Ticket

The Magic of Disney Animation [F-2] A-OK!	**6** **7** **8**
Animation fans enjoy this renovated tour, now similar to the popular version in California. The "Drawn to Animation Theater" features Mulan's Mushu (Eddie Murphy) and a live animator. The studio tour (the animation studios closed in 2004) is replaced by hands-on exhibits. "Animation Academy" has 38 easels where an animator teaches you to draw favorite characters. Allie'skidTip: "The part with Mushu is funny!" TweenTip: "It sounds boring, but it's fun inside."	**Walk-thru** / D-Ticket / Ages 4 & up / No scares / Med. waits / Allow 45 min.

Walt Disney: One Man's Dream [D-2]	**8** **8** **8**
This attraction opened in 2001 to celebrate Walt Disney's imagination and creativity and ties in well with Disneyland's 50th anniversary celebration. See page 157 for more details.	**Walk-thru** / D-Ticket / Ages 10 & up

Playhouse Disney–Live on Stage! [E-3] A-OK!	**7** **6** **8**
Preschoolers love Bear (and his Big Blue House) and friends like Rolie Polie Olie, Stanley, and The Book of Pooh. A cast of costumed characters and puppets gives a live version of Disney Channel favorites. Seating is on a carpeted floor. Outdoor, covered queue. Wheelchair access. Allie'skidTip: "Get a lot of space to dance."	**Live Show** / C-Ticket / All ages / 20 min. show

Studios Backlot Tour [B-2] A-OK!	**6** **6** **7**
This is the park's backstage movie magic blockbuster. See how sea battles and storms are stirred up, tour Disney's backlot, and brave Catastrophe Canyon, a special effects tour de force. Stand in long lines not once, but twice. Outdoor queue is covered. Wheelchair accessible. Closed captioning. 6 min. intro. Allie'skidTip: "Sit on the left side to get wet!" TweenTip: "At the end you can view movie costumes." (Backdoor entry to costume exhibit via The Prop Shop.)	**Tram Ride** / D-Ticket / Ages 6 & up / Fires, floods / Long waits / 17 min. ride

Voyage of the Little Mermaid [E-2] FP A-OK!	**8** **7** **8**
Your little mermaid will flip, and so will you! Enjoy all your favorite tunes while live action, puppets, falling water, and amazing laser effects bring Ariel and her friends to life onstage, making you feel as if you're truly under the sea! Cool theater offers comfy seats. Middle rows are best for view of stage and special effects. Stand to right during 5-min. pre-show for up-front seating. No flash photos or video lights. Outdoor queue is covered. Wheelchair accessible. Assistive listening. Reflective captioning. Allie'skidTip: "I love this! Look up!"	**Live Show** / E-Ticket / Ages 3 & up / Dark, strobe / FASTPASS or long waits / 17 min. show

Who Wants To Be A Millionaire–Play It! [D-2] A-OK!	**10** **9** **9**
Join 599 fellow guests and buzz in for a chance to sit in the hot seat to rack up points and prizes (sorry, no cash). Everyone plays along and gets scored, too. We've both made it to the hot seat, and in 2002, Dave hit one million points and won the grand prize of a three-night Disney cruise and leather jacket! Play in a replica of the famous TV studio with real, live hosts. (FASTPASS removed in 2004.) Wheelchair accessible. Assistive listening. Allie'skidTip: "Look for your seat number on the (top ten) screen!" TweenTip: "I got on the screen twice."	**Live Show** / D-Ticket / Ages 7 & up / Exciting! / Medium waits / 30 min. show

(Side tabs: Planning, Getting There, Staying in Style, Touring, Feasting, Making Magic, Index, Notes & More)

Charting the Attractions in the Hollywood and Sunset Boulevard Areas

<table>
<tr><th></th><th>Jennifer's Rating</th><th>Dave's Rating</th><th>Readers' Rating</th></tr>
</table>

☐ Beauty and the Beast–Live On Stage [G-4]   A-ok! | 6 | 7 | 8 |

Be Disney's guest! See Belle, Beast, Lumiere, Mrs. Potts, Chip, and that other beast, Gaston, live and on stage. An enthusiastic cast sings and dances its way through musical numbers from the animated film. The original story line all but disappears, but you'll hardly mind, thanks to the good performances, eye-filling costumes, and fine staging. Lines are long, but the theater opens 25 minutes prior to show. Live, pre-show entertainment. Note that doves are no longer released at the conclusion of the show. Outdoor queue is uncovered. Wheelchair accessible. Assistive listening. Allie's Kid Tip: "Skips some parts."

| Live Show |
| E-Ticket |
| Ages 5 & up |
| Loud sound effects |
| Med. waits |
| 10 min. intro 25 min. show |

☐ The Great Movie Ride [D-3]   A-ok! | 6 | 6 | 8 |

Hollywood's famed Grauman's Chinese Theater sets the stage for a sedate ride through famous scenes from classic movies enacted by Audio-Animatronics characters. Some live-action excitement and two short films add a bit of Hollywood pizzazz. Long lines snake through a props and costumes exhibit. (Yes, that is a carousel horse from "Mary Poppins.") Following the pre-show film, the queue separates—each line gets a slightly different version of one scene. Indoor queue with overflow queue outdoors. Effects may be too intense for small children. Transfer from ECV to wheelchair. Wheelchair accessible. Allie's Kid Tip: "Snakes!"

| Film/Ride |
| D-Ticket |
| Ages 4 & up |
| Loud noises, scary scenes |
| Long waits |
| 3 min. intro 18 min. ride |

☐ Rock 'n' Roller Coaster [G-3]   FP 🚶 | 8 | 10 | 9 |

Experience Disney's first high-speed coaster launch. Hurtle through twists, 4-5G turns, and three inversions (yes, upside down)—in the dark! Rock band Aerosmith invites you to take a limo crosstown and join them backstage. Aerosmith also provides the soundtrack for your ride—five different tunes are possible depending upon which "limo" you get. Upon boarding, we recommend you press your head against the headrest to prepare for the very fast start (0-58 in 2.8 seconds). Beyond that, this may be the smoothest coaster you ever ride—even the coaster-shy have enjoyed it. Fascinating indoor queue area takes you through a recording studio's display of historic memorabilia. Take the "chicken exit" if you just want to enjoy the queue. 48"/122 cm height restriction. Transfer from ECV to wheelchair, and then transfer from wheelchair to ride. Allie's Kid Tip: "You won't believe how fast it goes! Make sure your stuff is safe and sound." Tween Tip: "The loops are my favorite. It isn't scary at all!"

| Coaster |
| E-Ticket |
| Ages 8 & up |
| Very fast, very dark, can cause motion sickness, headaches |
| FASTPASS or long waits |
| 2 min. intro 3 min. ride |

☐ The Twilight Zone Tower of Terror [H-4]   FP 🚶 | 3 | 9 | 9 |

Delight in the delicious spookiness of this haunted hotel, long before you ride its legendary "down and up and down and up again" elevator. The gut-wrenching drops are matched by wonderful visual effects. The queue splits in the basement—go left, it's typically shorter. To enjoy just the fabulous queue and pre-show, take the "chicken exit" before you board the elevator (ask a cast member). The "Tower IV" upgrade in 2003 added random drops and replaced the lap bars with lap seatbelts. Outdoor queue is mostly shaded. 40"/102 cm height restriction. Health warning. Young children should be accompanied by an adult. Transfer from wheelchair to ride. Closed captioning. Allie's Kid Tip: "I like the up and down part, but the rest is scary. I won't go again until I'm older." Tween Tip: "There are new handles to hold beside the seats if you're scared. (But I'm not scared anymore!)"

| Thrill Ride |
| E-Ticket |
| Ages 8 & up |
| Dark, scary, sudden drops |
| FASTPASS or long waits |
| 10 min. intro 4 min. ride |

Attraction descriptions and ratings are explained on page 127.

Disney's Animal Kingdom

Disney's Animal Kingdom is the newest and largest park (500 acres) at the Walt Disney World Resort. Part zoological park and part theme park, Disney's Animal Kingdom charms, delights, and thrills guests with a uniquely Disney look at the wild world. Disney's Animal Kingdom is located the farthest west of all the parks on the Walt Disney World property.

The Tree of Life towers above Disney's Animal Kingdom, reminding us of the wonder, glory, and fragility of nature's creations. This is the quietest of the parks out of respect to the animals who make their home here, but "quiet" doesn't mean "boring." Adventure awaits, as discoveries lurk around every bend. Like Epcot, Disney's Animal Kingdom is a place to explore with open eyes and eager minds. Lace up your boots, grab your safari hat, and load your camera—the adventure is about to begin!

To set the tone for the day, all guests pass through **The Oasis**, a lush jungle teeming with exotic wildlife, sparkling waters, and rocky crags. Then, standing on Discovery Island at the center of the park, the **Tree of Life** binds the four lands of Disney's Animal Kingdom in a circle of life (see map on page 164). The Tree of Life also hosts the popular attraction, "It's Tough to be a Bug!" See page 163 for a list of attractions, page 164 for our favorite itinerary, and pages 167–170 for attraction details.

Camp Minnie-Mickey *Headline Attraction:*	Hike into an evergreen forest reminiscent of Adirondack fishing camps, catching "critters" like Mickey and Tigger for hugs and autographs. *Festival of the Lion King*
Africa and Rafiki's Planet Watch *Headline Attractions:*	Come together in the port town of Harambe, complete with thatched huts and baobab trees, and set off on safaris, treks, and adventures. *Kilimanjaro Safaris, Pangani Forest Exploration Trail*
Asia *Headline Attractions:*	Step into the mythical kingdom of Anandapur (meaning "place of all delights") to experience the beauty, wonder, and peace of Asia. *Kali River Rapids, Maharajah Jungle Trek*
DinoLand, U.S.A. *Headline Attractions:*	Get tourist-trapped in the wacky world of an old dinosaur dig site, scattered with dino bones and evidence of the paleontology team's pranks, then meet the "real" dinosaurs on a thrilling ride. *Dinosaur, Tarzan Rocks!, Primeval Whirl, TriceraTop Spin*

Planning · Getting There · Staying in Style · Touring · Feasting · Making Magic · Index · Notes & More

AMBIENCE

PARK LAYOUT AND HIGHLIGHTS

Don't miss the fold-out map in the back of the book!

Entertainment and Shopping at Disney's Animal Kingdom

ENTERTAINMENT

The absolutely best entertainment at Disney's Animal Kingdom is its themed live **theater shows**, described in detail on pages 168–171. Roving entertainers take a back seat to the wildlife, of course. Fireworks shows don't fit in here, either— they would just scare the animals. The most recent addition is **Mickey's Jammin' Jungle Parade**,

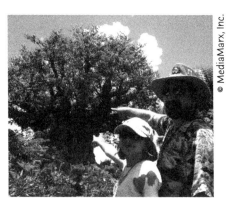

© MediaMarx, Inc.

Dave and Allie point out one of the hidden animals in the Tree of Life

which features your favorite Disney characters as they set out "on expedition." The "party animals" put on a wild street celebration and encourage guests to join in the action along the way! Other entertainment includes **The Adventure Begins** show, which starts 15 minutes before park opening every day—Rafiki, Mickey, Minnie, Timon, Terk, and characters from the Jungle Book arrive to start your adventure! In Africa's Harambe Village, **live bands** keep the Dawa Bar and Tusker House's outdoor tables hopping. Visitors to Rafiki's Planet Watch may get lucky and catch **live animal acts** on the outdoor stage or catch Pipa the talking recycling trash can! Also be on the lookout for **DeVine**, a ten-foot-tall, towering and wandering "vine."

SHOPPING

The best shopping at Disney's Animal Kingdom can be found in two places: Discovery Island around the Tree of Life and Africa's Village of Harambe. Of the two, Harambe offers more in the way of handcrafted and **imported goods**, while Discovery Island offers themed **Disney merchandise**. Here are our favorite shops:

Shop	Location	What makes it special
Outpost	Outside park entrance	Guidemaps, hats, sunglasses
Garden Gate Gifts	Inside park entrance	Film, stroller/wheelchair rentals
Beastly Bazaar	Discovery Island	Safari hats, logowear
Island Mercantile	Discovery Island	Disney-themed gifts
Disney Outfitters	Discovery Island	Upscale clothing, decorative items
Mombasa Marketplace	Africa	Crafts demonstrations
Out of the Wild	Rafiki's Planet Watch	Conservation-themed items
Chester & Hester's	DinoLand, U.S.A.	Kitschy, quirky gifts (and junk!)

Disney's Animal Kingdom
Attractions At-A-Glance

Attraction	Type	Allow	Page
☐ The Boneyard [F-5]	Playground	30–40+	170-DL
☐ Camp Minnie-Mickey Character Greeting Trails [A-5]	Pavilion	30–60+	167-CM
☐ Dinosaur [E-7]	Thrill Ride	20–40+	170-DL
☐ Festival of the Lion King [A-6]	Live Show	40–55+	167-CM
☐ Flights of Wonder [D-2]	Live Show	30–40+	169-Asia
☐ Kali River Rapids [F-2]	Raft Ride	25–40+	169-Asia
☐ Kilimanjaro Safaris [B-1]	Ride	30–50+	168-Afr
☐ Maharajah Jungle Trek [E-1]	Walkthru	30–45+	169-Asia
☐ The Oasis [C-6]	Walkthru	5–20+	167
☐ Pangani Forest Exp. Trail [B-1]	Walkthru	30–45+	168-Afr
☐ Pocahontas and Her Friends [B-6]	Live Show	20–30+	167-CM
☐ Primeval Whirl [F-6]	Coaster	30–60+	170-DL
☐ Rafiki's Planet Watch [off map]	Exhibit	60-90+	168-RP
☐ It's Tough to be a Bug! [D-4]	3-D Show	15–25+	167-DI
☐ Tarzan Rocks! [G-4]	Live Show	35–45+	170-DL
☐ The Tree of Life and Trails [C-3]	Walkthru	20–30+	167-DI
☐ TriceraTop Spin [F-6]	Ride	30–40+	170-DL
☐ Wildlife Express Train to Rafiki's Planet Watch [C-1]	Train Ride	20–25+	168-RP

The Allow column gives the amount of time (in minutes) you should allow for an attraction, assuming you do not have a FASTPASS and there are no ride breakdowns. The letters after the page numbers stand for the first two, three, or four letters of the land in which that attraction is located: DI=Discovery Island, CM=Camp Minnie-Mickey, Afr=Africa, RP=Rafiki's Planet Watch, Asia=Asia, and DL=DinoLand, U.S.A.

Finding the Animals at Disney's Animal Kingdom
Everyone has their favorite furry and feathered friends. The chart below shows typical locations of popular animals.

Animal(s)	Location(s)
☐ Parrots, macaws, turtles	The Oasis
☐ Gorillas, meerkats	Pangani Forest Trail
☐ Hippos	Pangani Forest Trail, Kilimanjaro Safaris
☐ Lions, elephants, rhinos	Kilimanjaro Safaris
☐ Crocs, cheetahs, zebras	Kilimanjaro Safaris
☐ Tigers, giant bats	Maharajah Jungle Trek
☐ Otters, giant tortoise	Discovery Island Trails
☐ Goats, sheep, llamas	Rafiki's Planet Watch
☐ Gibbons	Asia temple ruins

Tip: Keep your eyes open for live animal encounters with Disney naturalists. You're most likely to stumble across these on Discovery Island and Rafiki's Planet Watch.

Our Favorite Touring Plans for Disney's Animal Kingdom

NOTES

Like Disney-MGM Studios, Disney's Animal Kingdom has several attractions with specific showtimes, making it harder to fit the best attractions into one day. And even though Animal Kingdom has about the same number of attractions as Disney-MGM Studios, it's shorter hours make it just as hard to see and do everything you want. We've come up with touring plans—one for adults and one for kids—that takes the typical showtimes into account to minimize waiting and backtracking. If you plan to use this plan, or modify it, be sure to check your Times Guide or the Attraction Tip Board (just after you cross the bridge into Discovery Island from The Oasis) for showtimes. Use the fill-in-the-blank lines below to record showtimes on the day you visit to help you stay on track. As always, the touring plans work best if you go in the same order that we've listed, but you should feel free to skip an attraction or two (and return to it later) if that works best. You should be able to accomplish either of these plans in one day if you start by 9:00 am. Those with infants and toddlers, or less-adventuresome adults, may prefer to skip all attractions with asterisks.

ITINERARIES

Touring With Adults
Stroll through The Oasis
Enter Africa
Visit Kilimanjaro Safaris*
Visit Pangani Forest Exploration Trail
Have a snack at Kusafiri Coffee Shop
Enter Asia
Get a FASTPASS for Kali River Rapids*
Visit Maharajah Jungle Trek
Visit Kali River Rapids*
Eat lunch at Tusker House, Pizzafari, or Flame Tree BBQ (plan lunchtime for about 3 1/2 hours after you arrive)
Enter Camp Minnie-Mickey
Visit Festival of the Lion King @ _____
Enter DinoLand, U.S.A.
Get a FASTPASS for Dinosaur
Visit Tarzan Rocks! @ _____
Visit Dinosaur*
Visit Primeval Whirl*
Enter Discovery Island
Get FASTPASS for It's Tough to be a Bug!*
Watch Mickey's Jammin' Jungle Parade and have a snack
Visit It's Tough to be a Bug!*
(Tour duration: About 8 hours)

Touring With Kids
Arrive 15 minutes before opening to see "The Adventure Begins" ceremony
Stroll through The Oasis
Enter Africa
Visit Kilimanjaro Safaris*
Visit Pangani Forest Exploration Trail
Take Wildlife Express Train to Rafiki's Planet Watch
Visit Rafiki's Planet Watch
Take Wildlife Express Train back to Africa
Eat lunch at Pizzafari, Tusker House, or Flame Tree BBQ (plan lunchtime for about 3 hours after you arrive)
Enter Camp Minnie-Mickey
Visit Character Greeting Trails
Visit Festival of the Lion King @ _____
Enter DinoLand, U.S.A.
Visit The Boneyard
Visit TriceraTop Spin
Visit Tarzan Rocks! @ _____
Enter Discovery Island
Watch Mickey's Jammin' Jungle Parade
Visit It's Tough to be a Bug!* or Maharajah Jungle Trek
(Tour duration: About 8 hours)

Making the Most of Disney's Animal Kingdom

Disney's Animal Kingdom is a paradise, where delightful and often subtle details can work their magic if you **take the time** to notice. This is not a do-it-all-in-a-day-or-die park. Slow down, revel in the beauty, wonder at the animals, and enjoy yourselves!

Trails lead off in all directions—don't be afraid to explore them. A **new bridge and path** connects Dinoland and Asia (see map page 164). It's the perfect way to view the Expedition: Everest construction site and to dodge afternoon parade crowds on Discovery Island.

This park is one big photo op! Bring plenty of **film** and **batteries**, and even **binoculars** for viewing animals.

Dining options here are a bit more limited than at the other parks, but quality almost makes up for quantity. The counter-service eateries are particularly good here. See the listings on pages 218–219.

If it's open, the outdoor, sheltered **seating** by Flame Tree Barbecue is a wonderful spot, whether you want to dine or simply rest. Tables and dining pavilions are set amidst lush tropical gardens.

Not all **animals** can be seen all the time. On the plus side, you'll see new ones each time, making subsequent visits unique.

Beverages sold in Disney's Animal Kingdom generally do not come with lids and straws, for the animals' safety. Consider bringing your own covered mug or bottle if you want to keep drinks.

It always seems **hotter** at Disney's Animal Kingdom than at any other park, possibly because there are so few attractions with air conditioning. Be prepared with hats, sunglasses, sunscreen, and ways to keep yourself cool, like plenty of cold water and/or a personal misting fan ($16). Take advantage of the mist-spraying fans throughout the park when you need relief. Take frequent breaks in air-conditioned spots—try the eateries, shops, or attractions like It's Tough to be a Bug! or Rafiki's Planet Watch.

Seniors should go carefully when touring this park due to the heat. Nearly every attraction is outdoors, which means there's limited air conditioning. There's plenty of shade while you stand around or watch the shows, though. An ECV is particularly helpful at this park if you have any difficulty with walking or stamina.

TIPS

NOTES

Planning

Getting There

Staying in Style

Touring

Feasting

Making Magic

Index

Notes & More

Getting to Disney's Animal Kingdom

BEST TIMES TO GO

Most guests arrive in the mid-morning and leave in the afternoon, making the **early morning and late afternoon** the best times to visit. Not only are the crowds thinner, but the park's animals prefer the cooler temperatures found in the earlier and later parts of the day, so you're more likely to see them. You may have more luck spotting animals during and after a rainstorm, too. When you **first arrive**, head for Dinosaur or Kilimanjaro Safaris to pick up a FASTPASS (or just go ahead and ride if the wait is short enough). Another strategy is to ride one of the popular attractions early and then immediately get a FASTPASS for another attraction. Check the **Times Guide** for show times and durations, and plan your day accordingly—these shows can chew up more time than you'd expect. You can use our touring plans on page 163a to give you an idea of what you can expect to do in one day. Finally, if your park pass allows it, consider spreading out your visit over a **couple of days** rather than packing it all into one. Midday is best avoided due to the big crowds, the intense heat/sun, and sleeping animals.

GETTING THERE

By Bus—All resorts, Epcot, and Disney-MGM Studios have buses that take you directly to Disney's Animal Kingdom. From the Magic Kingdom, take the boat or monorail to the Transportation and Ticket Center (TTC) and catch a bus. From Downtown Disney, take a bus to an Epcot-area resort and catch a Disney's Animal Kingdom bus.
By Car—From I-4, take exit 65 (eastbound or westbound) and follow signs to Disney's Animal Kingdom parking. All-day parking is available for $8 (free to resort guests with resort I.D. and annual passholders). The parking lot is some distance from the entrance. You'll appreciate the free trams to the front gate.

Note: There is no boat, foot, or monorail access to this theme park.

Ratings are explained on page 120.

RATINGS

Our Value Ratings:		Our Magic Ratings:		Readers' Ratings:
Quality:	8/10	Theme:	9/10	44% fell in love with it
Variety:	7/10	Excitement:	7/10	33% liked it well enough
Scope:	6/10	Fun Factor:	6/10	15% had mixed feelings
Overall Value:	**7/10**	**Overall Magic:**	**7/10**	8% were disappointed

Animal Kingdom is enjoyed by... (rated by both authors and readers)		
Younger Kids: ♥♥♥♥♥	Young Adults: ♥♥♥♥	Families: ♥♥♥♥♥
Older Kids: ♥♥♥♥	Mid Adults: ♥♥♥♥	Couples: ♥♥♥♥
Teenagers: ♥♥♥♥	Mature Adults: ♥♥♥♥	Singles: ♥♥♥♥

Charting the Attractions at The Oasis, Discovery Island, and Camp Minnie-Mickey

	Jennifer's Rating	Dave's Rating	Readers' Rating

☐ The Oasis [C-6]   A-OK!   7 6 7

All guests pass through this lush jungle habitat of gurgling waters and exotic plants on their way in and out of the park. Many of the paths lead to small animal exhibits. Look for shady seats in a rocky grotto. Wheelchair accessible. **Allie's KidTip:** "Can you spot camouflaging lizards anywhere here?"

Walk-thru
A-Ticket
All ages
Allow 20 min.

☐ Camp Minnie-Mickey Character Greeting Trails [A-5]   A-OK!   4 4 6

Meet Mickey, Minnie, and other Disney characters in the shade of four rustic, open-air pavilions—each character has his/her own queue. Low-key atmosphere. Bring your autograph book or use PassPorter's autograph section, and have lots of film handy. Wheelchair accessible. **Allie's KidTip:** "Don't be shy."

Pavilion
A-Ticket
All ages
Med. waits

☐ Festival of the Lion King [A-6]   A-OK!   8 8 9

This colorful, dynamic pageant set to music from "The Lion King" features singers, dancers, acrobats, and floats, and really sets your hands to clapping! The 1,000-seat theater-in-the-round affords many great vantage points, but arrive early to sit down front. Try the first or last shows for shortest waits. Lots of audience participation and lots of fun! This theatre is now fully air conditioned. Outdoor queue is uncovered. No external video lights. Wheelchair accessible. Assistive listening. **Allie's KidTip:** "If you sit in the front you might get asked to play music!" **TweenTip:** "Try your best to make the animal sounds."

Live Show
E-Ticket
Ages 2 & up
Long waits (check showtimes in Times Guide)
30 min. show

☐ Pocahontas and Her Forest Friends [B-6]   A-OK!   4 2 4

Pocahontas and Grandmother Willow are featured in a conservation-themed live animal show. Seating is outdoors with light shade. First three center rows of seats reserved for kids under 11 (no parents), and volunteers are chosen. Brief glimpses of animals. Doors open 15 minutes before show. Check Times Guide for shows. Outdoor queue is uncovered. Wheelchair accessible. Assistive listening. **Allie's KidTip:** "If you're not too shy, sit with the kids in the front."

Live Show
C-Ticket
Ages 3 & up
Live animals and birds
13 min. show

☐ It's Tough to be a Bug! [D-4]   FP A-OK!   8 8 9

Long lines snake around the Tree of Life on Discovery Island for a humorous show hosted by Flik from "A Bug's Life" and featuring a pint-sized cast of animated and Audio-Animatronics characters. 3-D effects, creepy sensations, and yucky smells can terrify the bug-wary. The queue offers close-up views of the tree's animal sculptures. Look for hilarious movie posters in the "lobby." Air conditioned, 430-seat theater. Outdoor queue is uncovered. Special effects may be too intense for some. Wheelchair accessible. Assistive listening. Reflective captioning. Note that the entrance is marked on the map on page 163. **Allie's KidTip:** "Sit between two grown-ups just in case you get scared."

3-D Show
E-Ticket
Ages 6 & up
Dark, smells, bug noises, "stings"
FASTPASS or med. waits
8 min. show

☐ The Tree of Life and Discovery Island Trails [C-3]   6 5 8

Tropical gardens and exotic animals surround the Tree of Life at the center of the park. Walk the winding paths, and get a close-up view of the tree, too. How many animals can you see in the trunk and roots? (Hint: 325, including a "hidden Mickey.") Wheelchair accessible. **Allie's KidTip:** "The animals are cool."

Walk-thru
A-Ticket
All ages
Allow 30 min.

Attraction descriptions and ratings are explained on page 127.

Side tabs: Planning · Getting There · Staying in Style · Touring · Feasting · Making Magic · Index · Notes & More

Charting the Attractions at Africa and Rafiki's Planet Watch

Jennifer's Rating Dave's Rating Readers' Rating

☐ Kilimanjaro Safaris [B-1] FP 🕴 A-ok! | 8 | 8 | 9 |

Board a safari truck to explore 100 acres of African habitat teeming with lions, giraffes, crocodiles, ostriches, gazelle, and many other live animals. Wildlife may be plentiful or scarce, since it's free to roam. Disney also includes a story line in case the animals are feeling shy. The ride gets very bumpy, so hang on tight. We recommend you ride first thing in the morning, late afternoon, or after it rains, when the animals are more active. Sit in outside seats for best views and photos. The safari closes at dusk. Outdoor queue is covered and has overhead monitors. Height restriction for children riding in front two seats. Young children should be accompanied by an adult. Health warning. Transfer from ECV to wheelchair to ride. Wheelchair accessible. Assistive listening. Closed captioning. **Allie's Kid Tip:** "Be on the lookout for the baby elephant (Little Red)." **TweenTip:** "Look at the signs in the truck to identify the animals."

| Ride |
| E-Ticket |
| Ages 4 & up |
| Bumpy, live birds and animals, "close escapes" |
| FASTPASS or long waits |
| 19 min. vehicle ride |

☐ Pangani Forest Exploration Trail [B-1] A-ok! | 6 | 8 | 7 |

Animal lovers will stroll enthralled through this exhibit of African wildlife in an artfully built natural habitat. African birds, hippos, meerkats, and a troop of gorillas make their home here. Hands-on exhibits in the naturalist's hut add interest. A habitat—the Endangered Animal Rehabilitation Centre—calls attention to the African bushmeat crisis. The meerkat viewing area is especially popular, and plan to spend extra time in the aviary. Walk slowly or sit, and the wonders will unfold. Allow several hours if you love to watch animals. Early morning or late afternoon is the best time to visit. Wheelchair accessible. Closed captioning. **Allie's Kid Tip:** "You'll love all the animals and birds!"

| Walk-thru |
| D-Ticket |
| All ages |
| Live animals, birds flying overhead |
| Short waits |
| Allow at least 30 minutes |

☐ Wildlife Express Train to Rafiki's Planet Watch [C-1] A-ok! | 5 | 4 | 5 |

All aboard! This train at Harambe station is the only route into or out of Rafiki's Planet Watch (formerly called Conservation Station). Enjoy a ringside glimpse of the park's backstage animal care areas. A guide describes the sights as the train chugs slowly along the track. Note: Everyone must disembark at Rafiki's Planet Watch. As always, Disney's eye for detail shines forth around Harambe Station and onboard the train. The best seats are in the front row. Themed, outdoor queue is mostly covered. Wheelchair accessible. Assistive listening. **Allie's Kid Tip:** "Sit in the front row of the train to see better."

| Train Ride |
| B-Ticket |
| All ages |
| Glimpses of backstage |
| Short waits |
| 15 min. ride (each way) |

☐ Rafiki's Planet Watch [off map] A-ok! | 5 | 6 | 5 |

This is the park's most remote and most underappreciated attraction, a must-visit for animal lovers of all ages. Formerly called Conservation Station, it was renamed and jazzed-up with live Animal Encounter shows, more hands-on activities, and visits from Tarzan and Rafiki. The 5-min. walk from the train station to Rafiki's Planet Watch is interspersed with fun, conservation-themed exhibits and activities. See short films, use interactive video displays, and relax in darkened rain forest "soundscape" booths. View the park's nursery and veterinary hospital. Enjoy the cleanest, most animal-friendly petting zoo anywhere (it even has a hand-washing fountain at the exit). The Wildlife Express Train from Harambe is the only way into or out of Rafiki's Planet Watch. Wheelchair accessible. Assistive listening. **Allie's Kid Tip:** "Look for the fishes, lizards, and frogs. And go to the petting farm!"

| Exhibit |
| C-Ticket |
| All ages |
| Backstage, educational fun |
| Live animals |
| Short waits |
| Allow at least 90 minutes for a good exploration |

Charting the Attractions at Asia

Jennifer's Rating | Dave's Rating | Readers' Rating

☐ Flights of Wonder [D-2]   A-OK!   7 7 7

Duck! Owls or hawks may fly right above your head during a show starring more than 20 species of free-flying exotic birds and their talented animal handlers. Guano Joe, a tour guide from Anandapur Tours, adds some comic relief to this conservation-themed show. Guests are selected from the audience to join in the action. Afterwards everyone has a chance to come down to ask questions, view the "stars" up close, and take photos. Sit near the aisles for the closest animal encounters. Outdoor, shaded theater. Outdoor queue is uncovered. Theater opens 15 minutes beforehand. No food or drink allowed. Leave strollers at the door. Wheelchair accessible. Assistive listening. **Allie's Kid Tip:** "Volunteer to go on the stage! I'm too shy to do it, but it looks like fun."

Live Show	
D-Ticket	
Ages 3 & up	
Live birds overhead	
Med. waits (showtimes listed in Times Guide)	
25 min. show	

☐ Kali River Rapids [F-2]   FP 🧍 A-OK!   6 8 8

Drift through jungle mists, unexpected geysers, and smoking devastation on a somewhat daring ride in a 12-person raft. The roaring rapids boast one thrilling (albeit tame) drop. Just when you think it's all over, Disney tosses in one last little surprise. You will get wet—possibly damp, more likely soaked—and there's no way to predict (or control) how much. A small storage area is available on board, but it won't keep things very dry. Some guests wisely bring a poncho and a dry change of clothing—plastic ponchos are available for sale nearby. Shoes/sandals must be worn at all times. Long lines are common, but they snake through fascinating Asian architecture rich with fine detail. 42"/107 cm height restriction. Special effects may be too intense for some children and adults. Health warning. Must transfer from wheelchair to ride. **Allie's Kid Tip:** "If you go backwards on the drop, be prepared to get soaked." **Tween Tip:** "It's good when it's really hot out!"

Raft Ride	
E-Ticket	
Ages 7 & up	
Med. drop, flames, geysers, and you will get wet!	
FASTPASS or long waits	
5 min. cruise	

☐ Maharajah Jungle Trek [E-1]   A-OK!   6 8 7

Walk a winding path through ancient ruins in a lush Asian setting. Tigers, tapir, fruit bats, deer, antelope, a Komodo dragon, and a walk-through aviary filled with tropical birds highlight this beautifully designed zoo. Artfully hidden barriers make you feel like you can reach out and touch the animals, but fortunately for them (and us) you can't. Cast members are on hand to enrich your animal viewing adventure. We think the tigers, aviary, and bats are the highlights, but you'll find your own favorites. Be sure to pick up a guidemap on your way in. Animal lovers may be tempted to spend hours here—bring your camera! Wheelchair accessible. **Allie's Kid Tip:** "Tigers! How many can you find?"

Walk-thru	
D-Ticket	
All ages	
Live animals, birds overhead	
Short waits	
Allow at least 30 minutes	

🔟 Up and Coming: Expedition: Everest and Lucky the Dino

Disney's newest "mountain" is rising in Asia (see map on page 164). Called "Expedition: Everest," the new thrill ride will open in 2006. You'll ride up and into the 200-foot-tall Mt. Everest on a rickety tea plantation train for a startling encounter with the fearsome Yeti. You'll hurtle through darkness and even ride backwards before it's all over. On a lighter note, The Happiest Celebration on Earth (see page 191) brings a wondrous new visitor to the park—Lucky the Dinosaur, the first mobile Audio-Animatronics figure, who turned a lot of heads during his visit to Disneyland in California. Look for him once the celebration begins on May 5, 2005.

Side tabs: Planning | Getting There | Staying in Style | Touring | Feasting | Making Magic | Index | Notes & More

Charting the Attractions at DinoLand, U.S.A.

	Jennifer's Rating	Dave's Rating	Readers' Rating

☐ The Boneyard [F-5]   A-ok!   7 5 6

Kids can climb, slide, crawl, scamper, excavate, and explore to their hearts' content in a funky dinosaur dig. Parents are welcome, too. One of the places at Disney's Animal Kingdom with a water spray for hot days. Keep an eye on your young ones! Bring a towel and dry clothes. Wheelchair accessible. **Allie's Kid Tip:** "You can get wet here if you are hot. I love this place!"	**Playground**
	B-Ticket
	Ages 1 & up
	Allow
	30 min.

☐ Dinosaur [E-7]   FP 🚻 A-ok!   7 7 8

Intrepid riders are sent back through time to fetch a dinosaur before the dinos (and the riders) become extinct. Be prepared to be bounced, jostled, and scared as your Time Rover vehicle hurtles into the past and races through a dark forest. The "pre-show" and science exhibits in the indoor queue areas make the wait interesting. Front row "outside" seats for maximum thrills, inside seats for the less bold. No flash photography. 40"/102 cm height restriction. Young children should be accompanied by an adult. Effects may be too intense for some. Health warning. Must transfer from wheelchair to ride. Closed captioning. **Allie's Kid Tip:** "Cover your eyes in the dark parts if you're scared. Ask your grown-ups to tell you when a dinosaur shows up so you can look."	**Thrill Ride**
	E-Ticket
	Ages 7 & up
	Dark, loud, very scary, rough and bumpy ride
	FASTPASS or long waits
	3.5 min. ride

☐ Tarzan Rocks! [G-4]   A-ok!   7 8 7

This rockin' live concert extravaganza features hit tunes from the animated film, Tarzan, performed by a pumped-up cast of singers, dancers, acrobats, rollerbladers, and musicians. Tarzan, Jane, and Terk swing by for part of the show. Don't look for a plot—there isn't one, just loud, solid rock and roll. Shows every 75 minutes. The outdoor, covered theater opens 20 minutes before show time. No external video lights. Uncovered outdoor queue. Wheelchair accessible. Assistive listening. **Allie's Kid Tip:** "This is good, but very loud!"	**Live Show**
	E-Ticket
	Ages 4 & up
	Very loud
	Med. waits (check times)
	28 min. show

☐ Primeval Whirl [G-6]   FP 🚻 A-ok!   7 7 8

Chester and Hester cooked up a dizzy bit of fun for Primeval Whirl, a wild mouse coaster (with style). Your round "time machine" car spins as it goes around tight curves, over mild drops, and even through the jaws of a dinosaur. (What else?) Two identical coasters each boast 13 spinning, four-person ride vehicles. 48"/122 cm height restriction. Health warning. Must transfer from wheelchair to ride. **Allie's Kid Tip:** "The dips aren't as scary as they look."	**Coaster**
	D-Ticket
	Ages 7 & up
	Fast, drops
	FASTPASS
	2.5 min. ride

☐ TriceraTop Spin [F-6]   A-ok!   5 5 7

Dumbo morphs into a Dino! Sixteen dinosaur-shaped, four-rider cars swoop around a huge, spinning toy top. Part of Chester & Hester's Dino-Rama! (see description below). Must transfer from ECV to wheelchair to ride. **Allie's Kid Tip:** "Sit in the front and make the dinosaur tilt forward or backward."	**Ride**
	C-Ticket
	Ages 2 & up
	1.5 min. ride

🅛 Chester & Hester's Dino-Rama!

Chester & Hester, the operators of DinoLand's crazy roadside-style gift shop, have created a roadside "carnival" with two attractions and about a half-dozen games of skill or chance. Play midway games for $2 a pop and maybe win a prize. Games include Mammoth Marathon, Bronto-Score, and Fossil Fueler.

Typhoon Lagoon Water Park

Typhoon Lagoon is a 56-acre water park with lush foliage, lazy rivers, roaring waterfalls, and a huge surfing "lagoon." The water park is located near Downtown Disney West Side.

AMBIENCE

Legend has it that this was once the Placid Palms Resort in Safen Sound, Florida, a tropical hideaway nestled on a sparkling lagoon. Disaster struck when a typhoon raged through the sleepy resort, flooding the lagoon and tossing ships about. In its wake, they discovered sharks in the harbor, a surfboard through a tree, and ships scattered everywhere. Most amazing was the Miss Tilly shrimp boat, impaled on a craggy mountain (Mt. Mayday) that kept trying to dislodge the boat with a huge plume of water. Water was everywhere, forming waterfalls, rapids, pools, and surf. In true Disney form, misfortune was turned into luck and the Typhoon Lagoon water park was born. Or so the story goes.

PARK LAYOUT

The park's attractions are arrayed around its focal point, the gigantic, 2½-acre **wave pool** at the foot of Mt. Mayday. The "mountain" offers the advantage of height to several tube and body slides that slither down it. Around the perimeter of the park is a "lazy river" called Castaway Creek, offering a relaxing retreat to swimmers drifting lazily along in inner tubes. Finding your way around the park can be confusing at first—the dense foliage and meandering paths recreate the tropical look quite convincingly. Just keep in mind that one path encircles the park, and you can see Miss Tilly perched atop Mt. Mayday from almost everywhere. This park is worth exploring, too—the lush Mountain Trail on Mt. Mayday presents photo opportunities, and many hidden groves and glens offer quiet getaways.

EATING

Leaning Palms is the largest of the cafés, offering combos with burgers ($5.69), hot dogs ($6.49), sandwiches and wraps ($7.19), pizza ($5.49), salads ($6.39), and ice cream ($2.39). A kid's peanut butter and jelly sandwich meal is $3.99 and includes chips, drink, and a sand pail. **Happy Landings** has ice cream and a fun water play area where you can take aim at the guests drifting by on Castaway Creek. **Typhoon Tilly's Galley & Grog** has fish & chips, snacks, ice cream, and beverages. **Let's Go Slurpin'** offers soft drinks, alcoholic drinks, and snacks. **Low Tide Lou's** (open seasonally) has hot dogs, sandwiches, and drinks. **Surf Doggies** offers hot dogs and turkey legs. Three **picnic areas** have shade and tables.

Charting the Attractions at Typhoon Lagoon

	Jennifer's Rating	Dave's Rating	Readers' Rating

☐ Typhoon Lagoon Surf Pool [C-4] A-Ok! | 8 | 9 |

Waves in the world's largest inland wave pool at the base of Mt. Mayday change every half-hour, alternating between gently bobbing swells and six-foot body-surfing waves that arrive 90 seconds apart. Youngsters enjoy the two Bay Slides to the far left, and the small tidal pools (Blustery Bay and Whitecap Cove) near the front. Observe the waves before entering. **Allie's Kid Tip:** "Jump up when the waves come to get carried away, but don't scrape yourself on the bottom."

| **Pool** |
| E-Ticket |
| All ages |
| Surfing waves may scare kids |

☐ Castaway Creek [Entry points: A-3, A-2, D-2, D-3, D-5] A-Ok! | 9 | 8 | 8 |

Relax on a half-mile, 20-minute circuit around the park on inner tubes. Catch a free tube at one of five entrances. Note where you entered, too! **Allie's Kid Tip:** "This is nice and relaxing. Little kids will like the yellow inner tubes the best."

| **Pool** |
| D-Ticket |
| Ages 3 & up |

☐ Ketchakiddee Creek [A-2] 🧍 | 6 | 6 | 7 |

Several fountains, two body slides, and a 30-sec. tube ride—just for little squirts (48"/122 cm or under). Shady, thatched-roof shelters for waiting parents.

| **Playground** |
| B-Ticket |

☐ Keelhaul Falls [B-1] A-Ok! | 6 | 7 | 7 |

A slow, solo tube ride with a surprise! (Warning—ride spoilers ahead.) Rafters plunge unexpectedly into a pitch-black tunnel about half the way down. **Allie's Kid Tip:** "The waterfall is fun! You don't get as wet as you think you will."

| **Tube slide** |
| C-Ticket |
| Ages 7 & up |

☐ Mayday Falls [B-1] A-Ok! | 5 | 6 | 7 |

Like Keelhaul Falls, this tube ride is solo. Unlike it, Mayday Falls is fast and bumpy, twisting and turning through caves and waterfalls. **Allie's Kid Tip:** "This is bumpy. Think of something that is also bumpy and then you won't be scared."

| **Tube slide** |
| C-Ticket |
| Ages 7 & up |

☐ Gang Plank Falls [B-1] A-Ok! | 8 | 6 | 6 |

Bring the family on this three- to five-person raft ride down the mountain. Watch out for waterfalls and those twisty-turny rafts! **Allie's Kid Tip:** "This is fun! Hold on tight because you go a little fast, but that's no problem."

| **Raft slide** |
| C-Ticket |
| Ages 4 & up |

☐ Humunga Kowabunga [C-1] 🧍 | 1 | 5 | 7 |

This is the ultimate thrill slide at Typhoon Lagoon, shooting sliders down one of two slides in less than 10 seconds. Viewing bleachers at the bottom for observers. 48"/122 cm height requirement. Health requirement. Ages 9 & up. **Allie's Kid Tip:** "It's scary—don't go on it. P.S. It gave me a wedgie."

| **Body slide** |
| E-Ticket |
| Very fast, steep drop |

☐ Storm Slides [D-1] | 5 | 6 | 7 |

Three body slides (Stern Burner, Jib Jammer, and Rudder Buster) corkscrew through waterfalls and caves. Viewing bleachers at the bottom. Ages 8 & up.

| **Body slides** |
| E-Ticket |

☐ Shark Reef [E-1] A-Ok! | 9 | 8 | 8 |

Swim with the sharks! Line up at Hammerhead Fred's Dive Shop to get your snorkel equipment (free use with park admission), shower, listen to a five-minute lesson, then snorkel across the small, chilly, saltwater lagoon. You may see a variety of fish, perhaps even three kinds of passive sharks. Bring an underwater camera. Scuba-assisted snorkel for an extra fee. **Allie's Kid Tip:** "I love the sharks!"

| **Pool** |
| E-Ticket |
| Ages 6 & up |
| Cold, salty water |

Planning · Getting There · Staying in Style · Touring · Feasting · Making Magic · Index · Notes & More

Making the Most of Typhoon Lagoon

A **refillable mug** ($10) uses barcode scanners so you can refill without cast supervision. You can purchase a new refill barcode ($5) on future visits. A Typhoon Lagoon mug can be used at Blizzard Beach and vice versa as long as you buy the appropriate refill.

Avoid **two-piece suits** on slides—they may come down the slide at a different speed than you. Also, swimsuits with rivets, buckles, or exposed metal are not permitted at the park. Wear water shoes—the sand and pavement can get quite hot.

Use a single-use, **underwater camera** for great photos.

Get your first taste of **scuba** in a special section of the Shark Reef. Cost is $20 for the first 30 min. and $15 for the rest of your party or for repeat dives. Pay at the booth near the dive shop. Brief lessons are provided, and parents can attend their kids without renting.

Children under the age of 10 must be accompanied by an adult.

You can rent lockers ($5-7) and towels ($1 each). You may wish to bring hotel towels rather than rent them—they're practically the same size. Changing rooms are also available. Life vests are free (refundable deposit). Some personal flotation devices may be permitted.

At press time, **construction was well underway** for one or more new attractions, rumored to be a high-speed water slide and/or a rapids river ride. Specifics could not be confirmed, however.

Park hours: generally open by 10:00 am, closed at 5:00 pm or later. A one-day pass (with tax) is $33.02/adults and $26.63/kids 3-9.

Ratings are explained on page 120.

Our Value Ratings:		Our Magic Ratings:		Readers' Ratings:
Quality:	7/10	Theme:	8/10	76% fell in love with it
Variety:	8/10	Excitement:	7/10	21% liked it well enough
Scope:	3/10	Fun Factor:	7/10	3% had mixed feelings
Overall Value:	6/10	Overall Magic:	7/10	0% were disappointed

Typhoon Lagoon is enjoyed by... (rated by both authors and readers)		
Younger Kids: ♥♥♥♥	Young Adults: ♥♥♥♥♥	Families: ♥♥♥♥
Older Kids: ♥♥♥♥♥	Mid Adults: ♥♥♥	Couples: ♥♥♥
Teenagers: ♥♥♥♥♥	Mature Adults: ♥♥♥	Singles: ♥♥♥

Planning | Getting There | Staying in Style | Touring | Feasting | Making Magic | Index | Notes & More

TIPS | NOTES | RATINGS

Finding Your Way at Typhoon Lagoon

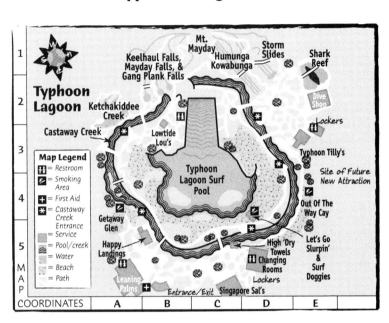

TYPHOON LAGOON PARK MAP

BEST TIMES

Typhoon Lagoon is very popular during the **hot months** and gets crowded fast—arrive early, as gates close when the park reaches capacity. It's also wise to stake out your beach chairs early as the good ones are grabbed quickly. We prefer to visit when it's a bit **cooler** as crowds are lighter and the water is heated. The park closes for part of the winter (January and early February)—call 407-560-4141 and confirm that it is open if you intend to visit the park. Beyond that, **weekdays** are better than weekends (locals love to visit the park). Visit in the **late afternoon** when the park empties a bit and the sun is less intense. The park may **close during storms**—when it reopens, it may be nearly empty. If you arrive when there are long lines, bypass them by getting your tickets at the Automated Ticket Vending Machines now available here.

GETTING THERE

By Bus—All Disney resorts have direct buses to Typhoon Lagoon. From Magic Kingdom, Epcot, Disney-MGM Studios, and Disney's Animal Kingdom, take a bus or monorail to a nearby resort and transfer to a Typhoon Lagoon bus (which may also be the Downtown Disney bus). Allow about 30-60 minutes if you travel by bus.

By Car—Take exit 67 off I-4, take the first exit and turn right on Buena Vista Dr.—the park is on the right. From Downtown Disney, turn right to Buena Vista Dr. and the park is on the left. Free parking.

Blizzard Beach Water Park

Is it a water park, or a ski resort? The Blizzard Beach water park brings the chills and thrills of a Colorado winter to the warm Florida sun. Ski jumps, toboggan rides, and slalom runs zip you past snow that never melts in Disney's most action-oriented water park.

Disney's Imagineers scattered magic white stuff over the rocks and pines of towering Mount Gushmore to create a water park that'll make you shiver on the hottest August day. Oh, don't worry, the water is always a warm 80 degrees, but just a look at some of those water slides can freeze your insides. Luckily, Disney never abandons the idea of family fun—even the meekest snow bunny will have a ball!

Before you "hit the slopes" you'll discover the park's **base lodge** facilities—the major food, merchandise, and locker room areas. Then, as you face the mountain the Tike's Peak children's area will be to your right. Straight ahead are two bridges over Cross Country Creek, the drift-along tube ride that encircles the mountain and most of the fun. Additional lockers can be found close to the action, near Downhill Double Dipper on the left, and Ski Patrol on the right. Of course, Mount Gushmore dominates the park in every way. Its slopes are home to nearly two dozen lanes of slides and flumes. Most slides can be seen from the Lodge area, but Runoff Rapids is tucked away on the back slope of the mountain. You can also watch your daredevils in comfort, from shaded grandstands at the bottom of many slides. Three footpaths and a chairlift scale the 90-foot (9-story) mountain. After your first ascent on foot in the hot, Florida sunshine, you'll know why folks wait patiently for the chairlift, which takes you to the top in the comfort of a three-person, umbrella-shaded chair (32"/81 cm height restriction, under 48"/122 cm must be with an adult).

Water park meals are never fancy, which is fine when you're only wearing a swimsuit. **Lottawatta Lodge** serves up cheeseburger combos ($5.69), hot dogs ($5.59), pizza ($5.49), chicken sandwiches ($6.79), chicken salads ($6.89), ice cream ($2.50), and kosher selections. A kid's meal is $3.99 with a choice of mac & cheese, hot dog, or chicken strips, plus chips, drink, and a toy. **Avalunch** and **The Warming Hut** offer hot dogs, sandwiches, ice cream, and usually close before dinnertime. The thirsty line up at **Frostbite Freddie's Frozen Freshments**, **Polar Pub**, and **The Cooling Hut**. There are also **picnic areas**.

AMBIENCE

ATTRACTIONS

EATING

Charting the Attractions at Blizzard Beach

Attraction		Jennifer's Rating	Dave's Rating	Readers' Rating	
Summit Plummet [D-2] 👤		2	5	9	
Only the boldest ride the world's highest body slide, which drops 120 feet. Go feet first, cross your arms, and it's over in eight seconds. Be prepared for a steep drop and a wedgie! 48"/122 cm height requirement. Health requirement.		**Body Slide** / E-Ticket / Ages 9 & up			
Slush Gusher [D-2]		3	6	8	
Ninety-foot-high double-bump slide is the second-tallest body slide in the park. One-piece suits recommended! 48"/122 cm height requirement. Ages 8 & up.		**Body Slide** / D-Ticket			
Downhill Double Dipper [C-2]		5	7	8	
Race head-to-head on a half-enclosed innertube slide. Your race results are flashed on a scoreboard. 48"/122 cm height requirement. Ages 8 & up.		**Tube Slide** / D-Ticket			
Snow Stormers [C-2] A-ok!		7	5	8	
Zig and zag your way down this three-flume, family-friendly slalom mat slide. 12-second ride. Allie's Kid Tip: "Fun, but it's a little bumpy." Ages 6 & up.		**Mat slide** / C-Ticket			
Toboggan Racers [D-2] A-ok!		6	5	7	
On your mark, get set, go! Race headfirst down an eight-lane mat slide. 10-second ride. Allie's Kid Tip: "Push yourself off to go down." Ages 6 & up.		**Mat slide** / D-Ticket			
Teamboat Springs [E-2] A-ok!		9	8	9	
Whitewater-loving families can pack up to six in a large, round, river raft for a long, twisting ride—at 1,400 feet it is the longest ride of its kind anywhere. Allie's Kid Tip: "Hold on to the bottom of the raft when you go down."		**Raft slide** / D-Ticket / Ages 4 up			
Runoff Rapids [D-2]		8	7	7	
Ride a tube down this twisty, turny, family-friendly course. Three different open and enclosed slides. Up to two can share a tube on the open slides. Allie's Kid Tip: "Pick up your behind over the bumps, or it won't feel good."		**Tube slide** / C-Ticket / Ages 6 & up			
Cross Country Creek [Entry points: B-4, A-4, B-2, C-1, E-3, D-4] A-ok!		8	7	7	
Float around the park on a moderately flowing creek. Enter and exit at any of six spots around the park. Return to your starting point in 20 minutes. Allie's Kid Tip: "Don't get wet under the freezing waterfalls."		**Pool** / D-Ticket / Ages 2 & up			
Melt Away Bay [D-4] A-ok!		7	6	7	
Bob in the sedate waves of a one-acre wave pool. Kids under 10 must be with an adult. Allie's Kid Tip: "The tide pools are cool to play in!" All ages.		**Pool** / C-Ticket			
Ski Patrol Training Camp [D-3] A-ok!		8	7	7	
Scaled-down area for kids 12 and under. Try Snow Falls slide, Cool Runners tube slalom, and Thin Ice Training Course—a walk across a field of "ice floes." Allie's Kid Tip: "If an iceberg is far away, lean back to move toward it."		**Playground** / D-Ticket / Ages 6-12			
Tike's Peak [D-5] 👤		6	5	7	
Even the littlest ones have a miniature version of the park, with slides, wading pools, and play fountains. Must be 48"/122 cm or shorter. Ages 0-6.		**Playground** / C-Ticket			

Making the Most of Blizzard Beach

Save time—buy your park passes in advance at Guest Relations.

There's **little shade** here—use waterproof sunscreen and cover-ups!

Play **miniature golf** at Winter Summerland, adjacent to the water park. See page 193 for more on this imaginative mini golf course.

Pick up a **map** on your way in to locate the lockers ($5-7) and towels ($1). Life jackets are free if you leave an ID card and/or deposit.

You'll find **chaise lounges** wherever you go, but on busy days, follow the path around the back end of the mountain, where you'll find secluded lounging areas and the main entrance to Runoff Rapids.

This is the "**big thrill**" water park, so it draws a young crowd. Typhoon Lagoon is a better choice for families.

Wear **water shoes** to ward off the heat of the sand and sidewalks.

If you ride the big slides, bikinis are a very risky fashion statement. You'll have better luck with a **one-piece suit**.

The **Beach Haus** near the entrance sells just about anything you may have forgotten or lost, from sunscreen to swimsuits.

When the **summer weather** is at its hottest, the parking lots fill up early. Use Disney buses instead, which can always drive in.

Children under the age of 10 must be accompanied by an adult.

Park hours: generally open by 10:00 am, closed at 5:00 pm or later. A one-day pass (with tax) is $33.02/adults and $26.63/kids 3-9.

Ratings are explained on page 120.

Our Value Ratings:		Our Magic Ratings:		Readers' Ratings:
Quality:	7/10	Theme:	8/10	94% fell in love with it
Variety:	8/10	Excitement:	8/10	2% liked it well enough
Scope:	4/10	Fun Factor:	7/10	2% had mixed feelings
Overall Value:	6/10	Overall Magic:	8/10	2% were disappointed

Blizzard Beach is enjoyed by...	(rated by both authors and readers)	
Younger Kids: ♥♥♥	Young Adults: ♥♥♥♥♥	Families: ♥♥♥♥♥
Older Kids: ♥♥♥♥♥	Mid Adults: ♥♥♥	Couples: ♥♥♥
Teenagers: ♥♥♥♥♥	Mature Adults: ♥	Singles: ♥♥♥♥

TIPS

NOTES

RATINGS

Planning

Getting There

Staying in Style

Touring

Feasting

Making Magic

Index

Notes & More

Finding Your Way at Blizzard Beach

BLIZZARD BEACH PARK MAP

Map Legend
- 🚻 = Restroom
- 🚬 = Smoking Area
- ✚ = First Aid
- ✳ = Creek Entrance
- = Service
- ≈ = Pool/creek
- = Water
- = Beach
- = Path

MAP COORDINATES: A B C D E

BEST TIMES

Thanks to the heated waters, you'll be comfortable throughout the **cooler months**, and the sun is kinder. The crowds are thinner, but the days are shorter, and an overcast, rainy winter day can make life miserable. Note that the park may be closed on Fridays and Saturdays in the cooler months. Summer at Blizzard Beach brings **huge crowds** that arrive early in the day. If the park reaches capacity, the gates close to all. By **mid-afternoon**, the crowds have thinned, as those who are worst-wilted have packed it in. That's a good time to arrive, refreshing yourself after a long morning at nearby Disney's Animal Kingdom. Operating hours vary with the season, so check before you trek. The park is generally closed in October and November.

GETTING THERE

By Bus—All resorts and Disney's Animal Kingdom have direct buses to Blizzard Beach. From Disney-MGM Studios, take the Coronado Springs bus. From Epcot, take the Disney's Animal Kingdom Lodge bus. From the Magic Kingdom and Downtown Disney, take a bus or monorail to a Disney resort and board a bus to Blizzard Beach. We recommend you take Disney transportation when you can, because the parking lot can fill up on busy days.

By Car—From westbound or eastbound I-4, take exit 65 (west on Osceola Parkway), exiting at Buena Vista Drive. Free parking.

Downtown Disney

If "heading downtown" is your idea of rest and recreation, the Walt Disney World Resort's Downtown Disney district is a major treat. From the world's largest Disney Store to mind-boggling Lego sculptures, super dining, and thrilling entertainment, you'll have a ball Downtown.

Downtown Disney has three unique **districts**. The **Marketplace** is a charming village of shops, **Pleasure Island** thrives on its vibrant night life, and **West Side** is the urban-style shopping, dining, and fun capital of the "World." Downtown Disney's pedestrian-only streets and sprawling layout avoid the "mall" feeling completely. This is one of the brightest, cleanest, safest, and most satisfying downtowns anywhere.

Downtown Disney satisfies the urge to "shop 'til you drop." Okay, so you can shop at every theme park, but there's no admission charge here, and you'll find much more than Disney merchandise. The **Marketplace** shops are Wonderful World of Memories (scrapbook center), The Art of Disney, Basin (bath and facial products), Disney's Days of Christmas, Eurospain (crystal shop), Disney at Home, Goofy's Candy Company, Once Upon a Toy, Summer Sands (resortwear), Disney's Pin Traders, Lego Imagination Center, Pooh Corner, Team Mickey's Athletic Club, and the World of Disney (the world's largest Disney Store). 2004 brought a new addition—Disney Tails (pet care and pampering items). **West Side** shopping features Sunglass Icon, Disney's Candy Cauldron, DisneyQuest Emporium, Guitar Gallery, Hoypoloi (sculpture gallery), Magnetron (magnets), Mickey's Groove (funky Disney gifts), Planet Hollywood on Location, Sosa Family Cigars, Starabilias (collectibles), Virgin Megastore, Wetzel's Pretzels, and shops at House of Blues, Cirque du Soleil, and DisneyQuest. Magic Masters offers top-flight magic gear, demos, and even a hidden room where guests can learn to use their magic tricks. **Pleasure Island** shops are discussed on page 188. Eateries and entertainment venues often have shops. Packages can be delivered to your Disney resort!

Downtown Disney builds fun into nearly every shop and restaurant, but four spots put entertainment first. Movie fans flock to the **AMC 24 Theatres Complex**, the Southeast's largest—their theaters sport stadium seating, most with retractable armrests. The innovative **Cirque du Soleil** also makes its home Downtown—see page 182. **DisneyQuest**, Disney's indoor "theme park," gets its own write-up on pages 183-186, as does **Pleasure Island** is on pages 187-190.

AMBIENCE

SHOPPING

PLAYING

Planning | Getting There | Staying in Style | Touring | Feasting | Making Magic | Index | Notes & More

Planning

Getting There

Staying in Style

Touring

Feasting

Making Magic

Index

Notes & More

Feeding Your Family
at Downtown Disney

DOWNTOWN DISNEY MAP

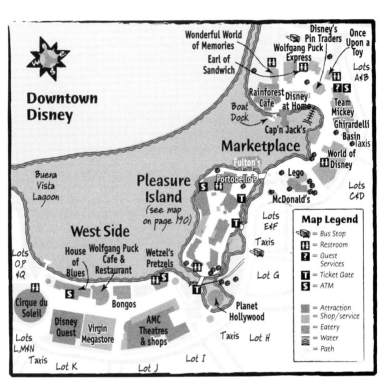

DINING

With the exception of Epcot, you won't find a more **diverse array** of dining experiences in the "World" than at Downtown Disney. For a heaping serving of showbiz, head to Downtown Disney West Side. The House of Blues serves up fabulous live music, Wolfgang Puck Grand Cafe offers famously innovative California fare, and Bongos Cuban Cafe has sizzling Latin rhythm and foods. Downtown Disney's showplace is the famous Planet Hollywood, which drips with movie memorabilia. Eateries are quieter at the Marketplace, a fine start for your night at Pleasure Island. Fulton's Crab House serves upscale seafood in a riverboat, the Rainforest Cafe cooks up imaginative fare, Portobello Yacht Club offers Northern Italian food in a casual atmosphere, and Cap'n Jack's Restaurant does seafood and steaks. Busy shoppers like the lighter fare at The Earl of Sandwich, Wetzel's Pretzels, Wolfgang Puck Express, Ghirardelli Soda Fountain & Chocolate Shop, and, of course, "Ronald's Fun House" (McDonald's). Complete descriptions of these Downtown Disney eateries begin on page 220.

Making the Most of Downtown Disney

Once Upon A Toy has amazing decor and unique toys, including make-your-own Tinkertoys and Mr. Potato Head sets, plus a Lincoln Log version of Wilderness Lodge and a Haunted Mansion Clue game.

Kids can **play for free** at the Lego Imagination Center and in the water play fountain near the Marketplace bus stop entrance.

Little-known **discounts and specials** may be available. Be sure to ask! For example, movies at the AMC Pleasure Island 24 are $6.50 before 6:00 pm, which makes them a cool hangout on a hot day.

Every November, the **Festival of the Masters** at Downtown Disney offers art exhibits, food specialties, performances, and kids' activities.

Christmas brings fun activities, including an honest-to-goodness ice skating rink. There's also a toy train ride that operates year-round. And don't forget the Disney's Days of Christmas shop, open year-round.

Of the eateries here, only Cap'n Jack's is run by the Walt Disney World Resort, so **reservations policies** differ, although many now offer Priority Seating through Disney. Most eateries and shops let you charge purchases to your Disney resort tab.

The Downtown Disney Marketplace and Pleasure Island **parking lots** are often packed. Try the huge West Side parking lot and use the shuttle boat (when operating) to reach the Marketplace.

Most **shops** in the Marketplace open at 9:30 am, while West Side shops open at 10:30 am. Closing is at 11:00 pm, with seasonal variations.

For **more information** and answers to questions, call Downtown Disney Guest Services at 407-828-3058.

By Bus—Buses are available from every Disney resort. From the Magic Kingdom, Epcot, Disney-MGM Studios, or Disney's Animal Kingdom, bus or monorail to a nearby resort and transfer.
By Car—From I-4, take exit 67, then take the first exit and turn right on Buena Vista Dr. Parking is free.
By Boat—Boats may shuttle between the Marketplace and West Side seasonally. Resort guests at Port Orleans, Old Key West, and Saratoga Springs can take a boat to the Marketplace, too.
By Foot—Guests at Hotel Plaza Resorts may find it quicker to walk.

TIPS

NOTES

GETTING THERE

Planning | Getting There | Staying in Style | Touring | Feasting | Making Magic | Index | Notes & More

Making the Most of Cirque du Soleil

A circus has come to Walt Disney World, the likes of which you've probably never seen—magical, musical, a little mystical, and poetically graceful. Cirque du Soleil ("Circus of the Sun") from Montreal, Canada, has redefined the concept of "circus" for millions around the world and has a company-in-residence at Downtown Disney West Side.

SHOWS

Cirque du Soleil weaves its magic with acrobats, clowns, jugglers, dancers, aerialists, lights, original music, and fabulous costumes (and not one animal). The current show, **La Nouba** (from the French "to live it up"), weaves a continuous, dream-like thread. There's a story here, but many guests hardly notice or care. This isn't Big Top-style circus, either. It has as much in common with modern dance as it does with circus. It's not for everyone (Dave likes it, Jennifer doesn't), but it adds yet another dimension to the magic. Note that this show has no intermission.

INFO

Housed in its own **1,671-seat theater** at the west end of the West Side, Cirque du Soleil presents its 90-min. shows at 6:00 and 9:00 pm, Tues.–Sat., and goes on brief hiatus four times during 2005. Tickets are $63–$91/adults and $42–$63/kids ages 3-11. Call 407-939-7600 or visit the box office. Seats are assigned based on availability, but you might get your pick at the box office. Premium seats are front center, cheap seats extreme left and right rear (see chart below).

SEATING PLAN

Cirque du Soleil Theater Seating Plan

Disney's Animal Kingdom Area | Epcot Area | Downtown Disney Area | Magic Kingdom Area

Chapter 4: Touring the "World" | Topic: DisneyQuest Introduction | 183

Planning
Getting There
Staying in Style
Touring
Feasting
Making Magic
Index
Notes & More

DisneyQuest

DisneyQuest is an indoor "theme park" housed in a big, blue, five-story building at Downtown Disney West Side. It features ride simulators, high-tech games, and hands-on activities for young and old alike.

Attractions run the gamut from simple video arcade games to a you-design-it, you-ride-it roller coaster simulator. Take the "Cyberlator" elevator to the Ventureport, where you can enter four zones: **Explore Zone**, **Score Zone**, **Create Zone**, and **Replay Zone**. Each zone organizes the attractions (described below) by theme. Each zone spans at least two floors, with various stairs and walkways linking them. This makes for a bewildering maze—study our map on page 186 to orient yourself before you go.

LAYOUT

■ **Aladdin's Magic Carpet Ride** [Floor 2]	A-OK!	6 4 6

Don virtual reality goggles for a wild, 4-min. ride on Aladdin's magic carpet. Swoop through Agrabah and the Cave of Wonder to search for jewels and free the Genie. Motion sickness warning. Explore Zone. **Allie's Kid Tip:** *"Make sure your helmet is on tight so it doesn't fall off when you play."*	Virtual
	D-Ticket
	Ages 6 & up
	Dizziness

■ **Animation Academy** [Floor 2]	A-OK!	7 7 6

Take your seat at a computer workstation as an instructor draws out your artistry. Hands-on lessons in drawing and/or animating characters. Several 20-minute lessons are offered. After the class, you can buy your creation. Create Zone. **Allie's Kid Tip:** *"Check the schedule for a class that draws a character you like."*	Hands-On
	D-Ticket
	Ages 6 & up
	Skill helps

■ **Buzz Lightyear's Astroblasters** [Floor 3]	🧍	7 5 7

Ride fully enclosed two-person bumper cars mounted with "cannons" that shoot large rubber balls. The driver pilots to scoop up ammo, and the gunner fires on other cars to make them spin out of control. 3-min. game. 51"/130 cm height restriction. Replay Zone. **Allie's Kid Tip:** *"Try to hit a lot of cars so they spin around."*	Vehicles
	D-Ticket
	Ages 9 & up
	Bumpy

■ **CyberSpace Mountain** [Floor 2]	🧍	9 8 9

Design and ride your own coaster! Start by choosing a theme and designing the coaster tracks on a computer screen. Then get strapped into a two-person flight simulator to experience your coaster, or choose from a ready-made coaster. Be prepared to be shaken, rattled, and rolled on a ride more dizzying than the real thing. Simulator seats are small. 51"/130 cm height restriction. Create Zone. **Allie's Kid Tip:** *"If you feel sick just hit the red stop button."*	Simulator
	E-Ticket
	Ages 9 & up
	Upside-down during inversions

■ **Invasion! An ExtraTERRORestrial Alien Encounter** [Floor 5]	A-OK!	6 7 5

Dash across the galaxy to rescue Earth colonists from an invading horde in this simulator ride that borrows characters and fun from the popular Magic Kingdom attraction. One teammate pilots the rescue vehicle, while three other teammates keep the bad guys at bay. Great pre-show film. Score Zone. **Allie's Kid Tip:** *"I think kids will have more fun being a gunner than a pilot."*	Simulator
	E-Ticket
	Ages 7 & up
	Violent theme

Attraction descriptions and ratings are explained on page 127.

Charting the Attractions at DisneyQuest

	Jennifer's Rating	Dave's Rating	Readers' Rating

☐ Living Easels [Floor 2]   A-OK!   **5** | **4** | **4**

Draw animated landscapes on a touch-sensitive screen. You can buy print-outs if you like. Create Zone. Allie's Kid Tip: *"Use your imagination!" Ages 3 & up.*
> Hands-On
> B-Ticket

☐ Magic Mirror [Floor 2]   A-OK!   **3** | **3** | **5**

Indulge your digital artistry as you turn a photo of yourself into a wacky portrait. Create Zone. Allie's Kid Tip: *"Use your parent's face! It's funny!" Ages 4 & up.*
> Hands-On
> B-Ticket

☐ Midway on the Moon [Floors 4 & 5]   A-OK!   **6** | **8** | **5**

Disney-themed versions of arcade games like Ursula's Whirlpool and traditional games like Skeeball. Purchase "points" to play ($5 for 20 credits) then redeem for prizes. Replay Zone. Allie's Kid Tip: *"Look at all the games before you play."*
> Arcade
> A-Ticket
> Ages 5 & up

☐ Mighty Ducks Pinball Slam [Floor 3]   🏃   **5** | **4** | **7**

Use body motion/weight to move a "puck" around a huge screen and "body check" opponents on this simulator. 3-min. game. 48"/122 cm height restriction. Score Zone. Allie's Kid Tip: *"If you're tall enough but skinny, it might not work."*
> Simulator
> D-Ticket
> Ages 9 & up

☒ Pirates of the Caribbean: Battle for Buccaneer Gold [Floor 1]   🏃 A-OK!   **8** | **8** | **9**

Yo ho, yo ho! DisneyQuest's newest attraction pits you and up to four shipmates in a 3-D simulated sea battle in quest of pirate gold. Fire virtual cannonballs against your foes, and feel the deck shudder when you take a hit. 35"/89 cm height restriction. Explore Zone. Allie's Kid Tip: *"Shoot the ships that you pass!"*
> Simulator
> E-Ticket
> Ages 7 & up
> Violent theme

☐ Radio Disney SongMaker [Floor 2]   A-OK!   **6** | **6** | **4**

Create your own hit song in a soundbooth. Combine styles and lyrics for laughs. You can buy a CD of it. Create Zone. Allie's Kid Tip: *"Don't be shy." Ages 4 & up.*
> Hands-On
> D-Ticket

☐ Ride the Comix [Floors 4 and 5]   **2** | **3** | **5**

Swing your laser sword to battle comic strip villains in this 4-min., 3-D virtual reality game. Heavy goggles, sword-play, and motion sickness make this hard to play. Score Zone. Allie's Kid Tip: *"The monsters might scare you." Ages 8 & up.*
> Virtual
> D-Ticket
> May feel dizzy

☐ Sid's Create-A-Toy [Floor 2]   **3** | **4** | **5**

Create a demented toy from spare toy parts—on a computer screen. You can buy a real version of your creation. Create Zone. Allie's Kid Tip: *"Boring." Ages 4 & up.*
> Hands-On
> B-Ticket

☐ Treasure of the Incas [Floor 1]   A-OK!   **5** | **4** | **4**

Drive a remote-control truck through an underground maze—a small camera mounted on the truck gives you a visual. Allie's Kid Tip: *"Have a grown-up watch your truck and call out directions." Create Zone. Closed (temporarily?) in 2004.*
> Maze
> B-Ticket
> Ages 5 & up

☒ Virtual Jungle Cruise [Floor 1]   A-OK!   **9** | **6** | **6**

Board a raft, grab a paddle, and take a 4-min. whitewater river cruise back in time on this motion simulator ride. Dr. Wayne Szalinski guides you and your teammates on this riotous journey over waterfalls and into the age of the dinosaurs. You may get a little damp. Explore Zone. Allie's Kid Tip: *"Paddle hard."*
> Simulator
> E-Ticket
> Ages 6 & up
> Paddling

Making the Most of DisneyQuest

You won't go hungry at DisneyQuest. The Cheesecake Factory operates two satisfying **counter-service eateries**: FoodQuest and Wonderland Café. Up on the top floor, FoodQuest (see page 222) offers an appetizing variety of pizzas, salads, burgers, sandwiches, and wraps, plus a few tempting desserts. On the floor below, Wonderland Café (see page 223) pleases the sweet tooth with a huge selection of cheesecakes and desserts, and all sorts of luxurious coffee concoctions. And while you sip your latté, you can browse the Internet on limited-use computer terminals.

First-time visitors should spend time exploring the entire place before splitting up. While you're at it, choose a **meeting place** and time. The Wonderland Café is a good choice with places to sit, and the Ventureport on the third floor is highly visible.

Allow at least **four to five hours** to tour, more if you love arcades.

Be sure to wear a **wristwatch**—it's easy to lose track of time! Also, it's faster to use the stairs to go up or down one level. On the other hand, the elevators are less disorienting than the curving staircases.

The Wonderland Café sports tables with **free Internet access**, but the custom browser makes it tough to surf at will.

Rumor has it DisneyQuest *may* become an **ESPN Zone**.

Best times to visit are during the mornings and afternoons and on the weekends. It gets pretty busy in the evenings, after other parks are closed. Crowds are huge on foul-weather days.

Discount admissions may be available after 10:00 pm.

Ratings are explained on page 120.

Our Value Ratings:		Our Magic Ratings:		Readers' Ratings:
Quality:	6/10	Theme:	5/10	78% fell in love with it
Variety:	4/10	Excitement:	5/10	22% liked it well enough
Scope:	3/10	Fun Factor:	6/10	0% had mixed feelings
Overall Value:	**5/10**	**Overall Magic:**	**5/10**	0% were disappointed

DisneyQuest is enjoyed by...		(rated by both authors and readers)
Younger Kids: ♥♥♥♥	Young Adults: ♥♥♥♥♥	Families: ♥♥♥♥
Older Kids: ♥♥♥♥♥	Mid Adults: ♥♥♥	Couples: ♥♥♥
Teenagers: ♥♥♥♥♥	Mature Adults: ♥	Singles: ♥♥♥♥♥

Finding Your Way at DisneyQuest

DISNEYQUEST PARK MAP

Map Legend
- **T** = Ticket Booth
- **?** = Guest Services
- 🚻 = Restroom
- **E** = Elevator

Floor 5: Invasion! Alien Encounter, Ride the Comix, Food Quest, Midway on the Moon

Floor 4: Midway on the Moon, Wonderland Café, Ride the Comix, Midway on the Moon

Floor 3: Mighty Duck's Pinball Slam, Ventureport (start), Buzz Lightyear's Astroblaster

Floor 2: Animation Academy, Living Easels, Sid's Create-A-Toy, Radio Disney SongMaker, Magic Mirror, Aladdin's, Cyberspace Mountain

Floor 1: Virtual Jungle Cruise, Pirates of the Caribbean, Treasure of the Incas, Cyberlators, Exit, Entrance, DisneyQuest Emporium

ADMISSION

In keeping with Disney's approach to park admission, you pay a **single all-day price** and enjoy unlimited use of all rides, games, and activities (excluding games that award prizes—a 20-credit card costs $5). Adults pay $33.02 for a full day admission, and kids ages 3-9 pay $26.63. Children under 10 must be accompanied by an adult, but feel free to leave the older kids here while you shop elsewhere. Annual passes are available—see page 116. DisneyQuest **admission is included** in Ultimate Park Hoppers and Premium Annual Passes, but it is not an option on the Park Hopper Plus passes. DisneyQuest hours are 10:30 am–11:00 pm Sundays–Thursdays, and 10:30 am–midnight on Fridays and Saturdays.

INFO

For more DisneyQuest information, call 407-828-4600 or visit http://www.disneyquest.com. There is also a DisneyQuest kiosk in Downtown Disney Marketplace that offers information.

Pleasure Island

AMBIENCE

Where can you celebrate a Times Square-style New Year's Eve every night at midnight, disco down until 2:00 am, lay back and listen to some cool, live jazz, laugh it up at a comedy club, or enjoy the camaraderie of a band of intrepid explorers? Pleasure Island! The party starts at 7:00 pm and continues until 2:00 am nightly, and admission to the clubs is required (see page 189). The clubs are described below.

8Trax — 8 5 6
Disco in all its Saturday Night Fever glory! The sound is classic 70s (Thursday is 80s night) the floor is packed and illuminated, and dancers are enthusiastic!
Dance — C-Ticket

Adventurers Club — A-OK! — 10 10 8
In all ways, this is the most "Disney" of the clubs on Pleasure Island (and our absolute favorite). Be prepared for the unexpected, the quirky, and the hilarious. The walls are encrusted with trophies, mementos, curios, and photos amassed by the club members—intrepid explorers and wannabes all. Look closely—this is Disney, after all! You may be greeted by the club's stoic butler, the matronly Club President, or even a French maid. Different shows are held throughout the night in the Mask Room, Treasure Room, and Library. **Allie's Kid Tip:** "The Yakoose moose drools! And they make you sing silly songs!"
Comedy — E-Ticket — Shows run continuously from 8pm to 1am — Audience participation

BET SoundStage Club — 6 4
Contemporary music and dancing for guests 21 and over. The club is one of the smaller ones, but the intimate atmosphere can be enjoyable.
Dance — C-Ticket

Comedy Warehouse — A-OK! — 9 7 9
Houses the Who, What and Wherehouse Players, a comedy troupe that delivers hilarious skits, standup acts, improv sketches, and adult humor "Disney-style." **Allie's Kid Tip:** "This is funny, but don't sit next to the telephone!"
Comedy — D-Ticket — Rib-tickling

Mannequins Dance Palace — 7 6 6
Voted the #1 dance club in the Southeast, this is the place for the hottest dance mix and the biggest sound and lighting system. Bouncers in tuxes proof you and let in a few people at a time. Very, very loud.
Dance — E-Ticket — Must be 21+

Motion — 2 5 7
A big dance floor and clean, open layout are all that distinguish this large club. Top 40 and alternative dance. Motion replaced the Wildhorse Saloon.
Dance — C-Ticket

Pleasure Island Jazz Company — 8 7 5
Offers a New Orleans setting for enjoying live jazz. There's a nice, elevated seating area outside. Wide choice of fine cigars (but you must smoke outside).
Music — C-Ticket

Rock 'n' Roll Beach Club — 8 7 6
Offers fans of classic and modern rock a crowded dance floor, live "cover" bands, and a DJ. You can also play pinball and munch-out on nachos.
Dance — D-Ticket

Eating and Playing at Pleasure Island

SHOPPING & EATING

Pleasure Island has its share of **small boutiques**, such as DTV (trendy fashions for all), Changing Attitudes (more clothing), Mouse House (Disney logo items and golf clothing), SuperStar Studios (star in a video/song), and Zen Zone (massage beds). On our last visit, shops like Suspended Animation were no longer selling merchandise. So it's not the best place to do serious shopping, and a good meal is even harder to come by. Eatery details are on page 221.

Adventurers Club members entertain on stage in the Library
(left to right: Butler Graves, Club Curator Fletcher Hodges, Club President Pamelia Perkins, Professor Otis T. Wren, Club Aviator Hathaway Brown)

© MediaMarx, Inc.

PLAYING

The West End Stage is the focus of the **nightly New Year's Eve** show at midnight. A live band rocks the stage for much of the evening, and at midnight, the streets are showered with confetti and fireworks. Every so often, the West End Stage plays host to **big-name acts**, too. Farther down the main street, the Hub Video Stage occasionally hosts performances by **smaller bands** and **energetic dancers**. The small Waterfront Stage is used on special occasions. Live and inside, you'll enjoy the **live jazz** every night at the Pleasure Island Jazz Company and straight-ahead **rock bands** at the Rock 'n Roll Beach Club. The Adventurers Club offers some **different kinds of fun**: sing-alongs, cabarets, "Fingers" the organ player, and "Balderdash" storytelling! Kungaloosh!

GETTING THERE

By Bus—Frequent buses are available from Disney resorts. From a park, bus or monorail to a nearby resort and transfer to a Downtown Disney bus. Get off at the second Downtown Disney stop.
By Car—Follow signs to Downtown Disney. Parking is free. If you intend to drink, please designate a driver. Tip for designated drivers: As you pass through a turnstile inside the first club you visit, let the cast member know that you're not imbibing and you may get two free soft drink coupons to use that evening.
By Boat—From Port Orleans, Old Key West, and Saratoga Springs, take a boat to the Marketplace and walk. All guests may use the boat between Marketplace and West Side, when it is running.

Making the Most of Pleasure Island

TIPS

Planning

Getting There

Staying in Style

Touring

Feasting

NOTES

Making Magic

RATINGS

Index

Notes & More

All Pleasure Island clubs are **non-smoking**.

Adventurers Club can seem a little confusing at first, but just wait a while—something's sure to happen wherever you are, when you least expect it. Come with a sense of adventure and be ready to join in. You can be inducted into the club, learn the secret greeting, and sing the club song! We absolutely adore the Adventurers Club and consider it one of our favorite places at Walt Disney World. We recommend the Kungaloosh and Jungle Juice drinks!

If you find the excitement too much, or just want to go somewhere romantic with that special someone, head for our **"hidden patio."** Go down the stairs beside the Adventurers Club, or go down the stairs beside the West End Stage and turn right before the bridge.

Alcoholic beverages are even served on the streets of Pleasure Island. Adults 21 and older get wristbands to show they can drink.

A good spot to watch the **New Year's Eve show** is from the access ramp in front of Adventurers Club. Just don't block it!

Pleasure Island clubs are open to guests **18 years and older** (younger kids can come with a parent or legal guardian). You'll need a valid driver's license or state I.D. (with photo). They really do "proof" you at the door, and if you're over 21 you'll get a special wristband that allows you to imbibe liquor. You must be over 21 to enter BET SoundStage Club and Mannequins Dance Palace (some nights)! If you bring kids, be prepared for some good-natured ribbing from performers.

Pleasure Island reduced its admission price to **$18.05/person** and is included in some passes. Ask about discounts. Clubs open from 7:00 pm to 2:00 am nightly, though some clubs may open later.

Ratings are explained on page 120.

Our Value Ratings:		Our Magic Ratings:		Readers' Ratings:
Quality:	6/10	Theme:	6/10	48% fell in love with it
Variety:	3/10	Excitement:	7/10	39% liked it well enough
Scope:	4/10	Fun Factor:	7/10	9% had mixed feelings
Overall Value:	**4/10**	**Overall Magic:**	**7/10**	4% were disappointed

Pleasure Island is enjoyed by...	(rated by both authors and readers)	
Younger Kids: ❤	Young Adults: ❤❤❤❤❤	Families: ❤
Older Kids: ❤❤	Mid Adults: ❤❤❤❤	Couples: ❤❤❤❤
Teenagers: ❤❤❤❤❤	Mature Adults: ❤❤	Singles: ❤❤❤❤❤

Charting Your Route at Pleasure Island

Planning

Getting There

Staying in Style

Touring

Feasting

Making Magic

Index

Notes & More

PLEASURE ISLAND PARK MAP

BEST TIMES TO GO

Time flies at Pleasure Island, so arrive **early in the evening** to really make the most of your visit. The clubs start hopping as soon as they open at 7:00-9:00 pm. **Comedy Warehouse** isn't the place to come for an entire evening's entertainment, but if you don't mind standing in line to enter, this is a fine place to go before you head out to other clubs. Note that Mondays and Thursdays are Cast Member Nights and tend to be crowded. To escape the crowds and noise, consider the Comedy Warehouse or Jazz Company during the **busiest times** of the evening—usually between 10:00 pm and midnight. Don't miss the nightly **New Year's Eve show** at the West End Stage, beginning at 11:45 pm. Note that the West End entrance (and the "hidden patio" mentioned on the previous page) is closed before and during the New Year's Eve fireworks show. Pleasure Island's streets are now admission-free at all times. Stroll through—some clubs may be open for a free "sample" and the live stage is rocking for all. Admission is now checked at the club entrances, and tickets can be bought at some shops as well as the ticket booths.

The Happiest Celebration on Earth

On July 17, 1955, Walt Disney cut the ribbon at his new California theme park, and a new era began. 50 years later, the Disney theme park empire spans the globe and the entire company is set to celebrate Disneyland's **50th birthday in grand style**. Dubbed "The Happiest Celebration on Earth," the party starts on May 5, 2005 (05/05/05) and will continue through the end of 2006.

You won't have to go to Disneyland to be part of the celebration (although you can be sure many will make the pilgrimage). Every Disney theme park around the world will be **observing the occasion**. At Walt Disney World Resort, every major theme park will have a new attraction of some sort, and while the details haven't been released at press time, the parks will undoubtedly be decked out in special decorations for the big occasion.

The Magic Kingdom is gaining **Cinderellabration**, a live show on the Castle Forecourt Stage in front of Cinderella Castle. The show is currently running to rave reviews at Tokyo Disneyland. Although it's opening in late 2004, Stitch's Great Escape! (see page 135) may be counted as a part of the celebration.

Epcot does especially well, with the opening of **Soarin'** (aka Soarin' Over California), one of the top attractions at Disney's California Adventure park at Disneyland Resort (see page 145). Epcot will also host the **Hong Kong Disneyland Preview Center**, spotlighting Disney's 11th major theme park (opening in late 2005).

Disney-MGM Studios gains the **Lights, Motors, Action! Extreme Stunt Show** (see page 158), a hugely popular show at Disney Studios Paris.

Disney's Animal Kingdom starts the celebration slowly, with a visit from **Lucky the Dinosaur**, the first free-roaming Audio-Animatronics creation and a star of Disney's California Adventure during his 2004 debut. In early 2006, the park will see the debut of **Expedition: Everest** (see page 169), the tallest peak in Disney's "mountain range" of coasters.

The Florida-based Disney Cruise Line also will participate. The Disney Magic will steam through the **Panama Canal** in May to bring the Disney Cruise experience to **California** for the first time. The ship will resume its East coast/Caribbean sailings in early September. Meantime, the Disney Wonder will continue with its normal 3- and 4-night Bahamian cruises.

It's going to be quite a party!

More Places to Play

BoardWalk—Pleasure Island doesn't have a monopoly on nightclubs in Walt Disney World—the BoardWalk resort has its own entertainment complex with clubs, restaurants, and entertainment. Jellyrolls is a dueling piano bar that serves drinks and free popcorn ($7 cover, 21 and up, smoking allowed). Atlantic Dance Hall serves specialty drinks while open-request DJ music lures you onto the floor (no cover, 21 and up, open Tuesday–Saturday). ESPN Club (page 224) is a popular sports bar. Midway games and street performers add to the fun. For details and directions to the BoardWalk resort, see pages 43–46.

Celebration, Florida—Imagine what would happen if Disney created a real town and you've got the community of Celebration, located on a corner of the Walt Disney World property just a few miles from the parks. Visitors to this quaint, small town may stroll or shop, have a bite in a restaurant, take in a movie at the theater, or stay in the luxury hotel. Others dream of moving to this carefully planned development. For more information, call 407-566-2200 or visit http://www.celebrationfl.com.

Golf—The Walt Disney World Resort boasts **99 holes of golf** on five championship courses and one nine-hole course, and consistently lands on a variety of prestigious "top golf resort" lists. All courses are open to the public and feature full-service facilities, including driving ranges, pro shops, cafes, and lessons. Guests at Disney resort hotels get free transportation to the links for their scheduled tee times. For details and tee times, call 407-WDW-GOLF. We recommend the Unofficial Walt Disney World Golf Site at http://www.wdwgolf.com.

Miniature Golf Courses—Disney has miniature golf, too! **Fantasia Gardens**, near the Swan Resort, has two 18-hole courses. One course is based on the scenes, characters, and music of Disney's classic animated film, "Fantasia." The other is a "grass" course (Fantasia Fairways) with wildly undulating par-three and par-four holes from 40-75 feet long. Waits for tee times for this challenging course are typically double the wait for the Fantasia course, so leave yourself some extra time. **Winter Summerland** is a miniature golf park at Blizzard Beach. It sports two 18-hole courses—one is blanketed in "snow," and the other celebrates the holidays in the tropics. Both are fun, and neither is particularly difficult. Tip: Ask about the "secret hole of the day" after you play at either course—if you get a hole-in-one in the secret hole, you may get a surprise. Cost is about $10 for adults and $8 for children (second round is half price), with discounts for Annual Passholders. Hours: 10:00 am to midnight.

More Places to Play
(continued)

Fort Wilderness Resort—Here's another resort with a lot to offer! Fort Wilderness is a respite from the bustle of the parks, offering canoeing, boating, fishing excursions, biking, tennis, horseback trail rides, horse-drawn carriage rides, and wagon rides. And you don't have to spend a penny to visit the petting farm (pony rides cost $3), blacksmith shop, and a nightly campfire program (with character visits and free movies). Jennifer, Dave, and Allie enjoyed their trail ride at the resort's Tri-Circle D Livery in 2002. It is a good entry-level horseback riding experience for riders age 9 and up and costs $32. Phone 407-824-2832 for reservations. For more information on Fort Wilderness, see pages 59–62.

Health Clubs & Spas—Many of the deluxe resorts have health clubs with exercise equipment—some even offer massage treatments, steam rooms, and saunas. If you've got relaxation in mind, we recommend the **Saratoga Springs Spa** and **Grand Floridian Spa & Health Club**. These world-class, full-service centers offer many beauty and wellness treatments, nutrition and fitness counseling, and lots of pampering. Call 407-827-4455 (Saratoga Springs) or 407-824-2332 (Grand Floridian Spa), or visit http://www.relaxedyet.com.

Tennis—Anyone for a game? Tennis enthusiasts won't be disappointed—seven sets of courts are available around Walt Disney World. Our pick is the Racquet Club at the Contemporary Resort, with six state-of-the-art hydrogrid courts. Call 407-939-7529.

Walt Disney World Speedway—Disney has its own speedway—a one-mile, tri-oval track for **auto racing**. The race track is home to the Richard Petty Driving Experience, in which participants get to drive or ride at speeds up to 145 mph! In July 2002, Dave strapped on his helmet and climbed in the passenger seat of a race car for a "ride around" experience. In a flash, the crew had his seat harness buckled, the photographer snapped his macho image for posterity, and he was headed out of the pit faster than you can say "zero to sixty." Dave's not a racing fan, but you don't really have to be to get a thrill out of this experience. For Richard Petty Experience details, call 407-939-0130.

Disney Nature Reserve—The Nature Conservancy runs this 12,000 acre hiking haven at the headwaters of the Everglades. For information, visit http://www.nature.org and search on "disney."

More Places to Play
(continued)

Waterways (Boating, Fishing, etc.)—Water, water everywhere—and lots of things to do! You can rent boats at nearly every deluxe and moderate resort and Downtown Disney. Probably the most popular rentals craft are little, two-person speed boats called Sea Raycers—the old Water Mice have been replaced by these more up-to-date craft. They're available at most marinas around Disney for $23 per half-hour (must be 12+ to pilot). Fishing excursions and cane pole rentals are also available in most of those same places. In 2004, Disney announced an enhanced bass fishing program, in association with BASS, the leading bass fishing organization. Guests can reserve two-hour, guided, catch-and-release bass expeditions at many Disney marinas. All equipment is provided (even a digital camera to document your catch), fishing licenses are not needed thanks to the state-licensed guide on board, and participants even get a free subscription to Bassmaster Magazine. Excursions accommodate up to five guests and cost $195-$215. Kids 6-12 can go on special one-hour excursions for $30. Phone 407-WDW-BASS for info. See page 244 for more on water-borne recreation at Disney.

Disney's Wide World of Sports Complex—Disney's state-of-the-art **athletic center** features a 7,500-seat baseball stadium, a 30,000-square-foot fieldhouse, a track & field complex, volleyball, tennis, baseball, softball, football, and more. In 2005, Disney opens a major expansion, adding another 20 acres of baseball, softball, and multi-sport fields under the sponsorship of Amerada Hess. The complex already hosts 170 youth, amateur, and professional sporting events annually, and clearly more are on the way. With admission ($9.69/adults or $7.46/kids 3–9), visitors enjoy the Multi-Sport Experience covering sports such as football, baseball, and basketball. The 200-acre center is also home to amateur and professional sports, including Atlanta Braves Spring Training and the Tampa Bay Buccaneers training camp. For more information, call 407-828-FANS or visit http://www.disneyworldsports.com.

Walt Disney World Running and Inline Skating Events—Disney's Wide World of Sports isn't just for spectators. Runners can register for the Walt Disney World Marathon, Half-Marathon, Family Fun Run 5K, and Kids' Races, all of which take place on a busy weekend in January (Jan. 8 & 9, 2005). April brings the Walt Disney World Inline Marathon and All Star Kids' (inline) Classic (April 30 & May 1, 2005). Skipping the hot Orlando summer, we next find Disney's International Distance Triathalon, which we expect to be held in September of 2005. October brings the Komen Central Forida Race for the Cure 5K and Disney's 10K Classic (October 9-10, 2004, 2005 date to be announced). Event volunteers are also needed. Visit http://www.disneyworldsports.com to learn more and to register.

Deciding What To Do

Whew! We bet you're now wondering how in the world (no pun intended) you'll find the time to **fit everything** at Walt Disney World into your vacation. It's simple: you can't do it. Even a month-long stay wouldn't be enough to do and see everything. Rather than try to fit everything into your vacation, make a practical plan.

Naturally, you can't plan everything in advance, nor should you try— spontaneity and discovery are two elements of a great vacation. Yet it is a good idea to get a feeling for the parks, attractions, and activities before you go and to make a note of the ones you simply "must" do. This helps you **create an itinerary** and keeps you from missing the things you've got your heart set on.

First, read the preceding pages carefully to gain a solid idea of what the Walt Disney World Resort is all about. Next, **make a list** of all the things you'd like to see and do. This can be a great family activity. Make it a free-for-all, no-holds-barred event—what we call a "blue-sky session." List everything, no matter how impractical, silly, or expensive. Once you've got a good list, pare it down to the things that are most important and copy them to the worksheet on the next two pages. List the activity, where in the "World" it is located (i.e., which park or resort), its approximate cost, and any notes (including why it's on the list).

When you're done with the list, take a good look at the locations. Are several located in the same park? If so, can you do them all on the same day? Go through the list and note other patterns. With luck, you'll have a better sense of where you're headed. Next, **assign the activities** to specific days of your vacation, using the Day/Date column on the far right. For example, on a recent trip, we wanted to visit Spaceship Earth, race around Test Track, and watch IllumiNations. All those activities are at Epcot, so we grouped them together on our third day. We wrote a "3" next to each of those items, but you could write "Wed" or the date instead. If you've planned too much for one day or place, your Cost and Notes columns may help you decide which activities to keep and which to throw out or schedule for another day.

Not all activities can be decided this way, nor should they. Some choices should be **spur of the moment**. Be sure to "schedule" some free time in your trip—preferably a whole day or two. Use these techniques as a general game plan to a great vacation!

Touring Worksheet

Use this worksheet to figure out the things you want to do most on your trip. Match up attractions to determine the parks you want to visit, noting the day/date (you may wish to refer to the Extra Magic Hour schedule on page 32). Fill in the park schedule grid at the bottom of the next page once you've picked days—the park schedule can help you complete your itinerary and choose eateries (in the next chapter).

Activity	Park	Land	Cost	Notes	Day/Date

Useful Abbreviations:

MK (Magic Kingdom)
EP (Epcot)
MGM (Disney-MGM Studios)
DAK (Disney's Animal Kingdom)
BB (Blizzard Beach)
TL (Typhoon Lagoon)
BW (BoardWalk)
DD (Downtown Disney)

DQ (DisneyQuest)
PI (Pleasure Island)
WWOS (Disney's Wide World of Sports)
DS (Disney Speedway)
FG (Fantasia Gardens)
WS (Winter Summerland)
DCL (Disney Cruise Line)
VB (Disney's Vero Beach)

OFF (Off-site)
USF (Universal Studios)
IOA (Islands of Adventure)
SW (SeaWorld)
COVE (Discovery Cove)
BG (Busch Gardens)
KSC (Kennedy Space Center)
CB (Cocoa Beach)
FH (Friend/Family's House)

Activity	Park	Land	Cost	Notes	Day/Date

Write your park schedule in this calendar grid—note the date in the corners.

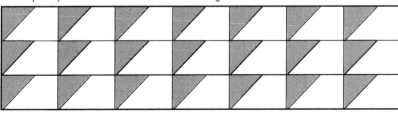

Planning

Getting There

Staying in Style

Touring

Feasting

Making Magic

Index

Notes & More

It's Not Such a Small World After All

If you've read this chapter, you know that touring Walt Disney World is no simple walk in the park. Here are some tips and tricks to help you:

- **Prepare your young child** for potentially "scary" things in the parks. For example, you could compare the troll in Maelstrom to the troll from "Dora the Explorer." We did this with our daughter and she didn't even get the slightest bit scared knowing what to expect.
  — Contributed by Tara Sydow, a winner in our 2004 Touring Tip Contest

- If you need to **keep in touch** with others, consider two-way radios, cell phones, or pagers. You may even be able to rent them for the duration of your stay from local companies. If you use radios or cell phones, remember to turn them off during attractions and shows.

- Disney attracts vacationers from around the world. Remember that other cultures have their own **customs**.

Magical Memories

"On our last family trip, the five of us were all seated for our first ride on Space Mountain. Dad was 'captain' in front, followed by the three boys, and I (Mom) brought up the rear. We were all breathless with anticipation and giddy with excitement as we waited for 'blast-off.' And it struck me: this is the ultimate moment. My family all together, happy, and in perfect sync with each other. I wished I could have bottled it so the next time there was a squabble over who sits in the front seat or whether we eat at McDonald's or Burger King, I could open that moment in time and we could all inhale the magic. That was one of the last times the five of us can all ride together. You see, we have added a new little Mouseketeer to our family: our one-year-old daughter from China. I look forward to the day when all six of us can ride Space Mountain together!"
...as told by Disney vacationer Jamie Dailey

"My son was about 3 ½ at the time of our Disney trip and really into Star Wars. For that reason, we were sure to take him to the Star Tours ride. He absolutely could not believe his eyes when we 'boarded our ship.' He fared rather well through the ride but the best part came when the ride ended. He ever so calmly looked over at me and in somewhat of a loud voice said, 'Where are we now, Mama?' Everyone on that ride heard him and the whole room errupted in laughter! I LOVE DISNEY!"
...as told by Disney vacationer Wendy Bloedt

"My wife and I took her parents for a once-in-a-lifetime trip to Walt Disney World. The first day at the Magic Kingdom was the best. As we came out from under the train station and entered the park, I saw their eyes as they looked up Main Street, U.S.A. It was worth all the money in the world. "How did they do all this?!" was uttered over and over by my in-laws. Seeing Disney through the eyes of two people who grew up not having much made us appreciate the wonder of Disney. You're never too old to experience Disney for the first time!"
...as told by Disney vacationer Thomas Blom

Feasting and Snacking

DISCOVER the fine points of dining at Disney

READ our reviews of restaurants and cafés

PLAN meals and reserve tables

LEARN about character meals and dinner shows

You can't have a good vacation without a good meal (or two), and your Disney vacation is no exception. Disney knows how to make your mealtimes as entertaining, adventuresome, and satisfying as the rest of your vacation experience. Disney eateries go out of their way to give everyone a unique and delicious dining experience, so you'll find that even the most exotic restaurant can please any taste, including the finicky eaters in your family. From the atmosphere to the service to the food itself, it has all been created to fill your imagination as well as your belly.

The choices can be awesome, ranging from basic hot dogs and burgers to once-in-a-lifetime elegance, from ultra-romantic dinners for two to foot-stompin' family hoedowns, and from exotic samplings of far-off places to the magic of a breakfast hug from Winnie the Pooh himself. One thing's for sure—you can't say, "There's nothing to eat around here!"

For us, meal planning is more important than choosing which attractions to visit. It's easier to jump in an unexpectedly short line at Space Mountain than it is to get a table at the better eateries.

The six basic types of Walt Disney World Resort meals are table-service restaurants, counter-service cafes, quick-service snack shops, "special experiences" (such as dinner shows and character meals), room service, and meals you fix yourself. We devote most of the space here to table-service and special dining experiences, which are more costly and require the most planning. We also include details on the counter service and snacks in the parks. Resort counter service and room service is discussed in the "Staying in Style" chapter. We can't say much about your home cooking until we're invited to your villa or campsite, though.

The chapter begins with a meal planning guide, then moves to mealtime tips, park-by-park and resort-by-resort eatery reviews, the low-down on the big shindigs, and ends with worksheets to plan your meals.

Bon appetit!

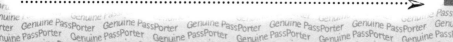

Deciding on Dining

If you thought selecting a restaurant in your hometown was tough, you haven't seen anything. The Walt Disney World Resort has more than **300 places to eat**. But before you go running for the exit, take heart. We've been to virtually every restaurant on property at least twice (usually several times) and we offer easily digestible descriptions and yummy ratings for you in this chapter. Better yet, we have a tried-and-true system for deciding where and when to eat.

First, decide **how often** you want to eat out. Many folks (including ourselves) bring or buy some food for in-room snacks or meals, with light breakfasts being the most practical choice. Most resorts can supply a refrigerator (sometimes for an additional fee), some include a coffeemaker, and home-away-from-home resorts have kitchen facilities, too. You can, of course, eat out every meal. We like to eat a light breakfast in our room with food we've packed or purchased, such as peanut butter and jelly on English muffins. We then do one or two special breakfasts "out" (such as a character breakfast—see pages 232–233). We often eat lunch and dinner at the parks, resorts, or Downtown Disney. Some vacationers prefer to eat a big meal mid-morning and another mid-afternoon to save time and money (it's easy to fill up at many restaurants). More money-saving ideas are on page 203.

Once you have an idea of how often you want (and can afford) to eat out, your next task is to decide **when and where**. Revisit your Touring Worksheet (pages 196–197) and check the parks you want to visit—it is much easier to choose a restaurant in or near your day's destination. Every park offers table-service restaurants, counter-service eateries, and snack shops and carts. To help you choose from the overwhelming number of dining choices at Walt Disney World, this chapter offers descriptions of nearly all eateries. Descriptions are organized alphabetically within each park and resort to help you focus on your choices. Pick the eateries that fall within your budget, tastes, and needs—you may find it helpful to highlight or circle those eatery descriptions that interest you.

As you make decisions about your meals and the eateries you want to visit, jot them down on your **Meal Worksheet** at the end of the chapter on page 238. Make note of those table-service eateries for which advance seating arrangements (priority seating) may be made. Continue on to the next page to learn the what, when, and how of priority seating arrangements at the Walt Disney World Resort.

Priority Seating

Virtually every table-service restaurant within Walt Disney World allows **advance seating arrangements**, known as "priority seating," or "P.S." These are not reservations. Rather, priority seating gives you the first available table upon arrival at your specified time. This system works better than traditional reservations, which require that guests wait while there is a table free because of latecomers and no-shows. The only Disney table-service restaurants that don't accept priority seating are some Downtown Disney restaurants, Big River Grille, and ESPN Club (see detailed listings in this chapter). Additionally, some restaurants take traditional reservations, such as Victoria & Albert's, the Swan & Dolphin restaurants (see pages 229–230), and the character breakfasts at Cinderella's Royal Table and Restaurant Akershus (see pages 232–233 for reservation details/policies).

Priority seating can be made in **advance of your arrival** by calling 407-WDW-DINE (407-939-3463). Call up to 90 days in advance for priority seating at most restaurants. (Disney switched most 60-day and 120-day restaurants to 90 days in 2003.) We list the number of days you may call in advance for priority seating with each restaurant's description in this chapter. We also suggest you visit Scott Thomas' handy Priority Seating Calculator at http://pscalculator.net for priority seating details. Arrangements can also be made the same day at the parks, and by touching "*88" on any Disney pay phone or "55" on your Disney resort phone.

When you call, you will be asked to supply the name of the Disney resort at which you are staying and your date of arrival—you can record this information at the top of your **Priority Seating Worksheet** on page 239. If you aren't staying at a Disney resort, no problem—you'll simply need to provide a daytime phone number. Also note that character breakfasts at Cinderella's Royal Table, some special dining experiences, and all Disney restaurants on major U.S. holidays (see calendar on inside front cover for dates) require a credit card deposit or guarantee. You will receive a **confirmation number** for each successfully arranged priority seating. Record this on a copy of your dining worksheet. If you later decide not to eat at a particular restaurant, just call Disney again and **cancel your priority seating**. If you are unable to get a priority seating, call back about one week before the desired date.

Due to the nature of priority seating arrangements, you should plan to **check in at the restaurant's podium 15 minutes before** your seating time. You may also need to wait anywhere from 5 to 30 minutes for a table to become available, depending upon how busy it is. Some restaurants issue a pager, and most have a comfortable waiting area or bar.

Restaurant Menu

Alcoholic Beverages—Most eateries serve alcoholic drinks, with the notable exception of those in the Magic Kingdom. Bars and lounges are located around the "World." Legal drinking age is 21 and they do check your identification. (Just ask Jennifer!)

Character Dining—Dine with Disney characters! See pages 232-233.

Children's Meals—Nearly every eatery has a children's menu at parent-friendly prices. Kid-staples like macaroni & cheese and chicken tenders can usually be had at the most exotic of restaurants—ask your server.

Counter Service—Most food at Disney is sold fast-food style. The quality does vary—it's generally worse at the Magic Kingdom and best at Disney's Animal Kingdom, the two parks where counter service is most common. At Magic Kingdom, we like Pecos Bill Cafe in Frontierland and Columbia Harbour House in Liberty Square. Disney's Animal Kingdom only has one table-service restaurant, but the counter-service food is several cuts above the ordinary. We especially like Tusker House's great rotisserie chicken and the Flame Tree Barbecue at Disney's Animal Kingdom.

Coupons/Discounts—Don't plan on finding coupons for restaurants. Discounts for early dinners and Annual Pass and Disney Vacation Club do exist—be sure to ask your server. See the money-saving tips on the following page for more information on available discounts.

Dietary Requirements—Low-cholesterol, low-salt, low-fat, and/or vegetarian meals are a regular part of the menu in most restaurants. With 24 hours of advance notice, kosher and other special dietary needs can be met. Cosmic Ray's at Magic Kingdom has a no-advance-notice kosher menu at the check-out (ask for this at other counter service restaurants, too). We also recommend the guidebook, "Vegetarian Walt Disney World and Greater Orlando" by Susan Shumaker and Than Saffel, published by The Globe Pequot Press. We include Susan and Than's "vegebility" ratings here—see page 204 for details. Dietary "special needs" are also addressed in the "PassPorter Walt Disney World for Your Special Needs" guidebook (see page 284.)

Dinner Shows—Disney offers several dinner shows, combining all-you-care-to-eat meals with live entertainment. See pages 234-237.

Dress—Casual clothing is appropriate for all eateries in the "World" except Victoria & Albert's in the Grand Floridian (see page 228). Several spots have "no tank top" rules. We note this in the eatery's description.

Entertainment—Some restaurants supply entertainment, while others like the Whispering Canyon Cafe and 'Ohana provide activities for kids.

Menus—Many menus can be previewed at Guest Services. Deb Wills' AllEarsNet Web site (http://www.allearsnet.com) also has a wonderful collection of up-to-date menus.

Money—Cash, Disney Dollars, traveler's checks, The Disney Credit Card, Disney Visa Reward Vouchers, MasterCard, Visa, American Express, JCB, Discover, Diner's Club. Disney Resort room charge cards are welcomed, even at some of the smallest snack carts. Sales tax is 6.5%. Gratuities may be applied automatically to large parties.

Smoking—Florida law prohibits smoking in all enclosed restaurants and other indoor public spaces. Only outdoor establishments and free-standing bars (no restaurants or hotel lobbies allowed) can allow smoking, but Disney has chosen to ban smoking at most of these, too.

Time- and Money-Saving Dining Tips

✔ At counter-service eateries, there are usually several lines. The line furthest from the entry is often shorter. Look before you leap.

✔ Consider eating earlier or later than traditional mealtime hours. You'll be more likely to get a seat (if you haven't arranged priority seating) or simply find the restaurant less crowded and noisy.

✔ Disney's Animal Kingdom sometimes offers a discounted meal program. The "Meal Plus" program gives you a voucher for one counter-service meal, a small soft drink, a box of popcorn (or ice cream bar), and a bottle of water for just $11.95/adults and $5.95/kids. Look for this program at the park.

✔ Every item at counter-service restaurants can be ordered a la carte. If you don't want fries with that burger "meal," just ask, and you'll pay a reduced price.

✔ The Rainforest Cafe offers discounts through its Safari Club and an e-mail list—get details at http://www.rainforestcafe.com.

✔ The Disney Dining Experience is for Florida residents. It offers 20% discounts on select restaurants in the parks and resorts, reduced prices on wine tastings, and more. See page 10 for details.

✔ Resort eateries are frequently less crowded than those in the parks. Consider a visit to a nearby resort restaurant before, during, or after a park visit. The Contemporary, Polynesian, and Grand Floridian resorts are close to the Magic Kingdom, the Yacht & Beach Club, BoardWalk, and Swan & Dolphin restaurants are close to Epcot and Disney-MGM Studios, and Disney's Animal Kingdom Lodge is a short drive/bus ride from Disney's Animal Kingdom.

✔ Quick-service eateries have lines on both sides of the cash register. If you see a short or nonexistent line on one side of an open register, jump in!

Understanding and Using the Eatery Descriptions and Ratings

PassPorter's popular capsule reviews of eateries cover all table-service restaurants, as well as counter-service eateries at the parks. Our reviews include all important details, plus ratings by us and fellow vacationers. We even include snack carts. Below is a key to our eatery charts. Dig in!

Description Key

Ratings[7]

[1] Eatery Name [D-2[2]]	B/L/D/S[3]	$[4]	⏱[5] ♦[6]	#	#	#
Description offering an overview of the eatery, including comments on the theming, quality, and menu range. We try to give you an idea of what sort of foods you'll find at a particular eatery, along with typical prices and our recommendations. We also include information on the availability of lighter fare, children's meals, and alcoholic beverages. Whenever possible, we describe the type of seating (tables, booths, etc.) and whether it is indoor or outdoor.				Type[8] Cuisine[8] Noise Factor[8] Seating[8] Avg. Wait[8] Hours[8]		

[1] Each chart has an empty checkbox in the upper left corner—use it to check off the eateries that interest you (before you go) or those at which you ate (after your return).

[2] Map coordinates—match them up to park maps in "Touring the 'World'" for locations.

[3] Meals are indicated by letters: B (breakfast), L (lunch), D (dinner), and S (snack).

[4] Dollar figures represent the average cost of a full adult dinner. Table-service meal costs include appetizer, entree, dessert, soft drink, tax, and tip. Whenever possible, we also provide in parentheses the average cost of a lighter dinner, such as a sandwich, pizza, or entree salad plus dessert, soft drink, tax, and tip. Average counter-service meal costs include entree (with fries when appropriate), dessert, soft drink, and tax. Average counter-service snack prices include a snack, soft drink, and tax. Use these only as a guide.

[5] The orange symbol indicates an eatery is vegetarian-friendly and has a good "vegebility" rating from the "Vegetarian Walt Disney World and Greater Orlando—Second Edition" guidebook published by The Globe Pequot Press (see page 202). Please note that these veggie-friendly eateries are the best bets for vegetarians in each location, especially for folks who eat eggs and dairy—but these eateries are not necessarily the best veggie restaurants in the country. For information on vegan meals and to be certain that a menu has not changed since the time of publication, please call Disney to speak directly with a chef at the restaurant in advance of your visit. Remember, too, that all the table-service restaurants can accommodate special dietary requests with at least 24 hours notice.

[6] Eateries with a reasonable selection of healthy items (low-fat/low-sodium/low-calorie) are indicated with a tape measure symbol. These are also friendly to weight watchers!

[7] The three white boxes on the right show ratings on a scale of 1 (poor) to 10 (loved it!). The first rating is **Jennifer's**, the second is Dave's, and the third is our **Readers'** rating. We offer our personal ratings to show how opinions vary, even between two like-minded people. You can also use our ratings as a point of reference—Jennifer likes eateries with extensive theming and well-prepared foods that aren't too exotic or spicy. Dave has more cultured tastes, enjoys unusual, spicy, and barbecue dishes, and loves seafood!

[8] The boxes on the right beneath the numeric ratings give basic information: eatery type (Table, Counter, or Buffet), cuisine, noise factor (from quiet to very noisy), seating (if priority seating is accepted, needed, suggested, recommended, or required, and how many days in advance you can call for priority seating), average wait time, and the eatery's hours.

Magic Kingdom Eateries

				Jennifer's Rating	Dave's Rating	Readers' Rating

Casey's Corner [D-4] L/D/S $10 — 5 | 4 | 7

Casey's at the bat, and there's a hot dog at the plate. Old-time stadium foods—hot dogs ($3.79), fries ($1.79), brownies ($1.79), and soft drinks ($1.99 & 2.29). Most seating is outdoors; some indoor grandstands and tables near a big-screen TV.

Counter
American
11 am–closing

Cinderella's Royal Table [D-3] B/L/D $51 🏆 7 | 6 | 8

For Disney magic, you can't beat dining right inside Cinderella Castle! The character breakfast at "Cindy's" is easily the hottest ticket in the Kingdom ($21.99 or $11.99/kids 3-11)—see pages 232-233. While lunch and dinner aren't character meals (and not as popular), the princess herself may visit. Menu items including prime rib ($23-26), steaks ($25-26), seafood ($22-23), and chicken ($21) can please all, and every plate has inventive flourishes. Meals aren't quite as good as the better resort eateries, but the light through the stained glass windows makes it all worthwhile. If you'll be celebrating a special occasion, mention it at booking. Average price of full child's menu meal: $4.99.

© MediaMarx, Inc.

Jennifer enjoys Cinderella's Royal Table during her honeymoon

Table
American
Med. noise
Reservations/
priority seats
essential
Vegetarians
should make
requests
before
ordering
Call 90 days
~8-10:30 am,
11:30-2:45 pm
4 pm–closing

Columbia Harbour House [C-2] L/D/S $11 😋🏆 5 | 6 | 6

This cozy inn provides cool relief and attractive decor despite the inexpensive menu. Fried chicken strips and fish with fries ($6.79), clam chowder ($4.99), garden salad ($6.39), and sandwiches ($6.29-6.69) dominate the menu, but several veggie dishes—such as the vegetarian chili ($4.99)—create a rare port in the storm at Magic Kingdom. Quiet, upstairs dining room.

Counter
American
Med. noise
10:30 am–1 hr.
before closing

Cosmic Ray's Starlight Cafe [E-3] L/D $12 😋🏆 6 | 5 | 6

Ray runs the biggest cafeteria at the Magic Kingdom. There's a wide choice of chicken ($6.49-6.99), sandwiches ($6.79), soups ($1.99), burgers ($5.59-$6.89), and salad ($6.39), but not all items are available from all stations. Families enjoy the whole rotisserie chicken meal ($15.99). Kids can get corn dog nuggets ($3.49). Toppings bar. Kosher menu, too. Singer Sunny Eclipse is no more.

Counter
American
Very noisy
Med. waits
11 am–closing

The Crystal Palace [C-4] B/L/D $29 — 6 | 6 | 8

Little more than a stone's throw away from Cinderella Castle (but please, don't throw stones), this replica of a Victorian glass conservatory (see photo on page 232) serves character meals all day long. Breakfast is $17.99 ($9.99/kids 3-11), lunch is $18.99 ($10.99/kids), and dinner is $22.99 ($10.99/kids). Winnie the Pooh is your host at this popular buffet. The dinner menu changes weekly, but usually offers carved meats, regional specialties such as arroz con pollo or paella, roasted vegetables, peel-and-eat shrimp, and a wide variety of salads. There's even a separate kid's buffet and an ice cream sundae "bar." Potted and hanging plants and wrought-iron tables and chairs add to the authenticity of the lovely garden setting. See pages 232-233 for details on the character meal.

Buffet
American
Very noisy
Priority seats
suggested
Call 90 days
Long waits
~8-10:30 am,
11:30-2:45 pm,
4 pm–closing

Side tabs: Planning, Getting There, Staying in Style, Touring, Feasting, Making Magic, Index, Notes & More

Magic Kingdom Eateries
(continued)

	Jennifer's Rating	Dave's Rating	Readers' Rating

■ El Pirata Y el Perico [A-4] L/D/S $10

		6	6	7

Look to the sign of the Pirate and the Parrot for an informal meal near Pirates of the Caribbean. The brief menu includes tacos ($4.99), taco salad ($5.79), and beef empanada ($5.79). A kid's meal with a taco, cookies, and a drink ($3.49) is available. The indoor and outdoor themed seating area is shared with Pecos Bill's, so your group has more food choices. May close seasonally.

Counter
Mexican
Med. noise
11:00 am–
4:00 pm

■ Liberty Tree Tavern [C-3] L/D $33 🐾

		6	6	7

One if by land, two if by monorail! Disney's elegant, Colonial-styled inn serves a la carte lunches and all-you-can-eat character dinners. At lunch, choose from an assortment of enticing soups and appetizers ($3.99-7.49), sandwiches ($10.79-11.99), salads ($3.99-11.79), seafood ($14.99), turkey ($13.79), and New England Pot Roast ($13.79). Kids' meals are $4.99 including drink and dessert. The character dinner resembles a Thanksgiving feast and comes to the table on platters filled with turkey, flank steak, ham, and all the trimmings for $22.99 ($10.99/kids). See pages 232–233 for more details on the character meal. The pricey lunch menu is a good choice for an early, moderately priced supper. Seating is at tables and chairs, and the dining rooms are well-themed.

Table
American
Noisy
Priority seats suggested
Call 90 days
Short waits
12 pm-3 pm
4 pm-closing

■ Main Street Bakery [D-5] B/L/S $5 🐾

		5	6	6

This favorite Magic Kingdom quick-breakfast and snack shop offers ever-popular fresh-baked cookies, pastries, cakes, and desserts ($1.49-5.99), hot breakfast items and sandwiches, as well as specialty coffees and other beverages. Enjoy your treats in the attractive dining area with granite-topped tables and counters, or take it outside to the tables near The Plaza Restaurant.

Counter
American
Med. noise
Med. waits
Open all day

■ Pecos Bill Cafe [A-4] L/D/S $13 ♟

		7	6	6

Just the place to rustle-up a bowl of chili ($2.99), hot dog ($5.59), or cheeseburger ($5.69-6.89)—they even have a well-stocked fixins' bar. Chicken wraps and salads ($4.69-7.39) please the health-conscious. Sit on the covered porch to watch the parade. Themed rooms provide delightful indoor seating, including an atmospheric "courtyard at dusk" room. El Pirata Y el Perico is next door.

Counter
American
Med. noise
10 am-1 hour before closing

■ The Pinocchio Village Haus [D-1] L/D/S $11 ♟

		6	5	5

Burgers ($5.59-6.69), salads ($6.39), and a turkey sandwich ($7.19) don't have much to do with Pinocchio, but the Swiss-styled stone building fits perfectly with its surroundings. A burger fixings bar helps dress up your meal, and you can substitute raw carrots for the fries. Sit outside at a patio table for Fantasyland sights; some inside tables may have a view of "it's a small world."

Counter
American
Noisy
11 am-1 hour before closing

■ The Plaza Pavilion [E-4] L/D/S $12

		4	4	7

Pizza ($5.49-7.99), Italian "stacked" sandwiches ($5.79), chicken garden salad ($6.39), fried chicken strips with fries ($6.49), and kid's PB&J with chips and a drink ($3.49) are served on a shaded, open-air (not air conditioned) terrace that doubles as a shortcut between Main Street and Tomorrowland. The best tables have a panoramic view of the Castle, but the rest are unappealing.

Counter
American
Med. noise
11 am-1 hour before closing

Eatery descriptions and ratings are explained on page 204.

Magic Kingdom Eateries
(continued)

	Jennifer's Rating	Dave's Rating	Readers' Rating

☐ The Plaza Restaurant [D-4]   L/D/S $25   🍴   7 8 7

This small Main Street standby has all the old-fashioned ice cream parlor atmosphere you need, offering overstuffed hot and cold sandwiches, including a classic Reuben ($10.89), 6-ounce burgers ($10.49 plus .49 per topping), proper malts and milkshakes ($3.79-4.99), pie a la mode ($3.99), and fountain sundaes ($3.79-5.49). Non-fat, sugar-free ice cream is available. A fresh veggie sandwich ($8.99) and the chicken and pear salad ($9.99) are offered as "lighter" fare. Kids' meals are $4.99 with drink. Snackers and light eaters can easily split one of their huge sandwiches. Walk-up guests can expect a short wait before being seated. Tables and half-booths.

Table
American
Med. noise
Priority seats suggested
Call 90 days
Short waits
11 am–1 hour before closing

☐ Tony's Town Square Restaurant [D-6] L/D $45   🌂🍴   8 8 8

Tony's serves Italian cuisine in the heart of Main Street, U.S.A. Familiar dinner entrees include Tony's "special" spaghetti and meatballs from Lady and the Tramp ($18.49) and veal marsala ($23.49). Less familiar but perhaps more interesting are Zuppa alla Farantina (shellfish and baby vegetables in a saffron broth–$22.49) and a strip steak with gorgonzola "mac 'n cheese" ($23.99). Tony's no longer serves breakfast. The lunch menu offers pizzas, sandwiches, and salads ($11.29-$12.29), plus more elaborate entrees ($12.99-$14.99). Tony's lunch menu is a good choice for an economical, early supper. Kids' meals are around $5.00. This could be the best table-service meal at Magic Kingdom.

Table
Italian
Med. noise
Priority seating suggested
Call 90 days
12–3 pm 5 pm–closing

Selected Magic Kingdom Snack Shops and Carts

Name	Land	Specialties
Plaza Ice Cream Parlor	Main Street, U.S.A.	Hand-dipped ice cream
Aloha Isle* 🍴	Adventureland	Pineapple Dole Whips (frozen dessert)
Sunshine Tree Terrace* 🍴	Adventureland	Citrus Swirl, frozen yogurt, pretzels
Aunt Polly's Dockside Inn*	Frontierland	Ice cream, sundaes, pie (seasonal)
Frontierland Fries	Frontierland	McDonald's french fries
Liberty Square Market* 🌂 🍴	Liberty Square	Fresh fruit
Sleepy Hollow	Liberty Square	Ice cream, root beer floats, coffee drinks
Enchanted Grove* 🍴	Fantasyland	Fruit slushes, juices, Strawberry Swirls
Mrs. Potts Cupboard	Fantasyland	Soft-serve ice cream, shakes
Scuttle's Landing	Fantasyland	Shaved ice, soft drinks
Toontown Market 🌂 🍴	Mickey's Toontown Fair	Fresh fruit
Auntie Gravity's 🍴	Tomorrowland	Ice cream, smoothies
The Lunching Pad 🍴	Tomorrowland	Turkey legs, frozen drinks

Note: Some shops and carts may be seasonal. Eateries marked with an asterisk (*) close between 3–5 pm.

Tip: Remember, opinions vary widely, especially on what constitutes a good meal. If you'd like to read reviews of eateries by other vacationers to gain their unique perspective, we recommend you visit MousePlanet's Walt Disney World Restaurant Resource located at http://www.mouseplanet.com/dtp/wdwrr. Another excellent resource are the PassPorter Message Boards at http://www.passporterboards.com. Click the "Feasting & Snacking" forum and look for messages or post your own!

Epcot Eateries

	Jennifer's Rating	Dave's Rating	Readers' Rating

▪ Restaurant Akershus [B-3]   B/D $32   ♟ | 7 | 8 | 8 |

Browse an authentic Nordic buffet ($18.99 adults/$7.99 kids) in a replica of a rustic Norwegian castle. Many diners have been happily surprised by food that's both remarkably familiar and somewhat unusual. Cold items are on the buffet, hot specialties are brought to your table. Enjoy smoked salmon, herring, Swedish meatballs, venison stew, fish in cream sauce, macaroni and cheese, red cabbage, soup, and a variety of salads. Ask for the Mickey's Child Deal ($4.99) if the kids want simpler food. As of October 2004, lunch is no longer served. Drinks and dessert are extra. Try the Carlsberg beer! The Princess Storybook character breakfast ($19.99/$9.99) offers fruit, pastries, french toast, eggs, bacon, sausage, and hash browns—see pages 232-233 for details.

Buffet
Norwegian
Med. noise
Priority seats recommended
Med. waits
Call 90 days
8:30 am-11:40 am, 4:30-closing

▪ L'Originale Alfredo di Roma Ristorante [C-1] L/D $52   🍴♟ | 6 | 8 | 7 |

The trompe l'oeil murals will catch your eye and so will the menu, which offers upscale Italian fare in an elegant setting—veal, seafood, and unusual pastas ($17.50-$31.95). Our most recent meal in August 2003 was the best yet, with great food and service. The hottest item is their original Fettuccine Alfredo ($17.95/$9.50 appetizer). Other first-rate choices include a salad of tomatoes, mozzarella, and mushrooms ($9.95), sinful gnocchi with gorgonzola, arugula and walnuts ($17.95, another good half-portion starter), satisfying osso bucco ($27.50), and a superior tiramisu for dessert ($5.50). The rich, expensive lunch (entrees $10.25-21.95) makes an even better early dinner. Try for lunchtime seating in the bright and cheery gallery. Child's meals $4.99-6.99.

Table
Italian
Very noisy
Priority seats strongly recommended
Call 90 days
Med. waits
12-4:15 pm 4:30-closing

▪ Biergarten [B-1]   L/D $35 | 5 | 8 | 8 |

Willkommen! A Bavarian town square in the midst of Oktoberfest is the setting for a hearty and satisfying German buffet ($19.99/kids $7.99). Wurst (sausages) with weinkraut, pork loin, chicken schnitzel, and rosemary roast chicken reign supreme at lunch. A first-rate sauerbraten and a fish entree are added at dinner. Every dish and side dish is several cuts above the typical German eatery, and each is distinctively seasoned. Musicians in lederhosen are on stage to entertain. Can you say "Gemütlichkeit"? (It roughly translates to "good feeling.") A large salad bar may even please some vegetarians, but this isn't the place for a light meal. Desserts ($3.79-6.79) and beverages are extra. There's Beck's beer on tap and a good German wine list. Lunch buffet is $14.99 (or $5.99 for kids).

Buffet
German
Very noisy
Priority seats recommended
Call 90 days
Short waits
Noon-3:45 pm, 4:00-8:30 pm

▪ Bistro de Paris [F-2]   D $62 | 7 | 8 | 7 |

Around the corner, upstairs, and upscale from Chefs de France, this "bistro" serves a limited menu that's anything but informal. Expect a leisurely, quintessentially French meal in mostly quiet and elegant surroundings—a far cry from the bustling restaurant downstairs. The short, classically French menu features escargot ($10) and duck foie gras ($17) appetizers; a roasted lamb loin ($26), seared scallops ($29), a grilled tenderloin of beef ($32), roasted pork tenderloin ($23), and fish of the day (market price). Desserts are outstanding ($6.50-8.00). The wine list is excellent, but the cheapest bottle is $42. Service is generally excellent, but one bad night still sticks in our minds. Ask for a window seat and linger until IllumiNations. No kids menu. No tank tops permitted.

Table
French
Very quiet
Priority seats strongly recommended
Call 30 days
Short waits
6:00 pm-8:45 pm

Eatery descriptions and ratings are explained on page 204.

Epcot Eateries
(continued)

	Jennifer's Rating	Dave's Rating	Readers' Rating

Boulangerie Patisserie [F-2]   L/S $11

	7	7	9

A quaint French bakery. Ham and cheese croissants ($3.25), a cheese plate ($5.95) and Quiche Lorraine ($4.95) make a nice, light lunch, while croissants ($1.95-2.85), eclairs ($3.75), chocolate mousse ($3.35), and fruit tarts ($3.85-$4.25) satisfy sweet tooths. Seating outside and inside Galerie les Halles shop.

Counter
French
Long waits
~11 am-closing

Cantina de San Angel [B-4]   L/D/S $12   🚫 ♿

	6	5	7

The partly shaded, open-air patio by the lagoon is the best feature of this taco and burrito stand. Try various platters ($6.79-7.79), nachos ($6.79), and Mexican chicken salad ($7.99). Try churros ($1.99) for dessert. Vegetarians can make special requests. Enjoy a cold beer or margarita at the bar or watch IllumiNations from a lagoon-side table. Children's platter with drink is $3.50.

Counter
Mexican
Med. noise
Med. waits
~11 am-closing

Les Chefs de France [F-2]   L/D $50   🚫 ♿

	6	7	8

Traditional French favorites such as escargot ($8.25), onion soup ($4.95), tomato and goat cheese tart ($7.50), braised lamb shank ($22.95), and grilled beef tenderloin with black pepper sauce ($27.95) carry the imprint of some of France's most famous chefs. The bright, bustling brasserie atmosphere, crowded seating, and overtaxed serving staff can be at odds with the desire for a slow, enjoyable meal. Lighter lunchtime choices such as Salade Niçoise ($14.95), croque monsieur with side salad ($10.25), and Quiche Lorraine ($9.95) will keep things affordable—save the heavier entrees ($15.50-17.95) until dinnertime, even if they're more expensive then. Children's meals cost $5.45-$5.85. Chairs and half-booths.

© MediaMarx, Inc.

Jennifer and Dave study their menus at Les Chefs de France

Table
French
Very noisy
Priority seats
strongly
recommended
Call 90 days
Med. waits
Noon-3 pm
5 pm-
closing
Tip: Request
a window
table for a
great view

Coral Reef [D-7]   L/D $54   ♿

	6	7	7

Few restaurants are as breathtakingly beautiful as the Coral Reef—brightly glazed blue mosaic tiles and brushed metal shimmer in the light cast by the Living Seas aquarium, as fish of all sizes and colors swim by. The inventive seafood menu ($20-30) covers a variety of international tastes and styles and is generally well-prepared. Meat and veggie lovers will also find foods to enjoy here ($16-$29). If only there was more elbow room, the noise more restrained, and the service more consistent. Tip: Request a tank-side table for the best views. Sweets here are special, especially for kids (they have edible Peanut Butter Playdoh). Kids' meals are $4.99-8.99. Enjoy the same view at lunch (entrees $13-24).

Table
Seafood
Noisy
Priority seats
recommended
Call 90 days
Med. waits
Noon-3 pm,
4:30-8:00 pm

Electric Umbrella [C-6]   B/L/D/S $11   🚫 ♿

	4	4	6

If you're looking for basic burgers ($5.69-7.19) at Epcot, this is the place. It's also decent for healthier fare, like turkey sandwiches ($6.59) and veggie burgers ($6.09)—you can also swap your fries for an apple. The main seating area is noisy—look for quieter seating upstairs, or dine outside on the terrace and watch the fountain. Breakfast ($4.29-5.29) served seasonally.

Counter
American
Med. noise
Short waits
~9 am-9 pm

Planning
Getting There
Staying in Style
Touring
Feasting
Making Magic
Index
Notes & More

Epcot Eateries
(continued)

Jennifer's Rating / Dave's Rating / Readers' Rating

Fountain View Bakery [D-6] B/S $6 — 5 6 8

How cosmopolitan! Sip a caffe mocha ($2.79) or latte ($1.99-2.79) and nibble a croissant ($2.29-4.49), Black Forest cake ($3.99), or fruit tulip ($3.99) while watching crowds criss-cross Fountain Plaza. Mmmm! Dine inside or out. Noisy.

Counter / French / Hours vary

The Garden Grill Restaurant [F-6] L/D/S $28 — 8 6 8

Epcot's only lunch and dinner character dining experience is tucked away in The Land pavilion. Farmer Mickey, Pluto, Chip, and Dale make the rounds of this rotating restaurant. Watch an ever-changing American landscape while you enjoy an all-you-can-eat meal. At lunch ($20.99/$10.99) and dinner ($22.99/$10.99), the grown-ups get sliced flank steak, roast turkey and all the trimmings, plus dessert (apple cobbler with vanilla bean ice cream) and soft drink. A "homegrown" salad comes with dinner—veggies are from Disney's hydroponic gardens. Vegetarians can make special requests. Kids get chicken strips, mac & cheese, and "Dirt and Worms" (chocolate pudding with gummy worms in a cookie topping). Try for a booth on the lower tier, which is closer to the scenery. At 3:00 pm, you can join Mickey for a $7 ice cream social (get a priority seating). The "Re-hitchin' Ceremony" previously offered here was discontinued in fall 2004. See pages 232-233 for character meal details.

Table / American / Med. noise / Priority seating not always needed / Call 90 days / Short waits / Noon-3:30 pm, 5:00 pm-7:00 pm

Kringla Bakeri og Kafé [B-3] L/D/S $10 — 5 6 8

This is a must stop for veteran World Showcase visitors. Have a light meal with tasty turkey, smoked ham, or smoked salmon sandwiches ($3.79-5.59). Or treat yourself to a "kringle" (sweet pretzel-$2.99), waffle with strawberry preserves ($2.49), rice cream ($2.29), or other desserts ($1.49-3.99). Beer and wine by the glass. Nice outdoor tables. Popular before IllumiNations.

Counter / Norwegian / Med. noise / Long waits / ~11 am-9 pm

Le Cellier [E-4] L/D $50 — 8 7 7

Oh, Canada! This steakhouse-in-a-stone-cellar is one of World Showcase's gems. Warm lighting, brocade upholstery, and stained glass make this the coziest cellar around. The menu is very hearty, but it's not plain steaks, roast beef, and potatoes—everything is richly sauced ($18.99-$27.99). Seafood—a seared tuna appetizer ($10.99) and salmon with maple butter ($19.99)—get royal treatment, and the vegetarian entree ($15.99) is very tempting. Moderately priced lunches include excellent salads ($2.99-14.99), huge sandwiches ($11.99-16.99), and steaks, of course ($15.99-23.99). The luscious cheddar cheese soup ($4.99) is a big favorite at any time. You may also find duck, venison, and a very popular buffalo ribeye (seasonal). Leave room for dessert—chocolate "moose" anyone?

Table / Canadian / Med. noise / Priority seats strongly suggested / Call 90 days / Med. waits / Noon-3 pm 4:00-closing

Liberty Inn [C-1] L/D/S $12 — 4 4 5

Hot dogs, hamburgers, and chicken strips ($5.59-7.19) weren't as American as apple pie ($2.49) back in the Colonial days, but they are now. A toppings bar adds relish to the basic fare, while a turkey club ($6.39), veggie burger ($6.09), and chicken Caesar salad ($6.39) provide alternatives. You can get that apple pie "a la mode" ($4.09), too! Kosher items available. Seating indoors and out.

Counter / American / Med. noise / Short waits / ~11 am-closing

Eatery descriptions and ratings are explained on page 204.

Epcot Eateries
(continued)

		Jennifer's Rating	Dave's Rating	Readers' Rating

Lotus Blossom Café [B-3] — L/D/S — $11 — 3 4 5

Chinese food at Epcot leaves a bit to be desired, but the menu here has become more enticing. Try twice-cooked beef, orange chicken or Shanghai grilled chicken combo plates (each $6.59), beef and corn soup ($2.49), egg rolls ($3.19), fried rice ($3.99), and Sichuan chicken salad ($4.99). Desserts run $1.30-2.99. Kid's meal $3.59. Covered outdoor seating.

Counter
Chinese
Med. noise
Med. waits
~11 am-closing

Restaurant Marrakesh [F-1] — L/D — $44 — 9 7 8

Enjoy exotic food in an authentic Moroccan setting as modest belly dancers and live musicians lend even more atmosphere. Lamb and chicken are the backbone of the cuisine, either grilled, roasted, or stewed ($18.95-25.95). The flaky pastry-based appetizers ($5.95-6.95) are a must, especially the chicken bastilla ($5.95). If you've always wanted to try couscous, the Moroccan national dish of stewed meat and/or vegetables over steamed semolina, you'll find it is quite good here ($16.95-$23.95). Order a la carte, or choose from a variety of family-style feasts ($28.95-$29.95) at dinnertime. Plan to sample a variety of appetizers and desserts ($4.95-5.95). Check for bargain-priced specials at lunch. The kids' menu is a bit exotic, offering grilled chicken with fries, beef kebabs with fries, kefta (bun-less burgers) with fries, and veggie couscous ($4.25-5.95). Tables and chairs.

Table
Middle Eastern
Noisy
Priority seats not always needed
Call 90 days
Short waits
Noon-3:45 pm, 4 pm-closing

Matsu No Ma Lounge [E-1] — L/D/S — $37 — 7 7 8

It may be a cocktail lounge, but you can make a full meal from a variety of traditional hot and cold Japanese appetizers ($3.50-10.75) and a good selection of sushi and maki (rolls), either by the piece ($3.75-7.25) or on platters ($16.75-$21.95). The lounge is often blissfully quiet, and large picture windows overlook the World Showcase. Kick back with a sake or Kirin, and enjoy!

Lounge
Japanese
Med. noise
Med. waits
~11 am-closing

Nine Dragons [B-3] — L/D/S — $37 — 7 8 6

Nine Dragons, decorated in traditional Chinese style with red lacquered woods and accents of gold and black has greatly improved, but the prices are still nothing like Chinatown. Many regions of China are represented by familiar menu items, including pot stickers (fried dumplings-$6.50), hot and sour soup ($3.00), mu shu pork ($15.45), scallops with black bean sauce ($18.25), lemon chicken ($18.95), kung bao chicken ($16.50), and remarkably, a traditional three-course Peking Duck dinner for two ($39) that you don't have to pre-order! Lunch now offers traditional Dim Sum service—pick plates of dumplings and other items from a cart, at $3.50-14.95 per plate. A sampler meal for two is $29.95 at lunch and $42.50 at dinner. Kids' meals are $4.75.

© MediaMarx, Inc.

Lunching at Nine Dragons

Table
Chinese
Med. noise
Priority seats suggested
Call 90 days
Medium waits
12:00 pm-4:15 pm, 4:30 pm-park closing

Epcot Eateries
(continued)

	Jennifer's Rating	Dave's Rating	Readers' Rating

☐ Pure and Simple [B-6]   [Currently Closed]   🏵 | 6 | 5 | 7 |

This counter-service eatery closed in 2004 along with Wonders of Life. It may reopen seasonally, however. The menu included waffles, muffins, danish, cereal and milk, and a fruit cup ($1.79-$3.29) at breakfast. At lunch, hot dogs and chili in various forms ($3.69-5.19) and a seasonal soup ($2.89). Yogurt sundaes and shakes, fresh fruit, and smoothies are low-guilt desserts ($0.99-4.29).

Counter
American
Noisy
Med. waits
~9 am-7 pm

☐ Rose & Crown Pub and Dining Room [E-3]   L/D $37 | 7 | 6 | 8 |

They say "heck" is a place where the cooks are English, but the food in this boisterous, crowded pub is quite nice. It's so cozy inside you'd swear you just walked in out of a London fog. Traditional specialties include a meat pie sampler ($15.99), very nice salmon ($17.79), bangers and mash ($15.99), and American rib-eye with Yorkshire pudding ($19.99). Start your meal (or simply snack) on a fruit and cheese plate ($5.99). Pub-style entertainers put in a regular appearance. A quieter meal with a view of IllumiNations may be had out on the terrace—request a 7:30 pm (or earlier) priority seating, check in early, request an outside table (no guarantee you'll get one, but ask anyway), and have a leisurely dinner. Don't forget a pint of ale, porter, or stout, an' 'ow about the sticky toffee pudding for dessert ($4.29)?

Table
English
Very noisy
Priority seats strongly recommended
Call 90 days
Long waits
~11:30 am-4:00 pm, 4:30-closing

☐ San Angel Inn [B-4]   L/D $35   🏵 | 7 | 7 | 7 |

Where but Disney can you dine at noon in a romantic, twilit Mexican plaza, while a cool evening breeze caresses your skin, a volcano steams ominously on the horizon and boats float by on El Rio del Tiempo (see page 147)? Despite the fine, authentic Mexican food, it's the atmosphere that makes San Angel Inn (pronounced "San Anhel") a favorite. For appetizers, we suggest the Queso Fundido ($9.25/two) or ceviche (marinated seafood, $7.95). For your entree, try their wonderful Mole Poblano (chicken in unsweetened cocoa sauce, $18.00), mahi-mahi Veracruzana ($19.75), or the basic Plato Mexicano ($19.50). Check the Chef's Selections for tempting items that go beyond simple "Mex." Vegetarians should make special requests before ordering. The kids can choose from quesadillas, chicken strips, and cheeseburgers ($4.99).

Table
Mexican
Noisy
Priority seats strongly recommended
Call 90 days
Med. waits
Noon-4:00 pm
4:30-closing

☐ Sommerfest [B-1]   L/D/S $12 | 5 | 5 | 7 |

Hearty, German fare for light eaters? Sommerfest serves a bratwurst ($5.99), frankfurters (with sauerkraut, of course - $5.49), soft pretzels ($2.89), Black Forest cake ($3.69) and apple strudel ($3.69). Wash it down with Lowenbrau beer ($6.75) and schnapps ($5.75). Seating is outdoors (but covered), within earshot of the oompah bands. This eatery is seasonal.

Counter
German
Noisy
Med. waits
~11 am-closing

☐ Sunshine Season Food Fair [F-6]   L/D $12   🐾🏵 | 6 | 6 | 8 |

The food court in The Land pavilion has something for everyone—salads ($6.39), soups ($2.89), cold sandwiches ($5.49-6.59), smoked barbecue ($6.79-7.59), stuffed potatoes ($4.69-6.29), pastas ($6.29), fresh fruit, baked goods ($1.49-3.49), ice cream sundaes, and low-fat frozen yogurt ($2.36-4.29). Wide choice of beverages. Festive, indoor seating at patio tables. May be renovated in 2005.

Counter
American
Noisy
Long waits
~9 am-7 pm

Looking for Restaurant Akershus or Restaurant Marrakesh? See page 208 for Restaurant Akershus and page 211 for Restaurant Marrakesh.

Epcot Eateries
(continued)

	Jennifer's Rating	Dave's Rating	Readers' Rating

Tangierine Café [E-1]   L/D/S $14   🍴🍷 | 7 | 7 | 7 |

Tangierine Café offers traditional Middle Eastern sandwiches and combo platters served in a delightfully decorated, open-air café. Choose from shawarma (sliced grilled chicken or lamb), roast chicken or vegetarian platters, and sandwiches and wraps ($6.95-10.95). Desserts are a deal—for $2.50 you can add baklava to your meal. A coffee and pastry counter is tucked in the back, making this cafe an excellent choice for mid-afternoon espresso and flaky, nut-filled, honey-drenched desserts. Indoor and outdoor seating.

Counter
Middle Eastern
Med. noise
Med. waits
Noon-closing

Tempura Kiku [E-1]   L/D/S $40 | 5 | 6 | 8 |

This attractive and bustling tempura "bar" snuggles up alongside Japan's very popular teppanyaki restaurant (see below). Alas, every entree is deep-fried, or we'd visit more often. Start out your meal with a nice variety of traditional Japanese appetizers, including sushi, sashimi, and hiyayako ($3.50-8.75), then on to the tempura—Japanese-style battered and deep-fried seafood, meats, and vegetables in various combinations, served with soup, salad and steamed rice ($12.95-24.75). Wash it all down with beer or sake. The children's meal costs $8.95. Sushi bar-style seating only; a good choice for last-minute dining.

Table
Japanese
Med. noisy
No priority seating
Medium waits
~11 am-closing

Teppanyaki Dining [E-1]   L/D $42 | 6 | 6 | 8 |

Meat and veggies cooked on a hot, steel-topped table by a flamboyant chef is "American food" in Japan, but don't say that too loudly at Epcot's Japan pavilion. Choose from steak, chicken, shrimp, scallops, or lobster in a variety of combinations ($19.95-31.95), and watch as everything is cooked the same way and served with the same vegetables and rice. Regardless, it's tasty, fun, and a good "adventure" for timid eaters. Vegetarians will be steered to the fresh vegetable platter ($13.95). Appetizers include chilled tofu and sushi ($2.95-8.95). Desserts are $2.95-4.50. If you're aching for "real" Japanese food, duck into the Matsu No Ma cocktail lounge for some sushi. Teppan tables are often shared by two or more parties. Children's meal is $8.95.

Table
Japanese
Noisy
Priority seats strongly recommended
Call 90 days
Long waits
12-3:45 pm, 4:30-closing

Yakitori House [D-1]   L/D/S $13 | 7 | 7 | 8 |

Of the Japan Pavilion's four eateries, this is the place we visit most often for its tasty, filling, and economical fare. This classic Japanese quick meal spot serves skewers of grilled yakitori chicken and beef as a snack, platter, or in a combo with shrimp tempura ($1.98-6.99), satisfying beef curry over rice or noodles ($5.99-6.59), and big, filling bowls of Udon noodle soup ($4.89-6.99). Wash it down with hot sake or cold Kirin beer. Dine at tables indoors or out, and take a few minutes to stroll through the nearby bonsai display. Kids' meal is $3.49.

Counter
Japanese
Medium noise
Medium waits
~11 am-closing

Yorkshire County Fish Shop [E-3]   L/D/S $10 | 7 | 8 | 7 |

Crowds have been queuing up and strolling away with Harry Ramsden's legendary Fish & Chips ($6.29), and for good reason—it's the real thing! (Dave can't resist it!) An extra side of chips is $2.59. Wash it down with a Bass ale, Guinness, or try a refreshing, hard cider (sweet or dry). Seating at patio tables is often available to the right, or visit the United Kingdom gardens to eat.

Counter
English
Med. noise
Med. waits
~11 am-closing

Eatery descriptions and ratings are explained on page 204.

Epcot Eateries
(continued)

Snacking at Epcot is every bit as diverse and rewarding as feasting in its fine restaurants. The snack carts and shops seem to appear and change regularly, however, so a definitive snack list isn't practical. Instead, we've listed our favorite treats at Epcot and where you can find them—this will give you an idea of the variety of snacks available. If you can't locate one of our favorite munchies, chances are very good you'll find a new tidbit that we haven't yet discovered!

Our Favorite Snacks at Epcot

Treat	Found At
Churros (fried dough rolled in cinnamon sugar)	Mexico (Cantina de San Angel)
Rice Cream and Vaffler (waffle with preserves)	Norway (Kringla Bakeri og Kafé)
Italian pastries and cappuccino	Italy (along promenade)
Funnel cakes (deep-fried batter with powdered sugar)	The American Adventure
Kaki Gori (shaved ice with sweet flavoring)	Japan (along promenade)
Baklava (flaky pastry with honey, rosewater, and nuts)	Morocco (along promenade)
Wine by the glass	France (along promenade)
Trapper Bob's Beaver Tails (tail-shaped fried pastries) 🍴	Canada (along promenade)

Note: Some shops and carts may be seasonal.

International Food and Wine Festival

Eager to sample more international cuisine and exotic tastes? Visit the "World" in autumn, when Epcot hosts the International Food and Wine Festival. Just stroll around the World Showcase Promenade and sample food and drink at the various booths set up in front of each pavilion. The generously sized appetizer treats range in price from $1 to $5, while small plastic glasses of wine, beer, champagne, cognac, and port begin at $2 and go up from there. You can easily make a meal out of the offerings, stopping at booths whenever you discover another appetizing snack. Eating while strolling around isn't always the most relaxing, but there are plenty of benches and quiet nooks at which to munch away. In addition to the treats, you can watch cooking demonstrations by top chefs, participate in beer and wine seminars and tastings, and attend the Eat to the Beat concert series at the America Gardens Theater (no extra charge). For an additional fee (and advance reservations), you can join special wine tasting events, a Party for the Senses (a wine-sipping and food-sampling extravaganza), wine schools (day-long education programs), and one-hour Food and Wine Pairings. The ultimate VIP experience may be the $185 reserve dinners (Exquisite Evenings), held in a VIP dining room and featuring a VIP viewing of IllumiNations. The 10th annual festival runs from September 30 to November 13, 2005. For more information, call 407-WDW-INFO.

Disney-MGM Studios Eateries

(park map on page 153)

Jennifer's Rating
Dave's Rating
Readers' Rating

ABC Commissary [C-3]   B/L/D/S $12 | 5 | 5 | 5 |

Carpeted floors, potted palms, and sleek decorating make you feel like a special employee. The International menu features fish & chips, vegetable noodle stir fry, Brazilian stew, tabbouleh wrap, Cuban sandwiches, and burgers ($5.29-6.79). Kids can get chicken or fish nuggets, and mac and cheese ($3.49). One of the park's only breakfast spots. Kosher items available. Shady outdoor seating, too.

| Counter |
| American |
| Med. noise |
| Med. waits |
| Open all day |

Backlot Express [C-5]   L/D/S $11 | 5 | 5 | 7 |

Rarely crowded and often overlooked, this backstage-themed cafeteria serves up burgers, hot dogs, chicken strips, grilled turkey & cheese, and sesame chicken salad ($5.69-6.99). The children's meal is $3.99 (includes drink). Pleasant indoor and outdoor seating. Perfect spot for watching the parade—stake out a table about a half-hour beforehand. Not always open.

| Counter |
| American |
| Noisy |
| Short waits |
| 11 am-closing |

Catalina Eddie's [G-3]   L/D/S $13 | 4 | 5 | 6 |

Part of the outdoor Sunset Ranch Market mini food court on Sunset Blvd. Cheese, pepperoni, and BBQ chicken pizzas ($5.99-7.99), a side salad ($2.19), apple pie ($3.29), and chocolate cake ($3.49) make up the menu. Outdoor, shaded (and not so shaded) seating. Nearby food stands serve McDonald's fries, fresh fruit, smoked turkey legs, burgers, and ice cream.

| Counter |
| American |
| Med. noise |
| Short waits |
| 11 am-closing |

50s Prime Time Cafe [E-5]   L/D $32 | 8 | 6 | 8 |

Clean your plate in an old kitchenette, while "Mom" serves gussied-up versions of home-cooked meals like meatloaf, pot roast, grilled and fried chicken, salmon, grilled pork chops, pasta ($12.49-19.99), and scrumptious malts, milkshakes, and sundaes ($3.49-4.99). The lunch menu adds pot pie, sandwiches, and salads ($10.99-16.99) Vintage TV clips of "I Love Lucy" and "The Honeymooners" play while you eat, and your "brother" and "sister" (your servers) boss you around when your "Mom" isn't watching. This is a unique dining experience if you're willing to play along—not recommended for the overly shy. Veggie burgers on request. The dining areas and adjoining bar/waiting area are a wonderland of '50s-vintage Formica, television sets, and knickknacks. Table and booth seating.

| Table |
| American |
| Noisy |
| Priority seats |
| strongly |
| recommended |
| Call 90 days |
| Long waits |
| 11 am-4 pm, |
| 4 pm-closing |

Hollywood & Vine [E-5]   D $27 | 7 | 7 | 7 |

This 1940s-inspired "Cafeteria of the Stars" no longer has the "star power" provided by Disney characters (character meals were discontinued in 2003), but it's a tasty and economical choice for a pre-Fantasmic! dinner. Stainless steel serving areas, comfy half-booths, metal-edged Formica tables, checkerboard floor tiles, and a mural of Hollywood in its heyday set the scene. The menu changes regularly—buffet choices may include flank steak, roast prime rib, pork loin, seafood pasta, honey-citrus baked chicken, and a fish specialty. The kids have their own buffet, and everyone can make sundaes. Dinner is $21.99/$9.99. Breakfast and lunch stopped in 2003, but may reappear. Available with the Fantasmic! dinner package at the same price (see page 217).

| Buffet |
| American |
| Noisy |
| Priority |
| seats |
| suggested |
| Call 90 days |
| 4:00 pm- |
| closing |

Tip: The Disney-MGM Studios' table-service restaurants <u>may</u> open 30 minutes earlier on Wednesdays and Sundays—check at 407-WDW-DINE.

Disney-MGM Studios Eateries
(continued)

					Jennifer's Rating	Dave's Rating	Readers' Rating

☐ **The Hollywood Brown Derby** [E-3]   **L/D**   **$47**   🍸🍴 | *8* | 8 | 8 |

The famous Brown Derby, complete with "stars," serves enticing starters like lump crab cake ($7.99), lobster bisque ($5.99), and the yummy and original Cobb Salad ($12.99/two). Entrees include excellent pan-seared grouper with a citrus sauce, and first-rate roasts and chops ($16.99-26.99). Desserts like the famous grapefruit cake ($5.99-7.29) are quite good, and this is the place for a celebratory bottle of bubbly. The Brown Derby is the Studios' most elegant establishment. Off-white walls covered with caricatures of the stars, dark wood trim, crisp, white table linens, and attentive, formal service set the tone. Hollywood "personalities" may jazz up the show. This restaurant offers some special meals—for information on the Fantasmic! Meal Package, see page 217; for the Meal with an Imagineer experience, see page 237.	**Table**
	American
	Med. noise
	Priority seats
	strongly
	recommended
	Call 90 days
	Long waits
	11:30 am-3 pm
	3:30 pm-
	closing

☐ **Mama Melrose's Ristorante Italiano** [A-4]   **L/D**   **$38 ($30)**   🍸🍴 | *6* | 5 | 7 |

Mama's is a bare brick wall and checkered tablecloths sort of place. A wide variety of individual wood-fired pizzas ($11.79-12.99), light pasta specialties, and simple meats grace the menu at Mama's, which changes regularly. Veal osso bucco with risotto ($21.99), chicken parmesan ($15.99), or a grilled beef filet ($19.99) may catch your eye. The seafood pasta Fra Diavolo ($17.99) wasn't devilishly spicy or briny, but there was plenty of shellfish. Sangria, a Bellini cocktail, and desserts like spuma di cioccolata ($6.49) may catch your attention. Ask about the Fantasmic! Dinner Package, which offers a three-course dinner plus seating at Fantasmic! (see pages 153 & 217). Your little "bambini" can get spaghetti, chicken nuggets, burgers, or pizza for $4.99.	**Table**
	Italian
	Med. noise
	Priority seats
	suggested
	Call 90 days
	Short waits
	11:30 am-3 pm,
	3:30 pm-
	closing

☐ **Rosie's All-American Cafe** [G-3]   **L/D/S**   **$12**   🍸 | *7* | 4 | 6 |

Part of the outdoor Sunset Ranch Market mini food court on Sunset Blvd., Rosie's is really a hamburger stand offering burgers ($5.69-6.69), veggie burgers ($5.69), chicken strips ($6.49), soup ($2.59), salad ($2.19), and desserts ($3.29-$3.49). Seating is outdoors at covered picnic benches. Other stands nearby offer pizza, smoked turkey legs, ice cream, McDonald's fries, and fresh fruit.	**Counter**
	American
	Med. noise
	Med. waits
	11 am-closing

☐ **Sci-Fi Dine-In Theater Restaurant** [C-4]   **L/D**   **$36**   🍸 | *7* | 7 | 6 |

Build a drive-in theater in a movie soundstage, seat folks in replica vintage cars, serve souped-up drive-in fare, and show old sci-fi movie trailers. Would anyone buy that script? You and the kids will at this fanciful eatery. The menu is fun and portions are huge. Definitely get a shake ($3.29)—you can get "adult" (alcoholic) shakes, too. The kid's menu is classic "drive-in," but the adult menu has upscale choices like pan-seared salmon on wild rice ($16.99) and shrimp penne pasta ($16.99). At lunch, try the Flat Iron steak sandwich ($14.99) or blackened catfish sandwich ($12.99). The desserts are out of this world ($4.99-5.29). Everyone faces the screen, so chatting is hard. Not all seats are "parked cars"—request one if you want it. Kids' menu $4.99.	**Table**
	American
	Noisy
	Priority seats
	strongly
	recommended
	Call 90 days
	Med. waits
	11 am-4 pm
	4 pm-closing

© MediaMarx, Inc.

Allie at Sci-Fi Dine-In

Eatery descriptions and ratings are explained on page 204.

Disney-MGM Studios Eateries
(continued)

				Jennifer's Rating	Dave's Rating	Readers' Rating

☐ **Toluca Legs Turkey Co.** [G-3]	**L/D/S**	**$8**	**4**	**4**	**5**

Part of the outdoor Sunset Ranch Market mini food court on Sunset Blvd. As you may have guessed, you can get a turkey leg ($4.69) to munch on. You can also get foot-long hot dogs with chili and/or cheese ($3.69-4.89). Seating is outdoors at covered picnic benches. Other stands nearby offer burgers, chicken strips, soup, ice cream, McDonald's fries, and fresh fruit.	**Counter**
	American
	Noisy
	Med. waits
	11 am–closing

☐ **Toy Story Pizza Planet** [B-5]	**L/D**	**$11**	**3**	**4**	**6**

The name is familiar, but this pizzeria/arcade doesn't look all that much like the pizza palace in Toy Story. Choose from individual pizzas ($5.49-5.99) or "meal deals" that combine pizza, a side salad, and drink ($7.49-7.99). There's also a Greek Salad ($5.29) and cookies ($1.79) It's an OK place to eat and rest while your little "Andy" or "Jessie" hits the arcade. Seating upstairs and outside.	**Counter**
	American
	Very noisy
	Long waits
	11 am–closing

Studio Catering Co. Comeback? Starring Rolls, Superstar

The Studio Catering Co. counter-service eatery may return with a new menu and maybe a new name in 2005 when Lights, Motors, Action! opens. Meantime, Starring Rolls Bakery on Sunset Boulevard has added yummy sandwiches to its menu—have a nice lunch!

Fantasmic! Dinner Package

If you're thinking about a table service dinner at Disney-MGM Studios, consider the Fantasmic! Dinner Package. You get a meal at Hollywood Brown Derby, Mama Melrose, or Hollywood and Vine *plus* seats in the reserved section at the Fantasmic! nighttime show, at the price of the meal alone. To qualify, everyone in your party must order the fixed-price meal—$21.99-36.99 (kids are $9.99-10.99). Credit card deposit required. Call 407-WDW-DINE to make reservations up to 90 days in advance, or ask about it at Guest Services at your Disney hotel or at Guest Relations in the park (see map on page 153 for location). Availability is very limited. Note: Restaurants and details may change, lunch may be available seasonally (ask) and Fantasmic! may be cancelled in bad weather. Note that no rain checks are issued for your Fantasmic! seating if it is cancelled.

Disney-MGM Studios Snack Shops and Carts

Name	Location	Specialties
Dinosaur Gertie's Ice Cream	Echo Lake	Soft-serve ice cream
Min & Bill's Dockside Diner	Echo Lake	Shakes & malts, stuffed pretzels
Peevy's Polar Pipeline	Echo Lake	Frozen slushes, bottled drinks
Tune-In Lounge	Echo Lake	Alcoholic beverages, snacks
Anaheim Produce ♻ ⊗	Sunset Boulevard	Fresh fruit, drinks
Hollywood Scoops	Sunset Boulevard	Hand-dipped ice cream
Starring Rolls Bakery	Sunset Boulevard	Baked goods, coffee, sandwiches
Fairfax Fries	Sunset Boulevard	McDonald's fries, beverages
Studio Catering Co. ♻	Mickey Avenue	Ice cream, popcorn (may be closed)

Note: Some shops and carts may be seasonal.

Disney's Animal Kingdom Eateries

(park map on page 163)

| | Jennifer's Rating | Dave's Rating | Readers' Rating |

Flame Tree Barbecue [E-4]   L/D/S $13   6 6 6

Although we're not sure how barbecue fits in with the Animal Kingdom motif, at least one of us can't knock it, because it's good stuff. Pork, chicken, and beef is smoked right on premises and is available sliced on sandwiches ($6.79) and arrayed on platters ($7.99–8.49). The condiment stations offer traditional and mustard-based barbecue sauces. A green salad with BBQ chicken in a garlic bread shell ($6.99) and the fresh fruit salad ($7.29) are light alternatives. PB&J and "Beanie Weenies" for the kids ($3.49). Shaded outdoor seating in a lovely Asian garden or on decks overlooking the lake. May be open seasonally.

Counter
American/ Barbecue
Quiet
No priority seating
Med. waits
10 am–5 pm

Pizzafari [B-4]   L/D/S $9   4 4 7

This popular pizzeria serves individual cheese and pepperoni pizzas ($5.49–5.79), chicken Caesar salad ($5.99), and a hot Italian sandwich ($6.19). You can also get a basket of breadsticks ($3.99). There's lots of indoor, air-conditioned seating in brightly decorated, uniquely themed dining areas. Not surprisingly, the menu makes this a popular family dining spot. Many folks love Pizzafari, but we find the noise levels and crowds to be a bit much. Look for quieter seating towards the back of the restaurant or outside on the patio. Kosher items available here.

Allie loves her pizza

© MediaMarx, Inc.

Counter
Italian
Very noisy
No priority seating
Long waits
10:00 am– 5:00 pm

Rainforest Cafe [B-7]   B/L/D $45 ($32) 🐾 🦍   5 6 7

Environmentally conscious dining in an artificial rainforest hidden behind a two-story waterfall? It even rains indoors! The Rainforest Cafe puts on quite a show and piles your plate with tasty, inventive foods representing many different cuisines. Hearty breakfasts ($7.99–12.99), enormous sandwiches ($10.99–12.99), personal pizzas ($9.99–11.99), pastas ($12.99–21.95), steaks ($22.99–23.99), comfort foods ($13.99–19.99), and mountainous salads ($11.99) overflow the menu. Smoothies and specialty alcoholic drinks are very popular. Located just outside the gates (no park admission required). This is the only table-service restaurant at Disney's Animal Kingdom. There's a special entrance for folks exiting and re-entering the park. For discounts, see page 203.

Table
American
Very noisy
Priority seats strongly suggested
Call 90 days
Long waits
8:30 am– 6:30 pm

Restaurantosaurus [E-6]   B/L/D/S $11 🐾   5 5 8

Disney and McDonald's teamed up to bring you DinoLand's only sit-down meal. Choices include "Dino-Size" ½-lb. burgers with McDonald's fries ($6.59), hot dogs with fries ($5.49), grilled chicken salads ($5.99), veggie plates (on request), and Chicken McNuggets ($5.49). McNuggets Happy Meals are $3.79. Donald's "Breakfastosaurus" is a fun character buffet ($17.99/9.99 kids) serving traditional morning fare (vegetarians can make special requests) and featuring that lovable duck, Donald (see pages 232–233). Priority seating accepted and recommended at breakfast. The food is not thrilling, but the indoor, air-conditioned dining areas are fun—it's a weathered, dig site bunker with broken equipment, humorous signs, and educational displays.

Counter
American
Very noisy
Priority seats at breakfast
Call 90 days
Long waits
8:00-10:30 am 11:30 am– 3:30 pm

Eatery descriptions and ratings are explained on page 204.

Disney's Animal Kingdom Eateries
(continued)

	Jennifer's Rating	Dave's Rating	Readers' Rating

☐ **Tusker House Restaurant** [B-2] **B/L/D/S** **$14** 🏆 **7** **7** **8**	
Savory, moist rotisserie chicken ($7.99) with garlic potatoes and veggies takes center stage at our favorite eatery at Disney's Animal Kingdom. A marinated vegetable sandwich ($7.29), a turkey wrap ($7.29), a huge grilled chicken salad in a bread bowl ($7.29), fried chicken sandwich ($6.99), and grilled salmon ($7.99) round out the menu at this no-red-meat establishment. Try the carrot cake ($3.29) for dessert. Kids can order macaroni and cheese or a peanut butter & jelly sandwich ($3.49). Breakfast plates are $3.89–5.29, cereal is $1.99, and the scrumptious cinnamon rolls are $2.79. There's lots of cool, indoor seating, but tables on the dining terrace or by the shaded Dawa Bar are a pleasant alternative, especially when there's a live African band playing.	Counter American Noisy inside Quiet outside No priority seating accepted Med. waits 8:30–10:30 am 11am–3:30 pm

Where Are All the Restaurants?

You may have noticed that Disney's Animal Kingdom doesn't offer many eateries, and it has only one table-service restaurant. Why is this? We think it's because Disney's Animal Kingdom closes in the late afternoon, before most folks sit down for dinner. This makes for slim pickings during your day, but it provides an excellent opportunity to sample the eateries at your resort or Downtown Disney in the evening. You could even take a direct bus to Epcot for an excellent meal and IllumiNations. Another option is to arrive early and leave in mid-afternoon, stopping for lunch when you return to your resort or hop to a new park. If you do eat in the park, look for a special discount meal program (see page 203).

Disney Animal Kingdom's Snack Shops and Carts

Name	Land	Specialties
Chip 'n' Dale's Cookie Cabin	Camp Minnie-Mickey	Cookies, ice cream sandwiches
Dawa Bar	Africa	Beer, cocktails
Harambe Fruit Market ⌀ 🏆	Africa	Fresh fruit, juices, beverages
Kusafiri Coffee Shop & Bakery	Africa	Pastries, cappuccino & espresso
Tamu Tamu Refreshments	Africa	Ice cream, sundaes, floats
Anandapur Ice Cream	Asia	Ice cream and floats
Chakranadi Chicken Shop ⌀	Asia	Chicken stir-fry, pot stickers
Dino Bite Snacks	DinoLand, U.S.A.	Ice cream, sundaes, nachos
Dino Diner 🏆	DinoLand, U.S.A.	Ice cream, drinks
Petrifries	DinoLand, U.S.A.	McDonald's French Fries

Note: Some shops and carts may be seasonal.

Tip: Want to enjoy the flavors of Walt Disney World at home? Pick up "Mickey's Gourmet Cookbook" (Hyperion Books) or download recipes at http://familyfun.go.com/recipes/disney/.

Downtown Disney
Marketplace Eateries
(map on page 181)

			Jennifer's Rating	Dave's Rating	Readers' Rating

☐ Cap'n Jack's Restaurant — L/D — $49 — 🍷 — 7 / 4 / 6

This casual, nautically themed restaurant hovers over the Lake Buena Vista Lagoon. Tables and chairs line the outer rim of the six-sided main dining room, giving each table glittering views through floor-to-ceiling picture windows. The lights of Downtown perform an enchanting dance on the waters, providing a romantic setting that the lackluster kitchen can't quite match. The menu includes crab cake ($14.99) and shrimp cocktail ($10.99) appetizers, chowder ($4.49), sandwiches at lunch ($7.99–11.99), and entrees that include seafood pasta in a lobster sauce ($20.99), steak ($19.99), smoked pork ribs ($21.99), seared salmon with caper vin blanc ($23.99), and a pound of king crab legs ($29.99). Consider Ghirardelli for dessert and Fulton's for superior seafood.

Table
Seafood
Med. noise
Priority seating not accepted
Short waits
11:30 am–10:30 pm

☐ Earl of Sandwich — B/L/D/S — $10 — 6 / 6 / 7

Yes, the current Earl of Sandwich is involved in this attractive establishment that replaced the Gourmet Pantry. Perfect for a lunch or a light supper in cozy British decor, the menu offers a dozen appetizing hot sandwiches on specialty bread (roast beef & cheddar, ham & brie, and a turkey, bacon & swiss club—all $4.95 each), Cobb and Chinese chicken salads ($5.95), and refrigerated, grab 'n go items—sandwiches ($3.95), wraps ($4.45), and tuna, fruit, or chicken salads ($4.95). Hot breakfast sandwiches ($4.95) in the morning, and a kids' menu ($4.95).

Counter
Eclectic
Noisy
Medium waits
8:00 am–11:00 pm

☐ Ghirardelli Soda Fountain & Chocolate Shop — S — $8 — 🍦 — 6 / 6 / 8

Who can resist the pleasures of San Francisco's famed chocolatier? Sundaes, sundaes, and more sundaes ($4.95–6.50) tempt dessert fans, or share an eight-scoop Earthquake ($19.95). If that's too much, cones, shakes, malts, and frozen mochas beckon ($3.75–4.50). Their whipped cream topped hot chocolate ($2.75) is perfect on cool winter evenings. Sugar-and-fat-free ice cream, too.

Counter
American
Med. waits
9:30 am–12:00 am

☐ Rainforest Cafe — L/D — $45 ($32) — 🍷 — 5 / 6 / 7

Another Rainforest Cafe? Yes, and it's very similar to the one at Disney's Animal Kingdom (see page 218 for menu items and descriptions). Differences include a smoking volcano atop the restaurant (rather than a waterfall) and lunch and dinner only (no breakfast). This is a very popular stop for families. Show up, sign up, and be prepared to wait. And wait. And wait. Occasional live animal demonstrations help pass the time. If the wait is too long, you can sit at the Juice Bar and order from the regular menu, or browse the Rainforest gift shop or the nearby Art of Disney shop. Near the Downtown Disney Marketplace bus stop. Open until midnight on Fridays and Saturdays. Priority seatings accepted at 407-827-8500. For discounts, see page 203.

Table
American
Very noisy
For priority seating, call 407-827-8500
Very long waits
11:30 am–11:00 pm

☐ Ronald's Fun House (McDonald's) — B/L/D/S — $8 — 2 / 2 / 5

This is a classic "Mickey D's" with Big Macs ($2.69), McNuggets ($2.69–6.29), and fries ($2.09–2.79) at familiar prices. What sets it apart from the typical Golden Arches is the imaginative, Disneyfied architecture. The eatery is a huge McDonaldland-styled clockworks, filled with oversized gears and springs connected to a clock tower outside. It's next door to Lego and World of Disney, so it's a happy stop for young families. Open 'til 2 am on Fridays and Saturdays.

Counter
American
Very noisy
Med. waits
8:00 am–1:00 am

Eatery descriptions and ratings are explained on page 204.

Downtown Disney Marketplace & Pleasure Island Eateries

(map on page 191)

Marketplace Eateries (continued)

Wolfgang Puck Express	B/L/D/S	$14		6 6 7

Fast food for the trendy, upscale set. Puck's famous wood-fired pizzas ($8.25–9.25), rotisseried rosemary garlic chicken ($9.95), pastas ($5.25–11.95) and soups ($4.95) are served hot. Salads ($6.25–8.25), sushi ($8.95), and appetizing sandwiches ($6.95) are available in the refrigerator cabinet. Desserts are $1.50–4.25, and childrens items are $4.50–5.50. Drink homemade lemonade, frozen cafe mocha, wines by the bottle and glass, and beer on tap. Dine outside, or take-out. See page 223 for Wolfgang Puck Grand Cafe over at the West Side.

Counter
American
Med. noise
Med. waits
8:30 am–11:30 am,
11:30 am–10pm

Pleasure Island Eateries

D-Zertz	S	$6	6 5 7

End your evening on Pleasure Island with a sweet something from this little cafe. Baked goods, ice cream, and frozen yogurt ($1.95–4.95), plus cappuccino and espresso to wash it down. Or pick up pastries for your breakfast the next morning. As at other Pleasure Island snack shops, convenience trumps quality.

Counter
American
Med. waits
7 pm–2 am

Fulton's Crab House	L/D	$65	6 7 8

A boatload of seafood, served in a replica of a riverboat (sans paddlewheel) outside the gates of Pleasure Island. The fish is flown in fresh every day, and the prices suggest it flew First Class. If you're looking for a fish feast, this is the right place. Preparations are straightforward—grilled, steamed, fried, or raw, with appropriate sauces. Crab lovers will be in seventh heaven, with nearly a dozen entrees featuring crab ($22.95–44.95). Twin Maine lobsters ($39.95), and the finest seasonal fish, shrimp, oysters, and clams ($24.95–31.95) also appear in many forms. Steaks make a strong showing, too ($32.95–$46.95). Dave just might dive into the Seafood Boil (lobster, clams, mussels, and snow crab–$32.95). Prices aren't too bad if you avoid crab and lobster. Kids' menu $4.95–12.95. Priority seating arrangements may be made at 407-WDW-DINE.

Table
Seafood
Very noisy
Priority
seating
accepted
Call 90 days
Med. waits
11:30 am–4:00 pm,
5 pm–11 pm

Missing Link	S	$10	3 2 7

Quick, cheap eats at Pleasure Island, for those who can't stand to leave the party. Greasy cheeseburgers, uninspiring nachos, cheese steaks, hot dogs, grilled sausage, and chili cheese fries make for an artery-clogging dinner (we admit to having done this more than once). Patio tables outdoors. Go down the stairs next to the Adventurers Club for quieter outside dining.

Counter
American
Noisy
Med. waits
7 pm–2 am

Portobello Yacht Club	L/D	$57 ($29)	5 6 8

This is a nice way to start your night at Pleasure Island. Contemporary Italian specialties are served in a bustling setting. Meals are robust and flavorful, and sometimes memorable—we've been disappointed by mediocre meals and excess noise, but we enjoyed our most recent dinner and loved our first. Specialties focus on grilled meats and fish, including veal chops ($31.95), rack of lamb ($27.95), and prosciutto-wrapped yellow fin tuna ($25.95). Pastas from $15.95 to $25.95. There's a fine, if expensive, wine list. Desserts include sinful chocolates, fresh fruits, and sorbet ($4.95–6.95). Call 407-WDW-DINE for priority seating.

Table
Italian
Very noisy
Priority seats
accepted
Call 90 days
Med. waits
11:30 am–11 pm

(Side column ratings header: Jennifer's Rating, Dave's Rating, Readers' Rating)

(Side tabs: Planning, Getting There, Staying in Style, Touring, Feasting, Making Magic, Index, Notes & More)

Downtown Disney
West Side Eateries
(map on page 181)

			Jennifer's Rating	Dave's Rating	Readers' Rating

Bongos Cuban Cafe — L/D — $33 — 🏆 — | 4 | 6 | 7 |

The lively Latin sounds and flavors of Miami's South Beach make Gloria Estefan's Bongos a popular choice for Downtown Disney dining. This is robust, savory fare, with not a chili pepper in sight. Black bean soup ($4.95), seafood stew ($27.95), garlic shrimp ($21.95), skirt steak ($18.95), ropa vieja ($12.95), fried plantains ($3.25), and flan ($5.25) are some of the authentic Cuban choices. The lunch menu offers mainly sandwiches ($6.95-8.50). Tastes may be too exotic for some diners, and our most recent meal was disappointing. The bar serves classic rum drinks, including the Mojito, a refreshing mix of white rum, mint, and sugar. An outdoor counter serves sandwiches and snacks (avg. meal cost=$16) from 9:30 am-midnight. Lunch served on Fri.-Sat. only. Open to 12:00 am on Fri. and Sat.

- Table
- Cuban
- Noisy
- No priority seating
- Long waits (allow 20 to 60 min.)
- 11:00 am-11:00 pm

FoodQuest — L/D/S — $12 — 🏆 — | 5 | 6 | 6 |

FoodQuest serves a wide, appealing variety of salads ($3.95-6.50), hot wraps ($6.95), sandwiches ($5.75-6.95), hot dogs ($3.95), and burgers ($4.95) to guests at DisneyQuest (you must have DisneyQuest admission to dine here). Kids' hot dog available for $2.75. FoodQuest is operated by the Cheesecake Factory, which means there's also a good selection of desserts and beverages.

- Counter
- American
- Noisy
- 11:30 am-10:30 pm

House of Blues — L/D — $39 ($30) — 🏆 — | 8 | 7 | 8 |

The funky House of Blues' menu is "Nawlins" Blues, with enough Cajun and Creole dishes to chase the blues away. The fried catfish starter ($8.95), gumbo ($3.95/5.25), and jambalaya ($16.95) are two beats ahead of any place similar in the "World," and you can get fine burgers ($9.95), Cajun meatloaf ($14.95), steaks ($23.95), ribs ($19.95), salads ($5.00-12.95), and sandwiches ($9.95), too. Located near Cirque du Soleil and DisneyQuest, "HOB" looks like a weatherbeaten wharfside dive. Inside is an equally aged interior with comfy booths. Live blues bands keep the joint cookin' (and make conversation difficult). Headliners play at the concert hall next door. A Gospel Brunch is held every Sunday (see page 236 for details). Open to 2:00 am on Thu.-Sat.

- Table
- American
- Very noisy
- Priority seats at 407-WDW-DINE
- Call 90 days
- Long waits
- 11:00 am-11:00 pm

Wetzel's Pretzels — S — $4 — | 6 | 5 | 5 |

Former Disneyland Jungle Cruise Cast Member Rick Wetzel has become king of the gourmet soft pretzel. This shop in the former Forty Thirst Street Cafe offers a variety of fresh, hand-rolled soft pretzels, "pretzel dogs" (pretzel dough-wrapped weiners), fresh-squeezed lemonade, fruit drinks, and Häagen-Dazs ice cream. A second kiosk can be found at Downtown Disney Marketplace.

- Counter
- American
- Med. noise
- 11:00 am-11:00 pm

Eatery descriptions and ratings are explained on page 204.

Tip: We enjoy eating at Downtown Disney West Side before or after a night out, but we find the lack of priority seating and the long lines frustrating. To offset the waits, try visiting at times least likely to be crowded (late afternoon and late night). If you can't avoid the peak times but need a good meal, try the bar seating at Wolfgang Puck Grand Cafe—seats open up frequently and you usually don't need a host to be seated. You can order any item off the regular menu at the bar, too.

Downtown Disney West Side Eateries
(continued)

			Jennifer's Rating	Dave's Rating	Readers' Rating

Planet Hollywood — L/D — $40/28 — 5 5 6

Everyone will be entertained and well-fed inside Planet Hollywood's big, blue globe full of movie and TV memorabilia. Every visitor gets the Hollywood treatment—you have to pass by the bouncers at the bottom of the stairs and walk under a long awning to reach the front door. There's seating on several levels, with views of projection video screens showing TV clips and movie trailers. You don't really come for the food, or do you? The menu can please almost anyone, with entree salads ($8.95-$12.45), sandwiches and burgers ($8.95-13.95), pastas ($10.95-15.95), fajitas ($13.95), and grilled and roasted meats ($13.95-19.95). Kids' meals run about $11.00. Portions are huge, quality is average, and service can be slow. You won't get bored, though.

Table
American
Very noisy
Priority seating at 407-WDW-DINE
Call 90 days
Med. waits
11 am–1 am

Wolfgang Puck Grand Cafe — L/D — $41 ($32) — 7 6 7

Puck is famous for nearly single-handedly popularizing California cuisine and for putting wood-fired, individual pizzas on the map. Menu favorites include Chinois Chicken Salad ($10.95), four cheese pizza ($11.95), stir-fried Pad Thai noodles ($12.95-16.95), ribeye steaks ($20.95), seafood ($19.95) and rotisserie chicken ($13.95). Ooops! Let's not forget his fabulous sushi and California Rolls ($4.95-$24.95)! The decor is trendy, the tables for two are too small, service is spotty, and dinnertime seating requires long waits. If you're in a rush, dine at the bar or outdoors. Conditions are much nicer at lunch. Note: "Grand Cafe" refers to the three restaurants under one roof. Priority seating can be made for dining times between 11:30 am-6:00 pm and 9:30 pm-closing.

Table
American
Very noisy
Priority seats at 407-WDW-DINE
Very long waits
11:30 am–11:00 pm

Wolfgang Puck Dining Room — D — $56 — 8 8 8

Climb the broad staircase inside Wolfgang Puck Grand Cafe and you'll reach the upscale Dining Room. This is a popular site for private parties, but when it's open to the public, it offers refined respite from the crowds below. Seafood items include tuna tartare, smoked salmon, pan-seared rare tuna "Nicoise," and sushi ($10-27)—notice a trend? Main courses include tandoori-spiced lamb chops ($28), pumpkin ravioli ($18), honey-lavender pork tenderloin ($26), and Wienerschnitzel ($25). Call 24 hours in advance for the five-course Chef's Table menu ($80). Call 407-WDW-DINE for reservations and parties.

Table
American
Noisy
Reservations recommended
Call 60 days
Long waits
6-10:00 pm

Wolfgang Puck Express — L/D — $13 — 5 6 8

Fast food for the trendy, upscale set. Puck's famous wood-fired pizzas, rotisseried rosemary garlic chicken, real macaroni and cheese, soups, and pastas are served hot. Enjoy a wide choice of salads and appetizing sandwiches, soft drinks, and alcoholic beverages. Part of Wolfgang Puck Grand Cafe. Dine outside, or take-out. See page 221 for Wolfgang Puck Express at Marketplace.

Counter
American
Med. noise
Med. waits
11 am–11 pm

Wonderland Cafe — S — $8 — 7 7 7

This is truly a coffee and dessert wonderland! This is the place to go for virtually every possible kind of hot and cold coffee drink plus to-die-for desserts, such as cheesecakes ($4.75-5.50), mud pie blackout cake ($4.95), and hot fudge brownie sundae ($4.95). Comfy seating. The Cheesecake Factory runs the joint. Located inside DisneyQuest—admission required.

Counter
American
Med. noise
10:30 am–11:45 pm

Resort Restaurants
(Disney's Animal Kingdom Lodge and BoardWalk Resorts)

Jennifer's Rating | *Dave's Rating* | *Readers' Rating*

Disney's Animal Kingdom Lodge Resort Restaurants

☐ Boma–Flavors of Africa B/D $31 🦓🍷 7 8 9

Savor the many flavors of Africa at a fabulous buffet (breakfast is $15.99/adults and $8.99/kids; dinner is $24.99/adults and $10.99/kids). At dinner, a dazzling array of unusual soups, stews, salads, veggies, and wood-grilled meats tempt both timid and adventuresome diners (including kids and vegetarians). The wood-burning grill and exhibit kitchen adds extra flavor to the marketplace décor. And the dessert station is fabulous—be sure to try the Zebra Domes. Breakfast is equally wonderful but more down-to earth. This has become one of Disney's most talked about restaurants. Diners are consistently amazed by the wide variety of pleasing new tastes, and even plain meat and potatoes lovers are delighted. Book ahead and arrive early. Even the line to check in can be long. Enjoy the Animal Kingdom Lodge's lobby and animal overlooks while you wait to be seated.

Buffet
African
Very noisy
Priority seats strongly suggested
Call 90 days
Long waits
7:30 am–11:00 am, 5:00-10 pm

☐ Jiko–The Cooking Place D $54 🦓🍷 9 9 9

African flavorings meet Californian and Asian influences with grace and style at Jiko. Savory appetizers like crispy cinnamon-spiced beef roll and duck firecracker come from wood-burning ovens ($7.00-12.75). Entrees include pan-roasted monkfish ($24.00), buttermilk-curry shrimp ($25.00), pomegranate-glazed quail ($25.00), grains and veggies with tandoori tofu ($17.50), and wood-grilled pork tenderloin with mushroom ragout ($24.00). Star chef Anette Grecchi Gray can now boast of a AAA Four Diamond rating, among other honors. Under her direction, fish and vegetarian items are now taking the limelight, and you'll also find a stronger Afro-Mediterranean influence. For dessert, try the Tanzanian chocolate candies ($7.00). Phenomenal South African wine cellar. The kids have their own menu with appetizers ($1.75) and entrees ($5.50-8.75).

Table
African
Noisy
Priority seats strongly suggested
Call 90 days
Short waits
5:30 pm–10:00 pm

BoardWalk Resort Restaurants   *See pages 230-231 for Beach Club eateries*

☐ Big River Grille & Brewing Works L/D $41 ($37) 🍷 3 4 4

No, you won't see Brewmaster Mickey, but this brewpub chain is a popular family dining spot at the BoardWalk (ESPN Club seems to siphon-off the rowdier drinking crowd). Choices range from chicken quesadilla ($8.99) to a grilled chicken cashew salad ($10.99), barbecue sandwich ($7.99, lunch only), burgers ($8.99-10.99), or grilled porkchops ($19.99). Steaks and ribs are also plentiful ($13.99-24.99). The decor and seating is simple—we suggest you dine outdoors on the boardwalk in good weather. Our most recent visit was disappointing, with lackluster service, mediocre food, and a dirty floor. They do take reservations 24 hours in advance and priority seatings on the same day at 407-560-0253.

Table
American
Noisy
Reservations 407-560-0253
Med. waits
11:30 am–11:00 pm

☐ ESPN Club L/D $37 4 4 7

100 TVs pipe the big games into every nook and cranny of this very popular (and loud) sports bar. You can even go on camera for a live sports trivia quiz. The lineup is familiar—hot wings ($8.99), chili ($5.99), burgers and sandwiches ($7.99-11.99), grilled meat or fish ($13.99-15.99), plus beer and mixed drinks. Sit at booths or on stools. Open until 2 am on weekends. No priority seating.

Table
American
Very noisy
Med. waits
11:30 am-1 am

Eatery descriptions and ratings are explained on page 204.

Resort Restaurants
(BoardWalk, Caribbean Beach, and Contemporary Resorts)

Jennifer's Rating · *Dave's Rating* · *Readers' Rating*

BoardWalk Resort Restaurants *(continued)*

■ Flying Fish Cafe	D	$65		8	8	8

This is a Disney dining hot spot and one of our favorites, serving uniquely prepared, fresh seafood in a trendy-but-fun atmosphere. The menu changes to suit the season and the catch. Appetizers are special. Dave was blown away by plump steamed mussels in a pastis-flavored cream. The "Chef's Thunder" portion of the menu offers daily specialties, such as coriander-crusted Yellowfin Tuna ($28), while the main menu may offer a remarkable red snapper in a crispy, sliced-potato wrapper with leek fondue ($29), or pan-roasted grouper with clams and salt cod brandade ($32). There's strip steak, chicken, and pasta for the fish-shy ($18-38) and not-to-be-missed desserts. The crowds here are loud—ask for a quieter table under the "canopy" in the back. Open to 10:30 on Fri. and Sat.	**Table** Seafood Very noisy Priority seats strongly recommended Call 90 days Med. waits 5:30 pm-10 pm

■ Spoodles	B/D	$47		6	7	6

Fresh seafood, grilled meats, oak-fired flatbreads, pastas, and other Italian, Greek, and Spanish specialties grace the menu. A satisfying breakfast offers popular items plus Italian frittata and breakfast flatbread ($5.99-8.99) and an all-you-can-eat breakfast platter ($10.99). At dinner, start with flatbread ($6.99-9.49) or tapas ($4.99-7.99), share a tapas platter ($19.99), or make a meal of these Spanish-style appetizers. Entrees include a Moroccan spiced tuna ($21.99); chicken breast with couscous, spinach, and lemon olive sauce ($16.99); and grilled pork porterhouse with polenta and figs ($19.59). Desserts ($1.99-6.99) include a chocolate velvet cake and pistachio creme brulee. A take-out pizza window is available, too.	**Table** Mediterranean Noisy Priority seats recommended Call 90 days Short waits 7:30-11 am 5-10 pm

Caribbean Beach Resort Restaurant

■ Shutters	D	$40	6	6	6

Serving American cuisine inspired by the flavors of the Caribbean, this 120-seat, casual family restaurant has a breezy, island atmosphere. In all ways, a big improvement over the old Captain's Tavern. Menu items include a delicious black bean soup ($4.29), grilled shrimp skewers ($18.99), and citrus marinated pork chop ($17.99). Their signature smoked prime rib ($17.99/$19.99) is just average. For dessert, go with the French toast bread pudding ($7.99—serves two).	**Table** Caribbean/American Priority seats suggested 5:30-10 pm

Contemporary Resort Restaurants

■ California Grill	D	$59		8	8	8

High atop the Contemporary, overlooking the Magic Kingdom, the California Grill pours fine wines, serves yummy California cuisine, and keeps getting better! The noise can be deafening, but the fireworks bursting over Cinderella Castle are spectacular. The menu changes weekly, but count on inventive sushi ($11.75-$22.75), flatbreads ($9.00-10.50), grilled or roasted seafood and meats ($21.75-$34.50), and sinful desserts. Perennial picks include Yellowfin Tuna ($25.00) and oak-fired beef filet ($34.50). Vegetarians do well. Three creams with three berries ($8.25) is a sinful dessert. When available, the peaceful Wine Room has the same menu, and you may see Epcot's IllumiNations. Sushi bar seating, too. Kids' menu $6.75-9.00. "Smart casual" dress (slacks rather than shorts). Note: Diners now check in on the second floor of the Contemporary and are escorted up to the 14th floor when their table is ready.	**Table** American Very noisy Priority seats strongly recommended Call 90 days Long waits 5:30 pm-10:00 pm

Sidebar tabs: Planning · Getting There · Staying in Style · Touring · Feasting · Making Magic · Index · Notes & More

Resort Restaurants
(Contemporary, Coronado Springs, and Fort Wilderness Resorts)

Jennifer's Rating   *Dave's Rating*   *Readers' Rating*

Contemporary Resort Restaurants *(continued)*

Chef Mickey's	B/D	$33		6	6	8

Chef Mickey's fills the Contemporary's cavernous lobby with all sorts of Goofy antics (not to mention Mickey, Minnie, and friends). Mickey's offers separate adult and kid's dinner buffets ($26.99/11.99 kids 3-11) and a sundae bar. Breakfast buffet ($17.99/9.99) includes omelettes and pancakes cooked to order. Dinner items change, but on our last visit, we had flavorful roast beef, tasty pork loin, and cod with a curry crust, all of a quality and presentation befitting a deluxe resort. Note that your picture is taken before you're seated—you may purchase the photo during your meal. The place is huge, but it's broken up into smaller areas. See pages 232-233 for character meal details.	**Buffet** American Very noisy Priority seats suggested Call 90 days Med. waits 7-11:30 am, 5:00-9:30 pm

Concourse Steakhouse	B/L/D	$42		6	7	8

Appealing touches on the appetizers and entrees lift the Concourse a cut above your typical steakhouse. Situated in the towering lobby of the Contemporary, you may see Goofy at neighboring Chef Mickey's, but it's a sane alternative when the California Grill upstairs is busy. Concourse's appetizing morning menu ($6.99-16.99) includes a breakfast quesadilla ($8.99). Lunch brings pizzas and sandwiches ($7.99-11.99) and salad with seared tuna ($15.99). The dinner menu includes shellfish bisque ($5.99), pasta pesto with veggies ($13.99), steaks and prime rib ($16.99-27.99), and herb-crusted salmon ($18.99). If noise is a concern, ask to be seated at a table away from Chef Mickey's.	**Table** Steakhouse Noisy Priority seats suggested Call 90 days 7:30-11 am, Noon-2:00 pm, 5:30-10 pm

Coronado Springs Resort Restaurant

Maya Grill	B/D	$48		5	6	5

Alas, this formerly inventive spot has become a nearly ordinary steakhouse with appealing Mexican/Southwestern items among the appetizers, catering to the resort's conventioneers. If you're hankering for Mexican food, try the resort's food court instead. The restaurant is almost too elegant for a moderate resort, with grand, soaring architecture evoking a Mayan temple in warm yellows and accents of deep blue, shimmering gold, and rich woods. The breakfast buffet offers the standards with a Southwestern flair ($11.99/6.99). The dinner menu includes steaks and mixed grill ($22.99-27.99), BBQ ribs ($18.99), marinated rack of lamb ($23.99), and salmon filet ($19.99). Kids' menu available ($8.25-8.50).	**Table** American Med. noise Priority seats suggested Call 90 days Short waits 7-11 am, 5-10 pm

Fort Wilderness Resort Restaurant

Trail's End Restaurant	B/L/D	$21		7	6	6

One of the best dining deals on Disney property. While the vittles at Trail's End won't win awards for elegance, the food is plentiful, fresh, and tasty. Breakfasts ($10.99/6.99 kids 3-11) are hearty and heavy on home-style classics—eggs, french toast, Mickey waffles, hash, donuts, biscuits and gravy, cereals, yogurt, and fruit. Lunch ($10.99/6.99) brings rib-stickin' fare like fried chicken, mac and cheese, BBQ, pizza, turkey wraps, and a passable salad bar. Dinner is a gentle $16.99/7.99 and you still get a tasty soup, salad bar, peel and eat shrimp, chicken, ribs, a carved meat, fish, good veggies, pizza, a daily regional specialty like venison stew, and fruit cobbler for dessert. Soup & Salad bar is $10.50.	**Buffet** American Med. noise No priority seating Short waits 7:30-11 am, Noon-2:30 pm, 4:30-9:30 pm

Eatery descriptions and ratings are explained on page 204.

Resort Restaurants
(Grand Floridian Resort)

Jennifer's Rating
Dave's Rating
Readers' Rating

Grand Floridian Resort Restaurants

Cítricos	D	$57		9 8 9

A grand restaurant at the Grand Floridian, Cítricos blends the fresh flavors of Florida and the Mediterranean with simplicity and elegance. Warm colors, tall windows, and well-spaced tables make this a very comfortable place. The menu changes frequently, but the sauteed shrimp ($12) and pan-seared quail ($9) are appealing appetizers. A wonderful braised veal shank is available as an entree ($33), along with seasonal fish specialties ($25-$28), roasted duck breast ($25), and basil-crusted rack of lamb ($29). The wine pairings—three wines selected to match your meal ($25)—are a fine idea, and the desserts ($8) are gorgeous! Closed Mondays and Tuesdays. Kids' menu ($6-12) available.

Table
Floridian
Med. noise
Priority seats suggested
Call 90 days
Short waits
5:30-9:30 pm

Garden View Lounge	S	$25		8 7 5

If you've ever yearned for afternoon tea, this is the place for it. The quiet, genteel Victorian setting is perfect for tea sandwiches, scones, and pastries ($2.75-12.75), or do it right with an all-inclusive tea "offering" ($12.50-24.50). A good variety of teas is served. A kids' "Mrs. Potts' Tea" is available for $8.50.

Lounge
English
Priority seats
2-6 pm

Grand Floridian Cafe	B/L/D	$33		5 6 6

This "informal" cafe features an American menu with all the extra flourishes found in finer restaurants. Hearty breakfasts include corned beef hash or eggs Benedict ($10.99), and a traditional Japanese breakfast ($19.99). Lunch brings entree salads ($10.99-13.99), shrimp and pasta ($14.99), and sandwiches including a Reuben, Catch of the Day, and turkey club ($9.99-13.99). Dinner offers a short menu with steak, prime rib, grilled fish, and pasta ($12.99-20.99), plus burgers ($9.99).

Table
American
Very noisy
7-11 am, 11:45 am-2 pm, 5-9 pm

Narcoossee's	D	$69		8 8 8

Narcoossee's open kitchen serves an ever-changing menu of grilled seafoods with savory accompaniments. Perched on the edge of Seven Seas Lagoon, the restaurant has a sedate and casual dockside atmosphere, with lots of bare wood and windows affording views of the Magic Kingdom fireworks and the Electrical Water Pageant. The huge appetizer of steamed mussels was heavenly ($14.75), as were the grilled salmon ($32) and pan-roasted red snapper (no longer on menu). Sesame-crusted Ahi tuna ($30), steamed Maine lobster ($54), and jumbo scallops ($30) are also tempting choices, and meat lovers can order filet mignon ($33) or roasted free-range chicken breast ($25). Desserts ($6-7) include assorted berry pyramid and Key Lime créme brulée. Kids' menu ($6-12) available.

Table
Seafood
Noisy
Priority seats recommended
Call 90 days
Short waits
6-10 pm
(lounge open 5-10 pm)

1900 Park Fare	B/D	$34		7 7 7

Daily character meals in a jolly Victorian setting, complete with an orchestrion ("player" organ). The upscale buffet breakfast ($17.99/10.99 kids 3-11) features Mary Poppins, Alice in Wonderland, and their friends. Waits can be long, but Mad Hatter may be on hand to keep the little ones occupied. At dinner time ($27.99/12.99), Cinderella and friends take their turn hosting. You don't really come for the meal, but this is one of Disney's finer buffets (keep your eyes open for the strawberry soup—it's scrumptious). The Wonderland Tea Party is held here for kids on Mondays-Fridays. See pages 232-233 and 244 for details.

Buffet
American
Very noisy
Priority seats recommended
Call 90 days
8:00-11:00 am
4:30-8:20 pm

Sidebar (right margin): Planning · Getting There · Staying in Style · Touring · Feasting · Making Magic · Index · Notes & More

Resort Restaurants
(Grand Floridian, Old Key West, and Polynesian Resorts)

Jennifer's Rating
Dave's Rating
Readers' Rating

Grand Floridian Resort Restaurants *(continued)*

| Victoria & Albert's | D | $121 | | *10* | *10* | *9* |

You have to dress up for Walt Disney World's five-star dining experience—jackets are required and a tux or gown isn't entirely out of place. The continental, five-course, prix fixe menu ($95) is redesigned daily, a harpist fills the air with music, and all the hosts and hostesses answer to "Victoria" or "Albert." For an extra-special evening, reserve the "Chef's Table," an alcove in the kitchen where you observe and interact with the chef and staff ($125, reserve six months in advance). Consider a wine pairing ($60) to perfectly match your meal. Is it all worth it? Without a doubt! Your dinner is elegantly prepared, and each course brings new delights. We held our wedding dinner here. Need we say more? State special dietary needs in advance. Call 407-824-1089 to confirm 24 hours in advance.

Table
French
Quiet
Reservations required—call 407-824-1089
Call 90 days
Short waits
5:45 pm & 9:00 pm

Old Key West Resort Restaurant

| Olivia's Cafe | B/L/D | $40 | | *6* | *6* | *5* |

Olivia's Cafe serves an enticing array of Southern- and Caribbean-tinged specialties in a homey, small-island atmosphere. Breakfast includes the classics and a lineup of healthy items ($7.29–10.79). Lunchtime brings conch chowder ($4.49), salads ($4.59–13.59), BBQ pork and Po' Boy sandwiches ($8.99–11.99). At dinner the shrimp fritters ($5.99), filet mignon with scampi-style shrimp ($21.99), seafood ($16.99–19.99), and jerk chicken ($18.99) will make you smile, and don't pass up the Key Lime tart ($5.29). The character breakfast here was discontinued in 2001. Priority seats not always necessary.

Table
Floridian
Med. noise
Short waits
Call 90 days
7:30-10:30 am, 11:30 am-5 pm, 5-10 pm

Polynesian Resort Restaurants

See page 235 for the Polynesian Luau

| Kona Cafe | B/L/D | $42 | | *8* | *7* | *8* |

A stylish spot for coffee and full meals. Its Asian/eclectic menu brings welcome sophistication to the Polynesian Resort. Breakfasts include banana-stuffed "Tonga Toast" ($7.99) and tropical fruit punch ($3.59). Lunch offers a huge teriyaki beef salad ($10.99), a satisfying Asian noodle bowl ($12.99), and a tasty blackened fish sandwich ($9.99). The appetizers are attractive, and dinners offer steaks, chicken, and seafood with an Asian flair ($13.99–24.99), including Macadamia-crusted Mahi Mahi ($19.99). Fabulous coffee bar and desserts, too! (The specialty is "Ko Ko Puffs.")

Table
International
Noisy
Priority seats recommended
Call 90 days
7:30-11:30 am, Noon-3:00 pm, 5-10 pm

| 'Ohana | B/D | $40 | | *8* | *6* | *7* |

Aloha, cousins! The Polynesian Resort welcomes you warmly to 'Ohana, a great, fun spot for families and groups. This is an all-you-care-to-eat feast ($24.99/$10.99 kids 3-11). Appetizers (salad, wonton, and wings) and veggies are served family-style, then the enthusiastic cast members circulate with long skewers of grilled steak, turkey, shrimp, and pork. Kids can participate in coconut races and hula hoop contests, and live entertainers sing Hawaiian melodies. It's a fun place for the outgoing, or just to relax and enjoy. If you work things right you may even see the Magic Kingdom fireworks! Soft drinks included. Desserts ($4.99) cost extra, as do the tropical drinks in unusual containers. 'Ohana also hosts a character breakfast (see pages 232-233) for $17.99/$9.99 kids.

Table
Polynesian
Very noisy
Priority seats strongly recommended
Call 90 days
Long waits
7:30-11 am, 5-10 pm

Eatery descriptions and ratings are explained on page 204.

Resort Restaurants
(Port Orleans and Swan and Dolphin Resorts)

Port Orleans Riverside Resort Restaurant

			Jennifer's Rating	Dave's Rating	Readers' Rating

Boatwright's Dining Hall   B/D $38   **7 5 7**

Cajun cooking from down the bayou fits the bill perfectly. In keeping with the restaurant's theme, a wooden boat hangs overhead and boat-builders' tools hang on the rustic walls. This is a place for hearty, Southern-style breakfasts such as the breakfast calabash ($8.99), big omelettes ($7.59), and stuffed french toast ($7.99). Dinner offers chicken gumbo ($4.99), cajun wings ($6.99), jambalaya ($16.99), blackened seafood pasta ($17.59), bourbon-glazed chicken ($14.59), prime rib ($19.99), and crab-stuffed salmon ($17.29). Kids' menu ($5.29).

Table
American
Med. noise
Call 90 days
Short waits
7:30-11:30 am, 5-10 pm

Swan and Dolphin Resort Restaurants

bluezoo [Dolphin]   D $69   **6 7 7**

Star chef Todd English presents upscale, inventively prepared seafood at this visually striking establishment. The scallop appetizer with braised short rib ($12) was a savory adventure, the "Dancing Fish" ($30) disappointing, filo baked salmon a winner, and other choices ($22-54) were satisfying. Separate, lighter menu at the crowded cafe/bar. Not kid-friendly. Dave prefers nearby Flying Fish Cafe.

Table
Seafood
Noisy
Call 90 days
5 pm-11 pm

Fresh Mediterranean Market [Dolphin]   B/L $24   **8 7 8**

This cheery and appealing variation on a buffet offers a wide variety of cooked-to-order items at breakfast ($16.95/9.95) and lunch ($17.95/10.95). The very attentive chefs ply you with all sorts of temptations, both Mediterranean-style and American, all prepared with a light, "fresh" hand. Grilled and rotisseried meats, pastas, cold salads, veggies, and lots of desserts, too! Worth a special trip!

Buffet
Mediterranean
Med. noise
Call 90 days
6 am-2 pm

Gulliver's Grill at Garden Grove [Swan]   B/L/D $49 ($41)   **5 6 8**

By day, this is the Garden Grove Cafe, offering breakfast and lunch. There's a satisfying breakfast buffet ($13.95/8.50 kids 3-11), a Japanese breakfast ($17.95), a la carte selections, and a character breakfast on weekends from 8:00-11:00 am ($16.95/$8.50). Lunch offers salads, sandwiches, and light entrees ($8.50-14.95). Each night of the week, this eatery is transformed into Gulliver's, a character dining experience (see pages 232-233). Dinner offers a buffet ($23.95/$10.95 kids 3-11) with a rotating theme. A la carte also available. Reserve at 407-934-1609.

Table
American
Noisy
Call 90 days
6:30-11:30 am, 11:30 am-2 pm, 5:30-10 pm

Kimonos [Swan]   D/S $44   **6 7 6**

In search of excellent late-night sushi, drinks, and karaoke? Try the Swan! Dinner is possible ($19.00-$22.50), or snack on sushi by the piece ($3.00-12.95) and hot appetizers ($3.25-9.95) while you get up the nerve to sing (if you want). Very noisy. No priority seating; reservations for 6+ (call 407-934-1609).

Table
Japanese
Noisy
5:30 pm-12 am

Palio [Swan]   D $54 ($41)   **7 8 9**

The Swan resort is home to this refined Northern Italian restaurant. Service is gracious and attentive, and the decor honors Palio, Siena's famed horserace. The menu features an enticing list of appetizers, including carpaccio (thinly sliced raw beef) with parmesan ($10.50) and risotto with mushrooms ($8.50). Wood-fired pizzas are $13.95-14.75. Pastas and entrees include tortellini with lobster ($23.50), veal saltimbocca ($24.25), osso bucco ($24.95), and marinated swordfish ($23.50). Excellent choice of Italian wines and desserts ($6.50-10.50).

Table
Italian
Quiet
Priority seats call Disney or 407-934-1609
6-11 pm

Planning | Getting There | Staying in Style | Touring | Feasting | Making Magic | Index | Notes & More

Resort Restaurants
(Swan and Dolphin Resorts, Wilderness Lodge, and Yacht and Beach Resorts)

Swan and Dolphin Resorts Restaurants *(continued)*

Shula's Steak House [Dolphin]	D	$75	8	8	9

This is the most upscale steakhouse on Disney property. Beautifully grilled, flavorful beef is the focus (if you finish the 48-oz. porterhouse, they'll engrave your name on a plaque!) but perfectly succulent fish ($22.95–24.95) gets the utmost respect. Grilled meats cost from $21.95 to $71.95. If you need to ask the "market price" of the 4-lb. lobster, you can't afford it! With dark wood paneling, Sinatra on the speakers, gilt-framed football photos, and formal, attentive service, you may prefer to wear a jacket or dress. Veggies are $6.95–7.95 (split an order, and get the potato pancake, too) but the "garnish" of peppers, watercress, and mushrooms on every plate may be enough. The wine list is expansive and expensive. And order the chocolate soufflé for two ($13)!

Table
Steakhouse
Med. noise
Priority seats suggested; call 407-WDW-DINE
Call 90 days
Short waits
5 pm-11 pm

Wilderness Lodge Resort Restaurants

Artist Point	D	$56	🏆	10	9	8

This visually stunning restaurant serves flavorful contemporary fare from the Pacific Northwest and is among our favorites. The dining room is a soaring, log-beamed space graced by large murals of Western landscapes and furnished with comfortable, Mission-style tables and chairs. The menu changes seasonally. For starters, try venison spring rolls ($8), braised mussels with lemon and fennel ($12), or smoky portobello soup ($6). The old-standby Cedar Plank Salmon ($28) is always rewarding, or try pan-seared pork chop ($24), grilled buffalo sirloin ($30), grilled beef tenderloin ($30), or seafood and vegetarian entrees ($19–29). For dessert, the hot berry cobbler is a must ($12). The wine list is excellent—try a wine pairing. "Smart casual" dress (slacks rather than shorts).

Table
American
Med. noise
Priority seats suggested
Call 90 days
Short waits
5:30 pm-10:00 pm

Whispering Canyon Cafe	B/L/D	$37	8	6	8

If you hanker for really fine barbecue in a rustic Wild West setting, sashay over to the Wilderness Lodge. There are a la carte choices ($15.99–22.99 at dinner), but most get the family-style, all-you-can-eat "skillets." The breakfast skillet is $9.69/$5.89 kids 3–11. Lunch ($13.99/$7.39) and dinner ($21.99/$8.79) bring barbecued chicken, ribs, pork, sausage, and all the fixin's. This is "dry" barbecue—marinated and smoked, with four sauces on the side. Just don't ask for ketchup. Trust us! There are activities for the kids, and the servers make sure all have fun. Hours: 7:30–11:00 am, Noon–3:00 pm, and 5:00–10:00 pm.

Table
Barbecue
Very noisy
Priority seats recommended
Call 90 days
Long waits
7:30 am-10 pm

Yacht and Beach Club Resorts Restaurants

Beaches and Cream	L/D/S	$20 ($9)	👶🏆	8	6	8

This small, seaside-style ice cream parlor is always jammed. Sure, you can get classic luncheonette items like burgers ($6.99–8.99), prime rib subs ($10.99), veggie burgers ($6.99), and hot dogs ($5.99), plus shakes and malts ($4.99), but you know everyone is here for the ice cream. Why not cut to the chase and go for an ice cream soda, float, ice cream, frozen yogurt, or sundae ($2.49–7.99). Or get the Kitchen Sink ($21.99), a huge sundae with every topping. Sit at tables, booths, or at the counter. The average meal costs above are for a "light" meal and a snack (dessert and soft drink). No priority seating. Take-out also available.

Table
American
Very noisy
No priority seating
Long waits
11:00 am-11:00 pm

Jennifer's Rating
Dave's Rating
Readers' Rating

Resort Restaurants
(Yacht and Beach Club Resorts and Miscellaneous)

Yacht and Beach Club Resorts Restaurants (continued)

Ratings columns: Jennifer's Rating / Dave's Rating / Readers' Rating

Cape May Cafe [Beach Club] — B/D — $33 — 7 7 8

It may not be outdoors, but it's a real nice clam bake! Seafood lovers line up for this dinner buffet ($24.99/10.99 kids 3-11), which is within walking distance of Epcot and five resort hotels. An endless supply of chowder, steamed hard shell clams, mussels, baked fish, prime rib, corn on the cob, and all the trimmings will make any seafood lover happy as a clam (although it's not quite genuine New England). They'll also steam up crab legs for an extra $11.99. There's plenty for the fish-shy, a kids' buffet, a dessert bar, and they bring taffy with the check. A character buffet ($17.99/9.99) is held in the mornings that is prized for its relaxed atmosphere (see pages 232-233). Chairs and booths.

Buffet | Seafood | Noisy | Priority seating recommended | Call 90 days | 7:30-11 am, 5:30-9:30 pm

Yacht Club Galley [Yacht Club] — B/L/D — $35 — 4 5 8

This casual-yet-typical hotel café offers pleasant surroundings at breakfast, lunch, and dinner. Traditional favorites and a healthy helping of meat and seafood dishes are the specialty here. Breakfast offers a buffet ($13.99/6.99 kids 3-11) and predictable a la carte selections ($4.99-15.99). Lunch brings salads ($6.99-12.99), half-pound cheeseburgers ($9.99), a crab and shrimp cake sandwich ($12.99), and a Yacht Club sandwich ($9.99). Dinner resembles lunch, with sandwiches, dinner salads, and a few basic entrees ($9.99-16.99).

Table | American | Med. noise | Short waits | 7:00-11 am, 11:30 am-2 pm, 6:00-10:00 pm

Yachtsman Steakhouse [Yacht Club] — D — $68 — 7 7 9

Until Shula's opened, Yachtsman Steakhouse was considered to be the best steakhouse in the "World," and it still comes close. Hardwood-grilled steaks are the main attraction at dinner, but vegetarians ($20 daily special) haven't been neglected. Appetizers include Oysters Rockefeller ($12), chipotle bbq shrimp ($12), and salads ($8-11). Plain and sauced meats ($23-48) including a popular bourbon-glazed strip steak ($32), rack of lamb ($35), and prime rib ($32) fill the menu, plus salmon salad, sea bass, and a steak/lobster tail combo ($32-55). Excellent wine and beer list. It's been reported that this is Michael Eisner's favorite restaurant on Disney property.

Table | Steakhouse | Med. noise | Priority seats strongly suggested | Call 90 days | 5:30 pm-9:45 pm

Miscellaneous Restaurant
(Wide World of Sports)

All-Star Cafe — L/D — $30 ($26) — 4 5 8

Super Star-powered decor fills this sports bar offering American cuisine, 55 televisions for watching the game, a video game arcade, and unique sports memorabilia. The predictable lineup of munchies ($4.99-8.99), salads ($4.49-9.99), sandwiches ($7.99-9.99), rib-eye steak ($16.99), chicken tenders ($9.99), and smoked ribs ($10.99/18.99) is available, along with some pasta and seafood. Desserts ($3.99-4.99) include a warm apple crisp. Ask for one of the rooms off to the side to cut down on the noise levels. Expect long waits at game time. Open Thurs.-Sun.; closed when no events are held at Wide World of Sports.

Table | American | Very noisy | Priority seats not accepted | Short waits | 11:30 am-9:00 pm

Eatery descriptions and ratings are explained on page 204.

Character Meals

Disney offers many opportunities to dine with characters, both those in full guise (like Mickey Mouse) and "face characters" in costume (like Cinderella). While they don't actually sit with you throughout your meal, they do roam around the restaurant and visit your table for interludes. Character meals are generally more expensive than regular meals (usually $17–35 for adults and $9–18 for kids), but the chance to meet the characters in an unhurried atmosphere makes it worthwhile. Even if characters aren't at the top of your menu, character dinners are a good deal—the cost of these buffets and family-style meals is usually less than comparable full-service meals when you factor all costs. Character meals are *extremely* popular—make priority seating arrangements as far in advance as possible at 407-WDW-DINE. Bring your camera and an autograph book!

Be aware that there's a mad rush for priority seating at Cinderella's Royal Table for breakfast in the Magic Kingdom. Folks start phoning at 7:00 am Eastern time, exactly 90 days prior to their desired date, and tables are often gone in a matter of minutes. If you get a table at Cinderella's, expect to pay a deposit of $10/adult and $5/child by credit card—this deposit is refunded if you cancel 24 hours in advance. If you miss out, don't despair. Try again once you get to Walt Disney World. Cancellations are common, so it never hurts to ask for a table, even as you're walking through Cinderella Castle. If you are set on dining with a princess, try the Princess Storybook Breakfast at Restaurant Akershus or the character dinner at 1900 Park Fare.

✔ Some character breakfasts start prior to park opening. All Disney resorts offer special Disney bus transportation to the early character breakfasts.

✔ For the best character experience, dine off-hours. While Mickey may only give you a quick hello during busy mealtimes, you might end up with a close, personal relationship when tables are empty.

✔ Don't be shy, grown-ups! Even if you aren't dining with kids, the characters visit your table. If you'd rather sit things out, they will simply give you a nod or handshake.

✔ The "head" characters don't speak, but that doesn't mean you have to keep quiet. Talk to them and they'll pantomime and play along!

© MediaMarx, Inc.

Dave and Allie wait for Tigger to bounce over to their table at the Crystal Palace

Character Dining Location Chart

To help you pick the meal that best suits you, we've created a chart of all the character meals known at the time of writing. The location of each meal is given in parentheses, along with the meal served (B=breakfast or brunch, L=lunch, D=dinner, All=all three meals), the type (buffet=buffet-style, family=family-style, plate=buffet items brought to you on a plate, menu=from the menu), and the prominent characters (note that a specific character's appearance is not guaranteed). Note: As of 2003, Hollywood & Vine no longer offers character meals.

Restaurant	Meal	Type	Characters
Cape May Cafe (Beach Club)	B	Buffet	Goofy, Chip, Dale, Minnie
Casual, beach party atmosphere and good, standard breakfast foods. (Page 231)			
Chef Mickey's (Contemporary)	B/D	Buffet	Mickey, Minnie, Goofy, Chip
Bustling, popular destination. Superior food. Try to dine at off-hours. (Page 226)			
Cinderella's Royal Table (MK)	B	Plate	Cinderella, Peter Pan, Belle
Gorgeous setting, hottest reservation at WDW. Original "princess" meal. (Page 205)			
Crystal Palace (MK)	All	Buffet	Pooh, Tigger, Eeyore
A favorite spot for satisfying meals in bright and airy surroundings. (Page 205)			
Donald's Breakfastosaurus (AK)	B	Buffet	Donald, Mickey, Goofy
Crowded and noisy, but lots of fun. Hearty, DinoLand-themed foods. (Page 218)			
The Garden Grill (Epcot)	L/D	Family	Farmer Mickey, Chip, Pluto
Tasty dining in an unusual setting. Good spur-of-the-moment choice. (Page 210) Also: An ice cream social is offered with the same characters–see page 210.			
Gulliver's/Garden Grove (Swan)	B/D[1]	Buffet/Menu	Timon or Goofy
A la carte menu makes this the most expensive character dinner. (Page 229)			
Liberty Tree Tavern (MK)	D	Family	Donald, Daisy, Minnie
Thanksgiving-style feast with Colonial-garbed characters. (Page 206)			
1900 Park Fare (Grand Floridian)	B/D	Buffet	Mary Poppins (B) Cinderella (D)
First-rate food, comfy Victorian surroundings, and lots of character. (Page 227)			
'Ohana (Polynesian)	B	Family	Mickey, Goofy, Chip, Dale
Aloha, Cousins! A relaxed atmosphere (no more Minnie, alas!). (Page 228)			
Princess Grand Tea Party (GF)	Tea[2]	Snack	Princess Aurora
A special tea and brunch, plus a My Disney Girl doll. (Pages 227 and 244)			
Restaurant Akershus	B	Family	Snow White, Belle, Jasmine
Dine in a castle with princesses (but don't expect Cinderella). (Page 208)			
Wonderland Tea Party (GF)	Tea[3]	Snack	Alice in Wonderland
"Tea," stories, and cupcakes with Alice at 1900 Park Fare. (Page 227)			

[1] Character breakfasts are weekends at 8:00–11:00 am; dinners are held 6:00–10:00 pm every night (Timon and Rafiki on Mon. and Fri., and Goofy and Pluto on all other nights).
[2] Princess Grand Tea Party has limited availability–see page 244 for details.
[3] Wonderland Tea Parties are held Monday through Friday, 1:30–2:30 pm.

Dinner Shows

Hoop-Dee-Doo Musical Revue

The Hoop-Dee-Doo Musical Revue is a **hilarious hoedown** in an Old West-style dance hall at the Fort Wilderness Resort. The song-and-dance vaudeville act relies heavily on slapstick humor, hokey gags, corny puns, and lots of audience participation. The Wild West performers interact with the audience, and guests celebrating birthdays and anniversaries may be singled out for special attention. The all-you-care-to-eat meal includes salad, barbecue ribs, fried chicken, corn, baked beans, and bread, with strawberry shortcake for dessert (kids can request mac and cheese and hot dogs instead). Complimentary beverages include soda, beer, and sangria—cocktails can be ordered but they are not included in the price. The dinner show costs $49.01/adults and $24.81/kids 3–11 (prices include taxes and gratuities). Shows are at 5:00, 7:15, and 9:30 pm nightly. Inquire about discounts for the last show. Note that a family photo is taken before the show, and you can purchase photo packages from a cast member who circulates during dinner. This show is very popular—reserve up to two years in advance at 407-WDW-DINE. Full payment is required with reservation, refundable up to 48 hours in advance. Hoop-Dee-Doo Musical Revue is located in Pioneer Hall at the Fort Wilderness Resort. See travel directions below.

Mickey's Backyard Barbecue
This old-fashioned, open-air barbecue features good ol' Disney characters (Minnie, Mickey, Goofy, Chip, and Dale), live country music, carnival games, and line dancing. Vittles include chicken, hot dogs, ribs, salads, corn, cole slaw, beans, vegetables, rolls, and (of course!) watermelon—all served buffet-style at picnic tables under a huge pavilion. Typically held on Tuesday and Thursday at 6:30 (ends at 9:30 pm). Cost: $39.01/adults and $25/kids 3–11 (prices include all taxes and gratuities). Call 407-WDW-DINE to inquire about availability and reservations. Full payment is now required with your reservations, refundable up to 48 hours in advance.

Getting to the Fort Wilderness Dinner Shows
To get to either Hoop-Dee-Doo or Backyard Barbecue, take the boat to Fort Wilderness from the Magic Kingdom, Contemporary, or Wilderness Lodge. Special buses run to and from some resorts, or take any Fort Wilderness-bound theme park bus. Driving (parking is free) is an option, too. The Hoop-Dee-Doo is in Pioneer Hall; Backyard Barbecue is next door to Pioneer Hall (around back). Allow 60 to 90 minutes for travel.

Disney's Animal Kingdom Area | Epcot Area | Downtown Disney Area | Magic Kingdom Area

Chapter 5: Feasting and Snacking | Topic: Dinner Shows | 235

Spirit of Aloha Dinner (Polynesian Luau)

Aloha! The Spirit of Aloha Dinner is an exotic, South Pacific-style celebration of color, style, history, music, and dance. Everything you expect from a luau is here—women in "grass" skirts, men in face paint, fire dancers, plus traditional music and a little bit of Elvis—showcasing the cultures and traditions of Polynesia and connecting them all to the modern Hawaii seen in Lilo and Stitch. The show is held together by Auntie Wini, the heart of a group of young islanders who have learned to love traditional values including 'ohana (family). The show is held nightly in Luau Cove, an outdoor stage surrounded by a torch-lit garden. Upon arrival, guests are presented with a complimentary lei and entertained in the garden before dinner. While you wait for the show, you can buy drinks and souvenirs, and have a family photo taken. Guests are seated at long, wooden tables that fan out from the stage, all under shelter in the event of rain. The all-you-care-to-eat meal, served family-style for your party, includes salad, fresh pineapple, roasted chicken, bbq ribs, rice, and sautéed vegetables, with a special "volcano dessert" (the name is the most exciting part). Included with your meal is your choice of unlimited soda, coffee, iced tea, milk, beer, and wine. Specialty drinks are extra. The show begins after dinner with Hawaiian music and plenty of South Seas dancing by both men and women. Children are quite welcome at the Luau. Although it's not as kid-friendly as the long-departed Mickey's Tropical Luau, the Lilo and Stitch tie-in helps, and the young ones will be invited on stage for a special dance number. Photos can be picked up after the show. The Polynesian Luau costs $49.01 for adults and $24.81 for kids 3–11 (prices include taxes and gratuities). Shows are held at 5:15 and 8:00 pm, Tuesdays through Saturdays. We prefer the later seating as the darkness adds to the mystique and romance of the show. Ask about discounts for the late show. In the cooler months, the late show may be cancelled. We highly recommend you make your reservations as early as possible—the best tables near the stage go to those who reserve first. Full payment is required with your reservation, refundable up to 48 hours prior to the show.

Getting to the Polynesian Dinner Show

To get to the Polynesian Luau, you can drive directly to the Polynesian Resort. From the Magic Kingdom, take the resort monorail. From other parks, bus to the Polynesian. From other resorts, bus to the Magic Kingdom and take the monorail (daytime) or bus to Downtown Disney and transfer to a Polynesian bus. Once inside the resort, follow signs to Luau Cove. Allow plenty of time for travel, especially if coming from another resort.

Special Shows

Holidays

Holidays are always special at the Walt Disney World Resort. The parks and resorts overflow with special entertainment and decorations that vary from season to season and year to year (see pages 256–257 for details). The Christmas and New Year's season is especially magical, with all kinds of celebrations throughout the property. One big Christmas favorite is the Candlelight Processional at World Showcase in Epcot, which is available free to Epcot guests (show only) or as an Epcot dinner package offering special seating for the show (call 407-WDW-DINE).

House of Blues

House of Blues has a concert hall separate from its restaurant (page 222) which features performances by top musicians. On Sundays at 10:30 am and 1:00 pm, they serve an all-you-care-to-eat Gospel Brunch with soul food and glorious gospel music—price is $30/adults and $15/kids 3–9. Reservations can be made up to a month in advance at the House of Blues box office (or call 407-934-2583). Tickets for evening performances are available through the box office or Ticketmaster, and range from $15 to $30. The House of Blues is located at Downtown Disney West Side.

MurderWatch Mystery Dinner Show

The Grosvenor Resort, a Hotel Plaza Resort on Disney property (see page 104), stages a popular murder mystery dinner show at 6:00 and 9:00 pm on Saturday nights in Baskervilles restaurant. The show includes an all-you-care-to-eat roast beef buffet and a healthy serving of (optional) audience participation. Tickets may be reserved in advance ($39.95/adult and $10.95/kids 9 & under) at 407-827-6534. Ask about discounts, too! Visit http://www.murderwatch.com for more information.

Restaurants With Entertainment

Several Disney restaurants offer performances or entertainment during meals. At the Magic Kingdom, a piano player may tickle the ivories at Casey's Corner. At Epcot, Biergarten has traditional German music and dancing, Restaurant Marrakesh features belly dancing and Moroccan musicians, and Rose & Crown plays host to pub performers. At Disney-MGM Studios, 50s Prime Time Cafe has TVs, the Hollywood Brown Derby may have cast members impersonating Hollywood personalities, and the Sci-Fi Dine-In Theater Restaurant shows old movie trailers. Both 'Ohana (Polynesian Resort) and Whispering Canyon Cafe (Wilderness Lodge Resort) offer fun activities for the kids (big and little).

Special Dining Opportunities

During Epcot's International Flower & Garden Festival (April 15–June 5, 2005) you can experience the **Food Among the Flowers Brunch**. This is an elaborate meal offering dozens of inventive and tantalizing choices—some may even include edible flower blossoms. Then, during the Epcot Food & Wine Festival (September 30–November 13, 2005), there are special **wine tasting dinners** and other special meals (see page 214 for more about the Festival). Finally, during **Christmas season**, when all the familiar eateries are overflowing, there is often a **holiday buffet** at a special location. For all these meals, call 407-WDW-DINE for information and reservations, but walk-up diners are often welcome at the holiday buffet.

Holiday dinners at the resorts and selected theme park restaurants usually go unheralded. Disney has no need to promote attendance during its busiest seasons, but you can be fairly certain that many resorts will have something happening on Easter Sunday, Mother's Day, Father's Day, Thanksgiving Day, Christmas Day, and New Year's Eve. Start by phoning your Disney resort to see whether the restaurants there are serving a special holiday dinner. If you strike out at your resort, call around to the various Deluxe resorts (holiday meals aren't always listed with 407-WDW-DINE). Magic Kingdom and Epcot full-service restaurants are also good candidates. Call 407-WDW-DINE to see if special meals are being offered at the theme parks during your visit.

The restaurants and cafes around Epcot's World Showcase are also likely to celebrate one or more of their **national holidays**. Check your park times guide and keep your eyes open as you travel about the World Showcase.

Dine with a Disney Imagineer is a special part of the Disney-MGM Studios dining lineup and offers a close-up peek at the people who create Disney's entertainment, attractions, parks, and resorts. These special meals are typically available three days a week, and feature intimate conversations with an Imagineer. Held in a private room at the Hollywood Brown Derby (see page 216), guests are served a special four-course meal while they learn about "their" imagineer's work. Each guest receives a souvenir that may be autographed. Available for groups of 2–10 guests, and groups may be combined. Lunch is $60.99/adults ($34.99/kids 3–11) and dinner is $99.99/adult ($34.99/kids 3–11), though it's not really a kids' event. Lunches are held on Mondays and Fridays; dinners on Wednesdays. Reserve up to 30 days in advance at 407-WDW-DINE.

Looking for the **Fantasmic! Dinner Package**? See page 217.

Planning | Getting There | Staying in Style | Touring | Feasting | Making Magic | Index | Notes & More

Meal Worksheet

The first step in planning your meals is determining your needs. Start by checkmarking the meals you'll need in the worksheet below. Next, write down where you would like to eat your meals—be specific ("cereal in room" or "Brown Derby at MGM"). Circle the meals that require priority seatings, then use the worksheet on the next page to make the arrangements.

Meal	Location	Meal	Location
Day One–Date:		**Day Six–Date:**	
☐ Breakfast		☐ Breakfast	
☐ Lunch		☐ Lunch	
☐ Dinner		☐ Dinner	
☐ Other		☐ Other	
Day Two–Date:		**Day Seven–Date:**	
☐ Breakfast		☐ Breakfast	
☐ Lunch		☐ Lunch	
☐ Dinner		☐ Dinner	
☐ Other		☐ Other	
Day Three–Date:		**Day Eight–Date:**	
☐ Breakfast		☐ Breakfast	
☐ Lunch		☐ Lunch	
☐ Dinner		☐ Dinner	
☐ Other		☐ Other	
Day Four–Date:		**Day Nine–Date:**	
☐ Breakfast		☐ Breakfast	
☐ Lunch		☐ Lunch	
☐ Dinner		☐ Dinner	
☐ Other		☐ Other	
Day Five–Date:		**Day Ten–Date:**	
☐ Breakfast		☐ Breakfast	
☐ Lunch		☐ Lunch	
☐ Dinner		☐ Dinner	
☐ Other		☐ Other	

Priority Seating Worksheet

Once you've determined what meals you plan to eat in table-service restaurants, note them in the chart below along with your preferred dining time. Next, call 407-WDW-DINE to make priority seating arrangements. Note the actual meal time and confirmation number below. You have our permission to make a photocopy of these two worksheets.

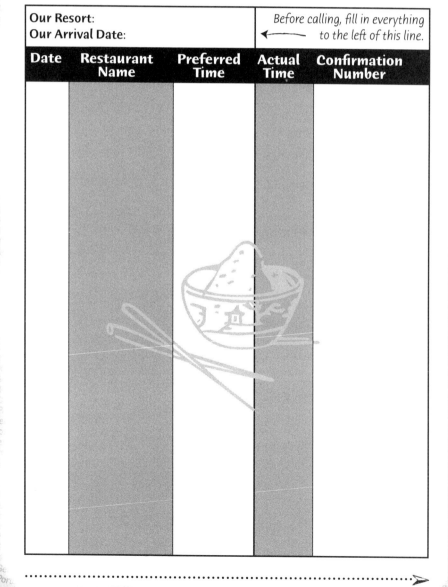

Our Resort: Our Arrival Date:			Before calling, fill in everything ← to the left of this line.	
Date	**Restaurant Name**	**Preferred Time**	**Actual Time**	**Confirmation Number**

Planning | Getting There | Staying in Style | Touring | Feasting | Making Magic | Index | Notes & More

Genuine PassPorter Genuine PassPorter Genuine PassPorter Genuine PassPorter Genuine PassPorter Genuine PassPorter Genuine PassPorter Genuine PassPorter Genuine PassPorter Genuine PassPorter Genuine PassPorter Genuine PassPorter

A Recipe for Fun

Make the most of your dining experience at Walt Disney World with these tips and tricks we've collected over the years:

If you're not sure how your younger children will react to the Disney characters, try a **trial run at the Ice Cream Social** with Mickey and Friends at the Garden Grill in The Land in Epcot. Although my older son has been to Disney many times, this trip was the first for my two-year-old twin daughters. Their first experience was great—the restaurant was almost empty and the characters came by the table multiple times. Luckily for us, the girls loved the characters. It was a great trial run ... and a lot less expensive than a full-fledged character meal or an overcrowded meeting in the parks.
— Contributed by Pamela Etheridge, a winner in our 2004 Dining Tip Contest

It isn't always necessary to make a priority seating for a restaurant. The more "exotic" eateries like Restaurant Akershus and Restaurant Marrakesh are **rarely booked to capacity**. It is also easier to get a last-minute table later in the afternoon or later in the evening. Just ask at the podium.

If you are celebrating a **special occasion**, be sure to mention it at the podium before you are seated. You may be pleasantly surprised.

If you want to **linger over your meal**, don't place your entire order all at once. This keeps your food from arriving too fast. Do let your server know you intend to order a full meal, however, or they might assume you're just snacking on appetizers and leave you alone.

Magical Memory

"When we were planning our trip, we knew we wanted one thing that had always eluded us on our previous trips: breakfast at Cinderella Castle. We started calling Disney 90 days prior to the first day of our trip and finally got through and booked on the fourth day! We were elated, and we decided that we would surprise the kids after our arrival. On the second day of our vacation at Walt Disney World, we asked our kids what they would like to do most and they both said, "Eat in the castle!" We told them that Cinderella picks her favorite guests and phones them to ask them to come for breakfast. We then headed to the wishing well near Cinderella Castle and both kids wished for the same thing ... to eat in the castle! We had my mom call us at our hotel the next morning and we pretended it was Cinderella inviting us to breakfast. When we got to the park, the kids were flabbergasted! This was by far the best part of our trip and the one thing that they remember. They told all their friends to wish in the wishing well and your dream will come true!"
...as told by Disney vacationer Karin Dunn

Planning | Getting There | Staying in Style | Touring | Feasting | Making Magic | Index | Notes & More

Making More Magic

Once you've tasted the Walt Disney World Resort, you'll hunger for more. Most visits can only *nibble* at the many wonders the "World" holds. There is much, much more that can be done to make your vacation magical. We've been to Disney more than most and yet there are *still* things we haven't done, and we add new discoveries to the wish list after every trip. It can all be a bit overwhelming, not to mention habit-forming. If you tried to keep up with each new activity on the Disney horizon, you'd have a full-time job on your hands.

To help you undertake your own magical explorations of the Walt Disney World Resort, we present a collection of useful information about some of its lesser-known aspects and attractions. This is our "everything else" chapter. To begin, we give you a backstage pass to the guided tours, special classes, and educational programs Disney offers—from peeks behind the scenes to dives under the seas. From there, we lead you on a treasure hunt for fun tucked away inside the parks—both real "treasure hunts" and hunts for items you'll treasure. We've even added a mini worksheet for those of you who love to shop! Next we share our special tricks for feeling and looking like a VIP on your trip—a little extra-special attention can go a long way! Then we give you the lowdown on childcare programs. Your kids may find these more fun than the theme parks themselves—no kidding! Special occasions and events aren't forgotten either, with ideas, tips, and details on celebrating birthdays, engagements, honeymoons, anniversaries, holidays, and more. Before we say goodbye, we'll leave you with information for explorations beyond the Walt Disney World Resort at other Disney vacation spots—from exotic ports of call, to foreign lands, to home lands.

So get out that pixie dust and don your sorcerer's hat—we're making magic, Disney-style!

Side tabs: Planning · Getting There · Staying in Style · Touring · Feasting · Making Magic · Index · Notes & More

Backstage Passes

Disney does such a good job of hiding the figurative ropes and pulleys that you'll be disappointed if you hope to catch a glimpse of what makes Disney really work. To meet the growing demands of interminably curious guests, Disney offers tours and programs that satisfy the need to "peek."

Guided Tours

Unless otherwise noted, advance tour reservations may be (and should be) made up to 90 days in advance at 407-939-8687, or through your resort's Guest Services desk. Some discounts are available to Annual Passholders, Disney Visa cardholders, AAA Diamond, or Disney Vacation Club. Tours are only open to guests 16 and older unless otherwise noted. Many tours require substantial walking and most are wheelchair accessible. In general, no photos of backstage areas are allowed on the tours. Cancel 48 hours in advance to avoid penalties. Tours that require regular park admission are noted with the ticket (🎟) icon. Important: Bring photo I.D. with you for tour check-in.

▪ Around the World at Epcot (The Segway Tour) [Epcot] 🎟

This new two-hour tour offers a unique opportunity to ride a Segway (a self-balancing, two-wheeled "vehicle"). Learn to use the Segway for the first hour, then practice riding around the World Showcase. Max. weight is 250 lbs.; pregnant and special needs guests may not participate. Offered daily at 8:30 and 9:30 am.	**$80** Ages 16 & up On-stage only

▪ Backstage Safari Tour [Disney's Animal Kingdom] 🎟

A three-hour, behind-the-scenes peek at the Disney's Animal Kingdom park to see how they care for our four-legged friends. No photography is allowed in backstage areas. Tours depart at 8:30 am on Mondays, Wednesdays, Thursdays, and Fridays. Park admission is required (not included in price).	**$65** Ages 16 & up Backstage peek

▪ Backstage Magic [Magic Kingdom, Disney-MGM Studios, and Epcot]

This seven-hour tour of three major parks explores how Disney's magic is created and maintained. Go beneath the Magic Kingdom to explore the underground "utilidors," enjoy a special lunch at the Disney-MGM Studios, and see the computer systems at Epcot. Tours depart Monday–Friday at 8:45 am. Price includes lunch. Park admission is not required. Reserve well in advance.	**$199** Ages 16 & up Backstage peek at three theme parks

▪ Family Magic Tour [Magic Kingdom] 🎟

This fun, two-hour tour offers guests an interactive adventure through the Magic Kingdom in search of a Disney character (such as Captain Hook or Maleficent). The popular tour is open to everyone and is offered daily at 10:00 am. Reservations are accepted, but those without reservations may still find room by asking at City Hall. Park admission required.	**$25** All ages On-stage only (no backstage)

▪ Gardens of the World [Epcot] 🎟

This three-hour walking tour explores the lush gardens of Epcot's World Showcase pavilions. A Disney horticulturist explains the basic concepts, theming, and practices used in creating the gardens, and offers ideas for home gardens. Tours leave at 8:45 am (same-day and advance reservations accepted) on Tuesdays and Thursdays. Park admission is required. A special version of this tour is offered during the Flower and Garden Festival (see page 256).	**$59** Ages 16 & up On-stage with possible backstage peeks

Looking for Epcot's Aqua Seas, Dolphins in Depth, or Divequest? See page 245.

Hidden Treasures of World Showcase [Epcot]

This three-hour walking tour focuses on the unique design and construction of the World Showcase pavilions. Tours leave at 8:45 am on Tuesdays and Thursdays. Park admission is required. 20-person maximum tour size.	**$59** Ages 16 & up Backstage peek

Keys to the Kingdom [Magic Kingdom]

This 4½-hour guided tour of Magic Kingdom gives an overview of the park's highlights, history, and backstage areas, plus lunch at Columbia Harbour House. The route varies, but usually visits five attractions and two backstage areas (even a peek in the "utilidors"). Offered daily at 8:30, 9:00, and 9:30 am. Guests without reservations can inquire at City Hall, but the tour is very popular and we recommend you book it well in advance. Park admission is required.	**$58** Ages 16 & up Backstage peek (including the utilidors)

The Magic Behind Our Steam Trains [Magic Kingdom]

Railroad fans get an inside look at the Walt Disney World Railroad in the Magic Kingdom. Join the opening crew, view the roundhouse, and explore Walt's passion for steam trains. The three-hour tour is held on Mondays, Tuesdays, Thursdays, and Saturdays at 7:30 am. Park admission is required.	**$40** Ages 10 & up Backstage peek

Undiscovered Future World [Epcot]

This 4½-hour walking tour of the pavilions in Future World goes backstage. Tour highlights include a visit to a VIP lounge, a walk-through of the Cast Services building, an opportunity to meet an International Ambassador, and a peek at where the IllumiNations barges are stored. Guests may receive a limited edition trading pin, discounts on lunch and purchases in the China pavilion, and/or special seating for IllumiNations that evening. Tours are offered on Mondays, Wednesdays, and Fridays at 9:00 am. Park admission is required.	**$49** Ages 16 & up Backstage peek (including Epcot marina)

VIP Tours

Custom-designed five- to eight-hour tours may be booked by individals or groups of up to ten people. Tours must include a meal. Cost is about $85 per hour per tour guide and does not include park admission. VIP Tours may be booked from 24 hours to three months in advance. Blackout dates apply; call 407-560-4033 for availability and reservations.	**$85/hour** All ages On-stage only (no backstage)

Welcome to the Magic Kingdom [Magic Kingdom] (English & Japanese)

Get a great introduction in English or Japanese with this 90-minute walking tour. Japanese tours leave at 9:30 am on Sunday–Wednesday and Friday; English tour leaves at 8:30 am on Thursday. Kids under 10 are free.	**$20** All ages On-stage only

Wild By Design [Disney's Animal Kingdom]

This three-hour walking tour takes you around Disney's Animal Kingdom to learn about the represented cultures, historic artifacts, and storytelling. Guests wear headphones to hear the tour guide better. Tours leave at 8:30 am on Thursdays and Fridays. Price includes a light continental breakfast.	**$58** Ages 14 & up On-stage only

Yuletide Fantasy [Theme Parks and Resort Hotels]

Offered daily during the holiday season at 9:00 am, this 3½-hour tour gives a behind-the-scenes peek at the magical holiday transformations. The tour visits theme parks and resorts to view and discuss the decorations. Guests under 16 no longer allowed. Park admission is not required. Meet at Epcot Guest Relations.	**$59** Ages 16 & up Backstage peek

Side tabs: Planning, Getting There, Staying in Style, Touring, Feasting, Making Magic, Index, Notes & More

Children's Tours, Parties, and Activities

Fun stuff for kids! You can reserve fee-based activities by calling 407-WDW-DINE up to 90 days in advance; free activities take no reservations.

Disney's Pirate Adventure [Grand Floridian Resort]

Ahoy, mateys! Cast off from the Grand Floridian marina on a cruise around the Seven Seas Lagoon in search of treasure. Little buccaneers get a bandanna to wrap around their heads, hear a reading of "The Legend of Gasparilla," learn pirate songs, and receive a bag of a "loot" (treats). Lunch is included.	**$28.17** Ages 4–10 9:30–11:30 am M, W, Th, Sa

Wonderland Tea Party [Grand Floridian Resort]

Take tea with Alice in Wonderland! Kids make and eat cupcakes, participate in projects, and meet Alice, the Mad Hatter, and friends. Held in the 1900 Park Fare restaurant in the Grand Floridian Resort on Monday–Friday.	**$28.17** Ages 4–10 1:30–2:30 pm

My Disney Girl's Perfectly Princess Tea Party [Grand Floridian Resort]

Pure pampering for your little princess. This five-part party is held in the Grand Floridian's Garden View Tea Lounge and features a visit from Princess Aurora. Includes tea, brunch, dessert, a My Disney Girl doll, and other gifts. Siblings or friends can attend for $135 each and adults are $65 each. Limited availability.	**$200.00** Ages 3–10 10:30–noon Su, M, Th, F

Grand Adventures in Cooking [Grand Floridian Resort]

Kids listen to a story, get aprons and chef's hats to decorate, then share their kitchen creations. Offered from 10:00 to 11:45 am on Tue. and Fri. in the Mouseketeer Clubhouse. Cancellations less than 24 hours before charged the full amount.	**$28.17** Ages 4–10 10–11:45 am

Boma Kids' Activities [Disney's Animal Kingdom Lodge]

Daily activities for kids—such as cookie decorating—are available in the restaurant (Boma) and lobby of Disney's Animal Kingdom Lodge. Ask for the daily schedule of events at the hotel's front desk or at Boma.	**Free** Ages 3–12 Times vary

Junior Chef Program at The Land [Epcot]

Don your chef hats and help make a batch of yummy chocolate chip cookies! Just go to the bright yellow "bakery" down stairs in The Land to participate. Offered at 12:30, 1:30, 2:30, 3:30, and 4:30 pm daily. Limited to 20 participants.	**Free** Ages 3–10 Times vary

Recreation and Water Sports

A wide variety of recreation options are available at many of the resort hotels, water parks, and the Downtown Disney marina. While not all activities are offered in all locations, you can expect to find biking (regular and surrey), fishing, canoeing, boating, sailing, parasailing, waterskiing, wakeboarding, tubing, surfing, horseback riding, and carriage rides somewhere in the World. Call 407-WDW-PLAY or your resort to get details on recreation. Sammy Duvall's Watersports Centre at the Contemporary offers personal watercraft excursions, waterskiing, parasailing, and wakeboarding (included in some vacation packages)—call 407-939-0754. Tip: Look for money-saving programs at your resort's marina: the Captain's Plan is $125 for four hours of self-drive boat rentals, while the Family Plan is $239 and gives up to 5 resort guests the use of self-drive boats for 10 consecutive days. See page 194 for more places to play.

Classes and Educational Programs

Behind the Seeds: A Special Guided Greenhouse Tour—This one-hour walking tour delves deeper into the innovative greenhouses seen in the Living With the Land exhibit at Epcot. Cost is $10/adult and $8/child age 3-9 (no minimum age), 13 people max. per tour. Park admission to Epcot is required. Sign up at The Land's Green Thumb Emporium or call 407-WDW-TOUR. Tours leave between 10:20 am and 4:00 pm. (Note: This tour was closed at press time but scheduled to reopen in January 2005.)

Dolphins in Depth—This unique three-hour program highlights the dolphin research at the Living Seas in Epcot. Guests play an active part in the research as they learn about dolphin behavior. Guests must be 13 or older, and 13-17 year olds need a signed waiver. Offered on Mondays–Fridays beginning at 9:30 am. Cost is about $150/person and includes a photo, soda, and a souvenir T-shirt. Dolphin interaction is not guaranteed. Park admission to Epcot is not required to participate in this program.

Epcot Divequest—Open Water SCUBA-certified divers ages 16 and older can dive the 6-million-gallon pool at the Living Seas. The three-hour program includes a presentation on marine research and conservation. Divers suit up and are guided in small groups for a 40-minute dive. The cost includes use of gear, refreshments, a certificate, a dive log stamp, and a shirt. Proof of certification must be shown and divers have to sign medical and legal waivers. Dives are daily at 4:30 and 5:30 pm. Cost is $140/person. Park admission to Epcot is not required. Advance reservations are required.

EpcotSeas Aqua Tour—A 2 1/2-hour SCUBA-assisted snorkel dive that takes place in the largest indoor aquarium in the world at the Living Seas pavilion. You do not need to be SCUBA certified; equipment and instructions are provided. Actual snorkel time is 30 minutes. Offered daily at 12:30 pm for guests ages 8 and up (8-16 year olds must be with an adult). Cost is $100/person and includes use of gear, a shirt, and a group photo. Park admission not required.

Typhoon Lagoon Learn-to-Surf Program—Surf's up! This exciting class at Typhoon Lagoon water park teaches guests surfing basics. Learn on dry land for the first half-hour, then try your new skills on the big waves in the park's huge wave pool for the remaining two hours. The 2 1/2-hour class is offered on Mondays, Tuesdays, and Fridays at 6:30 am, though starting time may vary with park operating hours (class is held before the park opens). Class is open to resort guests ages 8 and up who are strong swimmers. Cost is $135/person, and park admission is not required. Call 407-WDW-PLAY for reservations. See pages 171-174 for details on Typhoon Lagoon. (You can book special surf events at Typhoon Lagoon—call 407-WDW-SURF for details.)

Planning

Getting There

Staying in Style

Touring

Feasting

Making Magic

Index

Notes & More

Treasure Hunts

There is hidden treasure at the Walt Disney World Resort. While it may not consist of golden doubloons, it is every bit as priceless. There are countless sets of often-hidden and always-valuable Disneyesque items for you to find during your vacation. Sometimes these items are purposefully hidden; other times they are out in plain view for all to see but few to notice. Hunting for your favorite item can add a new dimension to your vacation! Here are our favorite things to collect:

Disney Characters and Autographs

Live Disney characters abound, and kids of all ages delight in spotting them. You can discover where some characters are "hiding" by checking with Guest Relations at each major park. If you want to "bag your catch," take photographs—and try to get yourself or your family in the picture! Keep in mind that characters are popular and crowds will form. If you know when your characters will appear, show up early to greet them. (Tip: Ask a Disney Cast Member about character appearances for the day.) You can also collect autographs from characters who are able to sign their name. Special autograph books are available at most shops, or you can bring your own. Or use the PassPorter's autograph space on pages 274-277. Try to bring a wide-barreled pen or marker so the character can hold it easily—their costumes may cover their fingers. You can also have the characters sign hats or shirts (which must be Disney or non-commercial), but shirts cannot be worn while they are being signed and you need something to slip under the fabric to provide a writing surface.

Pressed Pennies and Quarters

One of the least expensive souvenirs at the Walt Disney World Resort is pressed coins. Souvenir Pressed Coin machines, found throughout the "World," press different Disney designs onto pennies or quarters. Cost is 51 cents for a pressed penny and $1.25 for a pressed quarter. Designs differ from machine to machine, making a complete collection a worthy achievement. Bring rolls of shiny pennies and quarters along with you—the hunt for a money-changing machine isn't as much fun. While there are good lists of pressed coin machine locations on the Internet (try http://www.intercot.com/infocentral/coins), finding them is half the fun! **Tip**: Buy a keepsake book at Disney's gift shops to store your coins.

Free Stuff

Disney may seem to be a mecca to capitalism, but there are still free things for the taking and they make great souvenirs! Some may even become collector's items one day. You can collect guidemaps, brochures, napkins, paper cups and plates, containers, bags, menus, resort "newsletters," and more.

Hidden Mickeys

Believe it or not, Disney intentionally hides "Mickeys" all over the place! The internationally recognized Mickey Mouse head (one big circle and two smaller circles for the ears) has been discovered hidden in murals, fences, shows—you name it, you can probably find a Mickey hidden somewhere in it! Disney fans maintain lists of these hidden Mickeys—try http://www.hiddenmickeys.org for one of the largest collections. You will also enjoy the "Hidden Mickeys" field guide by Steven M. Barrett, available in bookstores and at our Web site (http://www.passporterstore.com/store). We made a list of our favorite Hidden Mickeys for a rainy day activity—how many hiding places can you find? Write your answers below.

#	Location	Hint	Hiding Place
1.	General	Isn't it good to know Disney cares for the environment?	
2.	General	Ka-ching! Look at what you get when the cash register rings!	
3.	General	Bubble, bubble, toil, and trouble, look to laundry for three bubbles.	
4.	Magic Kingdom	Clippity clop, clippity clop! I pull a trolley past the Main St. shops.	
5.	Magic Kingdom	Look to your feet for the holes in the street.	
6.	Magic Kingdom	A Mickey up a sleeve—no joke—check the Grim Reaper's cloak.	
7.	Epcot	Test the Track, can you cope? Find the Mickey in the rope.	
8.	Epcot	As you stand in Maelstrom's line, find him in the hands of time.	
9.	Epcot	Now turn your glance to the gardens of France.	
10.	Disney-MGM Studios	Look for a tower and we'll bet if you say "terror" you're all wet.	
11.	Disney-MGM Studios	All around the park I run, my thin black bars protect the fun.	
12.	Disney-MGM Studios	On your tour of the backlot put the refrigerator on the spot!	
13.	Disney's Animal Kingdom	Amid the trees near Simba's fest hangs a house that holds a nest.	
14.	Disney's Animal Kingdom	Near Pangani you'll pass some fruit. Don't squish Mickey under your boot!	
15.	Disney's Animal Kingdom	There is a froggie near Pizzafari. Now that's the end of this safari!	

Hidden Mickey hiding places are found on page 259.

Photographs and Memories

Many vacationers bring a camera or a camcorder to record their trip. Most seem content to simply take pictures as the mood strikes them, but you can also "collect" pictures as well! Here are some ideas for fun photograph collections: Disney puns and visual gags that often go unnoticed (try "holding up" Spaceship Earth in your photos, as we did on page 138); your favorite spot at different times of the day; all of the "Kodak Picture Spot" signs; and pictures through the eyes of your children (give them their own camera). How about a photo of each family member next to their favorite attraction? If you take these same photos on return trips, you can make a "growth chart" over time. Another idea is to hold a family photo scavenger hunt for fun things and places around the "World."

Souvenirs

If you enjoy taking home souvenirs but you're tired of the usual T-shirts or postcards, consider beginning a new collection. Chances are that if you can collect it, Disney has it somewhere on their property. Here are favorite collectibles: enamel pins (see page 251 for details), patches (you can sew them onto your packs), mugs (our favorite), figurines, hats, clothing, stuffed animals, mini bean bags, and Pal Mickey (see below). Love shopping? Here's a mini worksheet to help you organize the items you want to purchase for yourself and others at Walt Disney World!

Who	What	Size/Color	$$	✔

Pal Mickey – "The Talk of the Parks"

Who's 10 inches tall and is destined to become the most popular tour guide at Walt Disney World? Pal Mickey! Pal Mickey is Disney Imagineering's plush innovation, a soft, loveable toy that plays games wherever he goes, and becomes an instant tour guide whenever he enters a Disney theme park. While Pal Mickey is no substitute for a real tour guide (be that a person or a guidebook) and he mainly appeals to kids, he's still an amusing diversion. We recommend you rent one first ($8/day), and then apply the rental towards an outright purchase ($60) if you decide to keep it—this also means you turn in the rented one and get a new, boxed Mickey to take home. Be sure to keep his black nose pointed outward and uncovered, as he is literally guided by his nose. Pal Mickey is available in English or Spanish.

In Search Of...

Quite often we're on the lookout for specific items, whether they be souvenirs or necessities. To help hunt down your treasures, here is a partial list of places to find some of the more sought-after items:

Alcohol—You can buy a mixed drink or beer at any of the resorts or parks with the notable exception of the Magic Kingdom. You can also purchase alcohol at most resort general stores and at Downtown Disney.

Baby Needs—The baby care centers in the four major parks sell common baby items, such as diapers, powder, and formula. Your resort's gift shop stocks these items as well.

Groceries—Snacks are available at most of the resort stores, and a small selection of groceries is available at resorts with in-room cooking facilities. For more serious marketing, visit Goodings Supermarket at the Crossroads Shopping Center near Downtown Disney.

Gum—Gum is not sold on Disney property nor at the airport to avoid messes. If you need it, bring it with you or buy it off-property.

Lost Items—Lost and Found centers are located everywhere you go—generally near the front of the park or complex. Jennifer dropped a favorite scarf at Downtown Disney and within 15 minutes she had recovered it at Lost and Found (much to her relief). You can also call Lost and Found at 407-824-4245. Lost and found items are generally kept at each park only until closing. After that, they are usually transferred to Central Lost and Found at the Transportation and Ticket Center (inside the Kennel).

Medicine—Order prescription and over-the-counter drugs through Turner Drugs at 407-828-8125 from 8:00 am to 8:00 pm. Deliveries are available between 9:00 am and 9:00 pm. Over-the-counter medicine and band-aids are kept under the counter at many Disney shops—ask a Cast Member. Aspirin and band-aids are also available at no charge at the first-aid stations located in each park, which are staffed by licensed medical personnel.

Missing or Lost Persons—Should the unthinkable happen, immediately alert a Cast Member or go to Guest Relations. Teach kids how to recognize Cast Members. A message system is available at Guest Relations and Guest Services to help coordinate things, even if you aren't lost (yet). It's a good idea to choose a meeting place each day in the event you are separated from your family or friends. You may also find it helpful to give each member of your party a two-way radio or cell phone to stay in touch with one another.

Money—ATMs (cash machines) are located in all the parks and resorts. See our park maps or Disney's guidemaps for locations. The Walt Disney World Resort accepts American Express, MasterCard, Visa, Discover, The Disney Credit Card, JCB, Diner's Club, traveler's checks, cash, Disney Dollars, and Disney Visa Reward Vouchers (see page 10 for details on the Disney Visa card). Personal checks are also accepted (with two forms of identification) in most spots.

Rain Gear—If you didn't bring an umbrella or poncho along, Disney will sell you one at virtually any shop. You may need to ask, but chances are they'll have something. Tip: If your poncho rips, bring it back to any shop and they'll replace it. Note: In late 2003, Disney began selling clear ponchos (instead of the traditional yellow) to make it easier to spot your companions in the rain. No more "sea of yellow!"

VIP Tips

Wake-Up Call
If you're staying at a Disney resort, start your day with a call from Mickey. Just use the phone system to arrange a wake-up call, and when the phone rings, Mickey or one of his friends welcomes you to the new day! When the phone rings with your wake-up call, press the speakerphone button so everyone in the room can hear it! Tip: Make your wake-up call for an off-time, such as 7:03, to help ensure you get Mickey.

Box Seats
Monorail—If you're at one of the monorail resorts, ask the Cast Member on the platform about riding in the front cab. The view is fabulous! Keep in mind that you may need to wait for a specific monorail to arrive. Monorail cab rides are available on the Express and Epcot lines when traffic and crowds permit, too. Seating is limited to four guests. The front cab is not available when boarding a resort monorail from the Magic Kingdom or Transportation and Ticket Center (TTC). Note that wheelchairs cannot ride in the front cab; ask for a "license" in lieu of riding up front!

Contemporary Resort—Enjoy a meal in the California Grill during the Magic Kingdom fireworks (the music that normally accompanies the fireworks is broadcast in the restaurant). Note that the California Grill observation deck is once again open only to diners. There's another viewing area on the north end of the Grand Concourse (4th floor).

Fireworks Cruises—Do you have something to celebrate? Rent a pontoon boat, the Breathless speedboat, or the Grand 1 Yacht to view the fireworks at the Magic Kingdom or Epcot. Cruises are booked per boat rather than per passenger, and all include a pilot. Call 407-WDW-PLAY for rates and reservations. You can book up to 90 days in advance, and we recommend you call at 7:00 am Eastern Time exactly 90 days in advance, as these cruises are extremely popular. Note: These are sometimes called "specialty" cruises by Disney, as they can't promise that the fireworks won't be cancelled.

Leave a Legacy
Leave a Legacy is a huge, outdoor photo gallery at Epcot. Row after row of polished granite monuments line the entrance plaza. The monuments are decorated with shining metal plaques, each displaying dozens of one-inch-square, laser-etched portraits. We were among the first to leave our legacy—find our smiling faces at West 6-A-3-10-8 (west side, sixth monument, column A, 3rd plaque, 10 images up, and 8 images from the left). Leave your own legacy for $35 (one face) or $38 (two faces in one image). Annual Passholders may get a buy-one-get-one-free discount—ask about it.

Trading Pins

Colorful, enameled commemorative pins are a favorite Disney collectible, available at nearly every shop. Disney designs hundreds of these colorful, cloisonné pins, which commemorate the theme parks, resorts, attractions, characters, and events. Over the years, Disney stepped up pin trading activity by introducing Pin Trading Stations at the parks and the Disney's Pin Traders shop at Downtown Disney, where you can buy and swap pins. Bring (or buy) your own Disney pins, and trade pins with other guests

and with cast members wearing special pin-trading lanyards. Look for "Scoop Sanderson" (see photo), a special Main Street, U.S.A. cast member who offers pin trading classes and tips. Note that cast members wearing green lanyards trade only with children. Pin trading is a fun way to meet fellow vacationers and learn more about the world of Disney. Buy a Disney pin lanyard, or display your pins in a scrapbook, or on a vest or hat.

Scoop Sanderson and Allie trade pins— note how Allie presents her pin lanyard for viewing

Name Badges and Pins

Show everyone how special you are with an oval Disney name badge, personalized with your first name. The badges make great conversation starters—you may even get more personal attention from Cast Members while wearing one. You can purchase badges in the parks and at Downtown Disney for $6. Have an unusual name? Visit the engraving shop at Disney-MGM Studios or at Disney's Days of Christmas at Downtown Disney. Another option is our own PassPorter Badge, which our readers requested to help them spot fellow fans in the parks. PassPorter Badges are $4 and also come with free personalization. You can order PassPorter Badges at our Web site. We also issue our own collectible, cloisonné PassPorter Pins each year for $6 each (tip: we give them away free with a coupon when you order online—see page 281).

Park Passports

Disney has passports, too! The Epcot Passport is a great way to tour the World Showcase. Once you have a passport, you can get it "stamped" at each pavilion or land by a Cast Member. The passports—which kids love—can be purchased at shops and carts for about $10, and include an "I'm a World Showcase Traveler" pin and a set of stickers. A similar passport is available at Disney's Animal Kingdom.

Planning
Getting There
Staying in Style
Touring
Feasting
Making Magic
Index
Notes & More

Childcare Programs

"We're going to Walt Disney World. Why in the 'World' would we need childcare?" The Walt Disney World Resort is an adult playground, too! The "World" offers an exciting nightlife and leaves lots of room for romance. All you need is a sitter. Not surprisingly, Disney delivers with a variety of childcare options and a few programs that may seem like childcare to you (but don't tell the kids). The two main options are childcare programs at the resorts and private, in-room baby-sitting.

Many of Disney's deluxe resorts offer childcare programs. These childcare programs are a good bit like daycare, but unlike daycare, their "day" usually starts at around 4:00 pm and runs until midnight. They offer a variety of structured activities and entertainment and usually include a full meal. All programs accept children from 4 to 12 years of age, and all children must be potty-trained. Rates are $8–10/hour, and some programs have minimum stays. Programs usually also have an overtime rate—the kids won't be evicted if your coach turns into a pumpkin on the way back from Cinderella Castle. Parents are given pagers, too. Some programs are available only to Disney resort guests, and some only for guests staying in that particular resort. Make your status clear when you phone so there are no disappointments. No matter which program you contact, we recommend you call well in advance and ask plenty of questions. Reservations can be made with the club itself or at 407-WDW-DINE. Each resort offers different services and rules, and all are subject to change. Cancel at least 24 hours in advance to avoid a $15/kid fee. **Allie's KidTip:** "It's cool to stay at the kids' clubs so you can do what you like to do and grown-ups can do what they want to do." Read on for more of Allie's KidTips on the clubs she's visited.

Childcare Near Epcot and Disney-MGM Studios

Sandcastle Club [Beach Club]	407-934-3750
Large club with plenty of Legos, games, computers, and video games (free) to play with. Meals are served at 6:00, 7:00, or 8:00 pm. This club is available only to Disney resort guests. **Allie's KidTip:** "There are fun games to play."	$10/hour 4:30 pm-midnight

Harbor Club [Boardwalk Inn & Villas] (currently closed)	407-939-6301
Smaller club with kid-friendly activities. Price includes a meal and a snack-meals are served at 6:00, 7:00, or 8:00 pm. Note that this club was closed at the time of writing and it is not known if it will reopen.	$10/hour 4:00 pm-midnight

Camp Dolphin [Swan and Dolphin]	407-934-4000 ext. 4241
Kids have fun with arts and crafts, video games, and movies. Price includes a meal at 7:00 pm-kids are taken to either Tubbi's or the Dolphin Fountain eateries in the resort. Note that participation is limited to Swan and Dolphin guests.	$10/hour 5:30 pm-midnight

Childcare Near Disney's Animal Kingdom

■ **Simba's Cubhouse** [Disney's Animal Kingdom Lodge]	407-938-4785
The club with a view of the savannah and animals. Plenty of movies and games. Price includes a meal (serving time varies). **Allie's Kid Tip:** "This is my first choice! I liked the people and the decorations. And I loved watching the animals."	**$10/hour** 4:30 pm– midnight

Childcare Near the Magic Kingdom

■ **Mouseketeer Club** [Grand Floridian]	407-824-2985
A medium-sized club with movies, games, and crafts. Price includes a meal if child is checked in by 6:30 pm (meal is at 7:30 pm). Two-hour minimum stay. This club is available only to Grand Floridian resort and restaurant guests.	**$10/hour** 4:30 pm– midnight

■ **Cub's Den** [Wilderness Lodge]	407-824-1083
A smallish club with structured activities, movies, arts and crafts, and games. Price includes a meal (choice of hot dog, hamburger, cheeseburger, chicken strips, mac & cheese, or PB&J, plus ice cream) served between 6:30–8:00 pm.	**$10/hour** 4:30 pm– midnight

■ **Never Land Club** [Polynesian]	407-824-2000
This is the largest, most creatively themed club! Price includes a meal (buffet of kid-friendly items) served 6:00–8:00 pm. Open house daily from noon to 4:00 pm for Polynesian resort guests. **Allie's Kid Tip:** "I like the people here, and the toy stairs are fun to sit on and watch movies. The TV here is big!"	**$10/hour** 4:00 pm– midnight

Note: The Mouseketeer Clubhouse at the Contemporary closed on October 1, 2004.

Other Childcare Options

Kids Nite Out offers Disney-sanctioned, private in-room baby-sitting, 24 hours a day. Two other independent childcare agencies, **Fairy Godmothers** and **All About Kids**, offer similar services. The professional sitters will take kids to the theme parks if you make arrangements in advance (ask at time of reservation) and watch infants and children with some special needs. The sitters show up equipped to keep the kids occupied with games and activities. They are well-trained, bonded, and insured. Rates vary, depending on the age and number of kids under care. For reservations, call Kids Nite Out at 407-828-0920, the Fairy Godmothers at 407-275-7326, or All About Kids at 407-812-9300.

In January 2005, KinderCare will close its **childcare facilities** on Walt Disney World property. Our understanding is that Florida YMCA will operate two centers from 6:00 am to 11:00 pm daily for children of Cast Members, but it's unclear if these centers will accommodate Disney day guests. For more information, watch our book update list on our Web site (http://www.passporter.com/customs/bookupdates.htm).

Planning

Getting There

Staying in Style

Touring

Feasting

Making Magic

Index

Notes & More

Special Occasions

It seems natural to celebrate a special occasion at Disney. It's designed for fun and comes pre-decorated! So whether you plan a trip around a special day or want to celebrate one that falls during your vacation, you can do it at Disney! Here are our tips and tricks for a magical celebration:

Birthdays—What better place to celebrate a birthday than at Disney? If you're at a Disney resort, press "0" and ask for the special "birthday message." Be sure to request a free "It's My Birthday!" pin at the Guest Relations desk at the theme parks. If you want to celebrate in style, all sorts of birthday parties and cruises can be arranged in advance—you can even "invite" Disney characters (though they're very expensive). For kids ages 4-12, you can arrange a birthday party at the BoardWalk or the Yacht & Beach Club—call 407-WDW-PLAY. For parties in other restaurants, call 407-WDW-DINE. Birthday cruises (407-WDW-PLAY) are also available—we surprised Dave's father with one and he loved it! And in March 2003, Jennifer surprised her mom Carolyn with a special birthday event, planned in part by Gifts of a Lifetime (see sidebar below).

Engagements—Disney is a magical place to propose to a loved one. Alas, you'll have to devise your own scheme as Disney no longer offers official assistance.

Weddings—Of course you can get married at Disney—in fact, we tied the knot at a delightful "Intimate Wedding" with our immediate family at the Polynesian in May 2004! From intimate to traditional to themed, Disney's Fairy Tale Weddings have something for virtually every budget. Visit http://disneyweddings.com or call 407-828-3400. Visit http://www.yourfairytale.com, where you can get unofficial Disney wedding and honeymoon details, and order the "Disney Weddings" e-book by Andrea Rotondo Hospidor ($20).

Jennifer and Dave walk up the "aisle" at the Polynesian Resort

---

⚠ Special Services for Special Occasions

It's a challenge to organize a special occasion long distance. An innovative company, **Presentations: Gifts of a Lifetime**, helps you shop for that perfect gift, arrange a magical event, and even put on the whole show! To learn more, visit their Web site at http://www.giftsofalifetime.com or call 407-909-0593.

You can also have the **Walt Disney World Florist** (407-827-3505) prepare a fruit or snack basket and deliver it to a guest room.

Need a little help remembering that special occasion? Another unique service, **MouseMemories**, can create custom memory albums from your own photos. If you prefer to create your own memory albums, they offer scrapbooking supplies. To learn more, visit http://www.mousememories.com.

Honeymoons—Walt Disney World is the #1 honeymoon destination in the world, believe it or not. Not only are romantic spots found around virtually every corner, but Disney goes out of its way to make newlyweds welcome. Special honeymoon packages, romantic rooms, candlelit dinners, and adult-oriented entertainment abound. Even if you do nothing more than mention that it is your honeymoon to cast members, you're in for a special treat. For details, call Disney at 407-934-7639. We recommend the book "Walt Disney World for Couples" by Rick and Gayle Perlmutter for an excellent guide to romance at Disney.

© MediaMarx, Inc.

Jennifer and Dave share a Mickey Rice Krispie Bar on their honeymoon

Anniversaries—Like birthdays, anniversaries are always in style at the Walt Disney World Resort. You can plan a special night out at a romantic restaurant or shape an entire vacation around your special day. Be sure to mention your anniversary when making priority seatings (especially at Cinderella's Royal Table)—you may be pleasantly surprised. (Note that the "Re-hitchin'" ceremony at The Garden Grill has been discontinued.) If you're staying at a resort, mention your anniversary at check-in, too.

Group Events—With all the conventions they host each year, Disney is a pro at group parties and functions. We've planned several ourselves and found plenty of options and many helpful Cast Members. And with the introduction of "Magical Gatherings" (see sidebar below), group events are even easier to plan! You can have a private party virtually anywhere in the "World," for small or large groups. For parties in any of the resorts, call 407-828-3074. If you're interested in having a private party at one of the parks, including Pleasure Island (can we come?), call Group Sales at 407-828-3200. We can't say it'll be cheap, but you can plan one within a reasonable budget if you're careful. Of course, you can go all-out, too—companies rent entire theme parks. Planet Hollywood at Downtown Disney hosts private functions, too. In fact, your authors host special gatherings for readers who want to meet us and other like-minded folks who just can't get enough of Disney. If you'd like to learn about our next PassPorter Gathering, please visit us at http://www.passporter.com/gathering.htm and see page 282.

Magical Gatherings

Disney's Magical Gatherings program is designed to help bring friends and family together at Walt Disney World. If you've got eight or more people staying at a Walt Disney World resort, you can book special experiences only available to groups. These events include the International Storybook Dinner (with storytelling and a VIP viewing of IllumiNations at Epcot), Good Morning Gathering (a Magic Kingdom character breakfast with Mickey Mouse), Safari Celebration Dinner (an end-of-day safari followed by a dinner reception at Tusker House with characters, live entertainment, and animal experiences), and the Magical Fireworks Voyage (an evening cruise to view the new Wishes fireworks show over Magic Kingdom). Disney also provides helpful services to plan your gathering, such as Web-based tools to help your group stay in touch and build consensus. And Disney has increased the number of restaurants that accommodate larger parties. To plan a Magical Gathering, call 407-WDW-MAGIC, 800-327-2989, or visit http://www.disneyworld.com/magicalgatherings.

Special Events and Holidays

Disney really knows how to celebrate. Nearly every holiday seems to have at least one event, and Easter, Halloween, Christmas, and New Year's Eve spark extended festivities. Disney also is a master at battling periods of slow attendance with specially themed events throughout the year. Call Disney's main information line at 407-824-4321 or visit their Web site at http://www.disneyworld.com for more information.

Sports
January brings the sell-out **Walt Disney World Marathon** (Jan. 9, 2005) as well as the Family Fun Run (Jan. 8) and the Health and Fitness Expo (Jan. 7–8)—call 407-939-7810. For inline skating fans, there's the **Walt Disney World Inline Marathon** on April 30–May 1, 2005. The **Atlanta Braves** baseball spring training begins in February, and the **Tampa Bay Buccaneers** football team may have their training camp again in July and August. PGA Tour golf professionals play in the 35th Annual **FUNAI Classic** in October 2005. Many more sport opportunities are available at Disney's Wide World of Sports Complex—for more details, visit http://www.disneyworldsports.com.

Celebrations at Pleasure Island
Pleasure Island throws special parties throughout the year. **Mardi Gras** is February 8, 2005, and the island throws a party to celebrate for several days. Pleasure Island typically celebrates Valentine's Day, St. Patrick's Day, and Cinco de Mayo (May 5), too. Honor **Black Music Month** in June. Get a jump on Independence Day with **July 3 fireworks**. September sees salsa during **Latin Rhythm Nights**. And November has the **Pleasure Island Jazz Fest**.

Festivals and Fun
Magic Kingdom, Epcot, and Disney-MGM Studios host special events. The **Epcot International Flower & Garden Festival** (April 15–June 5, 2005) fills the park with exhibits, seminars, tours, demonstrations, the Food Among the Flowers Brunch (see page 237), and special entertainment at the America Gardens Theatre. On selected dates in May, Disney-MGM Studios has **Star Wars Weekends** with celebrity appearances and special events. **Grad Nights** party down at the Magic Kingdom (April 22, 23, 29, and 30, 2005) from 11:00 pm to 5:00 am—for details, visit http://www.disneyyouthgroups.com. The Friday and Saturday after Labor Day bring the popular **Nights of Joy** to Magic Kingdom to celebrate contemporary Christian music ($37; see http://www.nightofjoy.com). The 10th Annual **Epcot International Food & Wine Festival**, which will be held September 30–November 13, 2005, turns the World Showcase into an even greater gourmet delight (see page 214). November is also heaven for soap opera fans—**ABC Super Soap Weekend** brings many favorite soap stars to Disney-MGM Studios.

Easter (March 27, 2005)
Spring crowds reach a peak during Easter week. Easter egg hunts and candy scrambles may be held at some of the resorts for their guests (in 2004, the Animal Kingdom Lodge, BoardWalk, Caribbean Beach, Contemporary, Coronado Springs, Fort Wilderness, Old Key West, Pop Century, Wilderness Lodge, and Yacht & Beach Club all held Easter events for their hotel guests). Check with your resort for details. Some restaurants offer Easter dinners, such as Chef Mickey's (see page 225). Note that Magic Kingdom no longer has an Easter parade.

Independence Day *(July 4, 2005)*
Magic Kingdom traditionally puts on a spectacular fireworks show, as does Disney-MGM Studios. Pleasure Island also ramps up its fireworks and adds patriotic entertainment as well. Epcot's IllumiNations is enhanced with Fourth of July fun, too!

Halloween *(October 31, 2005)*
Mickey's Not So Scary Halloween Party brings kid-friendly spookiness to Magic Kingdom for 13 nights (7:00 pm–midnight) in October (usually the Fridays and Sundays in October before Halloween, plus Halloween night). Enjoy Disney's Halloween Parade, a kids' costume parade, trick-or-treating around the park, Halloween-themed fireworks, storytellers, fortune tellers, a complimentary family photo, and access to most rides. We recommend you make time for the Liberty Belle Riverboat, which offers Halloween cruises with storytellers and live entertainment—it was the highlight of our night! Advance tickets are $31.95/adult, $25.95/child, plus tax. Call 407-934-7639 well in advance as tickets sell out, especially for Halloween night—tickets usually go on sale in May.

Thanksgiving *(November 24, 2005)*
Crowds take a bump-up for this All-American holiday. Disney's holiday decorations are on their way up, and a number of the full-service restaurants at the parks and almost all of the Disney resorts host special holiday dinners, with and without Disney characters.

Christmas *(December 25, 2005)*
Christmas is a very special time, with delightful decorations, holiday entertainment, and countless ways to enjoy the season. Decorations go up around Thanksgiving, so there's more than a month of merriment. Try to come during the first two weeks of December when the crowds are thinner, the party is in full swing, and the "World" is decked with holiday cheer. **Mickey's Very Merry Christmas Party** is a big favorite. Packed full of special shows and special fun, the Magic Kingdom is open for five extra hours for 12 nights in early December. Snow falls on Main Street, fireworks and music fill the air, and the big rides are open. And let's not forget the Main Street tree lighting ceremony, holiday-themed shows in the Galaxy Palace Theatre (in Tomorrowland), strolling carolers, and complimentary cookies, hot cocoa, souvenir buttons, and family photos. Advance tickets are $36.95/adults, $26.95/kids, plus tax (add $6 if you buy at the gate). At Epcot, the **Candlelight Processional** runs 2 to 3 times nightly. A celebrity narrator, chorus, and orchestra present the Christmas tale. No extra admission required, but a special dinner package offers reserved seating (call 407-WDW-DINE). Be sure to **view the resort decorations** (try the Yuletide Tour—see page 243) and enjoy merriment at **Downtown Disney**. The **Osborne Family Spectacle of Lights** sparkles throughout the Streets of America Set at Disney-MGM Studios—see page 158.

New Year's Eve *(December 31, 2005)*
Magic Kingdom, Epcot, Disney-MGM Studios, Pleasure Island, and Atlantic Dance at the BoardWalk all host big New Year celebrations. The theme parks overflow during the Christmas-New Year's week, and reservations at resorts are extremely hard to get. Disney charges regular admission to the parks on New Year's Eve, but Pleasure Island hosts a $84/person event featuring headline entertainment, food, and a holiday toast. Recent celebrations have been extra busy, with Disney promising park admission only to resort guests. When we visited in 1999/2000, the roads and parking lots closed early and only Disney buses got through.

Other Holidays and Observances
All parks participate in February's **Black Heritage Celebration**. Of significance is **The Happiest Celebration on Earth**, beginning May 5, 2005—see page 191. The first long weekend in June (June 2–5, 2005) is the **Gay Days** event (visit http://www.gayday.com).

Beyond Walt Disney World

We're pretty infatuated with Disney, but there is life beyond Walt Disney World. At least that's what we hear. We don't venture far beyond the gates, preferring to spend more time immersed in Disney's magic rather than battle traffic to get to another park. We do know that families hope to visit other theme parks during their visit to central Florida, so here is a list of Florida parks and attractions, along with their numbers and Web sites. You may also be interested in "The Other Orlando" guidebook by Kelly Monaghan, available at our Web site and at your local bookstore.

Name	Number	Web Site
Busch Gardens	813-987-5082	http://www.buschgardens.com
Cypress Gardens	863-324-2111	http://www.cypressgardens.com
Gatorland	800-393-JAWS	http://www.gatorland.com
Green Meadows Farm	407-846-0770	http://greenmeadowsfarm.com
Kennedy Space Center	321-452-2121	http://kennedyspacecenter.com
Medieval Times	407-396-1518	http://medievaltimes.com
Sea World	407-363-2613	http://seaworld.com
Universal Studios/Islands of Adv.	407-363-8000	http://www.usf.com
Wet 'n' Wild	407-351-1800	http://www.wetnwild.com

Note: Splendid China closed at the end of 2003. Cypress Gardens is scheduled to reopen in late 2004, but it could be delayed due to the hurricanes of 2004.

Beyond Orlando

Like any other forward-thinking organization, The Walt Disney Company has expanded into other locales. Here are a few of them:

Disney Cruise Line—"Take the magic of Disney and just add water!" The Disney Cruise Line set sail in 1998 with the same enthusiasm and energy you find at the Walt Disney World Resort. See pages 100–101, and pick up a copy of our popular guidebook, "PassPorter's Field Guide to the Disney Cruise Line and its Ports of Call" (available in bookstores or order at http://www.passporter.com/dcl—more details on page 285).

Disneyland Resort (California)—The original "Magic Kingdom," near Los Angeles. Disneyland was the model for the Magic Kingdom in Florida and still keeps a step or two ahead of its offspring, since Disney's Imagineers live close by. The official Disneyland hotels are right next door if you want to make a week out of it. A whole new park, Disney's California Adventure, opened in 2001. We plan to cover the entire Disneyland Resort and other area attractions, such as Universal Studios, in a brand new book: "PassPorter® Disneyland® Resort." For details on the book's release and to pre-order a copy, visit http://www.passporter.com/dl (see page 285).

Disneyland Paris Resort (France)—The first (and only) Disney resort in Europe, the park has a similar layout to Disneyland, with the major change being a substitution of Discoveryland for Tomorrowland. It is said by many to be the most beautiful of all the Disney parks. In April 2002, the new Walt Disney Studios theme park opened, featuring a number of the most popular attractions from the Disney-MGM Studios in Florida. For more information, visit http://www.disneylandparis.com. We plan to visit in February 2005 for Dave's 50th birthday!

Tokyo Disney Resort (Japan)—Disney, Japan-style! Tokyo Disney Resort is located in Urayasu, just outside Tokyo. It is similar to Disneyland in California, incorporating the quintessential "American" things. When Jennifer visited in 1992, she found it squeaky clean and definitely Disney, with just a touch of Japanese peeking through. In 2001, the new Tokyo DisneySea theme park opened immediately adjacent to Tokyo Disneyland. The new aquatically themed park has seven lands and a new resort, Hotel MiraCosta. Visit http://www.tokyodisneyresort.co.jp and click English.

Hong Kong Disneyland—Set to open in 2005/2006, this new theme park will overlook the water of Penny's Bay, Lantau. For details, visit the preview center at Epcot or visit http://www.hongkongdisneyland.com.

Disney's Vero Beach Resort—Vero Beach, Florida, is Disney's first oceanside resort, a two-hour drive from Disney World. Relaxing and definitely laid-back compared to the parks, Vero Beach Resort offers the chance to get some real rest. But there's also plenty to do—nightclubs, theatre, movies, restaurants, cultural events, recreation, and, of course, walking on the beach (very important). Call 561-234-2000 for more information, or visit http://www.disneyvacationclub.com, and click Resorts.

Disney's Hilton Head Island Resort—For southern grace and charm, experience the Carolina Low Country lifestyle at Disney's Hilton Head Island Resort. Hilton Head is a golfer's nirvana, boasting 12 nearby golf courses. The tennis and beaches are also big draws. It's an ideal spot for small group retreats. For more information, call 843-341-4100.

DisneyQuest—Plans originally called for DisneyQuests around the country, but only one outside of Orlando was built—in Chicago. Alas, Chicago's closed in September 2001. Visit http://www.disneyquest.com.

Hidden Mickey Hiding Places (from list on page 247)

1) In the Disney Recycles logo on bags, napkins, etc.; 2) On cash register receipts; 3) The "Soap Stop" vending machines in the resort laundry rooms; 4) Main Street Vehicle horse harnesses; 5) In the center of manhole covers; 6) In the sleeve of a clock on a Grim Reaper ghost in the Haunted Mansion; 7) In coiled ropes on Test Track (visible in the ride photo); 8) Drilling platform worker's watch; 9) Hedges trimmed into circles; 10) EarFfel water tower; 11) The ironwork fence around Disney-MGM Studios; 12) The yellow refrigerator on the Backlot Tour; 13) Birdhouse near Festival of the Lion King; 14) On the sidewalk near the Harambe Fruit Market; and 15) On the frog statue outside of the women's restroom near Pizzafari.

Your Own Walt Disney World

Make Walt Disney World your personal playground with these tips:

Tour the parks with Tinker Bell! Get a container of yellow cake glitter (found in any arts and craft store which sells cake decorating supplies) and keep the glitter handy in a pocket or pack while you tour Walt Disney World. As you walk through the parks with your little one, talk about Tinker Bell and how she loves to play with a child or two during the day. When the unsuspecting child isn't looking, sprinkle them with a little 'pixie dust' and mention how she just flew off. Don't forget to send a post card home of Magic Kingdom signed by Tink with some glitter attached to it. My daughter still talks of the day Tink spent with her and looks forward to next year's trip so she can visit with her again.

— *Contributed by Elizabeth Shannon, a winner in our 2004 Magic Tip Contest*

Write to us and **share your experiences, memories, and tips**. If we use them, we'll credit you in PassPorter and send you a copy! Drop us a note at P.O. Box 3880, Ann Arbor, Michigan 48106 or e-mail us at memories@passporter.com.

Magical Memories

"When we were planning our first-ever trip for our daughter's birthday, we wanted to ensure that it would stay a surprise and no one would give it away. To do this, we decided that we would only tell the people who had to know: parents, bosses, teachers, etc. Then we had to figure out exactly how to tell our daughter. We had worked and snuck around for so long, it would seem anti-climactic to just say, 'Here, you're going to Disney World.' So, about six months out from the trip, we started hinting that she was going to get a HUGE surprise for her birthday. Each day, she could ask two yes or no questions before she went to bed, no more. 'Is it bigger than a book?' 'Is it red?' 'Is it alive?' The anticipation was thrilling for her. During those six months, I used GiftsOfALifetime.com to order little odds and ends, used the PassPorter (a lifesaver!!) to plan our days, and worked on the Internet until late in the night to get everything ready. Finally on her birthday, we set up a large treasure hunt for her. We started out with simple clues and as she became more comfortable with the concept, the clues were harder, some were even funny, such as: 'Oh no!! Rush, rush! Find your next clue where you have to flush.' At the end of the hunt, she found herself at her hope chest and found a large suitcase. When she opened it up, it was filled to the brim with Mickey hats, maps, water bottles, beach towels, etc. The look on her face was priceless! She still talks about the questions that she asked, and the treasure hunt making the trip that much better!"

...as told by Disney vacationer Dana Slusher

"I'll never forget the day I married my partner, co-author, and best friend in the most magical place on earth, Walt Disney World, on May 1, 2004. It's a dream come true!"

...as told by Disney vacationer and co-author Jennifer Marx (formerly Jennifer Watson)

Index

We feel that a comprehensive index is very important to a successful travel guide. Too many times we've tried to look something up in other books only to find there was no entry at all, forcing us to flip through pages and waste valuable time. When you're on the phone with a reservation agent and looking for that little detail, time is of the essence.

You'll find the PassPorter index is complete and detailed. Whenever we reference more than one page for a given topic, the major topic is in **bold** and map references are in *italics* to help you home in on exactly what you need. For those times you want to find everything there is to be had, we include all the minor references. We have plenty of cross-references, too, just in case you don't look it up under the name we use.

P.S. This isn't the end of the book. More nifty features begin on page 274!

Planning

Getting There

Staying in Style

Touring

Feasting

Making Magic

Index

Notes & More

fireworks 256
  at Epcot 150
  at Magic Kingdom 122
  at Pleasure Island 188
first aid 115
fishing 81, **194**
Fitness Fairgrounds 140, **143**
Flag Retreat 125
Flame Tree Barbecue
    164, 165, **218**
Flights of Wonder 164, **169**
Florida Orlando Tickets 117
Florida residents
  discounts **10**, 203
  passes 117
florist 255
Flying Fish Cafe 43, **225**
Food & Wine Festival 237
Food Among the Flowers
    Brunch **237**, 256
food courts 27
FoodQuest 185, **186**, **222**
ForeWord Magazine i
Fort Wilderness Resort
    27, **59-62**, 113
  activities 193
  dinner shows 234
Fountain of Nations 138, **146**
Fountainview Espresso and
    Bakery 140, **210**
Foxworth, Ben vii
France 140, **148**, 259
Francisco's 56
French Quarter **79**, 83, 84
Fresh 99, **229**
Friendships **118**, 140
Frontierland 121, 124, **130**
Frontierland Shootin' Arcade
    124, **131**
Frostbite Freddie's Frozen
    Freshments **175**, 178
Fulton's Crab House 180, **221**
Future World 137, 140, **143-
    146**

G

Galaxy Palace Theater
    124, **135**
Gang Plank Falls 172 174
The Garden Grill
    140, **210**, 233
Garden Grove Café 229
Garden View Lounge
    63, 64, **227**
Gardens of the World 243
Gasparilla's Grill and Games
    63, 64
Gatewood, Dene vii, **112**
gay and lesbian travelers
  Gay Days 257

Gaylord Palms 108
gear 283
Germany 140, **148**
Ghirardelli Soda Fountain
    180, **220**
Gifts of a Lifetime 254
Global Neighborhood
    140, **143**
The Globe Pequot Press 202
Gold, Stephanie i
golf 192
Gooding's supermarket 61
Goofy **131**, 154
Goofy's Country Dancin'
    Jamboree. *See Diamond
    Horseshoe Saloon*
Grad Nights 256
Grand 1 Yacht 250
Grand Adventures in Cooking
    245
Grand Floridian Cafe 63, **227**
Grand Floridian Resort & Spa
    27, **63-66**, 118
  Mouseketeer Clubhouse
    253
  pool bar 63, **64**
  restaurants 227
  Spa & Health Club 63
The Great Movie Ride
    154, **160**
Green Meadows Farm 258
Grey, Kristin vii
Greyhound 18
groceries 61, **249**
Grosvenor Resort **104**, 236
groups 255
Guest Relations 115
Guest Services 32
guidemaps 115
Guitar Gallery 179
Gulliver's 99, **229**, 233
gum 249
Gurgling Suitcase 68

H

The Hall of Presidents
    121, 124, **131**
Halloween 256, **257**
Haney, Jeff vii, **112**
Happiest Celebration on
    Earth 113, **191**
Harambe Village 162
Harbor Club 252
Hard Rock Hotel 107
Harry Ramsden 213
Hassle-Free Walt Disney
    World guidebook 6
The Haunted Mansion
    121, 124, **131**

Hawthorne Suites LBV 108
health clubs 27, **194**
healthy dining 204
Hendrickson, Debbie **vi**, vii
Hidden Mickeys 247
  field guidebook 247
  web site vii
Hidden Treasures of World
    Showcase 243
Hilton 104
Hilton Head Island 102, **259**
Hime, LauraBelle **vi**, vii
Holiday Inn (at Hotel Plaza)
    104
Holiday Inn Express 108
Holiday Inn Family Suites 106
Holiday Inn Maingate East
    108
Holiday Inn Nikki Bird 109
Holiday Inn SunSpree 109
holidays 256-257
  chart 14
  meals 237
Holland-Radvon, Christina vii
Hollywood & Vine 154, **215**
Hollywood Boulevard
    151, 154, **160**
The Hollywood Brown Derby
    154, **216**, 236
Hollywood Hills Amphitheater
    152
Homewood Suites 109
Honey, I Shrunk the Audience
    137, 140, **146**
Honey, I Shrunk the Kids
    Movie Set Adventure
    154, **158**
honeymoons 255
Hong Kong Disneyland 191,
    259
Hoop-Dee-Doo Musical
    Revue 60, **234**
Hotel Plaza Resorts 104-105
Hotel Royal Plaza 105
hotels. 25-112
  first night 11
  off-property 108
House of Blues
    179, **222**, 236
housekeeping 32
Howard Johnson Maingate
    109
Hoypoloi 179
Humunga Kowabunga
    172, 174
Hunter, Dave vii, 15
Hurricane Hanna's 94
Hyatt Regency Grand Cypress
    109

Planning

Getting There

Staying in Style

Touring

Feasting

Making Magic

Index

Notes & More

Planning

Getting There

Staying in Style

Touring

Feasting

Making Magic

Index

Notes & More

Web Site Index

Site Name	Page	Address (URL)
Adults at Walt Disney World	vii	http://www.adultsatwdw.com
All Ears Net	6	http://www.allearsnet.com
All Star Vacation Homes	108, 282	http://www.allstarvacationhomes.com
Along Interstate 75	15	http://www.i75online.com
Amtrak	18	http://www.amtrak.com
AutoPilot	15	http://www.freetrip.com
Busch Gardens	258	http://www.buschgardens.com
Care Medical Equipment	34	http://www.caremedicalequipment.com
Comfort Inn Lake Buena Vista	108	http://www.comfortinnorlando.com
Disney's Magical Gatherings	255	http://www.disneyworld.com/magicalgatherings
Disney Cruise Line	100–101	http://www.disneycruise.com
Disney Desktop	vii	http://www.disneydesktop.com
DisneyDollarless (The Mouse For Less)	7, 11	http://www.themouseforless.com
DisneyEcho	7	http://disneyecho.emuck.com
Disneyland (California)	258	http://www.disneyland.com
Disneyland Paris	259	http://www.disneylandparis.com
DisneyQuest	186	http://www.disneyquest.com
Disney Vacation Club	102-103	http://www.disneyvacationclub.com
Disney Visa	10	http://disney.go.com/visa
DisneyZone	vii	http://www.disneyzone.actusa.net
DoomBuggies.com (Haunted Mansion)	131	http://www.doombuggies.com
Drive I-95	15	http://www.drivei95.com
DVC By Resale	103, 281	http://www.dvcbyresale.com
EarPlanes	23	http://www.earplanes.com
eGuides To Go	vii	http://www.eguidestogo.com
Expedia	16	http://www.expedia.com
Florida Department of Transportation	15	http://www.dot.state.fl.us
Florida Orlando Tickets	117	http://www.floridaorlandotickets.net
Friends of Bill W. in Orlando	112	http://aaorlandointergroup.org
Gatorland	258	http://gatorland.com
Gay Days	257	http://www.gayday.com
Gifts of a Lifetime	254	http://www.giftsofalifetime.com
Green Meadows Farm	258	http://greenmeadowsfarm.com
Greyhound	18	http://www.greyhound.com
Grosvenor Resort	104	http://www.grosvenorresort.com
Happy Limo	19	http://www.happylimo.com
Hard Rock Hotel	107	http://www.hardrockhotelorlando.com
Hidden Mickeys of Disney	vii, 247	http://www.hiddenmickeys.org
The Hilton	104	http://www.hotel-inside-the-park.com
Holiday Inn (Hotel Plaza)	104	http://www.hiorlando.com
Holiday Inn Family Suites	106	http://hifamilysuites.com
Holiday Inn SunSpree	109	http://www.kidsuites.com
Hotel Royal Plaza	105	http://www.royalplaza.com
Howard Johnson Maingate	109	http://www.orlandohojomaingate.com
Iago & Zazu's Attraction of the Week	vi	http://aotw.figzu.com
Intercot	vii, 7	http://www.intercot.com
Interstate 95 Exit Information Guide	15	http://www.usastar.com/i95/homepage.htm
Kennedy Space Center	258	http://www.kennedyspacecenter.com
LaughingPlace.com	vii	http://www.laughingplace.com
Lynx (local buses)	19	http://www.golynx.com

Planning

Getting There

Staying in Style

Touring

Feasting

Making Magic

Index

Notes & More

Autographs

Kids and kids-at-heart love to get autographs from Disney characters! Autograph books are popular, but you can also make your own! You have our permission to make a photocopy of the next four pages so you can collect signatures, paw prints, and doodles from your favorite characters. We've even provided places to write the actual name of the character (they can be hard to read—they are autographs, after all), plus the location you discovered the character, and the date of your find. Be sure to see page 246 for tips and tricks on how to get character autographs, too!

Character: Location: Date:

Character: Location: Date:

Character: Location: Date:

Autographs

Character: Location: Date:

Character:
Location: Date:

Character:
Location: Date:

Character: Location: Date:

Character: Location: Date:

Planning

Getting There

Staying in Style

Touring

Feasting

Making Magic

Index

Notes & More

Autographs

Character:
Location: Date:

Character:
Location: Date:

Character: Location: Date:

Character: Location: Date:

Character: Location: Date:

Planning

Getting There

Staying in Style

Touring

Feasting

Making Magic

Index

Notes & More

Autographs Anonymous

We know. We understand. Bouncing tigers and giant mice can be intimidating. After several months of research and development, we came up with the following system that can help both the interminably-shy and the over-stimulated. Just write your name in the blank below, take a deep breath, and hold out your book. Now, wasn't that easy?

Hi, my name is _____. May I have your autograph?

(write your name here)

Character:
Location: Date:

Character:
Location: Date:

Character: Location: Date:

Character: Location: Date:

Register Your PassPorter

We are <u>very</u> interested to learn how your vacation went and what you think of the PassPorter, how it worked (or didn't work) for you, and your opinion on how we could improve it! We encourage you to register your copy of PassPorter with us—in return for your feedback, we'll send you **two valuable coupons** good for discounts on PassPorters and PassHolder pouches when purchased directly from us. You can register your copy of PassPorter at http://www.passporter.com/register.htm, or you can send us a postcard or letter to P.O. Box 3880, Ann Arbor, Michigan 48106.

Report a Correction or Change

Keeping up with the changes at Walt Disney World is virtually impossible without your help. When you notice something is different than what is printed in PassPorter, or you just come across something you'd like to see us cover, please let us know! You can report your news, updates, changes, and corrections at http://www.passporter.com/wdw/report.htm.

Contribute to the Next Edition of PassPorter

You can become an important part of the 2006 edition of PassPorter Walt Disney World! The easiest way is to rate the resorts, rides, and/or restaurants at http://www.passporter.com/wdw/rate.htm. Your ratings and comments become part of our reader ratings throughout the book and help future readers make travel decisions. Want to get more involved? Send us a vacation tip or magical memory—if we use it in a future edition of PassPorter, we'll credit you by name in the guidebook and send you a free copy of the edition!

Get Your Questions Answered

We love to hear from you! Alas, due to the thousands of e-mails and hundreds of phone calls we receive each week we cannot offer personalized advice to all our readers. But there's a great way to get your questions answered: ask your fellow readers! Visit our message boards at http://www.passporterboards.com, join for free, and post your question. In most cases, fellow readers and Disney fans will offer their ideas and experiences! Our message boards also function as an ultimate list of frequently asked questions. Just browsing through to see the answers to other readers questions will reap untold benefit! This is also a great way to make friends and have fun while planning your vacation. But be careful—our message boards can be addictive!

PassPorter Online

A wonderful way to get the most from your PassPorter is to visit our active Web site at http://www.passporter.com. We serve up valuable PassPorter updates, plus useful Walt Disney World information and advice we couldn't jam into our book. You can swap tales (that's t-a-l-e-s, Mickey!) with fellow Disney fans, play contests and games, find links to other sites, get plenty of details, and ask us questions. You can also order PassPorters and shop for PassPorter accessories and travel gear! The latest information on new PassPorters to other destinations is available on our Web site as well. To go directly to our latest list of page-by-page PassPorter updates, visit http://www.passporter.com/customs/bookupdates.htm.

PassPorter Web Sites	Address (URL)
Main Page: PassPorter Online	http://www.passporter.com
Walt Disney World Forum	http://www.passporter.com/wdw
PassPorter Posts Message Boards	http://www.passporter.oards.com
PassPorter: Best of Times Links Page	http://www.passporter.com/wdw/bestoftimes.htm
Book Updates	http://www.passporter.com/customs/bookupdates.htm
Luggage Log and Tag Maker	http://www.passporter.com/wdw/luggagelog.htm
Rate the Rides, Resorts, Restaurants	http://www.passporter.com/wdw/rate.htm
Register Your PassPorter	http://www.passporter.com/register.htm
PassPorter Deluxe Edition Information	http://www.passporter.com/wdw/deluxe.htm

Planning · Getting There · Staying in Style · Touring · Feasting · Making Magic · Index · Notes & More

Money-Saving Coupons & Offers

Money-Saving Coupons & Offers

Free PassPorter Pin with Online Purchase

Receive a free cloissone PassPorter Pin ($6 value) when you place an order of $17 or more in merchandise from our Online Store.

Add to your pin collection with our colorful, collectible cloissone pin!

To redeem, visit our special pin offer page (before you place your order) located at:

http://www.passporter.com/store/freepin.aspx and have this PassPorter handy.

The pin shown above is our 2004 version.

Valid for online purchases only. Limit one coupon per order, and one free pin per order. Our limited edition pins may sell out—if they do, another PassPorter Pin will be offered with this coupon.

More Offers and Opportunities

Celebrate Walt Disney World with Fellow Fans

Join PassPorter Authors Jennifer and Dave Marx, AllEarsNet's Deb Wills and a host of webmasters, guidebook authors and online communities for a grand gathering at Walt Disney World and on the Disney Cruise Line December 2–8, 2005.

What better time to visit Walt Disney World? Disney's holiday festivities are in full swing, lodging can be had at value season pricing, and crowds are a whole lot smaller than they'll be later in December. Spice up your regular family vacation by attending a couple of events, or build an entire vacation around MouseFest activities. It's a whole new way to enjoy Walt Disney World and the Disney cruise.

Come meet your online friends and make new friends who share your love of all things Disney • Choose from dozens of meets (most of them free) throughout Disney's parks and resorts • Find new ways to experience familiar attractions • Enjoy scavenger hunts and guided tours • Come together at the MegaMouseMeet, a grand meet-and-greet where you can meet friends from many communities and hobnob with dozens of authors, webmasters and other notables • Ask if your favorite online communities will be attending • Look for MouseFest vacation packages from favorite travel agencies like MouseEarVacations.com.

Be sure to visit http://www.mousefest.org to learn more about this great event!
MouseFest at Walt Disney World—December 2-5 2005
MouseFest at Sea (Disney Cruise)—December 4-8, 2005
MegaMouseMeet—Saturday, December 3, 2005

PassPorter Goodies

PassPorter was born out of the necessity for more planning, organization, and a way to preserve the memories of a great vacation! Along the way we've found other things that either help us use the PassPorter better, appreciate our vacation more, or just make our journey a little more comfortable. Others have asked us about them, so we thought we'd share them with you. Order online at http://www.passporterstore.com, call us toll-free 877-929-3273, or use a photocopy of the order form below.

PassPorter® PassHolder is a small, lightweight nylon pouch that holds passes, I.D. cards, passports, money, and pens. Wear it around your neck for hands-free touring, and for easy access at the airport. The front features a clear compartment, a zippered pocket, and a velcro pocket; the back has a small pocket (perfect size for FASTPASS) and two pen slots. Adjustable cord. Royal blue. $4\,^7/_8$" x $6\,^1/_2$"

Quantity:
____ x $7.95

PassPorter® Badge personalized with your name! Go around the "World" in style with our lemon yellow oval pin. Price includes personalization with your name, shipping, and handling. Please indicate pin name(s) with your order.

Quantity:
___ x $4.00

Name(s): _____

PassPorter® Pin is our collectible, cloissone pin. Our 2004 version depicted our colorful PassPorter logo, and we anticipate a new pin design for 2005. More details and a coupon for a free pin is on page 281. Watch for new pins to be introduced each year!

Quantity:
___ x $6.00

Please ship my PassPorter Goodies to:

Name ....

Address ....

City, State, Zip ....

Daytime Phone ....

Payment: ❏ check (to "MediaMarx") ❏ charge card
❏ MasterCard ❏ Visa ❏ American Express ❏ Discover

Card number ....Exp. Date. ....

Signature ....

Sub-Total:

Tax*:

Shipping**:

Total:

* Please include sales tax if you live in Michigan.
**Shipping costs are:
$5 for totals up to $9
$6 for totals up to $19
$7 for totals up to $29
$8 for totals up to $39
Delivery takes 1-2 weeks.

Send your order form to P.O. Box 3880, Ann Arbor, MI 48106, call us toll-free at 877-WAYFARER (877-929-3273), or order online http://www.passporterstore.com.

Sidebar tabs: Planning · Getting There · Staying in Style · Touring · Feasting · Making Magic · Index · Notes & More

More PassPorters

You've asked for more PassPorters—we've listened! We're adding three brand-new PassPorter titles in 2005, all designed to make your Disney vacation the best it can be. And if you're interested in a PassPorter with PassPockets, check out our Spiral and Deluxe Editions (described below). To learn more, please visit us at http://www.passporter.com.

PassPorter Walt Disney World Spiral Edition

The original! The spiral edition is our bestselling, award-winning version of PassPorter—it's an all-in-one travel guide, planner, organizer, journal, and keepsake in a compact, spiral book. The spiral edition has all the great content found in the Library Edition plus 14 organizer PassPockets, a sheet of tabs, labels, and stickers, a wraparound cover with elastic band, two-color pages, bookplate for personalization, planning calendars, and space for numbers and addresses. The spiral edition (ISBN: 158771020X) is stocked in most bookstores.

PassPorter Walt Disney World Deluxe Edition

Design first-class vacations with this loose-leaf ring binder edition. The Deluxe Edition features the same great content as the PassPorter Walt Disney World spiral guide. Special features of the Deluxe Edition include ten interior storage slots in the binder to hold guidemaps, I.D. cards, and a pen (we even include a pen). The Deluxe binder makes it really easy to add, remove, and rearrange pages ... you can even download, print, and add-in updates and supplemental pages from our Web site, and refills are available for purchase. Learn more at http://www.passporter.com/wdw/deluxe.htm. The Deluxe Edition is available through bookstores by special order—just give your bookstore the ISBN for the 2005 Deluxe Edition (1587710218).

PassPorter's Walt Disney World For Your Special Needs

New for Spring 2005! It's hardly a one-size-fits-all world at Disney's Orlando resort, yet everyone seems to fit. Consider the typical multi-generational family planning a vacation: pregnant and nursing moms, parents with infants, cousins "keeping Kosher," grandparents with declining mobility, a child with food allergies, an uncle struggling with obesity, a teenaged daughter recently "converted" to vegetarianism ... everyday people coping with everyday needs. Authors Deb Wills and Debra Martin Koma have prepared more than 400 pages of in-depth information for Walt Disney World vacationers of all abilities, delivering in-depth coverage of every ride, attraction and resort on Walt Disney World property from a distinctive "special needs" perspective. This is a perfect supplement to your favorite guidebook. Learn more and order your copy at http://www.passporter.com/wdw/specialneeds or get a copy at your favorite bookstore (ISBN: 1587710188).

Even More PassPorters

PassPorter's Field Guide to the Disney Cruise Line and its Ports of Call–Third Edition

Completely updated for 2005! Includes complete itinerary and port-of-call descriptions for the Disney Magic's 2005 West Coast and Panama Canal itineraries. Get your cruise plans in shipshape with our updated field guide! Authors Jennifer and Dave Marx cover

the Disney Cruise Line in incredible detail, including deck plans, stateroom floor plans, original photos, menus, entertainment guides, port/shore excursion details, and plenty of worksheets to help you budget, plan, and record your cruise information. Now in its third edition, this is the original and most comprehensive guidebook devoted to the Disney Cruise Line! Learn more and order your copy at http://www.passporter.com/dcl or get a copy at your favorite bookstore (paperback, no PassPockets: ISBN: 1587710226). Also available in a Deluxe Edition with organizer PassPockets (ISBN: 1587710234).

(February 2005)

PassPorter Disneyland Resort and Southern California Attractions–First Edition

New for 2005! PassPorter tours the park that started it all, just in time for Disneyland's 50th anniversary. California's Disneyland, Disney's California Adventure, and Downtown Disney get PassPorter's expert treatment, and we throw in Hollywood and Downtown Los Angeles, San Diego, SeaWorld, the San Diego Zoo and Wild Animal Park, Legoland, and Six Flags Magic Mountain. All this, and PassPorter's famous PassPockets and planning features. Whether you're making the pilgrimage to Disneyland for the big celebration or planning a classic Southern California family vacation, you can't miss. Learn more and order a copy at http://www.passporter.com/dl, or pick it up at your favorite bookstore (ISBN: 1587710048). Also available as a Deluxe Edition in a padded, six-ring binder (ISBN: 1587710056).

PassPorter's Treasure Hunts at Walt Disney World

New for 2005! Have even more fun at Walt Disney World! Jennifer and Dave's treasure hunts have long been a favorite part of PassPorter reader gatherings at Walt Disney World, and now you can join in the fun. Gain a whole new appreciation of Disney's fabulous attention to detail as you search through the parks and resorts for the little (and big) things that you may never have noticed before. Great for individuals, families and groups, with hunts for people of all ages and levels of Disney knowledge. Special, "secure" answer pages make sure nobody can cheat. Prepared with plenty of help from Jen Carter, famous for her all-day, all-parks scavenger hunts. Learn more about this fun new book and order at http://www.passporter.com/wdw/hunts or get a copy at your favorite bookstore (ISBN: 1587710269).

To order any of our guidebooks, visit http://www.passporterstore.com or call toll-free 877-929-3273. PassPorter guidebooks are also available in your local bookstore. If you don't see it on the shelf, just ask!

Note: The ISBN codes above apply to our 2005 editions. For the latest edition, ask your bookstore to search their database for "PassPorter."

Vacation At-A-Glance

You have our permission to make a copy of the chart below and create an itinerary overview. You can then make copies of it and give one to everyone in your traveling party, as well as to those who stay behind.

Name(s):	
Departing on: Time: #:	
Arriving at:	
Staying at: Phone:	

Date:	Date:
Park/Activity:	Park/Activity:
Breakfast:	Breakfast:
Lunch:	Lunch:
Dinner:	Dinner:
Other:	Other:
Date:	Date:
Park/Activity:	Park/Activity:
Breakfast:	Breakfast:
Lunch:	Lunch:
Dinner:	Dinner:
Other:	Other:
Date:	Date:
Park/Activity:	Park/Activity:
Breakfast:	Breakfast:
Lunch:	Lunch:
Dinner:	Dinner:
Other:	Other:
Date:	Date:
Park/Activity:	Park/Activity:
Breakfast:	Breakfast:
Lunch:	Lunch:
Dinner:	Dinner:
Other:	Other:
Date:	Date:
Park/Activity:	Park/Activity:
Breakfast:	Breakfast:
Lunch:	Lunch:
Dinner:	Dinner:
Other:	Other:

Departing on: Time: #:	
Returning at:	

Magic Kingdom Map

Fantasyland

located on the lower level of Cinderella's Royal Table in Cinderella Castle

Dumbo The Flying Elephant

"it's a small world"

Fort

The Pinocchio Village Haus

Ariel's Grotto

The Ma Adventur Winnie the

Walt Disney World Railroad

Big Thunder Mountain Railroad

The Haunted Mansion

4:00

Peter Pan's Flight

Cinderella's Golden Carrousel

Mike Fink Keelboats

Columbia Harbour House

Mickey's PhilharMagic

Snow White's Scary Adventure

Tom Sawyer's Island

Liberty Belle Riverboat

The Hall of Presidents

2:30

Fairytale Garden

Splash Mountain

Raft

1:30

Aunt Polly's Dockside Inn

Sleepy Hollow

2:00

Cinderella Castle

3:00

Frontierland

Liberty Square

Stage

2:00

Diamond Horseshoe Saloon

3:00

Liberty Tree Tavern

1:30

Hub

3:00

Pecos Bill Cafe

Country Bear Jamboree

Frontierland Shootin' Arcade

0:30

0:30

3:30

El Pirata Y el Perico

The Enchanted Tiki Room

The Magic Carpets of Aladdin

Aloha Isle

3:00

Tip Board

The Crystal Palace

Swiss Family Treehouse

Jungle Cruise

0:45

2:00

Pirates of the Caribbean

Casey's Corner

Ice Cream Parlor

The Plaza Restaurant

The Plaza Pavilio

Shrunken Ned's Junior Jungle Boats

3:30

Main Street Bakery

Main Street, U.S.A.

Barber Shop

Main St. Vehicles

Adventureland

City Hall

Tony's Town Square Restaurant

Town Square Exposition Hall

Walt Disney World Railroad

©MediaMarx, Inc.

Park Icon: Cinderella Castle

Monorail Station

Walk Around the World Path

Boat Docks

Ferry

M A P

COORDINATES

A	B	C	D	E

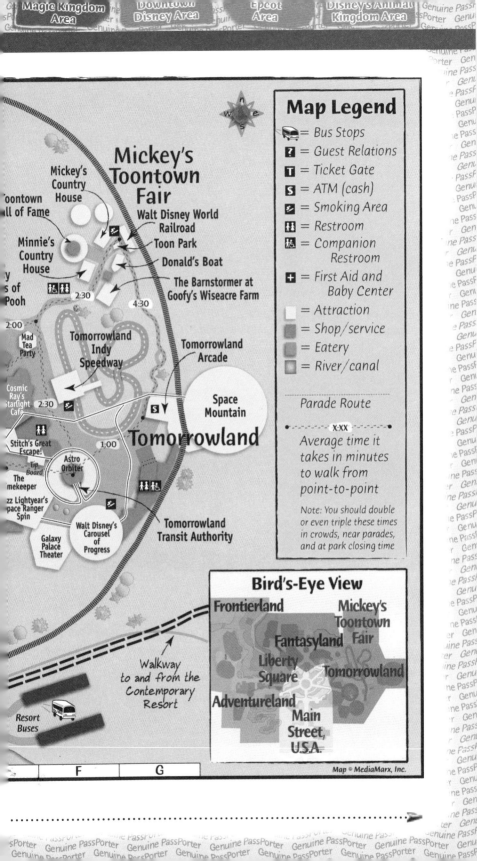

Mickey's Toontown Fair

Mickey's Country House

Minnie's Country House

...y ...s of Pooh

Toontown Hall of Fame

Walt Disney World Railroad

Toon Park

Donald's Boat

The Barnstormer at Goofy's Wiseacre Farm

2:30

4:30

2:00

Mad Tea Party

Tomorrowland Indy Speedway

Tomorrowland Arcade

Cosmic Ray's Starlight Cafe

2:30

Tomorrowland

Space Mountain

1:00

Stitch's Great Escape!

Tip Board

The ...mekeeper

...zz Lightyear's ...pace Ranger Spin

Astro Orbiter

Galaxy Palace Theater

Walt Disney's Carousel of Progress

Tomorrowland Transit Authority

Walkway to and from the Contemporary Resort

Resort Buses

Map Legend

- 🚌 = Bus Stops
- ？ = Guest Relations
- Ⓣ = Ticket Gate
- Ⓢ = ATM (cash)
- 🚬 = Smoking Area
- 🚻 = Restroom
- ♿ = Companion Restroom
- ➕ = First Aid and Baby Center
- ⬜ = Attraction
- ⬜ = Shop/service
- ⬜ = Eatery
- ⬜ = River/canal

- - - - - Parade Route

•·--·--·--·- X:XX ·--·--·--·•

Average time it takes in minutes to walk from point-to-point

Note: You should double or even triple these times in crowds, near parades, and at park closing time

Bird's-Eye View

Frontierland

Mickey's Toontown Fair

Fantasyland

Liberty Square

Tomorrowland

Adventureland

Main Street, U.S.A.

F   G

Map © MediaMarx, Inc.

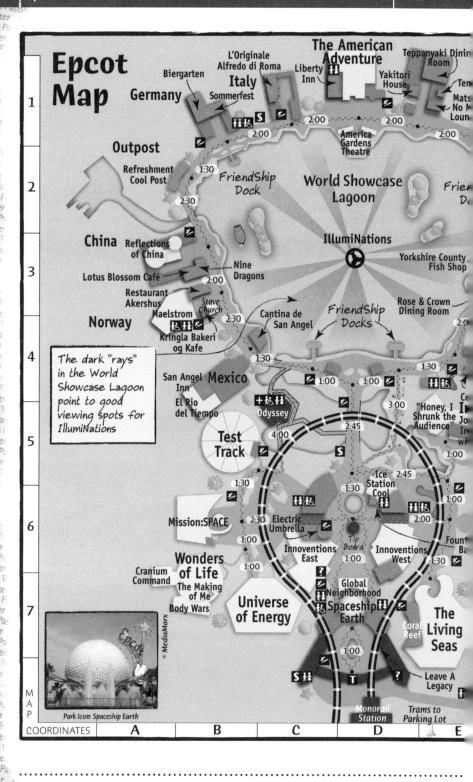

Epcot Map

Germany
Biergarten
Italy
L'Originale Alfredo di Roma
Sommerfest
Liberty Inn
The American Adventure
Yakitori House
Teppanyaki Dining Room
Ten
Mats No M
Loun

2:00
2:00
2:00

Outpost
Refreshment Cool Post
1:30
FriendShip Dock
World Showcase Lagoon
2:30

2:00

Frier D

China
Reflections of China
IllumiNations
Yorkshire County Fish Shop
Lotus Blossom Café
Nine Dragons
2:00
Restaurant Akershus
Stave Church
Rose & Crown Dining Room
Norway
Maelstrom
2:30
Cantina de San Angel
FriendShip Docks
2:0
Kringla Bakeri og Kafe
1:30
1:30

The dark "rays" in the World Showcase Lagoon point to good viewing spots for IllumiNations

San Angel Inn
Mexico
1:00
1:00
El Rio del Tiempo
Odyssey
3:00
"Honey, I Shrunk the Audience"
Ce I Jo In wi
Test Track
4:00
2:45
1:00
Ice Station Cool
2:45
1:30
Mission:SPACE
2:30
Electric Umbrella
1:30
2:00
Foun Ba
1:00
Innovations East
Tip Board
Innovations West
1:30
1:00
1:00
Wonders of Life
Cranium Command
The Making of Me
Body Wars
Universe of Energy
Global Neighborhood
Spaceship Earth
The Living Seas
Coral Reef
1:00
Leave A Legacy
Monorail Station
Trams to Parking Lot

© MediaMarx
Park Icon: Spaceship Earth

MAP COORDINATES   A   B   C   D   E

World Showcase

Japan

Tempura Kiku

Morocco

Restaurant Marrakesh

Tangierine Cafe

Bistro de Paris

Chefs de France

France

Boulangerie Patisserie

Impressions de France

Resort Boats

International Gateway

United Kingdom

World ShowPlace Convention Center

Canada

O Canada!

Cavalier

Imagination!

Journey Into Imagination with Figment

Soarin'
(opens spring 2005)

Future World

The Land

Sunshine Season Food Fair

The Garden Grill

Sunview Eatery

The Circle of Life

Living with the Land

To BoardWalk, Swan, and Dolphin Resorts

To Yacht and Beach Club and Villas

To Buses

2:30
2:00
1:00
7:00

Map Legend

- = Bus Stops
- ? = Guest Relations
- T = Ticket Gate
- S = ATM (cash)
- = Smoking Area
- = Restroom
- = Companion Restroom
- + = First Aid and Baby Center
- = Attraction
- = Shop/service
- = Eatery
- = River/canal

·····x·xx·····

Average time it takes in minutes to walk from point-to-point

Note: You should double or even triple these times in crowds and at park closing time

Bird's-Eye View

World Showcase East

World Showcase West

Future World East

Future World West

Map © MediaMarx, Inc.

F | G

Disney-MGM Studios Map

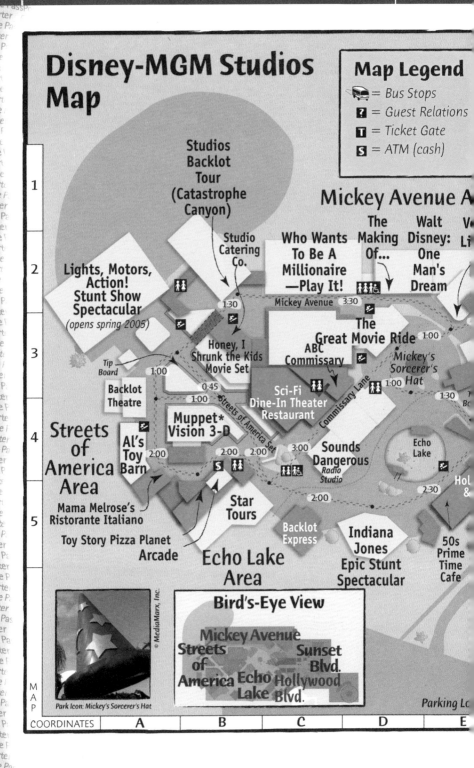

Map Legend

= Bus Stops
? = Guest Relations
T = Ticket Gate
S = ATM (cash)

1

Studios Backlot Tour (Catastrophe Canyon)

Mickey Avenue A

2

Lights, Motors, Action! Stunt Show Spectacular
(opens spring 2005)

Studio Catering Co.

Who Wants To Be A Millionaire —Play It!

The Making Of...

Walt Disney: One Man's Dream

V Li

Mickey Avenue   3:30

1:30

3

Tip Board

1:00

Honey, I Shrunk the Kids Movie Set

Backlot Theatre

0:45

1:00

The Great Movie Ride   1:00

ABC Commissary

Mickey's Sorcerer's Hat

1:00

1:30

4

Streets of America Area

Al's Toy Barn   2:00

Muppet* Vision 3-D

2:00   2:00

Sci-Fi Dine-In Theater Restaurant

Sounds Dangerous
Radio Studio

3:00

Echo Lake

Hol &

2:30

5

Mama Melrose's Ristorante Italiano

Toy Story Pizza Planet Arcade

Star Tours

Echo Lake Area

Backlot Express

Indiana Jones Epic Stunt Spectacular

2:00

50s Prime Time Cafe

Streets of America Set

Commissary Lane

Bird's-Eye View

Mickey Avenue

Streets of America

Echo Lake

Sunset Blvd.

Hollywood Blvd.

© MediaMarx, Inc.

Park Icon: Mickey's Sorcerer's Hat

Parking Lo

M A P

COORDINATES | A | B | C | D | E

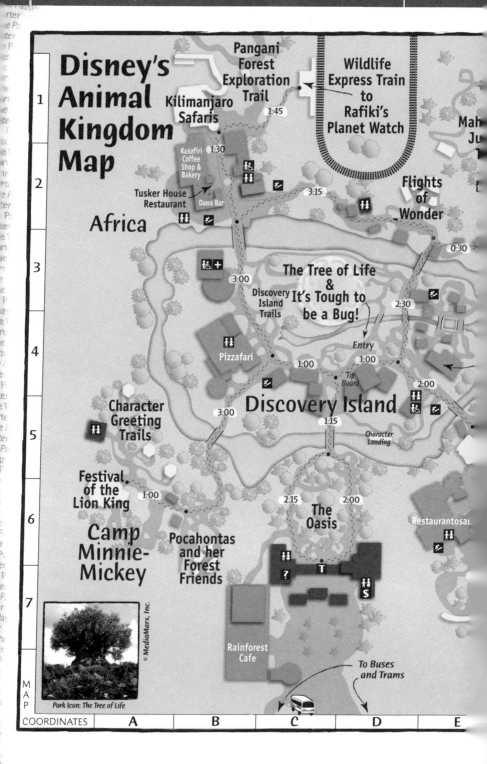

Disney's Animal Kingdom Map

Pangani Forest Exploration Trail 1:45

Kilimanjaro Safaris 1:30

Wildlife Express Train to Rafiki's Planet Watch

Mah Ju T

Kusafiri Coffee Shop & Bakery

Flights of Wonder

3:15

Tusker House Restaurant   Dawa Bar

Africa

0:30

3:00

The Tree of Life & It's Tough to be a Bug!

Discovery Island Trails

2:30

Pizzafari

Entry 1:00

1:00   Tip Board

2:00

Discovery Island

Character Greeting Trails

3:00

1:15

Character Landing

Festival of the Lion King

1:00

Camp Minnie-Mickey

Pocahontas and her Forest Friends

2:15   2:00

The Oasis

Restaurantosau

© MediaMarx, Inc.

Rainforest Cafe

To Buses and Trams

Park Icon: The Tree of Life

M A P

COORDINATES   A   B   C   D   E

Asia

arajah
ngle
rek

Exit

0:30

Enter

0:30

2:00

Kali River Rapids

Expedition: Everest
under construction

4:30

Flame Tree Barbecue

1:30

The Boneyard

2:00

Chester & Hester's Dino-Rama

TriceraTop Spin

Primeval Whirl

Tarzan Rocks! at Theater in the Wild

us

00

DinoLand, U.S.A

Dinosaur

F | G

Map Legend

🚌 = Bus Stops
❓ = Guest Relations
🎫 = Ticket Gate
💲 = ATM (cash)
🚬 = Smoking Area
🚻 = Restroom
👶 = Companion Restroom
➕ = First Aid and Baby Center
☐ = Attraction
☐ = Shop/service
☐ = Eatery
☐ = River/canal

- - - - - - - - - - - - - - - -

Parade Route

•—•—• X:XX —•—•

Average time it takes in minutes to walk from point-to-point

Note: You should double or even triple these times in crowded areas

Bird's-Eye View

Africa | Asia

Discovery Island

Camp Minnie-Mickey | The Oasis | DinoLand, U.S.A

Map © MediaMarx, Inc.

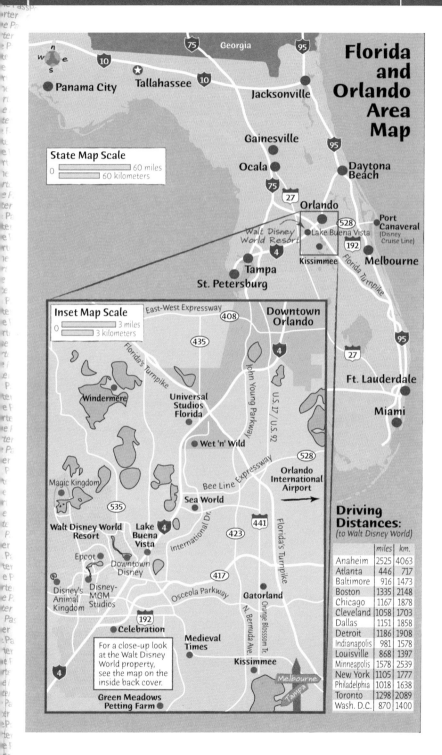

Florida and Orlando Area Map

Georgia

Panama City
Tallahassee
Jacksonville
Gainesville
Ocala
Daytona Beach
Orlando
Walt Disney World Resort
Lake Buena Vista
Port Canaveral (Disney Cruise Line)
Kissimmee
Melbourne
Tampa
St. Petersburg

State Map Scale
0 — 60 miles
— 60 kilometers

Inset Map Scale
0 — 3 miles
— 3 kilometers

East-West Expressway
Downtown Orlando
Florida's Turnpike
Windermere
Universal Studios Florida
Wet 'n' Wild
John Young Parkway
U.S. 17 / U.S. 92
Ft. Lauderdale
Miami
Magic Kingdom
Sea World
Orlando International Airport
Bee Line Expressway
Walt Disney World Resort
Lake Buena Vista
International Dr.
Florida's Turnpike
Epcot
Downtown Disney
Disney's Animal Kingdom
Disney-MGM Studios
Osceola Parkway
Gatorland
Orange Blossom Tr.
N. Bermuda Ave.
Celebration
Medieval Times
Kissimmee
Melbourne
Tampa
Green Meadows Petting Farm

For a close-up look at the Walt Disney World property, see the map on the inside back cover.

Driving Distances:
(to Walt Disney World)

	miles	km.
Anaheim	2525	4063
Atlanta	446	717
Baltimore	916	1473
Boston	1335	2148
Chicago	1167	1878
Cleveland	1058	1703
Dallas	1151	1858
Detroit	1186	1908
Indianapolis	981	1578
Louisville	868	1397
Minneapolis	1578	2539
New York	1105	1777
Philadelphia	1018	1638
Toronto	1298	2089
Wash. D.C.	870	1400

Walt Disney World Property Map

Map Legend

Resorts and Hotels on Property

- **MO** All-Star Movies
- **MU** All-Star Music
- **SP** All-Star Sports
- **AK** Animal Kingdom Lodge
- **BC** Beach Club
- **BE** Best Western Resort
- **BW** BoardWalk Inn & Villas
- **CB** Caribbean Beach
- **C** Contemporary
- **CS** Coronado Springs

- **D** Dolphin
- **DT** Doubletree Guest Suites
- **FW** Fort Wilderness
- **GF** Grand Floridian
- **G** Grosvenor Resort
- **H** The Hilton
- **HI** Holiday Inn
- **HR** Hotel Royal Plaza
- **OKW** Old Key West
- **P** Polynesian

- **PC** Pop Century
- **PF** Port Orleans French Quarter
- **PR** Port Orleans Riverside
- **SS** Saratoga Springs
- **SG** Shades of Green
- **S** Swan
- **WL** Wilderness Lodge
- **WP** Wyndham Palace
- **YC** Yacht Club

Golf Courses and Other Destinations

- **BO** Bonnet Creek Golf Club
- **CC** Centra Care Walk-In
- **EP** Eagle Pines Golf Course
- **FT** Fairy Tale Wedding Pavilion
- **FG** Fantasia Gardens
- **LBV** Lake Buena Vista Golf Course
- **MA** Magnolia Golf Course

- **OR** Osprey Ridge Golf Course
- **PA** Palm Golf Course
- **RC** River Country
- **TTC** Transportation & Ticket Center
- **DS** Walt Disney World Speedway
- **WS** Winter Summerland

Miscellaneous

- **Toll** Entrance/Toll Plaza
- **Gas** Gas Station
- **Park** Parking Lot

Map Scale

0 ▭▭▭ 1 mile
▭▭▭ 1 kilometer